RUNAWAY ME

A SURVIVOR'S STORY

*"We do not inherit the earth from our ancestors,
we are simply borrowing it from the children."*

RUNAWAY ME

A SURVIVOR'S STORY

a book written and lived by

Evan Karl Cutler

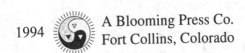

1994   A Blooming Press Co.
Fort Collins, Colorado

All inquiries regarding motion-picture, dramatic, translation, and other related rights should be addressed to the publisher:

A Blooming Press Co.
749 S. Lemay, Suite A3-223,
Fort Collins, CO, 80524-3900
(303) 482-0705

Manufactured in the United States of America on recycled paper
10 9 8 7 6 5 4 3 2 1

Quality Books Cataloging-in-Publication Data

Cutler, Evan Karl. 1968-
    Runaway me : a survivors story / Evan Karl Cutler.
    p. cm.
    Includes bibliographical references and index.
    ISBN 1-884607-15-2

    1. Cutler, Evan Karl. 2. Runaway teenagers--United States--Biography.
3. Runaway children--United States. 4. Abused children--United States.
5. Runaway children--Services for--United States.
I. Title.

HV1431.C87 1994   362.7'4'092
                            QBI93-22502 /AC

Library of Congress Catalog Card Number: 93-074729

Grateful acknowledgement is made to the Steve Miller Band for permission to reprint the lyrics of "Fly Like an Eagle" from *The Best of the Steve Miller Band.* Copyright © 1973-78 administered by Sailor Music, 1925 Century Park East, Suite 1260, Los Angeles, CA 90067.

Cover Art Credits:
    Back: *ENOCK* by Eric Hill
    Front: *Runaway* by Gretchen Wilson, a.k.a "Eris"
To contact artists, contact A Blooming Press Co, or consult the Artist Credits section at the back of the book.
Computerized Cover Design: John Schiller, Channel Z Graphics
Cover Copy: Ann Carr, Carr & Associates
Typesetting: Ethan Knipp

For
Mom
Dad
&
Jodie
in the hope
of family healing

For
Kelli
&
Kresta
in honor of your love

For
future generations
in the hope
we may create
a world
in which you will be
thankful
to be alive

Contents

Our Story:

A Guide:

A Gift:

Introduction

This book deals with one of the most serious problems of our time: teens running away from home. Each year between one half and two million kids run away in America. Too many suffer unnecessarily. It is past time for us to recognize the runaway crisis for the disaster it is, and work hard to bring it to an end.

Be you a teen, parent, friend or family member, or anyone else who cares, this book offers suggestions about what *you* can do to make a difference. How you and I deal with this problem will determine the future of our society. Wake up! Please.

My Story:

The first time I ran away from home was in the late spring of 1983. Only fifteen at the time, I remained independent of my family for three long months before conceding defeat and returning home. I left again about fifteen months later, when I was sixteen, and since then have only been back to visit.

The first half of this book is about what it was like for me the first time I ran away. In it, I describe much of what happened from the moment I ran until the moment I returned home, three hellish months older and a decade less naive.

Mine is not a pleasant story. However, it is true, and I hope it will be read by as many Americans as possible.

Our Story:

Neither is this my story alone. With but a few variations in plot, it is being lived by another generation of runaways right now. It will be lived again and again and again by literally millions of our friends, relatives, and neighbors until our society takes the necessary steps to declare, "The End."

As far as I can tell, this is the first book-length autobiographical account of the experiences of a teen runaway in America. This is in part because I was one of the lucky ones. For every scrape I was fortunate enough to escape or avoid, literally scores of American youth were simultaneously having worse luck.

Though many of their experiences are sure to have been far more gripping and depressing than mine, most of them never get to the point where they'd have any hope of putting together a project like this book. Unfortunately, those who survive often manage little more than survival, and could never hope to find the space needed to heal and share what they've been through. Even with all the support I've found, it has taken me two years to put this book together. Though it is the best I've been able to manage, it could and should be better. There is so much to say, and so much to do.

Like me, many runaways don't stay at shelters. I've personally witnessed hundreds of teens standing on the street prostituting themselves so they might eat or have a place to sleep for a night. In addition, I've met a sampling of the perverted child molesters for whom the selection on the street corners isn't enough. Invited into some of their homes under the guise of charity or friendship, I've beheld a bevy of other runaway kids conveniently housed where they could be regularly accessed by these molesters.

The longer our society puts off dealing with the severe reality of this crisis, the more kids will suffer, become warped, and even die while waiting desperately and in vain for people to decide they are worth saving. This is not an exaggeration.

A Guide:

The final chapters of this book consist of analysis, advice, and resource listings you can use to better cope with runaway crises in your life and community. The analysis chapter explains how the runaway "problem" at large is actually a *symptom* of a deeper problem. The advice chapters offer hundreds of practical suggestions to teens, parents, concerned citizens, and organizations alike on what they can do to better cope with runaway crises. The last chapter, "Resources," lists books, organizations, and toll-free hotlines that can help with many of the problems facing runaways and their families.

Why I Wrote This Book:

There are four significant reasons: to heal myself; to help heal other individuals and families; to help heal our society; and finally, to found the Fifteen Fund, a charity devoted to helping runaways heal and make something of themselves.

Writing my story has forced me to work through the garbage I accumulated as a runaway. By remembering and rethinking my experiences, I have begun to break the grip of denial, shame, and pain caused by my ordeal. It would be impossible for me to become a fully healthy and functioning person without this effort. What I survived left festering wounds and permanent scars. Thanks to my work they are now healing faster than ever.

Sharing my story and advice can help other teens and their families. If this book enables even a few kids to avoid the hell I and millions of others have lived through, writing it has been doubly worth the effort.

I hope children will read this book and through it learn some of what to avoid. For example, the whole experience of running away, if possible. Still, the sick truth for thousands of children each day is that life as a runaway, even including prostitution, may be a safer existence than that which they are offered at home. If they do run, this book may help kids avoid child molesters, incarceration, hunger, homelessness, disease, despair, prostitution, and shame.

Runaways should not be embarrassed about the socially disapproved actions engaged in the struggle to survive. Rather, this country should be embarrassed for providing a climate where such actions can seem the best options available to runaways. The people who take advantage of runaway teens' desperate situations, the people who molest and abuse runaways, should be the ones who are embarrassed, not the children.

Please hear this: *THERE IS NO SHAME IN BEING A RUNAWAY!* We must reject the shame to break through and heal.

Parents who read this can develop a little more understanding, compassion, love, and respect for their children. America's youth need this gift more than anything else. Parents will also gain insight into why kids run in the first place. Teens, families, and communities will benefit when parents stop perpetuating the intergenerational cycles that lead kids to run away.

The final advice chapter is for anyone else who cares about ending our runaway crisis. It has sections specifically addressing friends and family of teens, do-gooders in general, former runaways, shelters, schools, social workers, and governments. They contain enough food for thought and action to keep people who care busy for a long, long time.

My dream is that this society, our United States of America, can be inspired to gather the social will to overcome this problem. In my dream, I see our communities and governments, through the actions of individuals like you, putting more energy into working on the runaway crisis and the deeper problems that cause it. We can turn this crisis around.

Half of the profits from this book will be used to establish the Fifteen Fund, which as far as I know, is the first college and job-training scholarship fund specifically for runaway youth. (See the second to last page of this book for a description of how the Fifteen Fund will work.) It will take far more than this book can generate to create the support and opportunities runaways need, but it's a start.

Of course, I may be mistaken about this book helping anyone other than myself. Certainly some who read it will simply be titillated, excited, or thrilled in reading about my hell. Others will merely be shocked, upset, and sad for me and the other hordes of kids, before putting the book aside and going on to something else, never actually contemplating how to make a difference. But I don't believe all will follow these paths. I can't. You have to be better than that. Why? Because you are needed. Be you a teen, a parent, a neighbor, an important official, or anyone else, there is no one else who can help the way you can.

Hard Work:

There is so much to be done to help current and prevent future generations of runaways. This work has to be made a priority. The children of our society deserve at least as much attention as international issues, the Savings and Loan crisis, the national deficit, the environment, and health care issues currently receive.

This is one of the richest countries in the world! It is populated with millions of the most talented people on the planet. On top of this, we seem to command more material wealth than any other nation. If helping our children became a high priority issue, if we got more people like you involved in supporting positive, healing, change, then we could solve the problems causing the runaway crises. If we do, the generations to follow will thank us.

In the long run, the one that counts, it will cost us far less to make these issues an immediate priority than to continue to neglect them. Focusing our energies upon remedying the ongoing runaway crisis will require radical (root) change, but such change is certainly possible, and well worth it.

Unfortunately, our personal and societal priorities have been completely screwed up.

It hurts to know so many individuals keep constantly busy, hedonistically distracting themselves from the troubles that affect us all. We Americans spend billions upon billions of dollars and hours each year pursuing instant gratification through travel, entertainment, drugs, and anything else that will keep us from sitting still long enough to realize the truth which surrounds us. We become deaf, dumb, and blind to the enormous suffering, disparity, and disease right in front of us.

It also hurts to know our country can get so worked up about a problem that we'll send a half-million soldiers thousands of miles around the world (e.g. Kuwait, Grenada, Panama, and Somalia), purportedly in order to protect suffering people, while we are unwilling to mobilize an equivalent force to solve our own crushing problems.

During the Persian Gulf War we harnessed the resources to kill one-fifth of a million people: 200,000 human beings. By mid-1992 the aftermath of that effort had reportedly caused another 300,000 human deaths. In the process, we devoted tens of billions of dollars of equipment, and hundreds of billions in long term overhead, to support our armies.

Why don't we spend anything close to this kind of energy to save our children who are on the streets every day in the United States? Why do we let them continue to be abused by their families, by molesters, or by the weather, in every city, town, and village across America? Facing these issues won't be easy, but ignoring them is inexcusable!

Wisdom:
An ancient Native American proverb:
"We do not inherit the earth from our ancestors, we are simply borrowing it from the children."
It is time for us to listen to this wisdom and give the children the love, care, and trust that they deserve.

Why I Share Graphic Details of Sexual Encounters:
In my story I share more than a few intimate details of my sexual encounters along the journey. This is not intended to excite you. Instead, I have opened myself up in this very personal manner to give you an understanding of the turmoil and detachment that goes on for a kid when he or she is being molested. An element of terror and/or shame gets mixed in with an element of pleasure, and the result is a kind of confused insanity. If the details do excite you, I hope you will look within and challenge yourself to see why an act of child molestation shouldn't be a turn-on. Period.

This Book is Unique:
It breaks the silence and deals with the guilt and shame about what runaways find they must do to survive. It has been taboo for survivors to share and talk about certain aspects of the runaway experience. I hope to set an example by stating unequivocally, that regardless of the crummy things runaways go through, we are still good people, deserving of as much loving nurturance and acceptance as everyone else.

Pressure to Hide:
People have expressed concern that attaching my name to this book may invite life-long negative repercussions; it has been repeatedly suggested that I therefore don't write it, write it anonymously, or at least, leave out the more embarrassing or controversial details.

This attitude epitomizes the challenge we have in the United States with our runaway situation; almost no one wants to risk being honest, and too few are willing to directly help solve these problems themselves.

Meanwhile, thousands of runaway kids are homeless tonight. Fifteen will die within the next day.

I have a vision of healing, and the chance of transforming it into reality more than offsets the risk incurred by speaking out.

Pressure to Blame:

Several book publishers and film producers offered to take on this project, but only if I began the story with blame. They wanted it to start off with a bang, a traumatic scene with someone abusing me, so that readers and viewers would have someone to hate and blame for my running away. This way audiences would better sympathize with my "character" (me), and become that much more drawn in.

Hate and blame sell product. Americans are used to righteous anger and the violence it justifies. Most action movies and TV shows begin with the villain perpetrating a horrible crime, so we can cheer for the hero as he or she beats, kills, or imprisons the villain.

Wars begin this way too.

Hate, blame, and violence are destructive. They create more problems than they solve.

Judgement and finger-pointing aren't what we need. Love and personal responsibility are.

I Was Abused:

Yes, like many runaways, I was abused as a child. But I won't tell whether it was by family, teachers, counselors, friends, or acquaintances. The point here is not to shame or embarrass anyone — not to start things with a bang. Yet regardless of who perpetrated it, the abuse was a significant part of my development, and ultimately had a lot to do with why I ran.

My abuse came from more than one perpetrator and consisted of physical, emotional, and some sexual elements. It wasn't something that happened every day, but in the course of making it to age fifteen there were instances where I was:

whipped with a belt or paddle,

ignored,

beaten with fists and feet,

lifted by my hair,

kept in isolation for long periods of time,

called horrible names,

stripped naked and told I was a dog in front of others,

labeled as "lazy," "a liar," "a failure," and other denigrating names,

ordered to touch the naked body of an adult who undressed in front of
     me,

arrested when walking down the street with my friend, simply because it
     was five in the morning and state law said we weren't allowed out

until six,
slapped across the face when singing,
tickle-tortured until I literally couldn't breathe,
ganged up on and beaten by groups of people,
told through vicious accusations that my loved ones were rotten, incompetent, or inferior people,
publicly hung up on a nail wearing nothing but my underwear,
humiliated by having my stained underwear hung up out of my reach, clearly labeled with my name where others could see it,
robbed at knife point,
spit on in front of others,
and (unfortunately) so on, ad nauseam.

The world didn't seem like a nice place in which to live. I ran, not consciously seeking to avoid abuse, but simply to get away from an overwhelming burden of shame, confusion, pain, and guilt. One day something just snapped in me, and though I had no idea where I was going or what I'd do when I arrived, I couldn't handle going home. I wasn't running "towards" anything, merely away.

But running didn't help. Once I ran I found myself engulfed in the struggle to survive, to find food, shelter, and some safe space to simply be. I was alone and in a profound state of shock. The continual bombardment by one crisis after another prevented my catching my breath long enough to even begin to untangle the knot of emotions within. Wherever I went there were new threats, new people looking for an opportunity to abuse me further.

Many Reasons for Running:

There are a wide variety of "motives" kids have for leaving home. At base, the one thing all these motivations have in common is that kids are going through enough discomfort at home to make it seem worth the risk of running away. The causes span a spectrum ranging from sheer boredom, through drug, physical, sexual, psychological, and verbal abuse, all the way to suicidal depression. Some kids take off to explore the world. Others feel it's important to be independent and not be a further financial, time, or emotional burden on their already overloaded family. Still others feel their parents don't love or care about them or that running is the only way to get their parents' attention. All of these reasons, and many others, exist and are responsible for driving children to run away.

What is really important for you to know? Namely, when children do run away, they go through hell in our land; America.

Vision:

I have a vision of a world in which every child is blessed with all the love, opportunity, nurturance, and safety they need.

I have a raging anger and profound sadness because the world we share is so unnecessarily far from this vision.

I am filled with loving, peaceful joy because I know my vision will some-day come true.

And I have one nagging question: When?

Please read on.

"Coyote Lives"

By Evan Cutler

Coyote lives inside all
of our hearts,
minds,
habits and attitudes;
sometimes wakeful, alert,
snatching control;
sometimes sleeping lightly,
in its dormant domain.

Coyote is going to surprise us,
insidiously steering our actions,
stealing our self-control,
and creating changes we would never predict.

Coyote doesn't know itself
what it will create,
for that awareness always knocks Coyote
on balance
and into slumber once again.

Coyote says
aaoooohhh!! it hurts!
to be truly alive,
to dart our eyes around
and experience our surroundings,
to let ourselves feel the surging
gushing flow of feeling
that inundates us when we are awake.

Coyote needs
and wants to be alive;
to rouse from slumber and drink
from the river of life,
to lurch and leap
after nourishing soulfood,
and finally,
to complete the cycle in safe slumber,
in its dormant domain.

Flight

My face was still stinging from the five-fingered slap when I decided to jump out of the car. But the fire on my face was nothing compared to the burning I felt deeper inside. As the car slowed at the next red light I opened the door and took off. I didn't know where I was going or when I would be back; all I knew was that I couldn't take it anymore. I was getting away.

Blinded by a fury of frustrated rage, I bolted across a field and beyond some trees, and before I knew it, I was lost, weaving through a maze of people's backyards. The car was far behind me, out of sight, and I was too upset to care.

Everything is built far apart in Florida, almost too far for foot travel, and walking a mere mile beneath the blistering sun can be an ordeal worth avoiding. But off I went, through the first mile, and the next, and the next.

After running, then walking, the first couple of miles through fields, then a sprawling housing development, and later along a busy highway, I came upon a shopping center. Not knowing what else to do, I stopped at a pay phone and called Mike, a boy my age I'd partied with a few hours earlier. I didn't tell him I'd just run away from home. Instead, aiming to get myself asked over, I made up a story about how I had some unexpected free time to kill and could use some help.

Mike had nothing better to do so he invited me over. Good. I was relieved because it meant I could put off dealing with my family for a while. I had no idea what kind of trouble I'd get into for leaping from the car, let alone for drinking those beers with Mike before being picked up from school in the first place. That would have to wait until I could calm down.

Mike gave directions to his place in Cape Coral, adding that I'd have to get there by myself. Being only fifteen like me, he was too young to drive — legally that is. No problem. Cape Coral was just a few miles down the road and the rush hour traffic was still plenty heavy. And I welcomed anything that would take my mind off the trouble I'd just gotten myself into. I stuck out my thumb and hitched over within half an hour.

Mike's family had a small apartment in a plain, brick building. It was supper time when I arrived. At his mother's invitation I sat down and joined them. Between mouthfuls of food, his parents drilled me, asking too many questions about school, my family, and how I was getting home. I made up the sort of unverifiable bullshit answers I knew they wanted to hear: explaining how I was going to be picked up at a nearby shopping center when my dad came back from a late meeting.

After enduring some sorry excuse for a dessert, Mike and I were finally free to go out and have fun. We went to a nearby shopping center and busied ourselves looking at the stuff piled by the garbage cans in back, throwing rocks, and gabbing about nothing important.

It was as though I was just playing with a friend after school. I didn't stop to think about what I'd do afterward, until afterward came. Reality was right where I needed it, conveniently on hold, along with fear, insanity, and despair.

The evening rolled on quite smoothly for a while... until about eleven, that is. That's when Mike had to go home. Unlike Mike, I had no curfew. I was supposed to have been home hours ago and a few more wouldn't make any difference. I told him I'd hitch home and see him at school the next day. We had only three days of final exams left before summer break began. I never saw Mike again.

Not knowing where else to go, I decided to return home. I'd calmed down a bit and figured I'd face whatever medicine I had coming to me. Though terrified by what might happen, I didn't know what else to do. There was nowhere else to go.

After only a few minutes of walking with my thumb out, I was picked up by a ragged, hairy looking fellow headed back across the bridge to Fort Myers. The man had a rather remarkable invention with him, and in a burst of pride, offered a demonstration.

His device was nothing other than a typical red squeezy ketchup bottle, but instead of ketchup, it was used for marijuana. He unscrewed the lid, and in the hole on the underside, stuck the mouth end of a burning joint. Then he carefully screwed the lid back on so that the lit grass was suspended within.

Held a few inches from his face, a simple squeeze was all it took to project a narrow, yet potent stream of thick smoke through the nozzle and directly into his mouth. Mr. Squeezy explained that this gadget enabled him to get one hell of a "hit", getting him exceptionally high, much faster than by smoking joints in a more conventional manner.

First taking a couple of power-hits himself, Mr. Squeezy let me give it a

"Squeezy" By Chris DeHerrera

try. Indeed, as promised, I was soon utterly stoned. The man was a true inventor, and had the laws been a bit different, he could have made a humble living from sales of his special ketchup bottles.

Having shared his gadget and grass, Mr. Squeezy dropped me at the last intersection we had in common on our separate routes. He left me stoned out of my mind, needing at least four more rides to get home. I wished I could fly.

Hitchhiking wasn't new to me. I was doing it more often lately, instead of taking the bus to school. I'd always hated dealing with the jerks on the bus, and began riding my bicycle there as soon as I could. But when we moved to Florida, my daily trip grew to over twenty-six miles each way, between our house on Sanibel Island and the school on the mainland. Without wings, or even a car and a driver's license, hitchhiking was the only way to avoid the bus.

In fact, I'd been hitchhiking to school so regularly in the past few months that the same person usually gave me my first ride each day — a light-hearted little old lady who happened to be a teacher in one of the Fort Myers middle schools. Smiling even before the sun rose, she raced her sporty MG convertible all the way off Sanibel, to within five miles of my school. From there it usually was easy to snatch a couple more short rides.

But, night-time was different. Rides rarely happened to be turning the same way I needed to go, so it would probably take at least four more to get home. As the night wore on, and the roads grew more remote and rural, I could count on ever fewer passing cars. The last stretch would be the roughest; six miles bounded by thick, swampy forest on either side, a dense tangle broken only by an occasional intersection with a short, sandy access road.

It was about midnight now, and traffic was almost nonexistent. I stuck out my thumb and looked around with wide, bloodshot eyes. Feeling paranoid, afraid that any passing vehicle might be a police car, I prayed I'd get a ride soon. But I didn't.

Two hours passed and I had covered a mere handful of miles, including a long stretch alongside a palm tree studded golf course. None of the six or seven cars that passed had given into the fruitless plea of my extended thumb. When I finally did get home, I wondered, how would I sneak in without waking my dad. This anxiety-ridden walk was driving me crazy. When the next car approached, I boldly strode out in the street, waving my arms back and forth over my head to flag it down.

It worked! The driver stopped to ask what was wrong. I explained my frustration in trying to get a simple ride towards home, and once he had a chance to realize I was only a kid, he offered me one. It was a good thing I'd waited so long after all, because it allowed some of the pot to wear off. My head had cleared just enough to allow me to speak semi-coherently with the driver.

He was a thin, tired looking fellow with a neatly trimmed beard and an air about him that said he might be returning from a long, unromantic date. With a firm handshake, the man introduced himself as Robert and explained that he was going to Fort Myers Beach. Oh great, I groaned inwardly. That meant he could only take me a few more miles before turning onto another road. I would need a minimum of two more rides.

When I complained how, at the rate I was going, I wouldn't get home before sunrise, Robert offered me another choice. He said that if I wanted to, I could stay at his place that night, and he would drop me off at school when he returned to work the next morning. That way I could attend classes with a few hours' sleep under my belt and take the bus straight home from there. Alternatively, I was free to try my luck waiting for another ride.

It took less than a moment to decide. It was already past two, and my body and mind were drained from the day's misadventure. Putting off my return meant not having to face my father for another day. A part of me felt ever more afraid that I'd get it bad — real bad — when I got home. I accepted Robert's offer.

In my exhausted state, it never occurred to me to be the slightest bit afraid or suspicious of this man. In a sense, I felt safer with him *because* he was a stranger. For the first time in my life I would be staying away for an entire night without telling anyone where I was.

I felt a new kind of thrill. I knew I was digging myself a deeper and deeper hole, but at least it was me doing the digging, me taking control. During the ride, Robert and I exchanged few words, and I deluded myself into thinking I still was heading back, just by a longer route.

Robert's sofa was uncomfortable, and despite my fatigue it took a while to fall asleep.

Gnarled Hand

A moment later I awoke to Robert informing me it was time to get ready to go.

My first thought was, "Already?"

It was about six in the morning. I'd managed a bare three hours of fitful sleep, and the sun was shining a lot more brightly than I was. If I'd been in my own bed, I would have rolled back to sleep, ignoring my responsibilities. But I was a guest, and knowing my welcome was almost up, I rubbed the sleep from my eyes and forced myself to rise.

Using Robert's bathroom was an altogether awkward endeavor. It was filthy, rivaling some of the rankest gas station restrooms I'd used, and I didn't have any of my own shower stuff. The sticky floor only reluctantly released me from each step. There was no counter space and no place to hang my clothes either, so I balanced them on the relatively clean toilet lid while I showered. The shower curtain was coated with a slimy combination of mold and accumulated soap residue.

About two minutes into my shower I noticed the water had backed up to my ankles. Checking the drain, I lifted out a slippery clump of hair. This kept the water from rising any further, but wasn't enough to drain the tub. To finish without a layer of slime coating my supposedly clean feet, I had to clumsily straddle the tub and rinse them one at a time before placing them on the tiny, urine stained mat outside.

A sticky cloud of hot steam filled the room, yet I didn't want to open the door before dressing. At least Robert had given me a clean towel to dry off with, but it didn't have the same fresh smell I was used to at home. It was almost pointless to dry off anyway, as sweat immediately replaced any water I removed. Giving up, I wiggled into the clothes I'd worn for the past twenty four hours, making myself hotter still. The moisture brought out the stench of cigarette smoke from the fabric, causing it to reek like an ashtray. There wasn't much I could do about it, so I dove through the door to escape the bathroom as quickly as possible. For the first time in my life, I appreciated my nice, clean bathroom at home.

Robert was eating breakfast and offered me anything I wanted from the refrigerator, as long as I could finish it within five minutes. I wasn't all that hungry anyway, and just gulped a glass of orange juice. We left a few minutes later, and I smoked my day's first cigarette while he drove me the twenty miles back to Cypress Lake High.

Explaining that I wanted to get a candy bar before class, I had Robert drop me at the Seven-Eleven about a block from the school. The busses were just arriving, disgorging their cargos of tired looking kids, which meant I didn't have much time.

The bell for my first class would ring in about ten minutes. I smoked a cigarette and decided not to attend. Feeling smelly and depressed, I was in no mood to spend my day being herded around like a cow. Instead, I would skip school and find better things to do all day. Then, when school let out in the afternoon, I would act like I'd been in class all day, merge with the crowds leaving the building, and board the bus for a quick, free ride home.

It seemed wise to get out of the area for now. The trick was to manage this without being spotted by any bus drivers or faculty members who would recognize me as a student and bring me in for truancy. The quickest way out of there was to hitch another ride. I headed towards the state highway.

In Fort Myers, US 41 is bordered on either side by a variety of boring stores. Car dealerships and carpet stores were not my idea of fun. If there had been a video arcade and I had a decent supply of quarters, I would have been glad to play away the long hours till the bus could take me home.

But there were no arcades, and when I'd jumped out of the car and launched into this journey the day before, I only had about fifty-nine cents in my pocket. Besides this change, all I had with me were the clothes I was wearing (blue jeans, tee-shirt, socks, sneakers, and jockey shorts), my watch, and a pack and a half of cigarettes. I wished I had a good science fiction book to bury myself in until school let out.

Feeling an overwhelming sensation of dread and panic subverted under a layer of numb disorientation, and not knowing where I was heading exactly, I did my best to get on with the day. I waited at an intersection, thumb out, hoping to get a lift to somewhere else, anywhere else. A sense of timelessness, an almost trance-like state, overtook me.

My first ride out of the commercial zone was with an elderly man in an ancient, red beast of a pickup truck. The man looked well past retirement, with a thin, achingly hunched body and withered old skin. He was mostly bald, except for a wispy bit of white hair above his ears. He never said a word to me.

About ten minutes down the road, the man reached his arm over and put his gnarled hand on my left knee. Till then, I'd been spacing out, watching the never-ending forest drift by. I didn't know what to do, and just sat stock still for a moment, but he didn't remove his wrinkled fingers. A chill of confused apprehension surged through me while I debated whether to push away his hand or say something. The truck's engine continued its steady, hoarse whine and I still couldn't figure out what to do. Then the man dragged his bony appendage just a little bit further up my thigh.

That was too much for me, too freaky, and I breathed deep to gather some force. With all the strength and resolution I could muster, I managed to blurt out, "Stop the car! NOW!" And, "Let me out!"

A few seconds plodded by. I was panicking: what if he didn't do what I demanded? He didn't look very strong, but then, neither was I. The man wasn't much of a threat while he was driving, and I was pretty sure I could outrun him if I had to. But I didn't have any weapons...

He removed his hand and down-shifted as he pulled over, slowing the vehicle. Before it had come to a complete stop, I jumped out and backed off a few steps to see what the man was going to do.

He drove away.

So this is what they mean by "dirty old man," I thought.

I felt lucky. It was like the time when I jumped out of the bathtub just before the electric fan fell in, discharging so much energy into the bathwater that the fuse shorted. I'd seen the fan falling, slowly, inevitably, and wasn't sure if my motion to get out of the tub would hasten its fall. But I had to do something.

Like then, I was lucky to escape unscorched. What if the man hadn't listened? What if my yelling had only made him angry? But it was all over now, and "what if"-ing myself to death wouldn't get me where I was going.

Regrettably, I'd been dropped off miles from any traffic lights or stop signs. The empty road was flanked by a thick, swampy forest. Sweating under the mid-day sun, I took off my shirt and began what was to become the darkest tan of my life while I walked north and waited for the next ride.

The day drifted by with the miles, until a few rides later I was picked up by another unusual fellow, the Pipe-Man. The Pipe-Man smoked a typical wooden tobacco pipe, which he repacked with the contents of an ordinary zippered tobacco pouch. What made his pouch different though, was that it contained a mixture of one part pipe tobacco to one part marijuana.

The Pipe-Man explained that by mixing it like that, the police would never suspect he had pot. The tobacco masked the marijuana's smell, and once it was all blended together in a bag, it was difficult to distinguish the grass from the tobacco. By the smug and enthusiastic way he expounded upon his system, it was clear that the Pipe-Man was proud of his original idea. He was an innovator, the second I'd run into in less than twenty-four hours.

When the Pipe-Man asked where I was heading, I had to think for a while. Somewhere between this morning and this ride, my goal had unconsciously changed. I was no longer just skipping school. My fog was lifting and I became suddenly aware, knew for the first time, that I was no longer planning to return home; not this day, or any day in the near future.

In a voice I didn't recognize as my own, I replied that I had just turned eighteen, and was moving away from home to make it on my own. It was a lie, but maybe not a complete one; I *was* moving away. In fact, I'd already traveled over sixty miles. I told the fellow I wasn't sure where I was going, but my plan was to explore Florida until I found a good place to make a living.

The Pipe-Man suggested I check out Sarasota, the next major town in the direction we were heading. He figured the rich old folks who retired there would pay a lot for bellhops and other kinds of helpers. When he asked how much money I had, and I told him fifty-nine cents, he gave me a five dollar bill to help me get started. Then he dropped me off, stoned once again, near the bridge to Sarasota. He wished me luck.

Using pot wasn't a big deal anymore. I'd been smoking so regularly in the past months it had become a normal part of my day to day life. In fact, the lion's share of my experiences over the previous year were filtered through my drugged fog.

In the months before taking off, I was smoking pot several times a week, sometimes several times a day. Although I frequently enjoyed getting high, there was a big part of it I didn't like. Mainly the paranoia which set in after I'd smoked and started to worry about getting caught.

Pot was readily available at my high school. And it wasn't necessary to seek out dealers. They found me. This wasn't hard since I was a cigarette addict and smoking at school was against the rules. The bathrooms and a couple nooks outside were the only places on campus where kids could get away with it, and that's right where the dealers went to sell their wares.

For a buck apiece they sold us "pin joints," skinny cigarettes of terribly strong pot. It was of a variety called Sensimilia, so potent that one or two hits would sink me into a cushioning haze sure to last until classes let out.

When I didn't happen to have a dollar with me, the dealers extended credit. They'd offer to accept payment the next day. And they remembered exactly who owed them, and how much. They were efficient business-people, often selling up to twenty joints in just a couple of minutes.

That year there was also an abundant supply of what was commonly tagged "Sea-Weed." This was pot that had been washed up on the shores in giant rectangular bundles, about the size of hay bales. These enormous blocks of pot came from smugglers dumping their cargo overboard when they feared they were about to get caught by the Coast Guard.

In the spring before I ran, there was a giant incident of this sort right offshore. Shortly afterward there were literally tons of this dirt-cheap Sea-Weed available. It was harsh to smoke after days or weeks of floating in salty water, but it sure got me high. And at a mere thirty bucks an ounce, it was a bargain.

With everything from Sea-Weed to Sensimilia at such affordable prices, and with me being a lonely and depressed kid in desperate need of escape, I smoked all I could get. Consequently, it wasn't some unique, frightening, or novel experience to have strangers share their pot. It happened often.

It didn't take long to hitch the rest of the way to Sarasota. Once there, I wandered around until I found a strip of high-rise condominiums. I asked a few doormen if I could get any work, but there were no takers.

Nothing felt right about the area. Yes, there was plenty of wealth around — expensive cars, buildings, and property — but it was all so far from me, so private and out of reach. I found no public areas where I'd be allowed to mingle unchallenged. Every clean-cut curve of the town seemed to cry out, "Go away, Evan, you don't belong!"

Perhaps this repelling vibration was intentionally built into the design of the place. Or maybe I simply didn't feel far enough away from my family yet. In any case, I soon developed an overpowering urge to get out of Sarasota, and fast. I decided to forget the Pipe-Man's advice about the opportunities there and continued north.

Into the Castle

Several hours and forty miles later, I arrived at Saint Petersburg Beach. The sky was still a clear, cloud-studded light blue, yet softened the way it gets an hour or so before sunset. The driver who dropped me off had said I was about two blocks from the beach and had pointed the way before speeding away. As I followed his finger down the road, a huge, castle-like building caught my attention.

I approached, noticed luxurious automobiles pulling in under the entry awning where sharply uniformed bellhops opened the passengers' doors, and soon realized it was a ritzy hotel. Curious, I went inside to locate a bathroom and explore a little. I found myself awestruck at the sheer class and majesty of the place.

The lobby level had towering ceilings, from which dangled intricately ornate glass chandeliers. Fancy mirrors and plants were stuck here and there amid huge, heavily draped windows and handsome Asian-style carpeting. A cluster of people were busy checking in at the front desk, and others walked by, but no one seemed to notice me.

Continuing through the lobby, I found an enormous bar and lounge area with a cascading water fountain placed smack in the middle. People were sprinkled here and there, relaxing alone and in pairs on the comfortable furniture while reading, smoking, or drinking. Acting nonchalant, I gazed into an assortment of glass cases filled with beautiful little sculptures and pottery from around the world and wondered how much the stuff on just one of the shelves must be worth. Large, noiseless fans floating above caressed me with a gentle, cooling breeze.

Intrigued by the artful display of wealth, I continued exploring. There were several other restaurants and bars in the hotel, but the prices were far out of my reach. At eight dollars, a plain old hamburger and fries cost half again as much as I had to my name. Depressed, I kept exploring.

The bottom floor was occupied by an art gallery and ice cream parlor. I wanted a double decker on a sugar cone, with one scoop of strawberry, and a second of mint chocolate chip, but decided I'd better save my money. I walked on, past a small gift shop, a workout center with separate male and female exercise rooms, and a sign offering professional massage, "with appointment."

When I went out back to the pool deck, a buffet was being served for the guests. My stomach growled. That early morning glass of orange juice had long since been digested and I was more than ready to eat. I looked around, and as far as I could tell people were just going up and taking whatever food they wanted. No one seemed to be collecting money or checking names or room numbers.

Opportunity was knocking and I could either hide until it went away, or invite it on in. I resolved to welcome it with all that I had, and sauntered up to the buffet, seized a plate, and filled it with all it would hold. By the time I walked away, it was covered with meaty hors d'oeuvres, fruit salad, cheeses, breads, crackers, and two desserts. Unchallenged, I planted myself on a lounge chair near the pool, and relished my dinner. My safety lay in acting like I belonged there, merely doing what any other guest would do — lounge about the pool and eat.

Looking back, I saw the imposing structure of the pink and white hotel with its two wings branching off to either side. The center of the building ascended to castle like turrets on top of which appeared two separate bell towers. Several of the rooms had balconies overlooking the Gulf of Mexico. The scale and expense of everything was beginning to make me feel pretty small, and I figured I ought to split.

Once full, I lit a cigarette, inhaled, and cut through to the front of the hotel where I began hoofing it northward, along the road nearest the beach. After about a block I came upon George.

George was about my age, had tight, curly brown hair, and an anxious, yearning look like he was desperately seeking some way to escape his boredom. He sat on the front stairs of an expensive beachside home, and upon spying the cigarette in my hand bummed one for himself. We started talking, and I explained what I had just done back at the hotel, going on at some length about the richness of the place.

He didn't believe that just anyone could simply walk into the hotel and wander around like I had. Glad for a chance to show off, I offered to prove it. We went back into the hotel, and out towards the pool, and after a little coaching I demonstrated how we could pick whatever we wanted right off the buffet table. The two of us sat around and ate a few more hors d'oeuvres before the novelty wore off.

Like me, George appeared to be dazzled by the hotel's turrets and towers. "How would you like to go explore that?" I asked him. "I bet we could get up there!"

George stared at me for a second, then broke into a mischievous smile. We boarded the elevator and pushed the button for the highest floor. Once there, we wandered the halls, seeking a way onto the roof. That's when the manager found us.

The manager was an official, grumpy looking man. He had short-cropped dark hair and wore a well-fitting suit and a perfectly combed and mani-cured mustache. His face was knit into a serious, authoritative frown when he told us some people had complained that we didn't belong. He demanded to know what we were doing in the hotel.

We belonged as much as anyone else! What was so special about the so-called legitimate guests, that they were able to stay while others could not?

Money, of course. Other than having a few hundred dollars more to blow each day than we did, they weren't so different from us. Just folks. But their little rectangles of green inked paper and shiny plastic got them more privi-lege and respect than I could hope for in the next decade.

With a self-righteous anger born of desperation, I bluffed, telling the manager that our parents were staying at the hotel.

"What are their names?" he demanded.

Committed by this point, I made up a name. "The McGregers. My name's John McGreger."

He looked skeptical. "I don't know of any McGreger's staying here. What room are you staying in?"

George chimed in and made up a room number a few floors below. "Room two-seventy-two," he answered.

"We don't have any such room," the manager declared. "Look, if you don't start telling the truth right now, I'm going to call the police."

Why did George have to give a room number that didn't exist? The place was big all right, but it obviously didn't have over seventy rooms on each floor. If he had to make up a story, at least he could have taken care not to spawn an patently impossible one. I was pissed off at George, but it clearly wasn't a good time to tell him.

Instead, I gave up on our fiction, and in my most innocent voice told the manager that we were just trying to see what the building looked like in-side; we'd wandered by and been impressed by how much it looked like a real castle. We weren't trying to hurt anything, I assured him, and didn't want to get into any trouble.

The man told us we had to leave, immediately, and escorted us into the elevator. He took us downstairs and routed us out through the front door. We left willingly, of course, glad to receive only a lecture. George and I walked down the street a short way, and smoked a cigarette or two before he said he'd better go home for dinner. It was time to go our separate ways.

Twilight had arrived, and I knew not where to go or what to do. The place was new to me, and I'd never been alone for a night in a strange town before. My resources were limited. Thanks to the Pipe-Man my cash was up to $5.59, but my cigarettes were down to half a pack.

Confused, sick at finding myself engulfed in a second nightfall — this time over a hundred miles from home and without even a plan or destination in mind — I wandered along the beach, heading towards the hotels to the north. One after another the waves collapsed ever so softly upon the shore, each one impacting my hungering heart like a gentle nudge towards insanity. I'd never been so lost in my life.

Sometime later, well after the sky had turned to a deep black with myriad sharp specks of starlight, I found an all-night coffee shop in one of the hotels. Whether the chill came from me or the breezy night air, the prospect of crashing out in a warm place lured me into the dimly lit restaurant for a look at the menu. Without blowing the money needed for my next pack of cigarettes, the only things I could afford were a cup of coffee and some french fries.

Never having tried more than a sip of coffee before, I wasn't too excited about ordering it. The small quantities I had drunk had left an acid taste in my mouth. But it was the only thing on the menu that came with unlimited free refills. I figured if I ordered it, the waitresses would let me hang out for a while.

And I was right. Always being thirsty, and having more than a slight tendency to go to extremes, I learned how to drink coffee in quantity on this night; not by the cup, but by the pot. I spent the next five or six hours in that restaurant resisting the urge to sink horizontal and sleep on that cushy booth. Instead, I passed time reading a thick newspaper, slurping down my bottomless cup of coffee, and smoking cigarettes till my lungs ached, eventually buying a new pack from a vending machine in the lobby.

If I could, I would most likely have continued in this way until another five hours went by and a new day dawned. But at about two AM, things changed. When I looked up from my paper to get another refill I noticed two policemen coming inside the restaurant to soak up some coffee themselves.

An icy fear pulsed through my shaky frame as I imagined the officers questioning me. Why was I there all alone so late at night? Where were my parents? Where did I live?

It was time to leave. Unsure if they had noticed me yet, I left some money on the table, went to the bathroom, and slipped out by a side door. Perhaps they never would have even spoken to me, but I couldn't afford to take that chance.

I was charged to capacity after drinking seven cups of coffee and spying the police. Yet at the same time I was exhausted. It was now two or three in the morning, and I'd only had a paltry few hours of sleep the night before. The dark side of this day dragged into eternity while I roamed the beach and waited for morning to arrive.

Searching

The sun rose upon a new day. Tired from a sleepless night, I had no food, no place to stay, and was back to less than a dollar again. Finding a way to obtain these necessities was the obvious focus for the day. This couldn't be too hard, I figured; after all, everyone else managed.

I initiated my search by going from one store or restaurant to another, asking for work. Yet I kept running into the same problem everywhere I went. On every application form the first blanks asked for *Name, Address, and Phone Number.*

For the time being I only had one of these, a name, and I didn't want anyone to know it. Even if they were looking for new employees, they weren't considering homeless applicants.

The other blanks were even more of an obstacle.

Education: *Almost finished ninth grade, now truant.*

Previous Employment: *Occasional baby-sitting, and work in my grandfather's store.*

References: *None, though I could think of a few people who would attest to my general state of delinquency.*

These were all requests for societal connections which I now lacked completely. Answering honestly would only ensure I remained unemployed. I'd have to find work somewhere without one of these forms.

Further complicating matters, the first paycheck for unskilled work was usually issued at least seven days after completing the first week of work. I had neither I.D., nor any idea how I'd ever cash a check even if I could get hired, let alone work for two weeks before receiving my first cent. My hungry stomach and nicotine craving cells couldn't wait that long. I needed a way to earn some money now.

I tried asking if I could work for immediate cash. A typical response was, "Sorry, but we don't hire day laborers here." Another common one was "The manager's not here right now. Can you come back in six hours?"

Looking for a simple job had become one of the most frustrating experiences of my life.

After half a day's disappointments, I trudged into a poorly lit hotel restaurant. It was early in the afternoon, between the lunch and dinner rushes, and the place was nearly empty. My stomach growled painfully. When the waitress came to seat me I made an embarrassed half-smile and asked if I could work in exchange for some food.

That got her attention.

After a quick double-take, wherein she looked me over head to toe, the waitress solemnly stated, "Come with me." She escorted me to where the manager was sitting with some other people, and asked me to repeat my request. When I did, he asked why I needed food. I told them I'd just left home to start living on my own and had looked all morning for work, but couldn't find any. Since working for money didn't seem possible, I thought I'd try working for a simple meal.

The manager declared that they would help me out, but first he wanted to know a little more about my situation. From the way everyone was looking at me, I could feel their genuine concern; they wanted to find some way to give me a hand. I took a risk and told them the truth, that I'd just run away from home and was trying to get a good, honest start at taking care of myself.

They looked a bit shocked. The manager became excited. "Sure, we'll give you some food! Don't worry about working for it! Just wait here in the dining room and I'll have something cooked up for you in a few minutes. Then we'll try to work something out for you."

Wow! This was a bit more than expected. I'd honestly intended to work and felt ashamed to accept the free food, but I was too hungry to hold onto my pride. I offered my thanks with as much dignity as I could manage. They said they'd be right back and the group of them disappeared into the kitchen.

After waiting alone in the dining area for a while, I grew aware of a deep-seated doubt mounting in the pit of my stomach. There was no concrete proof, just a gut-level instinct, but I feared I was being set up somehow.

On an impulse, I slipped out through the side door. Just then, I spied two police cars pulling up in front of the hotel. Of course I couldn't be sure they were coming for me, but my strong feelings and intuitions had saved me from a slew of dangers before, and I was apt to trust them.

I stifled my urge to bolt, instead forcing myself into a casual pace in the opposite direction. A moment after ducking out of sight, around the corner of the building, I let go, darted up the beach, and vanished from the area. It was no longer safe for me to stay anywhere nearby. For all I knew the police would be looking for me. I was a fugitive, fearful of even being within eyesight of the police.

Despairing, I left Saint Petersburg soon after, and hitchhiked north into the sprawling city of Tampa. Unsure of where to go, I asked my next ride what other beach communities had lots of hotels. I reckoned I could make myself inconspicuous and survive better in a place with plenty of tourists. The driver said Clearwater Beach was the biggest resort area around. I determined to make it my next haven.

The driver happened to drop me off at an intersection by a huge indoor mall. It had several major department stores, and I decided to take a short detour inside to look around. My clothes felt and smelled like grimy rags after having been worn for two days straight without any change. I was used to being clean and fresh and the broiling waves of heat radiating from the asphalt parking lot weren't helping any.

As I opened the double doors to one of the gargantuan department stores, I was slammed by a powerful blast of cool, dry air. Relief! In no hurry, I relaxed within the airlock-like chamber for a few minutes before launching into the store itself.

When I got around to entering, the fresh looking outfits in the young men's department reached out and pulled me off course. I gazed around at the mannequins and shelves of clothing. There were piles of jeans and shirts just like what I was wearing, and I suddenly remembered how bored I'd always been when my mom dragged me out shopping each year to buy a new wardrobe.

New clothes. Clean clothes. After but a moment's deliberation, I decided to ignore the fact that I was broke and try something on. I took a new outfit to one of the fitting rooms, removed my dingy and damp attire, and tried on the clean stuff.

The new garb fit perfectly. It had to be mine! I resolved to steal it.

Just as in the big hotel on Saint Petersberg Beach, my challenge was to act like I belonged, like it was perfectly fine for me to leave whenever I pleased. I had to avoid giving any impression that would make people suspicious. But it wasn't easy.

My mind raced, repeating over and over again, "Did anybody see me? Will they know? Can they tell that these are clothes from the store? Am I gonna get caught? What happens if I get caught? Would I go to jail? Would my dad find out?" Whatever might happen, it seemed worth the risk. With any choice, I simply wasn't getting back into those gross old duds again.

I looked around to make sure no one could see me. I was the only one in the fitting room, so I took a chance and removed all the price and inventory tags. This was it! There was no going back now.

Acting as nonchalant as possible, I walked out of the changing room and, a minute later, out of the store, leaving my dirty clothes behind in exchange. I wandered around the rest of the mall for another twenty min-

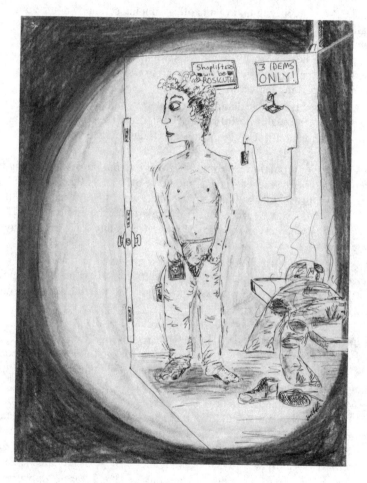

"3 Items Only" By Joel Heflin

utes or so, letting myself enjoy the luxury of clean clothing and cool air before heading off to Clearwater Beach.

A moment after abandoning the comfortable confines of the mall, my pores opened wide, soaking me in sweat once again. By the time I crossed the parking lot and began hitching towards Clearwater Beach, my new shirt was as damp as the one I'd left behind. At least it didn't smell like an ashtray.

"But stealing is wrong, right?" I guilted myself.

"Right, but so is being a complete reject." I answered.

It simply wasn't acceptable to walk around wearing the same clothes forever. Washing them seemed an obvious choice, but what was I to wear while doing so? As long as I didn't get caught, I decided, stealing seemed the way to go. If I couldn't come up with some way to make money I'd be using this clothes exchanging technique again.

Far more important than clothes, however, was my need for smokes; I was sucking down about a pack-and-a-half a day. This horrible addiction had already caused a pile of problems in the two years I'd been hooked.

Clothes could wait days, but running out of cigarettes wasn't allowed. My body wouldn't stand it. It always pleaded for another within twenty minutes of the last. In less than an hour, the withdrawal anxiety would get so bad that I could think of little else until I inhaled a few more breaths of nicotine rich smog. I would buy, borrow, beg, and, if I had to, steal to get my next fix.

When hitchhiking, the urge was stronger than ever, but I didn't want to give the impression that I was a delinquent (though I guess I was). I sensed that being seen smoking while waiting for a ride would scare away most of the non-smokers, and all of the people who had negative stereotypes about kids who smoke. With this in mind, I only smoked when there wasn't much traffic. Then, when a car approached, I'd throw the cigarette down where the driver wouldn't see it, only retrieving it if the car passed without picking me up.

Smoking wasn't an issue here by the mall, though, because the traffic was so heavy I could get a ride at any moment; my cigarette would just be wasted upon the ground. Once I'd actually found a ride and was safely on my way, I would ask the driver if it was okay to smoke. They might say no, but wouldn't kick me out of their car just for asking.

A couple of hours slid by, and I found myself in Clearwater Beach. It was indeed a more developed tourist trap than Saint Pete had been, with at least a hundred motels and hotels. One of the larger and more expensive hotels, a towering hulk of a building, seemed an especially promising place to explore.

Choosing a button at random, I exited the elevator on the eighth floor, and found about twenty evenly spaced doors, each with a different number, lining the halls. Further exploration of the floor revealed two that were unlocked, the first leading to a stairway, and the second to a small, cramped vending alcove with ice and soda machines. Nothing exciting.

While waiting for an elevator to take me to another floor, I noticed a plain, unmarked door a few feet away. No one was around, and overcome by curiosity, I tested the handle. It was unlocked.

Behind the door lay a barren, closet-sized room. The slight breeze from swinging open the door brought a putrid stench to my nose. One wall bore a two-foot-square metal plate with the word "GARBAGE" stenciled on it. I pulled the handle and peered down a dark, metal tunnel that stunk of decay and echoed the sounds of some distant wind. At the other end of the closet stood a folded roll-away bed. I closed the door on the stinky room and continued to explore the hotel, and then other places along the beach.

The next few hours merged together in a confusing blur of seemingly random searching, but I didn't even know what I was searching for. Then something happened to wake me from my trance.

I'd been walking along the beach, shoes and socks in hand, wading through ankle deep surf, and enjoying the sensual feeling of the endless, tumbling waves pulling cooling water and sand around my feet and through my toes, when I got into a conversation with a dark haired stranger. He seemed like a nice enough guy when I first met him.

The man introduced himself as Doug something and I said I was John McGreger, my new alias of choice. Doug was a tall, thin man, about twice my age. After we talked for a few minutes, he told me he was going back to his beachfront apartment to cook up some dinner. It was only a few blocks to the north, he said, and I was invited to come along.

Doug seemed alright and I was ravenous by this time, so I accepted his offer. His first-floor apartment was cramped. It had just one modest room, serving as a combination bedroom, living room, and kitchen, with a cramped bathroom to one side. I guess he willingly traded off indoor space in exchange for living on the beach. Besides, I didn't care how small his place was; I just wanted some free food.

True to his offer Doug cooked us an appetizing spaghetti dinner. I chowed down, devouring pasta and garlic bread until I was stuffed. In the course of conversation I told Doug how I was starting out on my own and had just arrived in Clearwater Beach that day. He invited me to sleep over that night, saying he could make up a small palette on the floor. What luck! Up to that point I had no idea where, or *if*, I was going to sleep that night. Once again, I accepted his offer.

Dinner With Doug

After dinner, Doug asked me if I smoked pot.

"Sometimes," I replied.

Then he said, "I have some we could smoke if you'd like."

"Sure!" I answered. "But just a little. I don't want to get too stoned."

Doug went over to his dresser and pulled out a baggie filled with dark, leafy marijuana and a pack of rolling papers. He brought it over to the table and rolled a joint while we spoke. When finished, he lit it, sucked in a deep drag, and passed it over.

I took a medium sized hit and held it as long as I could, until it came bursting out with a great cough. Wishing to appear grown-up, I was always embarrassed when I coughed on smoke, so I tried to suppress the reflex, which only made it worse. Despite my best efforts, I lapsed into an attack of spasmodic choking that made my eyes water, nose run, and body break into a cold sweat.

Handing the burning joint back to Doug, I did my best to recover. Still toking on the joint, Doug walked over to the bathroom and got a stretch of toilet paper for my leaking eyes and nose. We passed the grass back and forth two more times, and I made sure to take even smaller breaths and let them out more quickly.

Half a joint later I became afraid it might be a bit much. "That's enough," I said. "I don't want to get too wasted." Doug was in a mellow mood and didn't pressure me, seemingly glad to smoke the rest by himself.

Then, after chatting about different things for a while, Doug abruptly shifted the conversation over to sex. "Have you ever had sex before?"

His question might have been innocent enough, but I started to feel uneasy. Something about the way he looked when he said it reminded me of someone else who had turned out to be trouble. Ignoring my sudden impulse to get the hell out of there, I answered.

43

"Not yet, but I'm sure looking forward to it someday! I just haven't found any women who are willing yet."

"That's surprising," Doug declared. "I'd think a good looking guy like you would have no problem finding girls to have sex with." He paused a moment, then added, "How about guys? Have you ever considered having sex with other guys?"

Now I knew for sure why I was having that bad feeling. This wasn't the first time a man had asked me about sex with other guys. It had happened two other times before I ran away, and I had a good idea where this conversation was leading.

I'd thought about these questions before, and knew I was attracted to women and only women. Before leaving home I had found and read a secret cache of magazines containing sexually explicit pictures of, and stories about women and sex. And the more women the better, because I got the most excitement from the lesbian scenes.

After thinking about it, I realized the reason was that like most guys, I was afraid of anything gay; I didn't want to see any guys in the picture. As long as the scenes were limited to women it was okay to be turned on. Then I could safely imagine stepping into the scene and joining them in some exhilarating activities. It didn't matter if the women were gay, just that I wasn't.

On the other hand, no matter how sexy and inspiring the women were, I couldn't get turned on when a man was also in the picture. I was too afraid to associate any kind of sexual excitement with other males, afraid to be a "faggot." To enjoy such a mixed sex scene, I'd first have to figure out how to get rid of the guy who was already there. It was far easier to see a scene with two women and add myself, than to extract someone else.

Doug's question also brought into play some things I learned from the mountain of science fiction I'd consumed. While these speculative fiction books seemed innocent enough, they ultimately led me to be more critical of the society in which I lived.

Freed from the bounds of our "real world," the writers took a current trend or idea a bit further to create other worlds. Once in these new realms, these possible futures, they attempted to see how the people in them would cope with each other and their environment. In the process, they often revealed interesting things about my own universe.

Some of these story-visions were dreadfully depressing, such as post-apocalyptic future Earths where people were trying to survive a plague, nuclear war, or environmental catastrophe. Others took me to a future utopia, or showed what the world might be like after the introduction of a wonderful new technology. But all of them provided new lenses through which I could critically examine my own, current reality.

This mind opening altering of perspective was extremely provocative, because once I could look critically at my own society, I wanted to change it. For example, after reading of a planet where robots did all the tedious work, I found myself less inclined to accept the workaday ethic of having jobs for jobs sake; after reading vivid descriptions of what Earth could be like following a nuclear war, I became fiercely opposed to the continuing build-up and maintenance of nuclear weapons; and after reading about schools of the future, wherein kids learned without studying, I hated my prison called high school more than ever. Perhaps SF would be better named "subversive fiction."

Not that subversiveness is inherently bad; that depends on what's being subverted. Protesting the genocide in Hitler's Germany was considered subversive by those in charge at the time. So was the Boston Tea Party and the rest of the independence movement that created the United States. Thousands of people were killed for participating in these movements, but I was taught they died heroes.

The science fiction I'd read had made me more tolerant of other people. Like most kids, by grade school I'd learned that it was fine to be attracted to the other sex. Yet if I was attracted to the boys I'd be "Bad," a "Queer," and a "Fag," the most loathsome things there were. But through SF I learned how people in other times or worlds might view their sexuality differently than the ways approved of in mine.

Lazarus Long, a character in Robert Heinlein's books, was one of those people. He lived over four thousand years, and during these four millennia ended up fathering hundreds of children. Consequently, his descendants eventually amounted to over a quarter of all human beings, thanks to all the different wives that he'd bred with, and all of their kids, their kids' kids, their grandkids' kids, and so on. After a while, nearly every human alive was related to Lazarus, if not genetically, then by marriage.

In time, this presented Lazarus with the problem that when he met new women, he would probably be related to them through some distant lineage. He reasoned that it was ridiculous to rule out one-quarter of all the women in the universe just because he might have had sex with one of their distant ancestors. Lazarus's high ethical concerns, coupled with his eternal horniness, led him to reconsider the cultural taboo against incest, to think about where, and even whether, the socially ordained limits should apply.

Another thing Lazarus did in the course of his long life was to have his sex changed from time to time. This is already possible, but with the fictional technology of a thousand years from now, Lazarus could do it quite safely and completely. When Lazarus changed his gender, he also switched the gender of those he had sex with. Yet he was still the same person; he had the same soul, the same memories. When Lazarus first changed, a question arose: Which would make him gay, having sex with other women (now his same sex) or having sex with men (now the opposite sex)? It was confusing to say the least.

Through reading about Lazarus Long and a host of other charismatic SF characters whose concepts of "normal" sex were different from those in my own culture, I'd become used to the idea that perfectly interesting, friendly, and decent people can have diverse ways of expressing themselves sexually. It got so I really didn't care what kind of sex people had, as long as all the participants agreed.

But I had yet to express myself sexually in the way I wanted to, with women, and I wasn't about to do it with men, who didn't interest me sexually at all.

Doug's questions still rang in my ears: "How about guys? Have you ever considered having sex with other guys?"

"No, I only like women that way," I answered. "I don't care if other people are gay, but it's not for me."

"You really shouldn't knock it when you haven't tried it," Doug retorted. "Sex with another guy can be much better than sex with a woman, because he knows exactly how to touch you to make you feel really good. I'd be happy to show you, if you'd like."

Shit! This guy wanted to have sex with me; he'd crossed the line from general to specific, leaving no more doubt about his intentions. I was scared. The other two times men had expressed this interest, it was tricky getting away, and I wondered if I was about to have another one of those sticky situations.

"No, I wouldn't like to, thank you," I replied. I explained that I was a virgin and intended to lose my virginity to a woman. "I don't care if that's what you do in your spare time, but I just don't want to."

The pot had blown me away and I wanted Doug to just back off. The normally simple act of getting my thoughts out now seemed as insurmountable as a doomed bug's attempts to tear free from the sticky clutches of fly paper. The nauseating panic racking my stomach wasn't helping any.

He kept pushing. "Most men try sex with another guy at least once in their lives," he claimed. "What difference is it going to make whether you lose your virginity to a man or a woman if you're going to do it with a guy someday anyway? You should at least try it once to see if you like it."

He wasn't letting up! This was a rotten time to have to argue about my sexuality. I knew I should try to get out of there, but it was getting late and I didn't know where else to go. I felt far too wasted to deal with the outside world. I merely wanted a place to sleep for the night.

"Look," I expelled, "I don't have anywhere else to stay tonight, but if you won't accept my answer, I'm leaving! I don't know what `most men' do, just what I don't. Maybe I'll change some day, but I only want to have

"Percarious Perch" By Kevin Brewer

sex with women now. And I don't even want to *talk* about sex anymore, okay?" My heart pounded with the force of my message as I pushed it from my far too dry mouth.

Doug stared at me, appearing surprised by my outburst. Though he was reclining unthreateningly in his chair, I was becoming afraid he might not accept "No" for an answer. His relaxed posture didn't change the fact that he was much stronger then me. I weighed how quickly I could run to the door, open it, and escape, and calculated that I could beat him out of there if it came to that. At least, that better be the case, because it would take a miracle to beat him in a fight.

"Hey man," Doug started after a drawn out moment of awkward silence, "I just thought you might want to, that's all. It's cool, okay? You can still stay here, and I won't try anything."

He seemed to mean it. I needed him to. So from somewhere beneath my haze I decided to stay, but planned on splitting if he began pressing again.

"All right," I said. "I appreciate that. Thanks." I wondered if I might have been too harsh on Doug and felt a slight pang of guilt.

We talked about other things for a little while longer, but it wasn't the same. We were merely going through the motions. Before long, Doug said he wanted to go to sleep. He gave me some blankets and a pillow to make a bed on the floor. After a brief visit to the bathroom, he said good night and turned off the lights.

I was exhausted, but still too nervous to relax, unable to trust Doug not to try something. Quietly, I lay on my palette for a long time, straining to listen and stay awake. How insane my life had become. Not that it had ever felt the opposite. I wanted out, and imagined hitching a ride to some other planet, one of the utopian worlds described in my science fiction books. It wasn't until I heard him snoring that I finally let go of my worries and allowed myself to fall into a shallow sleep.

I woke up, instantly alert, to the sound of Doug's alarm buzzing. It was morning, and the light streaming in the windows revealed the same tiny apartment I'd fallen asleep in. Across the room, I saw Doug stretching his arm out to shut off the annoying clock-thing. We both got up, and I lit a cigarette while Doug headed toward the bathroom to clean up. He said he would make breakfast after he showered, but that I'd have to leave when he took off for work.

I'd made it safely through the night! Now all I had to do was figure out what to do with myself for the rest of my life, or at least for the rest of the day. The room looked rougher with the morning sun pouring in through the smudged windows.

When he finished, Doug offered me a crack at the shower, but I said "No thanks, I'm gonna be swimming soon anyway." There was no way in hell I was going to get naked in his house after last night.

Doug cooked up some eggs and toast for us. Afterwards, as we were heading out, he to work and me to the beach, he invited me to come back later, after he returned home.

"Sounds good, I'll see you then," I lied, with no intention of ever seeing him again. He'd managed to restrain himself this time, but that didn't mean he would if given a second chance. I began wandering along the beach to see what my fourth bewildering day as a runaway would bring.

Drifting along the beach, depressed after my encounter with Doug, I remembered a couple of other sticky situations I'd extracted myself from before this eternal week.

If ...

The first incident had begun on a rainy afternoon about a year earlier, when I lived with my mom up in Haverford, Pennsylvania. I'd been fourteen.

My friend Chris and I were in one of our favorite fast food hangouts, smoking cigarettes and acting silly, whiling away the slow hours after school. Before long we entered into a conversation with a stranger — a stocky, middle-aged man who reminded me of a cheesy actor from some TV sitcom. He introduced himself as Herb.

Herb happened to leave when we did, and when he saw us unlocking our rain-soaked bikes, he asked us where we were riding to. We told him we were returning to school, about three miles away, to pick up our things before heading home. Herb said that, coincidentally, he was heading that way himself, and since it was drizzling he would be more than happy to offer us a ride. His van had ample room for both us and our bikes. Chris and I looked at each other, knew our laziness, exchanged nods, and accepted the ride.

Along the way Herb started boasting that he was a producer of adult movies. With a self-important air he explained how he had made himself and a score of young actors rich by producing a series of high-quality sex flicks. In fact, he explained, although girls were in greater demand, more than a few good looking young guys had made their bundle starring in his films.

The bait half set, Herb paused, looking us over like he was considering the possibilities. After a drawn, almost audible "hmm"ing sound, he mumbled that he was looking for some decent actors for his next movie. Then, suddenly louder and more certain, as if he had just come to a new realization, he asked if we would be interested in that kind of work; if so, we'd get four hundred dollars a piece for having wild sex with a bunch of beautiful young women.

Chris and I had talked about the twin gods of money and sex plenty of times before. To earn that kind of cash and finally lose our virginities at the same time was an opportunity almost too good to be true. But on film? What if people recognized us?

I asked Herb and he responded that it wasn't a problem; he didn't have to show our faces in the movie because it was only our bodies the viewers cared about. Chris and I looked at each other again; we both wanted to go for it. We agreed to meet Herb later that evening.

He promised to pick us up later that night and bring us to the production studio for an initial screen test with some of the women. When he pulled to a stop at our school, we told him where and when to meet us, and he left.

Herb had pledged to pick me up near my mom's house around eight o'clock. I was grounded for one of my endless sins at the time, so at around seven-thirty I pretended I was tired and told my mom I was going to sleep early. This way she wouldn't be checking in on me while I was gone. After waiting in my room with the lights off for a while, I crept over to the window, slowly slid it open, and climbed out, moving as soundlessly as a rabbit sneaking past a sleeping panther.

It was a still, dark, and cloudy night, with the only illumination coming from an occasional porch or street light. I walked to the corner where I'd told Herb to meet me. He was supposed to pick me up first, then drive to Chris's to get him too. I waited.

At about eight-ten he drove up. A block into the ride Herb told me there was a slight change in plan; Chris and I would be having separate screen tests. After mine, Herb would take me home and go get Chris for his.

Part of me was frightened by this last minute change, but another part was relieved. My kid side wanted to talk it over with Chris, but there was no way while in the van. On the other hand, my bashful side was spared the embarrassment of being naked in front of my best friend, something I'd avoided up to now. Then my greedy side kicked in, and felt glee at having first crack at the women.

We drove around in his van for a time, along a winding, unfamiliar road, before he came to a stop at an especially dark and secluded place. I had no idea where we were and the frightened side was taking over again. Nothing was going according to plan.

Herb twisted his head towards me and said, "Okay, we're ready to do the screen test."

I was puzzled. "What do you mean? Where are the women?"

"First, we have to make sure that you're brave and that you can do all sorts of stuff for the movies." he replied. "So for your screen test, I have to lick your penis. There's a hidden camera in the dashboard of the van here, and we'll get it all on film."

"Well, I, um, I don't want to do that." I stammered, terrified at my loss of control. How could I have been so dumb as to think I'd ever had any control over this?

"I thought you wanted to make lots of money in the movies." Herb sounded surprised. "Well you can't expect to become a star without doing a screen test."

"I'll have sex with women, like you'd said before," I answered, "but I don't want to with you." I couldn't see a camera, or even a lens, anywhere. The dash looked like solid plastic to me. It was raining again, and all I could see outside were a few coldly dripping trees revealed by the headlights. I didn't know what to do and wished to all the powers that might be that my friend Chris were there.

Indignant, Herb retorted, "What are you, a Chicken? We don't want any babies doing this."

"No, no, I'm not a chicken," I came back. "I just don't want to do that; this is not what you said was gonna happen. I'll do it with women, but I just don't want to do it with you."

"If you want to do it with the women, you first have to prove that your dick is long enough and that you photograph well. We don't want to hire any fraidy cats with little weanies," Herb frowned. "We can't afford to have a whole filming crew there if you're not going to cut the mustard. If you let me do this, and the screen test comes out well, we can go ahead and arrange filming with the women for the day after tomorrow."

I didn't believe him anymore, and felt an almost paralyzing fear. It was looking like all the stuff Herb had said about having sex with women was just a load of crap, and I wanted out. "Would you please just take me home?" I pleaded. "I don't want to do this."

Herb looked and sounded furious. "If you're too wimpy to perform here, you're simply not going to get the job. Maybe your friend will be *man* enough to do it." Growling, he restarted the van and drove me back near my house. Along the way, I listened to the van's rattling engine, looked around at the battered interior, and realized that if Herb had truly made so much money producing these films, he'd probably own a newer set of wheels.

He let me off, snarling that I should look him up when I grew up, and pulled away to go get Chris. Herb must have figured he still had a chance with my friend. Now freed, I began to get mortally worried about Chris; I wanted to warn him.

Rushing down the street to my house, I snuck back in through the window, slinked into the kitchen, and tried to call Chris on the telephone. It just rang and rang and rang with no answer. No one was in, and I was over five miles away. There was no way I could get there before Herb did. I debated telling my mom what had happened, but was too afraid I'd get in trouble

"Pain" By Ragz T. Rejected

for sneaking out. I should have risked it, but when it came to involving my parents in something I'd done wrong, I *was* a chicken.

As it turned out, Chris was still standing in front of his house waiting for Herb, so he couldn't hear the phone ring. The next day, I spoke with Chris and told him what had happened to me. He said pretty much the same thing happened to him, but when I asked him for details he didn't offer any more.

My second encounter with a child molester was about nine months later, after I moved in with my dad in Florida. This time it happened where I worked. A huge resort nearby occasionally hired me to baby-sit for their wealthy guests. There was a steady business from parents who didn't want to be encumbered with their bratty little children throughout every moment of their vacation.

After a typically grueling day, I stopped by the main lobby to log my hours with Bill, the chief bellhop. Bill always seemed to be in a friendly, jovial mood and, as often happened, we got to talking. When I was leaving, he said he was about to get off himself, and casually invited me over to catch an after-work joint with he and his wife.

He couldn't have come up with a better lure. I was at the peak of my grass-smoking phase and welcomed any opportunity to land a free high. Twenty minutes later, after a quick round of my favorite video game in the arcade, I went to find his pad.

Bill and his wife were both there. and as promised, we smoked a bowl and hung out for while. I was a bit nervous at first, but their jolly attitude put me at ease. Nothing bad happened, and I left with the intention of returning another day.

Over the next few weeks I got in the habit of visiting their room whenever I finished a baby-sitting job. The pot was fine, and Bill's stunning twenty-year-old wife even finer. They were openly affectionate with each other, and I secretly yearned for the day when I'd find a myself holding a girlfriend who looked like that.

Then one day Bill's wife happened to be away when I arrived. We didn't let that stop us. We smoked a heap of Bill's weed, and as if that weren't enough, he was guzzling some kind of mixed drink. Evidently this combination of drink and drug was enough to help Bill ditch whatever inhibitions he might have had, because all of a sudden he asked me, in a strangely relaxed tone of voice, if I wanted him to "suck me off."

Bill's unexpected query shocked me, piercing my thick fog of pot-induced brain clot. I scrambled to figure out where he was coming from. He was married and had given every impression that he was entirely straight. I'd trusted him to be cool with me, but he'd just shattered my image of him, unveiling a hidden side that scared me.

Yet I was afraid to show my fear. If he could be so casual, so would I.

Hoping he would lose his spunk if put on the spot, I said, "What?"

It didn't work. He repeated his question. "I said, would you like me to suck you off?"

"No," I answered.

"Why not?"

I told Bill I just wasn't interested, much as I'd just told Doug in his apartment on Clearwater Beach. He didn't want to hear that answer, and like Doug, contended that I'd like it and ought to give it a try.

Fortunately, as we were arguing our different positions his wife returned. Just as abruptly as he'd brought it up, Bill dropped the matter and acted like nothing had happened. That was fine with me because I was running out of things to say on the subject. A few minutes later I fashioned some excuse about having to get home, and split.

Even after my two run-ins with Herb and Bill, my experiences with Doug and the man-with-the-gnarled-hand were none the less frightening! They had both happened within only two days of each other, and nobody would have known where to start looking, if...

Into the Closet

I used up my second day in Clearwater Beach aimlessly wondering around, lost in a fog of lonely depression, and avoiding contact with any new people. As usual, it became increasingly hot as the day wore on. My jeans were becoming uncomfortable. Though I could easily wear them swimming in the Gulf, I knew that afterwards they would feel like cold, squishy, deadweights and draw unwanted attention from passers-by.

It was time to score a bathing suit. I ventured into a clothing store and searched around until I found a nice pair of shorts. Hiding the shorts within a stack of full length pants I was purportedly trying on, I carried them into a changing room. Once safely behind the latched door I put the shorts on under my pants.

Upon exiting the fitting room, I approached the sales clerk and returned a jumbled mass of pants, deliberately messed up to look like I'd tried them on, and told her I'd decided not to buy any. She had no reason to suspect me of any wrong-doing. However, if she happened to glance down at my lower body, she might notice the outline of the shorts under my jeans. With this in mind, I slunk away, zig-zagging through as many clothes stands as possible, using them to block most lines of sight to my butt.

And I made it.

Now I could swim in comfort, without soaking the jeans I'd later need to keep warm. And the gulf was sensational! I passed the rest of the afternoon goofing off on the beach and in the surf, temporarily forgetting the rest of my survival needs.

By the time it grew dark again, I still didn't know where to go for the night. Thinking back over the places I'd explored since arriving in Clearwater Beach the day before, I remembered something I'd seen at one of the hotels. I resolved to go back there and check it out.

I'd remembered right. That night I began living in the fanciest hotel on the beach. However, unlike the paying guests who sojourned in first-class accommodations, I stayed there as a stowaway. My room was the musty garbage-chute closet I'd discovered on the eighth floor, the one with a folding bed stored inside.

It was in this little room that I slept each night for the next week. And as dirty as it was, with paint peeling off the sticky walls and the constant sour stench of garbage always at the edge of my perception, it beat risking another stay with Doug, the dirty young man. The room enveloped me, womb-like, its four solid walls surrounding the nest I made upon the bent bed.

Being a foot longer than the room, the bed couldn't unfold completely, and my sheets kept sliding down towards the center, no matter how carefully I tucked them in. I'd periodically awake from my nightmares, to find the monsters I'd been fighting were merely the tangled, sweat-soaked sheets that had become entwined around my arms and legs. A few minutes of bed making later, and I'd drift back off.

When I wasn't tired enough for slumber, I would read newspapers and smoke cigarettes. The light switch on the wall controlled the bare bulb projecting from the ceiling. But I was nervous about keeping it turned on. I feared some of the harsh light would leak under the door, and people walking by would come over to investigate. Consequently, whenever I heard the elevator arrive or people approaching from the main hallway, I would flip the switch and wait, barely breathing, in the dark silence.

Another dread was that people exiting the elevators just outside would see or smell my smoke and possibly try to open the door to investigate. If the person in question happened to be an employee, I'd be in serious trouble. Still, I had to smoke, and while I could go elsewhere, the room was all mine.

Keeping my smoking in the closet tended to become more than a bit suffocating. Even my nicotine addicted lungs required some oxygen, and I needed to open the door often to exchange the smog for a batch of fresh air. Before doing so, I would listen to make sure nobody happened to be right outside waiting for an elevator. When I felt safe, I'd open the door and fan it back and forth for a few seconds to hasten the ventilation.

Smoking was my number one priority. By the ninth grade cigarettes were no longer a matter of choice for me. I'd been branded by Marlboro, and my addiction was so strong that if I didn't smoke at least a cigarette an hour I would grow shaky and full of anxiety. I *had* to have a cigarette! It would become the overwhelming preoccupation of my body and mind until I got one.

At school I'd had to keep my smoking in a different closet. I made the utmost use of the five minutes of free time between classes, racing to a bathroom, blazing through a cigarette in the company of the dozens of other

"Prison" By Ann Miller

boys who were also hooked, then rushing off to my next class before the final bell. My new closet was far preferable, because at least I could take my time to smoke "right." At school I always had to smoke so fast that the filter would overheat and burn my lips, and the ember, lacking enough time to turn to ash, would grow too long for a good inhale.

Thinking back, I remembered the time one of the walkie-talkie-bearing Deans caught me and hauled me in to the principal. She gave me a choice — either two whacks with a wooden paddle, or three days of in-school suspension. I took the whacks, figuring that by the time my parents found out about it, the punishment would already be over.

The "paddle" was more like a board, a piece of wood about an inch thick, and for the rest of the day my backside served as a fiery reminder of institutionalized hypocrisy; if they caught me hurting myself by smoking, they would hurt me to show me I was wrong.

I couldn't stay in the closet during the day, because the housekeeping staff would need to dump their garbage there. To keep from breeding suspicion, I made sure nothing in the room would appear to change from one day to the next. Whenever I left the room I re-folded the bed and rolled it back to the end of the closet where I'd found it. The only thing I left behind was the strong stench of cigarettes, which probably just blended in with the rest of the smells emanating from the garbage chute.

Given my lack of employment or other support I was usually unable to obtain sufficient money to buy all the cigarettes I needed. I often bummed them from strangers, but in order to have enough to keep me going, I found it necessary to lift a few packs.

The easiest method was to go into a supermarket and grab a carton from the end-aisle dispenser. Then I'd take it with me into the employee bathroom, and while hidden in a locked stall, tear it open and stuff five packs into each sock. With a little care in the placement, when my pants were pulled back over my socks, there wouldn't be the slightest bulge visible to engender suspicion.

Food was garnered by any means necessary. Trusting to the hunter-gatherer instinct inherited from my ancestors, a good deal of my sustenance was harvested from happy hour buffets in some of the nicer hotels' bars, and by "grazing" through convenience stores and supermarkets. More than a few restaurant meals were purchased with tips quickly scooped up on the way to my table or, alternatively, by the establishment itself when they discovered that I'd finished my meal and snuck out without paying.

Over the next week I floated about in a state of shock, too overwhelmed by the reality of having run away to pay much attention to anything more than meeting my immediate needs and desires. The bulk of my daytimes were spent roaming the beaches, swimming in the Gulf of Mexico and some of the pools at various hotels, and occasionally meeting people and talking with them. My shirt off in the warm mid-day air, I often wore only my new swimsuit, and the baking sun soon cooked my skin darker than ever. To get clean, I rinsed my clothes and myself under the poolside showers at various hotels.

After a couple of nights in the trash chute room I returned from a long day on the beach to find that I couldn't turn the doorknob. The door was locked. I didn't know of anywhere else I could sleep that night, but not being a quitter, I attempted to open the door anyway. As Benjamin Franklin, a teen runaway himself, once said, "If at first you don't succeed, try, try again."

When I pulled on the door again, it gave a little. It turned out that the metal plate into which the door bolt slid was missing one of the two screws that held it on. I pulled harder and the plate pivoted ever so slightly, giving me access to the bolt from the side.

Thanks to the mysteriously missing screw I was able to open the door about three-quarters of an inch. This was just enough to expose part of the hole in the plate that the bolt stuck through. From the backside of the plate I worked the bolt back into the door and was able to regain my room.

My home was still safe, for the time being.

In my ongoing wanderings, I often met up with college-types drinking on the beach, enjoying a seemingly endless spring break (even though it was summertime now). These slothfully relaxed young adults were forever in a festive mood, and I could usually convince them to share their booze with me.

While crashing one such party I drank so much beer and then hard liquor that I got myself sick. Late that night I realized I wouldn't be able to hold down the sloshing contents of my stomach much longer. Attempting to avoid any undue attention, I withdrew from the beach party scene, and walked along the shore looking for a private place to retch. If it could be helped, I didn't want anyone to know I was about to lose it; I was embarrassed to be such a child that I couldn't even hold my liquor.

Just in time, I found a bush in an unlit area between the beach and a hotel, and kneeling into it, up-chucked all that I'd down-chugged. My world kept spinning and spinning and spinning. I stumbled back to my garbage chute room and eventually managed to sleep away the fat part of another night.

Bold Approach

Though I could forget about my family most of the time, a deeper core of pain and dread remained hidden inside. No matter how well I managed to distract myself from my insanely deranged situation with drinks, drugs, books, and the beach, the deeper truths remained. I continued to feel terrible shame for running away, and believed my parents must be angry, looking upon me as usual, as a bad boy. Running like I had merely added one more ugly stroke of paint to the disturbing picture they already had of me. When trying to imagine how they would react if I went back home, the fear became overwhelming.

Wandering at random around Clearwater Beach I reflexively ignored these uncomfortable feelings, keeping them out of my consciousness. I had to, because I was entirely unable to deal with the endless tide of emotions, fears, and thoughts. My time was spent running away from this monumental muddle of emotional confusion, as much as from my family.

In a sense, it was almost as if I were on holiday, like the thousands of tourists with whom I shared the beaches. It was a vacation from my former life at home and school. However, unlike the other tourists, some of whom seemed to be set for life, I still had to figure out how to eat, drink, and survive one day at a time.

Having failed in my search for work, I decided to start a business. Somehow, I came up with enough money to buy a six-pack of soda from the Seven Eleven. My plan was to carry it to the beach and try selling the cans for seventy-five cents apiece. With so many hot, sweaty, and thirsty people lazily basking under the sultry afternoon sky I figured I could double my money pretty quickly.

I was wrong.

Selling sodas on the beach was far more difficult than I'd expected. They were awkward to carry, and lacking a sign to attract attention, I had to keep walking up to strangers to inquire whether they wished to buy one. The selection was poor, as the six pack I'd bought was all one flavor. It was broiling out, which, while making the potential customers thirstier, also heated up the sodas making them less appealing.

To further complicate matters, I didn't have any change to give my first clients. Once they'd decided to buy a soda I had to bother a bunch of other people, asking if anyone could make change for the dollar before I could even complete the sale. It turned out that most of the beached tourists left their money back in their rooms; it was probably easier than trying to stow it in their swimsuits and risk its loss or water damage.

Then there was the established competition. At the hotels with beach-side beverage service, the guests could have drinks charged to their rooms and delivered to them complete with straws and frosty, ice-filled glasses. On top of that, these services offered far better selection and convenience.

Not to be deterred, I kept at it, figuring that if I could generate enough business, I'd be able to reinvest the earnings, expand my selection, and even buy a cooler to keep the drinks cold. It was just a fantasy though. Sometime later, after I'd annoyed a few dozen sun bathers, the mean-faced manager of one hotel's beach vending area told me it was illegal to sell anything on the beach without some kind of concessions permit. In a serious and condescending tone he added that if he saw me bothering anymore tourists he'd "have to" report me to the police.

I still had two luke-cool sodas left, and could have headed down the beach a few blocks to try selling them there, but decided it wasn't worth risking police intervention. I ended up drinking them myself. At least I had earned back my investment. If I'd had a permit, a beach-worthy vending cart with a big sign, and a small bankroll for making change, I bet I could have been quite successful.

At one point along my haphazard explorations through another hotel I found that the cleaning staff had, as usual, left some of their maid's carts unattended in the hallways. When the maids cleaned the different hotel suites, they often left their carts in the hallway instead of lugging them through the tight doorways, only taking from the cart what was needed to clean that particular room. This was a common practice at many of the larger hotels, and I'd already taken towels, sheets, soap, and matches from some of them before.

This time, however, I discovered a bunch of room keys on top of one of the carts. There were tags stamped with the corresponding room numbers connected to them. Apparently some of the guests left the keys in their rooms, instead of dropping them at the front desk when checking out.

No one was in the hall. On impulse, I grabbed about half of the keys, dodged into a stairwell, and left the building.

Later on in the day I returned to try some of the keys. At the first room, I knocked on the door to make sure no one was inside before actually testing the key. It was a good thing too. A voice answered my knock asking, "Who is it?"

"This is Johnny," I answered. "Is Abe there?"

There was a fumbling at the door as the chain-lock was set and the bolt turned. The door opened a crack and a woman's face peered out at me. "There's nobody named Abe here," she said. "What room are you looking for?"

I looked at the number on the door — 523 — and replied, "He said he was in room 532."

"This is room 523, not 532. You have the wrong room, " the woman responded. "Look down the hall."

I put on the cute little kid act. "Oops! I made a mistake... I'm sorry. Abe said we could go play by the pool. Sorry for bothering you, miss."

I walked down the hall, pretending to look at the different room numbers until out of the woman's line of sight. When she closed the door, I rapped on the next one I had a key for.

There was no answer. I knocked again and waited. There was still no answer, so I tested the key.

The door opened into an unoccupied room. It had been recently cleaned, and was furnished like any other hotel room, with a large color TV, two giant beds, and a full bathroom complete with fresh white towels and soap. There was even a band of paper around the toilet seat with the words "Sanitized For Your Protection," printed on it.

It was nice of them to protect me. I let myself get comfortable. Actually, I grew a bit too comfortable, enjoying the illusion that I was a paying guest and that this was really my room.

Stretching out across a bed that was a hell of a lot more comfortable than the bent one in my closet, I fell into a short nap. Upon waking, I allowed myself a lengthy shower, savoring the luxuriousness of having an immaculate bathroom all to myself. It was a pleasure not to have to wear swim trunks, as I did when showering on the pool decks outside.

Refreshed, I moseyed on down to the swimming pool. I left everything but my wristwatch, my bathing suit, and the room key in the hotel room, and rode the elevator to the pool level in bare chest and feet. Forgetting about the flow of time, I swam and lounged in and around the pool, concentrating on light things like how long I could hold my breath under water, and what the woman nearby would look like without her bikini.

When I eventually returned to what I now considered my room and opened the door without knocking, I found myself looking at the startled faces of a group of strangers: a tired looking woman with two small kids. A family had apparently checked into the room while I was busy loafing downstairs.

Surprised myself, I must have mirrored their shock as I felt my own flustering rush of adrenaline. I was afraid I was about to get caught, and raced to figure out a good excuse for having opened their door.

An alarmed timbre to her voice, the woman demanded, "Who are you?! What are you doing coming into our room?"

"John McGreger," I replied. Maybe a touch of bluff would help. "Who are you? This is supposed to be my room!"

At this point, a man emerged from the bathroom wearing nothing but boxer shorts and a towel. "What's going on here?" he challenged. The two kids had moved, and were now quietly clutching their mother's legs.

The woman pointed at me. "He just opened the door and came in; he says it's supposed to be his room."

"See, I have the key," I said as I held it up. I tried to seem calm, cool, and collected and asked them, "Where are my clothes and stuff? I left them here when I went down to the pool."

Once they realized that I wasn't some kind of mugger (at least not a credible one), but just a child, their mood changed from alarm to irritation. The woman told me they were supposed to be the only ones with a key to the room.

"We found your things laying all over when we first arrived and complained to the front desk. They told us the room was to have been cleaned already, and sent a man from Security to take them away. They also had a maid come to clean the bathroom and make the bed. This is our room."

The man added, dismissively, "You can go ask Hotel Security, but please leave; this is our room now, and we don't have your things."

Of course, I wasn't about to ask the security people for my things, as I wasn't supposed to be there in the first place. They'd probably arrest me. Pretending confused and indignant surprise I promised, "Okay, I'll go ask them. Sorry if I scared you, but I don't understand why they would give my room away."

It was time to leave the hotel, posthaste. I walked towards the elevator at a normal pace until I heard the door close. Then I took off, leaping and bounding five or six floors down a stairway, and darting out the door to the auto garage. The hotel was on stilts, with a ground-level parking area underneath. For all I knew the family was on the phone to security at that very moment. If that were the case, I had only a matter of minutes to be out of sight. I ran through the garage, onto the beach, and disappeared from the general vicinity.

Now my watch, swim shorts, and a key to a hotel room I didn't belong in were all I owned. I'd left a change of clothes, a half-read science fiction book, my comb, and a few other things behind in the room. It wasn't exactly a wealth in personal property, but its loss would make a hefty difference in my standard of living.

The other keys I'd taken had also been left behind. This was for the best though, as it would have been an act of supreme idiocy to show my face in that hotel again. This criminal wasn't returning to the scene of the crime. I was lucky to get away so easily, and I knew it.

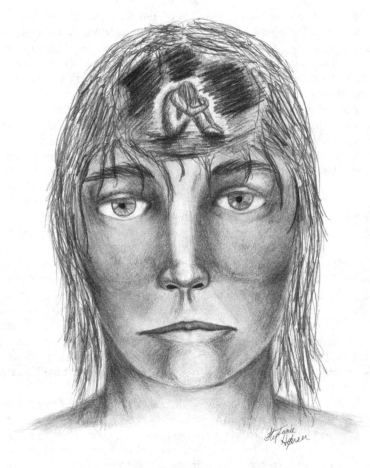

"Fetal Thoughts" By Stephanie Horser

The air was warm as ever. The soft, protective gulf waters called out to embrace me, to take me in and make me forget again, for a spell, but I'd heard the story of the ant and grasshopper, where the ant worked to prepare for winter while the grasshopper clowned around. In the end, the ant was cozy when the snows began to fall, and the grasshopper died a frigid, hungry, and lonely death. My first priority needed to be the rebuilding of my clothing supply so I wouldn't freeze after the sun set.

Feeling like an asshole for losing my stuff, I trod on up the beach and tried to develop a plan. Shortly, I came across some flip-flops laying unprotected on the sand. The thick plastic soles had three brightly colored layers. I spotted a man, the probable owner, swimming in the Gulf about a hundred feet away, and I acted. Barely slowing, I slipped into the sandals as smoothly as possible, and kept on moving.

Hopefully it wasn't obvious to anyone that I was stealing this guy's shoes. The man himself couldn't see me. His back was turned as he faced the gentle incoming swells. Nobody challenged me. Now I had shorts and shoes!

This wasn't enough, though; flip-flops wouldn't keep me warm. I needed more clothes soon, or I was certain to become extremely chilly in a few hours. As it grew colder, being inconspicuous in hotels, stores, and restaurants without at least wearing a shirt with my shorts would get difficult. Even in sunny Florida most indoor establishments had a "No Shirt, No Shoes, No Service" policy, especially at night. I left the beach and entered a crowded convenience store.

While browsing around I found a clothes rack. Feigning intense interest in the typically boring array of tacky pink, blue, and sea-green tourist tee-shirts, I waited. When the cashier was too busy with customers to notice, I slid one from its hanger, tore off the price tag, and stuffed the shirt down the front of my bathing suit. Then, taking the most roundabout route to the front door, and thereby gaining the extra visual shielding provided by the shelves, I slithered out of the store. The shirt made an obviously oversized bulge in my shorts, too big for a man twice my age, but either fortune or etiquette was on my side and no one challenged me.

Once safely outside, I smiled and slipped on the shirt. Now I had shoes, shorts, and a shirt. A full outfit again!

In time, I gained a new set of footwear using a similarly bold approach. By leaving my sandals hidden outside and walking barefoot into a discount store, I was able to try on a new pair of socks and sneakers and stroll on out the door without drawing any suspicious attention.

I wouldn't be returning to that hotel again, but figured I was still safe staying in Clearwater Beach for now. After all, I still had the trash chute room in the other hotel down the beach to sleep in. Given no force to drive me away, I kept sleeping there by night, wandering aimlessly by day, and falling deeper and deeper into the inviting trance of denial.

Capture

It was late in the sunny and hot afternoon a few days later, and once again I'd gotten drunk on the beach with a bunch of partying college students. I wondered what they did to finance their summertime festivities; maybe they were all daddy's little rich kids sent on all-expenses-paid vacations, or maybe they'd scrimped and saved to pay for their fun themselves. There were probably some of each. Most of the cheaper motels and hotels along the beach were overflowing with these kinds of people, a breed whose main concerns seemed limited to getting tan, getting drunk, and getting laid.

Though I could have cared less, I was getting pretty tan myself from constant exposure to the sun. Getting drunk wasn't so hard either, because whenever I hung with a group of these young guzzlers, they were glad to share a few cans of their beer.

It was easy to find people who thought it perfectly all right, or at least funny and entertaining, to get a fifteen year old drunk; a lot easier than finding a job. I was "cute," as some of the young women in these crowds kept saying. These were the same sort of folks who joked about getting "cute" little cats and dogs drunk.

Getting laid was an entirely different matter, of course. No matter who I hung out with, I was always alone at the end of the day. I was sick to my stomach of being "cute," because it meant I wasn't any kind of prospect to these women; I craved to be "a hot hunk," or "fine," or "Sexy" with a capital SEX, so I could enjoy the sensual pleasures I'd read and dreamt so much about. As long as I was merely cute, it was no surprise I was still a virgin.

On the other hand, at least I was cute enough to be a drunk virgin, and as long as I could manage that, I had something to do with part of the long day. As separate as I felt from those I lingered with, it beat being constantly alone.

This day, though, I had no idea of the trouble I was getting into until it was too late.

I had scarcely guzzled two or three beers before I developed a most serious need to go to the bathroom. Searching for an appropriate place, I went up to the pool deck of the nearest big hotel. There were a bunch of guest rooms with sliding-glass doors opening directly onto the pool deck. I noticed one with a group of people milling around, cocktail glasses in hand, chattering to each other. Unaware of where the closest public bathroom was, my bladder compelled me to ask someone to point me in the right direction.

As I approached their doorway I decided a slight change of question would be in order. The people were casually dressed, friendly-looking folks in their mid-thirties, smiling and laughing over their drinks. They were clearly a different crowd from the one on the beach — with an older and more mature air, getting tipsy instead of drunk — but they also seemed the same somehow. I lurched into their open doorway and asked if I could use *their* bathroom.

Some woman snubbingly responded, "Of course not! This is a private room! Go use the one everyone else does!"

One of the men then directed me towards the public restroom in the hotel lobby. It must have been apparent that I'd been drinking myself, because of my loud and abrupt approach, and my slightly slurred speech. My bladder was about to burst, but I saw no other option than to follow their directions, and quickly ran to the lobby.

I was leaving the bathroom a few minutes later, when an unfamiliar pair of thick, hairy hands came out of nowhere to land in a clamping grip upon my arm. A surging, sweaty flash of panic jolted me.

The man who grabbed me was wearing a suit with a shiny name-tag stuck to the breast; he was the hotel manager. He said someone had complained about me coming into the hotel, and he asked who I was and where I stayed. I said I was staying at another hotel with my family and was out on the beach when I realized I had to pee; I had simply come into the hotel to use the bathroom.

As the manager yanked my arm and forced me down the hallway, he told me some things had been stolen from a few of the rooms and that I fit the description of the alleged thief. He added that the police had been called and were on their way to the hotel to arrest me.

Nabbed for a crime I didn't commit, I was sobering up very quickly. The manager shoved me into his office, squashed me into a chair, and locked the door.

I told him I hadn't stolen anything, but had only come into the hotel to relieve myself. He had the wrong guy. My eyes scoured the room, but I saw no way out.

He sat down at his desk and demanded to know my name and where to find my parents. I gave him my favorite alias, John McGreger, and told him I had to use the bathroom again. He didn't believe me.

I had to find a way out of there before the police arrived. I was terrified of being arrested. If I was, it wouldn't matter that I hadn't stolen anything; I'd still be detained, locked up in some cell somewhere. They weren't likely to release me without telling my family where I was and what I'd been accused of. And once they knew my identity, I'd be in double trouble, first for running away, and second for stealing.

Desperate, I insisted that I really *had* to use the bathroom. I didn't actually, but thought if I could only get out of that office before the cops arrived, I might gain at least a chance of escaping.

The man wasn't buying it though. "You just came from the bathroom."

It seemed my only shot, so I insisted. "Look, I'm not kidding. I absolutely *must* take a leak! It's not like I have a choice about it." My heart throbbed convulsively in my chest, while my mind raced, fumbling for the right words, the key to persuade him. I began bouncing my legs up and down, as though I couldn't hold it in anymore.

"Come on man. You scared the hell out of me when you grabbed me, and I'm going to go in my pants if you don't let me use the bathroom." Whether he was afraid I'd ruin his nice office furniture, or just sick of my whining, he finally gave in and agreed to take me back to the restroom.

Again, the man tightly gripped my arm while forcefully escorting me around several corners to the bathroom. The hallways bent back and forth in that building in a maze. I whined some more, telling the manager he was hurting me with his tight hold, then asked him to ease up a bit.

"I'm not going to try to run," I lied. "I know I didn't steal anything. All you'll have to do is take my fingerprints when the police get here and compare them to the thief's and you'll see they're different."

My pleading worked. The man ever so slightly relaxed his iron hold on my arm. It was a start.

The manager began to accompany me into the urinal and I said, "Could you give me a break? Please? I'm just using the John. I don't need to be watched while I do this."

He backed off a little bit.

"Thank you," I said, as he left to wait outside.

There was only one door out of the room, anyway. I still didn't have to go, but tried, just to get some more time to think. Unfortunately, I didn't have any bright new ideas. The police would arrive any second now.

When I came out of the bathroom, the manager grabbed my arm for the third time in ten minutes, this time with only one of his hands, and started escorting me back toward the office. He'd relaxed that extra smidgen that comes with doing something repeatedly without any problems. It was now or never.

With no warning, I twisted my body towards him, ducking under his arm as fast as I could. My arm slipped from his grip, and I ran at breakneck speed back towards the bathroom. Now I had the advantage, because I was wearing sneakers while he wore dress shoes with slick soles; he had no traction. I could hear him shouting from behind, ordering me to stop.

I darted around a few corners and saw a swinging glass door into the hotel's restaurant. As I was halfway through it, I spotted two police officers entering the building and heading down a different hallway, towards the manager's office. I thought they'd seen me, but didn't slow for a second. Glimpsing an exit-way to the beach on the far side of the dining room, I quickly weaved through the cluttered tables, past the startled stares of the assorted diners, and then slammed my way through the door as swiftly as possible.

I was outside. Far from safe, I sprinted around the hotel next door, across the street, and past a string of other motels, finally entering a residential neighborhood. Springing over fences and twisting through scrubby bushes I cut through a series of backyards before slowing. I was in a small housing development that backed up to a long, straight canal.

It was difficult and risky getting from one yard to the next because each was tightly enclosed by metal or wood fence-walls and dense hedges. In most cases, the barriers extended from the street in front (where I might be discovered) right to the sheer cement wall that dropped into the waterway. To get from one yard to the next, I had to hold the edge of the fence and swing myself around without falling into the mucky canal water. At any point I expected to be confronted by someone who was rightfully lolling about in their own backyard. As I hurtled around each fence the hedges tore at me, leaving scratches and debris all over my arms, legs, and face.

After maneuvering through about fifteen backyards, with no sign of close pursuit, I found a particularly bushy place and hid, my heart racing. As I began to calm and catch my breath, thoughts began to trickle through my brain. I imagined the police would be looking for me all over Clearwater Beach now; I had to get out of the area without being nabbed. How? What if they actually caught me?

I stayed hidden for the next three or four hours puzzling through various scenarios, awaiting the cover of darkness. I tried to imagine what it would be like to be back home right then, but couldn't; the prospect of ever feeling "back home" seemed so distant as to be out of the question.

At last it was dark! I crossed the street and worked my way down another canal, creeping through more backyards until I was out of the residential area. I didn't want to risk the naked visibility of the street. Keeping out of sight, I passed a dozen of the cheaper motels set back about a block from the beach before risking a return to the open exposure of the shore. I was about half a mile from the hotel where I was almost arrested.

The thought of the police looking for me made me feel vulnerable around any people; it was like I was in the movie *Invasion of the Body Snatchers*, where anyone who spied me might suddenly turn towards me, point their finger, open their mouth, and unleash a hideous scream that would mark me as doomed. I did my best to stay off the busiest streets, where a cop might drive by at any moment.

It seemed far too dangerous to return to the garbage chute room. It was only a couple of buildings away from the scene of my escape. I trod north along the beach and decided to risk going back to Doug's to see if I could stay at his place for the night. I braced myself in case he tried to bully me into sex again, but I didn't know where else to hide; it seemed a necessary risk.

Doug wasn't around when I got there. I waited. It was getting cold out, but I stuck around for several hours, thinking he might come back any minute.

When one A.M. came around and he still hadn't arrived, I gave up waiting. I went back to the beach, and traipsed farther north into a more suburban residential section.

The beach was lined with quiet houses, many of which were unoccupied. The owners probably only lived in them during the winter. These were imposing and costly homes, often several stories tall, with beachside decks and lounge chairs.

After searching for a while, I found one that seemed likely to be unoccupied. The house and property were entirely unlit and closed up, with no signs of life. I snuck around the front and the driveway was empty, with no garage that could be hiding a car. If someone was there, they had walked like me.

Returning to the beach side, I noticed a cushionless lounge chair. I laid down on the cold, rigid chair intending to make it my sleeping place. But after shivering on it for a few moments, the chill breeze drove me to seek a warmer and softer place to wait out the night.

Since it was already near two in the morning, and no one was in the house, I assumed nobody was currently living there. I tried the doors, only to find them all locked tight. Looking up, I spotted a balcony on the second floor where there was another lounge chair, this one with cushions.

The potential comfort of those cushions inspired me to climb the house, and somehow I worked my way up the side and over the railing. I laid down feeling secure atop the wooden deck for a couple of minutes, but after cooling off again I began to freeze worse than ever. My shorts, sneakers, and tee-shirt provided scant protection from the relentless gulf breezes.

A sliding door led off this second-story porch. I tested it and was surprised to find it unlocked. The owners must have figured nobody would be ambitious enough to get into the house via the balcony. I slid the door open and crept inside. The interior was not what I expected.

Now I understood the real reason it had been left unlocked. The inside was spacious and very clean, but completely unfurnished. There was nothing to take!

After scouring the house, looking for anything to help warm me, I found a plastic tarpaulin I could use as a blanket in a downstairs utility closet. It wasn't the most comfortable way to sleep, especially since the tarp was sticky and gritty from exposure to sand and sea water. A part of me wanted to get away from it no matter how cold I was, but in the end, it was better than freezing to death.

When I couldn't stand another moment huddling and shivering in that house, I began walking back towards the town. By the light of the breaking day I noticed a "For Sale" sign in the front yard and wondered how much a house like this would cost; it would be a long time, if not forever, before I could have a home like that of my own. Any home would have been nice. I walked back to Doug's place one more time to see if he'd returned yet, but he hadn't.

Still covered with goose bumps, I bent into the gusting wind and walked over the bridge and along the causeway towards mainland Clearwater. It was time to leave Clearwater Beach and get as far away from the local police as possible. I knew I was especially vulnerable when crossing the open expanse of the bridge. If a cop happened to drive by, I would have nowhere to hide.

About halfway across the causeway I noticed a side road leading to another small island community. There was a big sign at the entrance emblazoned with the name "Island Estates." I ventured inside the community, and a few blocks in found a swimming pool by several of the condominium buildings.

The pool was heated, emitting a light fog that wisped just above the water. I tested it, and to my surprised delight found the water felt much warmer than the air. It seemed a good place to wait out the early part of the morning. My watch said it was still only six. I jumped in.

As I floated around and contemplated my situation, I decided my new goal was to get to the other side of the state, where I hoped to find a bigger and better resort town in which to live. Even though I kept getting into trouble, I felt there would be more opportunities in larger resort towns: food, jobs, places to hide, and whatever else I needed. It would be easier to disappear among the constantly changing masses of tourists, and with a little luck and skill, some of the vacationers' money might trickle down to me.

A part of me dreamt some rich family would adopt me and take me with them on their vacation, making my life better. We'd stay in the best hotels, eat at the fanciest restaurants, wear splendid clothes, and have lots of fun boating and diving and laughing together. Then we'd go home, and I'd have my own room and maybe even some friends to sleep over and watch good movies with now and then.

It seemed unlikely to happen though.

Shrimp Bait

After waiting for the rising sun to heat the morning air to a comfortable temperature, I left the swimming pool to search for an inconspicuous way out of the area. Only about half a mile off the Clearwater Beach island, I was still in danger of being recognized and arrested for the alleged crimes. I decided to wander around and find a decent place to ask people for a ride into Tampa.

About a block away, I found a church.

It was at this small Catholic church that I attempted to manufacture my escape. My hope was to avoid hitch-hiking on the open road. I needed a ride, but knew I couldn't tell the friendly people at the church the truth about my circumstance without their turning me over to some "authorities." So I lied, creatively.

I told them I'd been on my way to my grandparents' house in Daytona Beach, but that along the way I had been mugged by a gang of teenage thugs. Endeavoring to sound as innocent and naive as possible, I further developed my tale, explaining that my wallet, bus ticket, and suitcase full of belongings had been stolen, thereby making it impossible to continue the rest of the way to Daytona Beach without some help. This fiction wasn't all that far from the truth, I reasoned, because I had actually lost all my things a couple of days earlier.

I pleaded with them to either lend me the money for a "new" ticket, or let me do some sort of work to earn my way. The church people felt sorry for me and said they could help me out with a meal and bus ticket, and that my grandparents could send them a check once I returned. In reality, my grandparents were living in Philadelphia, about a thousand miles to the north, and I had no real intention of ever telling them about this day, let alone paying the church back. Of course I didn't let this stop me.

Displaying the most heartfelt thank-yous I could muster, I agreed to their generous offer. Even though I was conning them, it wasn't hard to muster a sincere display of gratitude. I was genuinely thankful. Without their help I would have to resort to considerably more conspicuous means of finding a ride, and stood a substantially increased risk of being caught and jailed.

But there was a catch. Before sending me off to the bus station, the minister wanted to contact my family to inform them of what had (ostensibly) happened to me, and let them know I would be okay. Sticky. If they actually managed to reach my family the whole scheme would be off and I'd quickly find myself on the run again.

Fortunately, I'd planned ahead. Before arriving at the church I had discovered a telephone number in Daytona Beach at which I was fairly certain there would be no answer; I gave it to them, claiming it was my grandparents' number. I'd found the number the previous week by making collect calls to randomly selected numbers in Daytona Beach. Using the area code and one of the three-digit prefixes found in that vicinity, I kept trying until I found a number that consistently gave no answer several days in a row.

Once I had a number that consistently rang with no answer, I knew I could use it as an alibi. Should I get nabbed for something, there would be no one at the other end to contradict whatever story I gave. And it worked. When the church attempted to call my grandparents, they got no answer, and therefore no-one to discredit my account.

A part of me thought, "God Evan, how could you *lie* in a *church* of all places?" But it was a small part, easily ignored. With all that kept going wrong it was hard to have much respect for "God" or religion. I certainly didn't see any way in which God had been helping me. I knew lying was "wrong," yet when I had told the truth about my situation at that restaurant half a moon earlier, they'd tried to turn me in to the police. Besides, I didn't know what else to do. This was a matter of survival.

My lying and conniving was worth it too. As promised, the people at the church bought me lunch and a bus ticket, and one of them drove me all the way to the bus station on mainland Clearwater, miles away from the beach and any police who might be waiting for me there. I had found safe passage.

The bus that carried me the one hundred fifty miles to Daytona Beach was one of those large, smelly buses with an engine that never seemed to stop idling, even when parked for a long layover at the terminal. Emanating from the smallish bathroom in back were the overpowering smells of urine mixed with one of those chemical air "fresheners" that itself makes you want to hold your breath. To further enhance the customer's olfactory displeasure, cigarette smoking was allowed in the last few rows. Non-smokers had no choice other than to live with the irritation of the smoke or find some other way to get where they were going.

Even though I too smoked, I sat as far forward in the non-smoking section as possible, thereby avoiding as much of the restroom and the smoking section stench as possible. The only times I ventured to the back of the bus were when I severely craved a cigarette, and when I needed to use the restroom. I tried my best to avoid the latter, but couldn't. Sometime after passing Orlando and the many signs for Disney World, I reluctantly heeded the call of my bladder and pulled myself up out of my seat to brave the walk back through the smoking section to the toilet.

The people occupying the seats by the bathroom were drinking cheap vodka from paper-bag-disguised bottles. They were having a jolly time and wanted the rest of the world to join in. These were the kind of loud, greasy, dirty, and malodorous adults with vulgar senses of humor that most people will go far out of their way to avoid. The crowd radiated a roughness most likely born from taking a few too many bus trips. Unfortunately, they seemed compelled to engage every rider attempting to gain entry into the bathroom. My case provided no exception.

I was waiting my turn by the bathroom door, wishing the current occupant would hurry up, when a drunken man began accosting me with his noxious presence. Mr. Lush stood up, leaned much too close, and mumbled something incoherently. It was obvious that the man was joyously intoxicated and wanted to share his booze with me, but I found myself unable to concentrate on his words; his rotting alcoholic breath and the spittle spraying from his mouth as he spoke proved too distracting.

Though I didn't wish to offend Mr. Lush, I wasn't about to drink out of the bottle his slobber soaked lips had slavered over. I did my best to resist my overpowering, reflexive urge to lean away, and uttered some excuse about not wanting any, but thanks anyway. His face contorted in disappointed confusion and his stubbled mouth began gyrating on further, but I had no idea what he was trying to say.

Mr. Lush wasn't the only one speaking during this uncomfortable encounter; his entire cohort seemed to writhe and contort to the swaying motions of the bus, like a bucket of shrimp bait on a floating fishing trip. They were laughing at slurred jokes I somehow knew I was the center of, but couldn't appreciate. Eventually, the bathroom door opened, and I waved a nervous good-bye to the group as I wiggled into the closet-sized space and locked the door behind me. After only a few minutes of enduring their company I'd begun to feel pretty incoherent myself. Even inside the bathroom, I could hear wave after wave of their grunted conversation and laughter buffeting the walls, and actually appreciated my isolation in the cramped and disgusting cubicle.

The toilet seat was in an absolutely appalling state, thanks no doubt to drunken men peeing to the constant bumping and rocking of the bus. I wouldn't have touched it no matter how intensely nature compelled me to assume a sitting posture. I wondered how women managed, and coming up with no ideas, just breathed as little as possible and felt thankful that I didn't have to figure that one out. Eventually, I managed to make it out of the sticky chamber, through the drunk and friendly people, and back to my seat, where I resumed gazing at the forested swampland rolling by. What, I wondered, was Daytona Beach going to be like?

Freedom

The first thing that struck me when I arrived in Daytona was the jam of cars driving both ways along the beach, right on the sand. I'd never seen a beach where cars were permitted to do this. A strip of the hard-packed shore was a virtual highway devoted to the hundreds of vehicles slowly streaming along the two designated lanes. As incongruous as it seemed, the traffic fit well with the seemingly endless array of hotels and motels that fronted both sides of the paved road closest to the beach.

The next thing that struck me about Daytona Beach was the huge number of young people there. For as far as I could see, there were thousands of people on foot, in the water, and sitting on their rears, most of whom were somewhere between college age and their late twenties. This presented a sharp contrast to the Clearwater and Saint Petersburg Beaches, both of which had much older tourist populations.

What surprised me the most though, were the women in Daytona Beach, and what some of them were wearing. More, what they weren't wearing.

The first two women I noticed were walking along with nothing but strings up their butt-cracks, leaving their cheeks totally exposed to the sun, the air, and my yearning gaze. At first glance I thought they were naked, but after a double take I realized they were wearing string bikinis. Seen from the front, they seemed to be wearing much more, and yet it was still lot less covering than I'd ever seen on people in public. Most of their breasts stuck out around the little triangles of yellow cloth they used to hide their nipples.

The only women I'd ever seen in such un-dress before were in movies and magazines, most of which I was too young to get access to legally. And though I'd heard of it before, this was my first visual introduction to the string bikini. When I looked around, I realized that not all the women wore so little, but more than enough did.

One of the feelings that increasingly characterized my journey as a run-

79

away was a growling sense of want and hunger for things I didn't have. Perhaps this feeling was so intense because of hanging out in resort communities where so many were living relatively extravagant lifestyles. Being in Daytona Beach only worsened my hunger.

I arrived broke as ever. What was left of the few crumpled bucks the church had given me to buy snacks on the way was already earmarked for my next pack of cigarettes. But here I was, amidst thousands of people who had enough money to stay in the hotels, eat at the restaurants, and enjoy, for a price, the many other amenities offered. This was a luxury vacation for these people, some of whom were millionaires.

It wasn't just the material wealth that taunted me, it was the power that the other people had merely by being beyond the age of majority. I was only a "minor." These people could show an ID card, sign their name, and get respect. Wherever they had come from, they were surely allowed to work, rent, and be out past curfew without first obtaining permission from someone else. All of these activities were called "status offenses" for me, meaning that though they were completely legal for adults, I could be arrested for doing them.

There was also the issue of sexual power and privilege. I was a lone fifteen-year-old boy; a scrawny, cigarette-smoking delinquent. All around me were beautiful women, as young as seventeen, yet much older than me in all the ways that counted. An endless barrage of images in magazines, commercials, movies, and books had taught me that these lovely women-creatures should be the objects of my affection.

Yet, these same educational sources also taught that I had to be a physically mature adult to attract any reciprocal passions. In addition, to get their loving attention I had to be a financial success, to hold a decent job, a nice home, and a sporty car. Using the right shampoo, deodorant, shaving supplies (not that I had anything to shave yet), and toothpaste was likewise supposed to help me score.

I didn't have any of these things. Not only was I alone, but I was barred (by many invisible barriers) from having access to these beautiful women whom I was taught to value above all else.

Mired in my insignificance, I didn't like Daytona Beach. I was very small there. And the constant flow of cars along the sand wasn't precisely my idea of a pleasant vacation environment. Somehow, being bombarded by the sounds of squeaking breaks and racing engines and the smells of exhaust fumes, while trying to dodge through lanes of moving cars to get from the hotel-front down to the waterfront just didn't appeal to me.

The town felt ugly, and even if I enjoyed cars on the beach, I couldn't be driving one. Supposing I could somehow afford a car, there was no way I could legally drive it. One had to be sixteen to get a driver's license in Florida, and even then, parental consent was necessary. Florida would surely

"Streets" By Travis Mitchell

freeze over before my parents would dare risk letting me drive.

So, what could I do in this city? I walked. I moved along the beach, walking and walking and walking, past a multitude of motels and hotels. Most of them were cheap, sleazy, and much smaller than the sort of hotels that I kept an eye out for. The limitless hordes of people were far too absorbed in pursuing their own activities and interests to give me a second glance.

When I found myself walking south of the Hilton Hotel at the southernmost end of Daytona Beach, I turned around and headed north again. I followed the beach about six miles to where there was a sign marking the northernmost end and the beginning of Ormond Beach. Then I turned around and walked south again.

The unnatural immensity of the place was overwhelming. The constant flow of people and cars blurred into the background as I became more and more alienated and depressed.

Now what? I didn't know what I was doing there or where I was going next.

The Hilton had been one of the biggest hotels I'd noticed. I decided to go back and explore it.

The same reasons that drove me to hang out in giant resort towns applied when choosing big hotels like Hiltons and Holiday Inns to investigate; it was easier to disappear among the masses. The more guests at a hotel, the higher the likelihood that the staff couldn't know who everyone was. In turn, I would be that much freer to run about the place without being questioned. Besides, the bigger resorts usually had gift shops, restaurants, swimming pools, hot tubs, game rooms, and a hell of a lot more to explore.

After hanging out on the Hilton's swimming pool deck for a time, I met a thin, fit looking middle-aged man, who was lazing around in the company of two sexy women. The women were both young, exceptionally attractive, and clad in tight, revealing bikinis. The trio were having a fine time drinking and being merry.

I must have been staring at them for a long time, with a longing look, because I soon found myself invited to join the man and his companions at their table. The fellow was some kind of multi-millionaire from what I gathered; one of the women laughingly explained that he was traveling around the world on a vacation that had already lasted over a year. Mr. Rich-Man's short, dark hair was receding a little, but he still had most of it.

When asked about myself I gave them some bullshit line about being on vacation with my family. That seemed to satisfy their curiosity. In the course of the next hour or so the man treated me to a giant, juicy quarter-pound burger with fries, and a couple of sodas, while we all lounged about chatting and enjoying the scenery.

Try as I might to appear easygoing and relaxed, my deeper attention was actually focused on two lines of thought. First, once I realized Mr. Rich-Man was a millionaire, a large part of my concentration was spent in a frantic attempt to figure out how I could get him to give me more than just a couple of drinks. I wanted to find some way to persuade him to pay for a hotel room for me.

Another part of my mind was wondering if anything could possibly happen between me and one (or both) of these two very beautiful women. At this point in my life I wasn't especially interested in females for their minds or what kind of conversations we might have. My thoughts about women centered on one area only: sex.

In the time before running away I had acquired quite an education about men, women, and sex from the secret cache of porno magazines I'd discovered. Breaking several rules of the house, I had found and repeatedly perused the entire assortment. The "Letters" sections in several of these publications contained letters-to-the-editor allegedly submitted by various readers and based upon their own true-life sexual experiences.

After reading dozens of these letters I surmised that the average length of the human penis must be something between eight and twelve inches, since that's pretty much the range all the writers had claimed their's to be. These letters gave the impression that casual sex with complete strangers was a perfectly normal experience, and that during the average sexual encounter a woman would have half a dozen or more orgasms, while the male might have "only" three or four.

These articles made me feel woefully inadequate as a male, who, being somewhere in the midst of puberty, didn't come anywhere close to measuring up to these grand penis potentials. Sometime later I was informed by a scientist acquaintance of mine that the actual average penis length of adult humans is somewhere between four and six inches, substantially smaller than those discussed in the magazines. I guess only the men with abnormally big ones wrote in to the editors.

In reading all of these articles I was studying my script. I believed they described the typical way sex was performed. What I gained from this miseducation was a fantasy life where my supreme goal was to play women's bodies to bring them as much pleasure as possible. I saw myself giving women so many wonderful orgasms they could barely stand it, and then, finally, allowing myself to have two or three. The idea of living out one of my fantasies with these women offered good competition to my fantasizing about a free hotel room.

While sitting by the pool with them, watching the ceaseless surf roll in, I kept having this screaming feeling of, "Can't you see, I'm like you!?! I have the success potential in me, too! I could be great! I could be a millionaire!"

Time passed while I sat and talked with the middle-aged millionaire and his two gorgeous friends. Sooner or later they said good-bye, excusing themselves to go back up to their room. I never figured out how to broach either subject, and my thoughts of getting the man to help or the women to make love remained only fantasies.

I had nothing to show for these fantasies. Only the irrational feeling that if I was given the right chance, I would be one of the wealthy ones too someday. The wealthy crowd was where I belonged, I thought, but I had no idea how to join it as more than a stowaway. It had seemed logical that if I just hung around enough expensive places and enough rich people some of it would have to rub off on me. However, reality was teaching that, so far, the only part that rubbed off was what I pulled off.

I wished for my own hotel room to relax in. Now that they'd left I was kicking myself for not finding some way to be more assertive and simply ask Mr. Rich-Man for help. At home I'd never had to ask special permission to stay over each night, to eat from the fridge when hungry, or for any of the other luxuries I now missed. I had taken it all for granted, then.

I stared out at the Atlantic. Maybe I should go back.

No. I was too ashamed to even call my family, let alone return. It didn't occur to me that they might be worried for me. Angry, yes. It seemed they were always angry. But not worried. And I just wasn't ready to face up to their anger.

Besides, apart from the material things I'd taken for granted, I'd hated my life at home and school before running. I'd wanted to die. It was just a few weeks earlier that I'd skipped school for a week and hid in the swamp with my dad's gun to my head, trying to muster the courage to pull the trigger. But I was too afraid I'd fuck it up like everything else and wind up wounded, not dead.

Up to now being a runaway sucked, but was still preferable to the problems of being at home. At least I was free. I could go whichever way I wanted, whenever I wanted...

Well, not exactly. More accurately, I was free to go whichever way I wanted, whenever I wanted, only as long as it didn't cost anything or require a legal identity.

I got up from my seat, began walking again, and moped the rest of the day away.

This is the Police!

Ironically, though I'd been unfairly accused of stealing from hotel rooms in Clearwater Beach, I became guilty of attempting a similar crime in Daytona Beach, less than a week later.

It all started when I was making another of my exploratory trips through the halls of one of the bigger hotels, and I came across yet another maid's cart sitting in the hallway. In the bins on top lay the standard assortment of soaps, shampoos, and disposable shower caps, and a more rare and useful bunch of room keys.

I didn't have to think about it this time. No one could see me, so I grabbed a quick handful of the keys and ducked into a stairwell. A minute later I was one floor up, waiting for an elevator to take me back to the ground floor.

A few hours later I returned and scouted the floor to make sure no one was around. Once I felt safe, I went to the first room. Using the approach that worked before, I knocked on the door to see if anyone was in the room. No one answered. I unlocked the door and slipped inside before anyone could enter the hallway and see me.

Unlike the fresh room at the last hotel, this one was clearly occupied. An opened suitcase sat on a bench in the narrow hall, and toiletries lay scattered across the bathroom counter. I locked the door behind me, and began searching. Advancing further into the room I noted an assortment of men's and women's clothing hanging in the closet, and a bunch of papers laying atop the dresser.

Lifting the papers I uncovered about two dollars in loose change. I scooped it up, eagerly, but wanted more. Two bucks wasn't enough to warrant all this risk, or the strain on my heart, which was pounding double-time in anticipation of getting caught.

My fantasy find, the treasure I most craved, was a fat wallet, stuffed full

85

of non-traceable, easy to spend cash. I required a jackpot, a cache of money that would feed and shelter me for the longer term, at least a few days. With one big score I wouldn't have to suffer the constant nagging of my stomach and nicotine craving cells, or the endless roaming in search of a safe hiding place, or the long, lonely nights of shivering in the chilly, pre-dawn winds.

Rifling through the drawers of the dresser, I found about five hundred dollars hidden beneath the jockey shorts and socks in the first drawer. But it was no good: the money was all in traveler's checks. To spend traveler's checks one needed to duplicate the rightful owner's signature, and I was not very good at writing legibly, let alone forging documents. And to make matters worse, if I was caught anywhere outside of the room with the checks on my person I could easily be traced back to this crime. Realizing all this, I gave up on the checks and continued my search.

Time was passing and I felt every second tear by. There was only one door out of that room. At any moment, the occupants could return from wherever they were, and catch me in the act. I was several stories up, so the window offered no escape.

I was playing a high-stakes game, gambling that I could be in and out of the room before anyone showed up. If successful, I'd have more options. If not, I'd be in deep shit. I was terrified, but did my best to ignore my fear and focus on looting.

I was guilty. I knew what I was doing was wrong, criminal. Still, I was desperate. When seen as a choice between stealing some rich tourist's money, or going on as a homeless, hungry, and broke boy for another day, the stealing option won. No contest. I was guilty all right, but given my perceived alternatives, it seemed the lesser evil.

A short search further revealed the jewelry. A couple of gold chain necklaces and a matching bracelet had been stuffed within a lightweight woman's sweater. I didn't know how to sell the stuff, but snatched it anyway, figuring I might be able to melt the metals down somehow and pawn them off as untraceable lumps of raw gold. As I shoved the loot into my pocket I grew dreadfully anxious, frantic almost. Another thirty seconds of furious ransacking failed to reveal anything else worth taking. It was time to make my getaway.

Withdrawing from the room was the riskiest part, especially now that I had the jewelry on me. There was no good excuse for being there, though I would surely try one if caught, perhaps explaining how I thought it was my room and I must have had the wrong key. If someone grabbed me on my way out, the jewelry in my pocket would provide proof of my villainy; cash would have been preferable, as it is almost impossible to prove original ownership without knowing the serial numbers.

I listened hard at the door, straining to hear if anyone was in the hall on the other side. Not a sound reached my ear, so I quickly unlocked and opened the door, then squeezed through and pulled it shut behind me in an almost liquid motion. Fortunately, no one was in the hall, and I walked as calmly as possible to the nearest stairwell, and from there out of the building. I'd made it!

That was more than enough burglarizing for one day and place. It wasn't worth pushing my luck. I ditched the rest of the keys into a trash can and vanished from the area.

Aside from not getting caught, it hadn't been an overly successful venture. The two bucks wasn't much to spend, but would have to do until I could hock the jewelry, or make some other score. It was better than nothing.

Another consideration in choosing beach towns, were the advantages of being near the water. I could stay clean by taking dips in the hotel swimming pools and the ocean. This wasn't as good as having my own bathroom, of course, yet it sure beat being a stinky mess. Sometimes I'd have an almost normal shower, using bars of soap snatched from the maid's carts. But most of those perfumed soaps had a horrible stench, worse than most anything my body could put out, so I usually avoided them.

A deeper, more important benefit of the coastline was the soothing effect of the waters. I would sit on the beach for hours, listening to the hypnotic sound of crashing waves, touching the drifting clouds with my eyes, and feeling a deep sense of calm. My problems would wash from my mind, and for the moment, I'd forget I was a runaway. Watching the seabirds hop around in the waves and wet sand made the difficulties lurking ahead in the remainder of the day float away to a safe distance. I could enjoy the luxury of being at peace for a while.

By about eleven one night, I still hadn't figured out where I was going to stay. With no particular plans or intentions I was walking about, aimlessly entering and surveying any stores or hotel lobbies I came across. I unconsciously sought something as yet unknown to me — namely, any kind of opportunity to improve my situation.

I found one, in the lobby of a small, run of the mill motel. Nobody was there.

As with the maid carts in the hallways at other hotels, I recognized an opening. I looked all around to make sure nobody could see me, then jumped up on the counter, balancing on my belly, legs sticking out behind me, and leaned over the front of the check-in desk. My head was upside down, and I could see into the numbered slots where they kept the keys and messages for various rooms.

I grabbed a couple of keys and dropped back to the ground. Noiselessly, I rushed outside. A quick glance over my shoulder revealed no signs of motion inside. I scanned the area and didn't see anyone who could have seen me taking the keys. It seemed I'd gotten away with it.

Next, I went around the building to find the rooms the keys were for. Most of the motels and hotels in Daytona Beach had direct entrances to all the rooms from the outside; there were few indoor corridors like they have in hotels in the colder climates up north. One of the keys was for a room facing the beach. No light leaked around the curtain. After knocking on the door and getting no response I felt certain there was nobody inside. I tried the key.

The room was clean and unoccupied. I entered and did my best to make myself at home, figuring no one would be checking in this late; I'd get up early and be gone before the maids started their morning rounds.

Wasting no time, I undressed and showered in the cramped, windowless bathroom. At home, I used to shower twice a day. Now, having warm, clean water rush over my body in a private space was a luxury I'd gone without for more than a week. The last private shower had been back where I'd lost my things in Clearwater Beach.

After drying off, I watched TV. Snuggling beneath the sheets, with my head propped up on the soft, fresh pillows, I let go. It didn't matter what I was watching. By midnight I'd fallen into a very relaxed sleep.

I awoke to a pounding on the door and the words, "Open up NOW! This is the police!"

It was two A.M. I remembered where I was, yanked on my clothes, and searched furiously for some way to escape. The sole window was next to the door. By the time I realized this I also noticed that somebody was prying it open with a crowbar. There was no way out. It was futile to resist at this point, so I announced I was coming out and opened the door. The police arrested and handcuffed me.

Arrest

I was caught.

They read me my rights and demanded my identification. I didn't have any. They asked me who I was, and I lied, "John McGreger."

"How did you get into this room, and what are you doing here?" they inquired.

I thought fast. "I didn't have a place to stay tonight, and a man on the beach said it was his room. He sold me the key for five dollars."

"Who was this man who sold you the key? Where did you find him?"

"I don't know who he was, but I was walking down the beach when this man told me he had decided not to stay in his hotel room after all, and offered to sell me the room for five dollars. I figured he must be on the level because he had the key, and since this seemed like a real bargain, I paid him."

"Can you describe what the man looked like?" asked the officer.

"I don't know. He had dark hair and a mustache, and he was taller than me," I fabricated. I continued, "He was taller than me and wore glasses too."

Then they asked me who and where my parents were.

"My name is John McGreger," I repeated. "But I don't want my parents to be woken up and bothered at this time of night. They'd just kill me. I'll tell you what hotel they're staying at in the morning, but not now."

The police officers took me to a juvenile detention center. Along the long, windy way I realized I'd blown my story. On one hand I'd claimed not to have a place to stay, but I'd also said my parents were in a nearby hotel. The cops didn't say anything about the contradiction, but just drove me, the silence along the way interrupted only by occasional cryptic chatter on the police radio.

Part of the booking procedure involved the confiscation and inventory

"Arrested" By Joel Heflin

of my few possessions, including my watch, the only thing I still owned from home. I got nervous when they got to the jewelry, but they just wrote it down like everything else. In the next half hour, I was fingerprinted, asked a lot of questions which I refused to answer, and then put into a grimy detention cell.

Aside from the bathroom on the bus across the state, the detention cell was the grossest room I had ever been in. Its only furnishings were a crude seatless toilet, a puny sink with a button that triggered a paltry flow from the faucet, and the small, striped mattress that lay over a barren concrete block. The stripes on the mattress looked just like pictures I'd seen of the stripes on the Nazi concentration camp prisoners' uniforms.

The room smelled like urine. The walls were covered with depressing graffiti from kids who had been there before me. And the door was locked shut, lacking any kind of handle or knob to open it from the inside.

The light in the room came from two sources. One was a small bulb behind a metal grill in the ceiling beyond my reach; the other was indirect light entering via the narrow window in the door. The window looked out into a plain hallway, and was filthy, as was the rest of the room, making it hard to see through. There wasn't much to see, anyway. Only the institutionally painted cinderblock wall on the other side of the hallway. I knew that a little further to my left, just out of sight, the hall opened into a larger office area.

I was trapped. I felt trapped. Being in the cell made me want to scream and punch things, but I knew that if I let myself, it would only make my situation worse; they might even tie me up and sedate me, like that time I flipped out when I was ten.

A layer of grit coated every surface, and I didn't want to contact any more of it than I had to by sitting down. I never minded sitting in "clean" dirt like on the beach or in a field, but this was a repulsive, sticky, and most foul type of dirt — the sort only humans seem to produce and accumulate.

I read all of the graffiti and explored every feature of the room. This took about five minutes. Then I waited. They left me in this unpleasant little room for about half an hour, then brought me out for an "intake" interview. I started to need a cigarette, bad.

The interviewer was an older woman with short, graying hair surrounding a concerned and grandmotherly face. She was the center director for the graveyard shift. The woman — I think of her as Granny — told the guard that I was alright, and asked him to leave us alone. This was a surprise. She was so much shorter than I, and seeing how the husky policemen had felt a need to handcuff me, surely Granny would too! I was only five-foot-two, but her tiny four and three-quarters feet made me feel like a giant. She was right though. I wouldn't attack her.

Her face solemn, Granny told me I'd been charged with illegal entry into a motel room, and that she wanted to notify my parents of my situation. In the morning, I would be brought before a judge for something called an arraignment, where he or she would ask me questions about the hotel room incident. This would, most likely, lead to a trial of some sort, and a possible sentence to spend time in Juvenile Hall.

The woman had convinced me. I was in major trouble. There seemed no point in pretending anymore. When she asked for my parents' names and number, I explained how I had run away a few weeks ago. The gig was up. I'd been caught, and with no escape possible it was time to face the music.

My parents were going to be pissed enough as it was, without the added insult of being woken in the middle of the night. That, at least, was under my control.

With a sudden twinkling of conviction I told Granny I wasn't going to help anyone wake my parents, especially to deliver a batch of bad news, then added that I was far too exhausted to deal with either my family, or lots of questions right then. For now, anyone who wanted to get any more information out of me would have to wait until I got a decent sleep.

If she'd just let me catch up on my rest, I promised I'd willingly answer all her questions and let them know my real name in the morning. Sticking to my story about buying the key from a man on the beach, I emphasized that getting some sleep was the reason I'd been in the room in the first place. The police waking me just an hour or two into my snooze only left me more tired than ever.

Once I'd stated my position, Granny remarked that I didn't look like I was even the fifteen years I'd claimed. She felt I looked more like twelve, and she didn't think I belonged in this harsh detention center environment. Something softened in her previously sobering expression, and Granny offered me a deal.

If I swore I wouldn't try to leave the shelter or pull anything funny, and if I promised to tell the judge who I really was at court in the morning, she would transfer me into the care of the local runaway shelter. She felt I'd be better off there, but it was only an option if I would promise to behave myself.

Of course, I was ready to promise just about anything at this point, as long as it would get me out of that hell-hole of a detention center! I'd never even heard of a runaway shelter before, but the thought of spending a long night back in that evil little cell sent a shiver through my gut. Almost anything would be better than that. And if I was transferred somewhere else I might even have a chance of escaping! It might not be over yet, after all.

Striving to look as cute and sincere as possible, I promptly promised to be on my best behavior. I pledged to tell the judge everything he or she wanted to know in the morning. What else did she expect? Given a choice between sleeping in an inescapable scum-pit, or being sent to a nicer, less secure space, only a masochistic idiot would choose the former.

Granny decided to trust me, probably before I'd even promised anything. I watched and listened from my chair as she made a few phone calls to arrange my transfer. Shortly afterwards, another officer drove me out of there, to a runaway shelter where I was swiftly checked in and given a place to sleep.

The officer and the shelter worker emptied the contents of a big manila envelope and returned almost all they'd taken during the booking procedure a couple of hours earlier. This included a few dollars and change, a half-pack of chewing gum, a paperback science fiction book, and even the jewelry. They had no way to prove I'd stolen the gold chains, and in fact, showed no indications of even suspecting me. It was a damned good thing that I had trusted my instincts and hadn't swiped those travelers checks after all. But most importantly, they returned my watch; the longer I'd managed to hold on to it, the more important it had become.

That they'd given back any of my things came as a surprise. Did this mean I was no longer a prisoner?

However, they didn't return everything. Despite my aching plea to the contrary, they kept my cigarettes and mangled pack of matches, lecturing me that I was "too young to smoke."

If there was one thing I was sick of hearing adults tell me, it was, "You're too young to smoke." Due to the overabundance of overzealous adults with nothing better to do than lecture at people they didn't know, I heard this sorry comment all the time. Adding to the ridiculousness, the irritating, judgemental opinions were most frequently delivered by adults who were themselves smoking, and thus seemed to lack the standing to tell *me* not to.

Oh, come off it! I'd been smoking for two years already, and at one to two packs a day, was just as addicted as most any adult smoker. Nicotine doesn't give a rat's ass about your age; it just grabs and hooks whomever it can.

If anything, adults are too *old* to smoke. After all, when you're older, aren't you supposed to know better than to destroy your body? And aren't you supposed to be strong enough to quit if you already started? Kids at least have an excuse for starting, in that they are supposedly so much less mature than adults, thus a mistake in judgement is more forgivable.

I'd started at an overnight summer school two summers earlier where I'd been put into an experimental algebra program for "gifted" thirteen year olds. There were about five of us there. Sharing the same dorms were a few dozen fifteen and sixteen year old "juvenile delinquents" who were taking remedial courses in a separate summer program; if they did well they wouldn't have to repeat ninth grade.

After dinner each night these older kids would sit and smoke outside the cafeteria. They seemed a whole lot happier and more mature than me. I watched jealously as they blew perfect smoke rings and were seized by frequent fits of raucous laughter. They were Cool with a capital "C," and I wanted to be like them. Like my hero Curious George (the little monkey from children's books) would have done, I procured some cigarettes and learned to smoke.

The harsh fumes made me choke and my coughing fit embarrassed me; I didn't want the older kids to look down on me as a little boy who couldn't handle smoking. I wanted, even craved their approval so much that I faked it, inhaling a lot of air with only a puff of smoke, while doing my best to suppress my cough reflex.

This approach helped. Soon, I also discovered that I could suck smoke into my mouth, and with a small half swallow, get it to exit from my nostrils, making it look like I'd actually inhaled. The resulting irritation in my nose was a small toll to pay on the road to becoming Cool.

After practicing for several days, I was finally able to inhale the smoke directly without choking. That's when I discovered a great side effect of smoking: The rush. When I stood up after a cigarette, my body felt tingly all over and I'd get a bit a dizzy.

As summer-school wound on, it became a nightly ritual to smoke a couple of cigarettes with the older kids after dinner. Afterwards, I would enjoy the vertiginous, light-headed buzz as I wobbled the quarter mile back to my dorm. The rush would taper off by this time, and I'd wash up and change clothes to ensure none of the adults in charge would smell the smoke and confront me.

Over the next few months my hobby became a habit, and my habit became an addiction. Before I knew it, my smoking reached about half a pack a day and I wasn't even getting the buzz anymore. I was hooked.

Now, two summers later, I smoked not for the buzz, but because I absolutely needed a cigarette to keep from going bonkers. It wasn't about being Cool anymore; it was about being able to calm down. I felt like a lump of shit if I didn't get to smoke when the urge came on strong.

So screw that "you're too young to smoke," bullshit. I was too young not to smoke; maybe if I lived long enough I'd find the strength to quit, but not now. A few years later I read that the U.S. Surgeon General had declared that cigarettes are as addictive as heroin, and equally hard to quit. Finally, an adult who understood! But those authoritative folks at the detention center and the runaway shelter didn't, and at the moment I lacked the energy to complain.

The officer, who was by far the more condescending of the two officials, wanted me to sign a receipt for the things they did return. I hastily scribbled John McGreger, doing my best to make even my fake name illegible. With the paperwork bullshit out of the way, the police officer left and the shelter worker guided me to my room at the end of the hall.

My situation kept changing. An hour ago I'd been a prisoner in a scuzzy, high-security detention center; three hours ago I'd been fast asleep in a clean, comfy bed; and five hours ago I'd had no idea where I'd be sleeping that night. Now here I was in yet another radically different situation.

It was near three-thirty A.M., and the man who showed me to my room said breakfast would be served at seven and that I'd be taken to court right afterwards. He told me to try to get some sleep because tomorrow was going to be "a big day." I thanked him and yawned.

He gave me some sheets and a pillow case and helped me make up one of the two beds. The other was empty, thankfully, so the room was all mine. On his way out, the man told me to turn off the light within a few minutes, and then said, "Goodnight, I'll see you in the morning." This was the first time anyone had said "Goodnight" to me since I'd slept on Doug's floor.

I was alone.

The room was fairly small. It had two windows, one in the door and one that actually faced the outside. I couldn't see anything on the other side, only a reflection of myself. It was too dark outside for any light to shine through, but even so, the room had a much more open feel than the cell I'd been in.

This door did have a knob on the inside. It also didn't have a lock. Could it be this easy to leave? I decided I'd better wait awhile before testing the limits of my new container.

My intention was to stay awake, but I set the alarm on my watch for five-thirty in case I couldn't. I lay down in bed to wait. Despite my best efforts, I fell asleep.

Beep-beep. Beep-beep. Beep-beep.

Two hours later I woke to the sound of my watch's alarm. Thank the engineers for digital watches! I pushed one of the buttons to turn off the beeping and crept out of bed. Tip-toeing to the door, I cracked it open to look out into the hallway. Nobody was there. Directly to the right of my door lay the end of the hall and what appeared to be an exit.

I dressed as quickly and quietly as possible and slinked into the hallway, closing my door behind me. Too afraid to breathe, I simply stood there a moment, listening to my blood throbbing in my ears. Other than my roaring breath and piercing heartbeat, and the quiet hum of a fluorescent light down the hall, there was an absolute silence. The hallway was dimly lit at this end and lined with nine more doors like mine.

Creeping the few steps to the exit I tested the bar handle. It wasn't locked and lacked any signs of an alarm. Very slowly, I pushed it open, fearing doing so would set off loud bells. I was in luck. Aside from the ferocious noise when the pressure on the push bar popped open the bolt, the door opened smoothly and soundlessly, allowing me to sneak out of the building.

Once outside, I felt the sticky sweat that had broken out on my entire body and my heart continued pounding, hammering like a jackhammer in my chest. Though I knew it was ridiculous, my every breath seemed loud enough to wake all who slumbered inside. As slowly as possible, I closed the door most of the way, leaving it open just a crack so as not to risk the extra noise of the bolt clicking back into place.

Looking around, I saw that I was in the shelter's backyard. The lawn smelled like it had been mowed recently. A tall, chain-link fence completed a circuit almost all the way around the yard, except for a good sized gap near where it met the building; a section had been torn from its support post, and was left hanging limply, like a partially peeled banana. Someone had gone this way before. At only six feet high, it wouldn't have been hard to climb over, but I choose the path of least resistance and slipped through the hole.

I found myself in the middle of nowhere. The runaway center was somewhere near Booniesville, Florida, at least several miles from the nearest town. The two-lane highway that passed by the shelter was bounded on both sides by a dense forest of pine. The shelter compound was open and brightly lit, shielded only by the light of the towering lampposts.

Wasting no time, I darted to the cover offered by the closest clump of trees. Although the sky above was brightening, it was still relatively dark at ground level, and nobody seemed to have seen me. At least I couldn't see anyone.

Making maximal use of my pounding heart and pumping adrenaline, I sprinted through the woods, staying out of sight of any drivers on the highway. Traffic was light, with a minute or two between each passing car. The road was so straight that I could spot the headlights long before they arrived. I thought of hitching, but was afraid a police car might drive by before I found a ride. By the time it was close enough to recognize, it would be too late to duck back in the woods without being spotted. Clutching my cramping stomach, I ran several miles along the side of the road, collecting more than a few cobwebs in my face and hair, while weaving back and forth, steering my body around the trees and bushes that kept sprouting up in my path.

After forty or fifty minutes of bolting through the tangled woodland with no signs of pursuit, I came upon a dinky little motel, the only building for miles. It was on the other side of the highway. I waited several minutes until there were no cars in sight before venturing across the open road and darting around behind the motel.

The term "dinky" was no exaggeration. The dingy white paint was peel-

"Night Forest" By Brett M. Damon

ing off the walls, and the small sign for the motel was faded, making it hard to tell what it advertised without standing still and staring at it for a while. A mere three or four cars were parked in the gravel parking lot.

There was a good chance my escape from the runaway center would be discovered within the next thirty minutes, when someone went to wake me up for the seven A.M. breakfast. That's if it hadn't been discovered already. I had to get farther, fast, but unaccustomed as I was to such long runs, the trek through the woods had already worn me out.

I needed a ride, yet had to get it without standing on the road. With the impending discovery of my unexcused disappearance, it would be riskier than ever to show my face. My best option was to wait near the motel until somebody was leaving, then straight away ask them for a ride.

An aged man came out of his room at about seven-fifteen. After fussing for a long moment with the lock on his door, he began moving his bent body, ever so slowly, towards one of the beat-up old cars in the parking lot. Marshalling every drop of persuasive force I could muster, I approached him and asked if he was heading out, and whether he could possibly give me a ride. In a tone of desperate frustration, I explained that I'd been hitch-hiking all night, but hadn't found a ride since about midnight when my last one dropped me off miles away. For now I would be happy to get a ride to any population center where I might find a bus to take me where I was going.

The man looked me over, slowly, finally fixing his gaze on my pleading, lying eyes. He said he was going up to Saint Augustine, about forty-five miles to the north, and that if I happened to be going that way, I was welcome to join him.

Great! I thanked him, making up a story about how I was trying to get to see my grandparents up north and at the rate I'd been walking I'd be lucky if they were still alive when I arrived. We got into his tired old tank of a car and left the parking lot, heading north to Saint Augustine, a town I'd never heard of before about a minute earlier.

I couldn't believe it, but knew I had safely maneuvered through my escape. I was starting to feel lucky.

Jane

When the old man dropped me off in Saint Augustine, I still couldn't believe I'd escaped. It was only about eight-thirty in the morning, quite early yet, and the rest of the day stretched ahead of me like one of those endless hallways in the horror movies. The old man had informed me that Saint Augustine Beach, just off the mainland from Saint Augustine proper, was the biggest resort beach around. He was heading inland himself, but pointed the way when dropping me off, claiming that it was only a few miles further down the road.

Without any better ideas, I resolved to go check it out. Hopefully, I was already far enough from Daytona to be safe from pursuit. If they managed to catch me yet again, I was sure escape wouldn't be so easy.

The beach surprised me. I'd expected another big tourist trap like the beach cities I'd already visited. But it wasn't one. In contrast, Saint Augustine's handful of hotels hardly qualified it as a resort town. It seemed a great place to get some true peace and quiet, if you could afford the price, with a far more pleasant environment than Daytona Beach.

Nevertheless, tranquil and beautiful as it was, Saint Augustine wasn't a place in which I would be inconspicuous. If only I had the kind of money to rent a nice beach home here. If only I knew someone who could help me. I found my mind endlessly repeating: if only, if only, if only...

But my various fantasy "ifs" wouldn't feed me or keep me out of trouble. If I didn't hurry up and figure out how to deal with my current reality, I'd soon find it dealing with me. Within a few long hours of exploring and sizing things up, I decided it would be best to move on.

According to the map at a nearby gas station, the next major metropolis to the north, with what looked to be a tourist beach, was the city of Jacksonville. Back to the south lay Daytona Beach. Returning to the scene of my demise was a bad idea; I didn't want to push my luck. Striking out towards

Jacksonville Beach in the opposite direction was my best option. Besides, judging from the large yellow splotch on the map, Jacksonville had a relatively dense urban population, which would give me a much better chance of blending in.

Wasting little time, I stuck out my thumb, put ever more distance between the Daytona area and myself, and made it to Jacksonville Beach with a few hours of daylight left to spare.

Soon after my arrival I began to get the distinct feeling that the further north I travelled in Florida, the further "South" I was getting in the United States. The beaches at Saint Petersburg, Clearwater, and Daytona were primarily vacation spots for wealthy Northerners who flew in from gargantuan cities like Philadelphia, Manhattan, and Chicago. However, Jacksonville was right up alongside the Georgia state line, and not being a major destination of the Northern travelers, it was its own town. It had a sharply alien feel, very different from the cities further south.

A large portion of the locals working in the shops, and scurrying to and fro around the town, spoke with the quintessential Southern accents I'd only heard on TV. Also, things weren't quite as polished and ritzy as they had been in the beach towns further south. The Jacksonville area struck me as being run-down, shabbier than any of the communities I'd already been through. Perhaps I simply didn't find the right neighborhoods, or perhaps this was more a reflection of the inner turmoil going on inside myself, but it felt like everything around me was in a morbid state of deathly decay.

I was afraid, my fears fueled by my stereotypes about The South. Stemming from these mass-media-fed preconceptions, I was concerned the cops would cause serious problems for me if I journeyed any further north, into The South. In the movies, southern police were either complete idiots, or much tougher and meaner than those in the north. I grew up hearing adults speak about how "you'd better not speed if you ever drive through The South; those cops will lock you right up!" My anxiety was heightened upon realizing that I would stand out more than ever here, as I'd be the one with the accent.

Three hours of wandering later, it was starting to get dark, and as was usually the case this summer, I had yet to find a place to stay the night. I was walking along the edge of the cloud covered beach, trying to sort out the faded images revealed by the dusky light of the setting sun, when I made out the silhouettes of two women rooting through a garbage dumpster. I'd almost missed them as the dumpster was hidden between a hotel and a separate apartment building. The women were almost comically corpulent, waddling around the dumpster under the stress of all their excess poundage.

Seeing nothing better to investigate, I went up to them and asked why they were picking through the trash, what treasure were they hoping to find. The younger one explained they were looking for aluminum cans, to sell to a recycling company for some extra cash. Each woman lugged her own industrial-size plastic garbage bag, almost entirely filled with soda and beer cans found while searching through a string of likely trash-cans and dumpsters.

After talking with the two women and watching them work for a while, I must have confided that I had no place to stay the night, because they ended up inviting me over to sleep in their home. I gratefully accepted their offer. In way of thanks, I did what little I could to help them, joining in on their search of a few more garbage bins for another handful of the precious aluminum cans. It turned out that the heavier of the two was the mother of the other. Her name was Jane.

With their bags finally stuffed to the limit, the women slung the rattling sacks of aluminum booty over their shoulders, and led me on a long walk back to their home. Their apartment was in the corner of a government housing project, an ugly, featureless brick structure with three other apartments in it. The other buildings located on their block were virtual mirror images of the one they lived in, cookie cutter construction differing in no readily discernible detail. All were equally ugly.

The inside of their particular abode consisted of a living room, a walk-in utility closet, a kitchen and a bathroom on the ground floor, and two bedrooms upstairs. There appeared to be about ten or eleven people living there altogether. The most striking peculiarity about their place, something that brought itself to my attention within seconds of walking through the door, was the unbelievably large number of bugs crawling around, everywhere.

There were all sorts of bugs: ants, spiders, palmetto bugs (also known as flying cockroaches), and a variety of other creepy-crawly creatures, all slithering, slinking, and swarming over the ceiling, walls, floor, and furniture. I was kind of afraid to sit down and subject myself to some sort of mass attack by the insects, but these people were being damned hospitable to me; I wasn't about to be rude by saying, "Hey! I can't stay here, you have bugs in your house!" or, "Thank you for letting me stay here, but I don't like your bugs, would you get rid of them?"

No, I had to be as gracious as possible. Disregarding my shuddering, instinctual urge to flee from the sight of these creatures, I made myself sit. Too embarrassed to reveal my fear and revulsion of the little beasts, I did my best to act like everyone else and ignore the constant movement in my peripheral vision.

From my limited experience of "Nuclear Families," this was a huge family. Jane shared the place with her many children, and it seemed that two of the older daughters had little babies of their own. The brood of youngsters spanned an age range from babies on up to late teens, most of whom were running from place to place in a random pattern not unlike that of the bugs. The oldest male in the apartment, other than me, was an eleven or twelve year old boy.

Just before dinner, a skinny, timeworn man arrived. Jane's husband. It looked like he was drained from a long day at work, and plopping himself onto the couch, he soundlessly made himself at home among the crowd. Once settled, this elder man nodded in my direction, giving me a gentle smile, but didn't say anything to me.

In fact, nobody there really said very much. I sat with them and shared what I assume was one of their typical home cooked meals. It was a simple supper, including plenty of pork, greens, and white bread and butter. We drank water.

The food was damned good, and I hungrily ate all that was offered, only slowing down to savor the tasty flavors sometime after starting on my second plate. And I obviously wasn't alone in my deep enjoyment of the meal, as most everyone else at the table ate with an equal relish and silent abandon. Looking around me I wondered: Could they have as much reason as I to so enjoy this modest food? This was the first real meal I'd eaten since before my arrest. It was hard to believe fewer than twenty hours had passed since being nabbed by the police.

It was also hard to believe that these people, over crowded as they were, had the mercy to take me in and furnish me with a spot to stay for the night. There were apparently only two beds and one sofa in the cramped apartment, just three sleeping surfaces to be shared by at least two adults and eight or nine kids. Even more incredible, they gave up one of their two bedrooms, and its half of the two beds, for me to have all to myself. There must have been people sleeping on the floors in order for me to have this luxurious space in privacy!

The unbelievable generosity exhibited by this family shattered my preconceptions about hospitality. Of course I'd been a guest at various friends' and relatives' houses up to that point, but no one had ever given up their own bed for me. Usually, if there was no extra bed, I'd be the one sleeping on the floor. But these people unselfishly let me, an outright stranger, sleep in one of their only two beds.

Such behavior would have been inconceivable in my own family, wherein almost all charity was administered through the mail; I couldn't think of anyone I knew who would risk bringing a stranger into their home like this, let alone give up their own bed. Jane and her family utterly and irrevocably impressed me with this act, one coming from their truly generous spirit. How could people so poor be so rich?

Given my own weary state, and having only gained a few hours of sporadic sleep the night before, I wasn't about to argue with them about accepting such a gift. After all the stress and excitement of being arrested and escaping, I needed a decent night's sleep more than ever. As defensive as I had become, I wouldn't have been able to let myself drift off nearly as quickly if I wasn't left alone. Fortunately, in addition to the privacy, there were fewer bugs in this upstairs bedroom. Before reaching for the switch I had a brief vision of hordes of bugs crawling all over me the moment I turned out the light, but was too tired to let myself worry. A scarce minute after extinguishing the light, I dropped into a deep, dreamless sleep, like a bag of rocks sinking in quicksand.

When I awoke, it was to a room brightly lit from a river of sunlight streaming in through the uncurtained window. Stretching my limbs to squeeze out the stagnant juices of sleep, I became aware of the thundering sound of some of the smaller kids stampeding up and down the stairs. A corresponding vibration was simultaneously transmitted by the slight shaking of the bed. I raised my arm to see what time it was.

My watch was gone. It had been on my wrist, but it wasn't there anymore. I knew I'd had it on when I went to bed, because I'd set the alarm to wake me in the morning before going to sleep. Somebody must have taken it in the night. It surprised me that I hadn't awoken, because even before running away I had always been an extremely light sleeper, waking up at the slightest sound.

As a little boy I'd always catch my mom as she snuck into my room, pretending to be the Tooth Fairy. Whenever I lost a tooth, she'd remind me to put it under my pillow for the Tooth Fairy before retiring for the night. The Tooth Fairy supposedly needed little boy's and girl's teeth and would leave a quarter or more in exchange for a fresh one. I'd usually feign a deep sleep to keep my mom from realizing that I knew it was her. I didn't want to spoil our game; besides, she might not leave any more money if she knew I was on to her. Secretly knowing it was her added to the fun.

Having my watch stolen wasn't any fun, though. To the contrary, it put me in a tough situation and brought up a host of emotions. I didn't want to make a scene by accusing my benevolent hostess and her family of stealing my watch, yet I had prided myself on holding on to it, not selling it no matter how bad things got.

The watch was the only possession I'd managed to keep since I left home. It had been a special gift to me from my dad. He always prided himself on giving practical presents that people would really use in their day to day life. When my dad he this fine gift, it represented the state of the art in digital watches, and did much more than just telling the time; it also had a count-down timer, stop watch, alarm, and night-light built into it.

However it wasn't the high-tech functions that made me treasure my watch so much; what made it special was that my dad had given it to me. I had quietly vowed to myself to always keep the watch in my possession, figuring that if and when I ever returned home, I could show it to my dad and tell him that even when things had gotten really bad for me, I hadn't sold it. In my mind's eye, I saw the watch proving my strength and integrity, earning my dad's respect. Up until now, holding onto the watch was one of the few things I had to be proud about. I couldn't let it slip away without a fight.

Mustering my courage I went to Jane and explained what had happened. Jane was the matriarch, a wife, mother, and grandmother, and it was crystal clear that she made all of the important decisions for her family. Once given, her word was final. If you couldn't respect Jane, you didn't stay under her roof, blood of her blood, or not.

As soon as I told her what had happened, she became furious and screamed, "Ain't NO body leavin' this place 'tills we finds you yo' watch!" She then yelled at all of her kids demanding that whoever stole my watch give it back, immediately.

I was horribly embarrassed. The watch had never fallen off my wrist before, and I knew someone must have taken it, but after telling Jane I just wanted to disappear. Averting my eyes, the last thing I wanted was to look accusingly at anyone in the room and wonder whether or not they were the guilty party, like I was some sort of judge or something. Jane insisted that she wasn't going to let me out of her place with the impression that her's were a bunch of thieving people. This meant that I wasn't leaving until she found it.

After Jane had interrogated each and every one of the children to find out if they had my watch or knew where it was, I tried to tell her it wasn't such a big deal to me after all, and that I would be willing to just leave. I pleaded that maybe I'd made a mistake, and had lost it before coming into their home. She replied that no, she had noticed the watch on my wrist at dinner and she was going to get it back for me, even if they had to turn that house upside down looking for it.

She went into a frenzied search upturning the whole apartment in her quest. Nobody seemed to know what to do. We all knew better than to try and open the front door to leave. Whenever Jane singled out one of her kids, they denied taking it. One of the babies started crying. I felt like crying, too.

After a while, I noticed that one of the older daughters, perhaps fifteen years old, appeared guilty when she looked at me. I kind of knew her guilty look because it was the same look that crossed my own face when I felt guilty of something. Before leaving home, when I was asked if I'd done something "bad" (against the rules), and I had, I'd often tell a lie to avoid being punished. I'd know I was lying, and despite my best efforts to control my expression, I would feel my face betray me; my eyes would open wider while a certain stretched expression would spread across my face; I'd fear anyone who knew me could tell as well, seeing right through my thin guise.

This pigtailed daughter of Jane's had that very same look.

After a while, I saw her go into the linen closet when Jane was in the other room, and come out again about a minute later. A few minutes later I decided to act on my hunch. I told Jane what I'd seen, and that though I couldn't be sure, I had a feeling that she might find my watch in the closet. I'd learned to trust my hunches. She decided to check it out. After about five minutes of rummaging around in there, she finally found it.

With some amount of ceremony, she gave it back to me.

Jane was very apologetic and clearly felt a lot of shame. I didn't blame her, and shared her shame. She insisted on my staying for breakfast, and remembering the scrumptious dinner from the night before, I did as requested, still keeping my eyes averted from everyone else's. Shortly afterwards, I left with a stuffed belly, my watch, and a sense of relief.

Not looking back, I walked straight away from that place. My aim was to find the main road and hitchhike back south. Given the increasingly depressed feeling I got as I approached the Georgia state line, I'd had it with going north.

Jane's hospitality had served to break some of my stereotypes about people who lived in housing projects. It also helped me shed another piece of my racism, incrementally decreasing my prejudice. Jane and her family happened to have brown skin.

Without harping on anyone in particular, I'd happened to grow up in an environment peppered by "white" people who were prejudiced against "black" people. As in all too many human families and communities, more than a few members of my own were also afflicted with the disease of bigotry. These particular relations never seemed to mind being waited on by darker skinned folks, but they condescendingly looked down on and didn't trust any of "them." Occasionally, people within my sphere of social intercourse would tell "black" jokes, just as people in other groups might tell Italian, or Polish, or Jewish jokes. And I'd always laughed; then.

Before the move to Florida, most of my growing up had been done in the suburbs of Philadelphia. At the time, there were probably over a million black people living in the city, and there was a correspondingly massive amount of hostility between the races. It was common for me to hear white folks complaining about how "the blacks" were moving out of the city into suburban areas, and thereby lowering the property values.

Over time I'd been trained to believe a host of stereotypes about how "they" were lazy, greedy, poor, and lived like slobs; about how they would move into a good neighborhood and completely trash it in less than a generation; about how they were natural criminals, with no control over their primitive urges; and so on, ad ridiculoso.

One white man even taught me a code he'd developed so he could secretly say nasty things about black people right in front of their faces. He called black people "trucks" and white people "cars." Then, while out in public places, he'd loudly tell me things like, "I hate trucks. They are big and smelly, and burn too much fuel! Cars are much better. I wish we could keep all the trucks off my street." We'd both chuckle when he did this, because we felt the power of saying these things right in front of people who had no idea we were insulting them.

It was when I was seven years old, in the second grade, that I first exhibited my learned racism. My teacher, Mrs. Shipley, had brought her wriggling puppies into class one day so that we could all take turns, two at a time, petting them. Like all puppies, they were divinely beautiful, soft, and cuddly, and I could barely wait for my chance to come around.

Eventually one of my classmates and I finally got our turn. Mrs. Shipley was at the other end of the classroom, busily focused on something else, when an older boy (about nine years old) peeked his head in from the hallway. He was one of the handful of black kids in our school.

There was a big smile on his face when he asked us, "Can I pet the puppies?"

"No!" I exclaimed. I wanted the puppies all to my greedy self.

His smile disappeared. "Why not?" he pleaded.

Without thinking about it for more than a second, I replied, "Because you're black!"

There was a moment of silence between us, while the puppies kept hopping around my outstretched hands, and then the boy ran away down the hall. The moment the words had escaped my mouth and I caught the look on the boy's face, I knew I'd done something dreadful. Was I going to get in trouble? Not knowing what was about to happen, I soon forgot about the whole thing and resumed playing with the pups.

It wasn't long until a strange teacher came to our classroom to tell Mrs. Shipley what I'd done. Before I knew it I was in the Principal's office, listening to a solemn lecture about how what I'd done was terribly hurtful and wrong, and how I had to apologize to the boy. Soon after, my parents were called and notified of what I'd done.

Ironically, even though it was family members who taught me racism, it was my family that punished me the most harshly now that I'd been caught publicly emulating its examples. As much as hypocrisy seems to abound in this world, this uncomfortable incident didn't bring my lessons in racism to a close. What was truly learned from the act of discipline was that it was only okay to say bigoted things when I was sure I could get away with it.

Fortunately people can change, and lessons learned can be unlearned. I'll never forget the help Jane and her family gave me. Their loving grace helped to move me one step further along, ever so slightly eroding those

"Kinder, Gentler Nation" By Nicole Gluckstern

walls of racial prejudice that I'd been taught to erect. It's much harder to be bigoted about people who have been decent to you.

Yes, Jane's family was poor, and in some ways fit the stereotypes I'd been taught. Yet, their behavior towards me showed a bit of who these people were inside, at their core. Jane taught me that her essence wasn't to be discerned or categorized by her physical surroundings, whether neighborhood or skin-tone. The idea that the daughter had stolen my watch because she had a darker skin pigment was patently ludicrous, as would be the equally absurd conclusion that my lighter skin was associated with my thievery. She, like me, stole simply because she was human, and had yet to grow up.

As I walked, I kept thinking about Jane. I felt a beginning. By challenging myself and looking deep within, I was able to acknowledge my own racism, and knew I still had a long way to go to end it.

What's It Gonna Be?

As I walked away from Jane's neighborhood, I decided to hitchhike to Key West, the southernmost city in Florida. Inasmuch as the world felt increasingly hostile and alienating the further north I headed, I figured the most hospitable conditions might lay in the extreme south. Unlike Jacksonville, I'd actually heard of Key West before, which meant it must be a big place. As I recalled, Key West was supposed to be a huge resort town, with plenty of wealthy artists and bigwigs like Ernest Hemingway.

According to the map, there were about five hundred miles separating Jacksonville Beach and Key West. Five hundred miles was a good bit further than I'd ever hitchhiked in a day, but I calculated that if I could average fifty miles an hour I'd arrive before sunset. It was doable.

I had two main hitchhiking techniques. Walking backwards, thumb out to the side, and waiting at a traffic signal or stop sign. Standing at intersections usually worked better as it gave whoever was stuck there more time to decide in my favor. However, both methods had their advantages and drawbacks.

Walking was guaranteed to get me in the direction I was heading, so even if nobody picked me up I would get there eventually. On the other hand, skirting the edge of the road, close enough to be seen by traffic, and yet far enough to avoid getting run-over could be tricky. And when cars were moving faster than about thirty miles an hour, their drivers were far more hesitant to disrupt the traffic behind them just to pick me up.

Waiting at a red light got around these problems. Standing at a well-defined curb or shoulder was safer and easier than walking. And since the cars had to stop there anyway, the drivers wouldn't have to block traffic in order to help me.

Still, while it solved one set of problems, it led to another. The biggest drawback was the awkwardness. I'd just stand there while people sat in their cars fully aware of my presence. Sometimes they'd stare, at others they'd do their best to ignore me, making sure to look at everything but me. When I was lucky, that awkwardness would make people feel sorry for me, guilty that they weren't helping me out, and after a few moments they'd break down and give me a ride after all. However, it worked both ways; I often became rather embarrassed myself.

Sometimes this awkwardness could grow to almost unbearable proportions, like when people locked their doors. There I'd be, a skinny fifteen-year-old boy with short brown hair, reasonably neat appearance, and harmless intentions, standing with my thumb out. A carload of people would be waiting, stuck at a light and I would hear a solid "CLICK!" the sound of all four doors simultaneously locking. Power-locks.

How could people be scared of me, a kid, I puzzled? All I wanted was a ride. I knew I wasn't going to hurt anyone; I was more worried they might try to hurt me!

It was bad enough to hear them flicking their locks, but it got worse because then I'd just have to stand there, knowing they'd locked their doors because of me. The rest of the light-cycle would entail a kind of uneasy distance, a gulf that, ironically, only contracted when the light changed and the people drove away; until then I'd be acutely aware of our mutual non-compatibility, of their conscious decision to further separate their reality from mine. The locked doors provided a sort of insulation for their comfy space, ensuring their environment wouldn't leak out and mine wouldn't leak in.

I found my way to Interstate 95, and stuck out my thumb. This was my first time hitching along an interstate. The sign at the foot of the on-ramp stated that no pedestrians were allowed. It was illegal to walk or stand beside the busy highway, hitching or not, so I had to wait at the beginning of the on-ramp.

Of course, this beat not being able to thumb at all, but it meant that most of the hundreds of motorists going my way wouldn't even see me. The only people who could stop to pick me up, were those entering the interstate right at my particular on-ramp. Though the interstate was a fast way to travel once I actually secured a ride, it ended up taking a prolonged wait to get on my way.

It was getting late and I was sitting in the passenger seat of someone's truck, continuing in my eternal push south. I'd managed to thumb a little over three hundred miles since leaving Jacksonville, spending at least as much time standing on the roadsides as actually riding in cars. The guy currently driving me was getting off the highway at the Pompano Beach

"Getting Out of Here" By Kevin Brewer

exit. This would mean yet another long wait at an on-ramp, this time in the dark. Just before he pulled off, I noticed a sign indicating we were getting close to Fort Lauderdale and considered changing my destination for the night.

Fort Lauderdale is about four-fifths of the way from Jacksonville to the southern tip of the Florida peninsula. But being an island, Key West is still farther south, and to get to it you still have to cross about a hundred miles of bridges, causeways, and islands. One of my rides had explained that Fort Lauderdale was a big tourist place, and since I didn't have the energy to hitch another two hundred miles at the moment, I decided to give into my fatigue and head for Fort Lauderdale instead. I could always continue to Key West the next day.

The driver was uselessly (from my viewpoint of course) heading further inland, to the west. This left me with a decision to make about which of two paths I should take. Unknown to me, this seemingly insignificant decision was to have a drastic impact on how I lived during the next two months.

I could have kept waiting at the on-ramp until I got a ride to take me eight miles south to the western edge of Fort Lauderdale, and then head east from there, another eight miles to the beach. However, the sun had set, the night was quickly becoming black, and the flow of traffic was some-what sparse at the on-ramp. There seemed to be more activity and illumination at the nearby traffic light so I walked over there to get a ride heading eastward. From the beach I would head south along the coast. Standing at the light I remembered the Pythagorean theorem from math class, and wished there was a diagonal road so I only had to get one short ride.

Much to my surprise, it was a woman who picked me up. It was ex-tremely rare for a female to risk giving me a ride, the last one being the teacher who used to help me get to school. What was even more unusual, was that this particular female was young and very pretty, probably some-where between 18 and 22 years old.

The woman was driving an aging VW bug. My seat felt a bit sticky and the rest of the car was a pigsty. There was so much garbage on the floor, that I had to wiggle my legs, shoving aside soda cans, eight-track tape cas-settes (already obsolete in 1983), and crumpled fast food wrappings, in order to worm a small space in which to place my feet.

I noticed a cluster of feathers dangling from her rear-view mirror, at-tached by a hinged metal clip. This implied that she was probably a Stoner of some sort, as Stoners often used such clips, known as "roach clips," to smoke the last bit of their joints. By pinching the clip onto the tail edge of the joint, one could smoke it without scorching their fingers, even when the very last centimeter was burning. This way, that one last breath of pot wouldn't be wasted, and in turn, the smoker would.

There was something else very strange about this woman, though I didn't pick up on it at first. Once we got to Pompano Beach she just kept driving around in circles, weaving around the same few blocks and parking lots again and again. I told her she could let me out anywhere, including the next stop sign, but she just mumbled, "Wait, um...wait."

The woman was stalling. I began to think she must be fried, thoroughly wasted on some kind of drug, perhaps permanently. Finally, at my insistence, she stopped the car in an unlit parking lot behind some stores, turned towards me, and said, "Well? What's it gonna be?"

What was she asking? She just sat there staring at me and I simply didn't get it. I stared back, not knowing what to expect or what I was suppose to do. It dawned on me that she might be asking if I wanted to have sex with her.

She was delightful to look at alright, but this wasn't my idea of a satisfactory way to lose my virginity: In a parking lot with some strange, tripped out woman, who couldn't even utter a coherent question. I wondered how many other people she so casually had sex with, and was worried that she might have some venereal disease. Someone had told me that one in six Americans had herpes or some other sexually transmitted disease, and I was not to eager to get one myself.

AIDS wasn't considered much of a problem yet, at least by most people; I hadn't even heard of it yet. I wasn't concerned about contracting something that would kill me, just something that would cause my favorite appendage to rot away. That was too scary.

Simply returning her gaze, I played dumb, mimicking the way she was behaving, until she finally snapped out of it enough to say, "Well, okay, you're here. You can go now, since you're gonna be that way."

I wasn't sure what "way" she was talking about, but I didn't bother to ask, and quickly got out of the car. After so many years of anticipation I'd never have predicted turning down my first chance to have sex with an attractive woman, yet I felt relief when I did.

She'd let me off close to the beach and I quickly found good old A-1-A again. A-1-A follows the beach along most of Florida's east coast, seldom more than a few blocks from the beach. One more brief ride would be my ticket to Fort Lauderdale.

A deep darkness had descended, broken only by islands of light projected from the buildings and street lamps. I'd been walking backwards with my thumb out for about five minutes, trying to get that one last ride, when I nearly stumbled into a guy who was minding his own business, waiting at a bus stop. Luckily, I caught a glance of him over my shoulder just in time to avert a collision.

Stopping for a moment, I offered a brief apology to the man for almost running him over. He was a slim fellow who looked to be in his early twenties, and with his dark hair and cleft chin, he bore a striking resemblance to

John Travolta, the actor I'd seen in a movie called Saturday Night Fever a few years before. The guy was friendly. He laughed off my apology in a good natured way, and introduced himself as "Pete."

Into the Sea

Pete and I got to talking. I told him I was heading down to Fort Lauderdale to find a place to spend the night, but that I didn't have any money. Forgetting about heading for Key West in the morning, I added that I was just starting out on my own, and hoped to find a job in Fort Lauderdale, and begin pulling my weight in the world.

Pete responded in a good-hearted tone. He said he had a friend named Frank staying here in Pompano Beach with an extra bed at his pad; he thought Frank might let me crash there until I got a job. He said Frank was friendly so it wouldn't hurt to ask. If I wanted to accompany Pete on a few brief errands in Fort Lauderdale, he'd be happy to introduce me to Frank on his way back.

I agreed to stick with Pete and give his idea a chance. It wasn't like I had any particular place or activity waiting for me when I made it to Fort Lauderdale anyway. All I would be risking was a little time if things didn't pan out.

Losing a little time was no big deal. The flow and passing of time had ceased to mean what it used to, as there was nowhere I had to be, nothing I had to do by a certain moment. The chorus from an old Steve Miller Band song kept going round and round in my head: *"Time keeps on slipping, slipping, slipping, into the future; time keeps on slipping, slipping, slipping, into the sea..."*

The lyrics were right on. Like the receding waves on the beach, time slipped away endlessly for me, one moment disappearing within the crashing surge of the next.

The rest of the lyrics were equally on target:

"I want to fly like an Eagle, to the Sea. Fly like an Eagle, let my spirit carry me... Feed the babies, who don't have enough to eat. Shoe the children, with no shoes on their feet. House the people, living on the

115

street. Oh, there's a solution."
I sure hoped there was.

My watch marked the passing of time with silent accuracy. But its value lay more in way of sentiment and pride. Sure, it displayed the day and date, but what did that mean exactly? Though I could track the passage of time with a glance at my watch, a few hours spent on a possible wild goose chase wouldn't matter in the grander scheme of things.

The stopwatch function allowed me to time the intermission between successive waves hitting the beach within the nearest hundreth of a second. Oh, wow. The alarm was the only function that was actually useful to me in this crazy life as a runaway. It allowed me to wake up early enough to avoid being caught sleeping somewhere I shouldn't. Time was only useful for avoiding those who kept track of it.

Accordingly, time being of little concern, off we went. Pete lent me change for the bus, saying I could pay him back at a later date, when I got a job. He had a great deal more faith in the future of our relationship than I. Everything was up in the air from my perspective; I could just as well be in Key West by the next evening, making tonight the last time I'd ever see Pete.

After a few stops I began to grow suspicious about Pete's errands. I imagined they involved something secret, something illicit, but couldn't figure out what, precisely. Pete and I walked from one building to another, where he had me wait on the sidewalk outside for a few minutes, while he went inside to "talk to a friend," or "pick something up." He claimed he was visiting friends, yet if they were simply casual visits, why did Pete find it necessary to leave me waiting outside each time? He never explained.

After a few hours of this bopping about, we took another bus back to where we'd started in Pompano Beach, and headed on foot towards Frank's place. As we wove down some dark streets I thought about how much bigger than me Pete was; he could kick my ass if it came down to it. I could try to run if he was jerking me around, trying to set me up in some way. But it was fun hanging out with Pete, and I felt I could trust him. I determined not to worry. As long as I stuck with him there was no point in it.

A few blocks from the bus stop, we came to a one story motel complex with a dingy, hand-painted sign boasting daily, weekly, and monthly rates. We went to a door and Pete rapped on it. A moment later a strong, spunky looking man in his mid-thirties opened it and inquisitively stuck out his head.

His mustached face broke into a great big smile when he recognized Pete. This had to be Frank. Pete introduced me as John McGreger, the name I'd given earlier, and Frank quickly shifted his beer to his left hand, sticking out the meaty right one for me to shake. I said "hi" and caught a whiff of his reeky beer breath as he invited us in.

The inside was shabby as motels go. The furnishings included a tiny

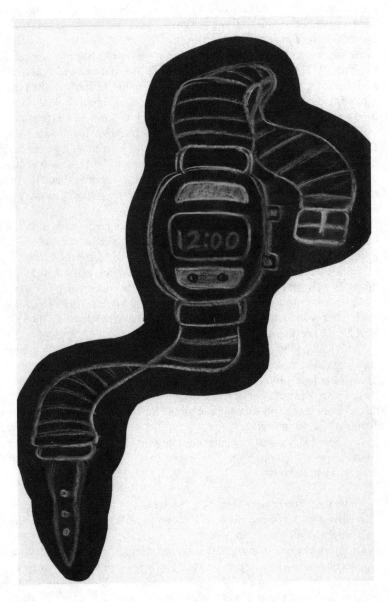

"Gift" By Nicole Gluckstern

kitchenette, some worn chairs, a peeling table, a dresser spotted with cigarette burns along the edges, two unmade beds, and a door leading to a small
bathroom off to one side. All the area on the timeworn table and dilapi-
dated dresser was covered by dozens of randomly strewn beer cans, junk
food wrappers, and at least five overflowing ashtrays. My eyes came to rest
upon the burly figure of another man.

He was a round man with a bushy head of grey-white hair and an equally
thick beard. The fellow was sprawled across one of the chairs next to the
table, holding a beer in one fat hand and a handful of cards in the other.
Squinting up at me with some effort, he introduced himself as "Big Bob;"
he'd come over to play cards from his room a few doors down the walk.

Frank joked that they called him Big Bob because he was so damned fat
that his clothes had to be tailor-made, then gave us each an icy beer from
the midget refrigerator under the kitchenette counter. He'd clearly had more
than a few himself. If his over-jubilant response to our arrival and the par-
tied-out decor of the room were any indication, he'd probably been at his
drinking for hours.

Pete relayed how we had met, and how I was new to town and didn't yet
have any money or a place to stay. Frank didn't need to be asked, and
immediately invited me stay there the next few nights, free of charge. He
explained that his rent was paid up for the next week and a half and he
might as well have company instead of letting the other bed go to waste.
Though wary of possible motives hidden behind his generous offer, especially after what had happened with Doug, I thanked him and said I was
glad for the hospitality.

In his slap-happy state, Frank expounded upon how he loved to imbibe,
stay in good company, and just have a fine old time. Up until about five
days earlier he couldn't drink or do anything else he liked; Frank had been
locked up in the state penitentiary for the past six years. Since his release
he had been going full-speed ahead, doing his best to make up for so long
devoid of serious partying.

As I heard him speak, my guarded state shifted to one of fear, my brain
pondering what heinous crime he'd committed to have been locked up for
so long. I had to know.

"Why were you in jail?" I meekly inquired.

A distant look crossed his face for a moment before he responded, "I
was caught holding up a store."

He returned from wherever his mind had drifted, and picking up on my
frightened and anxious expression added, "you don't have to worry, I'm
not gonna rob you! I only rob stores, not people." Then he burst into a
bellowing, friendly, drunken, chortling, with Pete and Big Bob joining in
soon after. The dreary room became alive with the trio's laughter.

Seeing and hearing them titter and guffaw helped me relax a bit. Frank seemed too amicable to be any kind of threat. The alcohol was making me aware of my exhaustion pent up from the long day of dealing with Jane, hitching over three hundred miles, following Pete around, and finally, meeting Frank and Big Bob.

An intense, almost overpowering craving for the release of sleep began to dominate my consciousness, but I knew I had to wait for the natural course of things to wind the little party down, whereupon Big Bob and Pete would finally leave. I waited, and the longer I waited the more at ease I began to feel. Contrary to all my stereotypes about "criminals," I could see that Frank wasn't some kind of ruthless, inhuman villain, simply because he'd been in jail; like he'd said, he was merely a guy who wanted to enjoy some good old happy times with his friends.

Actually, now I was a criminal. In the past few weeks I'd escaped from the police several times, shoplifted, trespassed, conned a church, and stolen jewelry. Oh yeah, and I ran away from home, yet another crime.

I didn't think of myself as a criminal though. I preferred to imagine myself as a survivor, a cunning loner who could navigate the depths of our society, and despite my unemployable "minor" status, still be able to eke out a living from the systems designed to shut people like me out.

In reality, I wasn't such the cunning survivor. And I knew it. I was more a confused and desperate kid, unaware of how to take better care of myself than I'd managed thus far.

Yet, however I tried to look at it, I was still a criminal by society's standards. That might be why I found myself feeling so comfortable around Frank. Maybe I was in my element.

The party wore on and on, and I did my best to stay alert despite my profound fatigue. After a while, it was explained that Frank had been released with his clothing and a small sum of money, about two hundred fifty dollars. He'd used some of it to pay for a couple week's rent here, and most of the rest to buy food and booze. Less than a week out of jail, he was almost broke. He was in no hurry to get a job though. Sooner or later he would get around to stressing about it, but there was too much relaxing to do first.

As usually happened with new acquaintances, they gave me the fifth degree about what I was doing, where I was from, where I was going, and why. I elaborated upon the story I'd given Pete, telling them I was eighteen, just out of high school, and had left home to start making it on my own. Mixing in a grain of the truth with a heap of fabrication, I said I was from Sanibel Island on the gulf side of Florida, and had been hitching around for a couple of weeks. Recounting the same story I'd given the church, I told them I'd been robbed in Clearwater and had thereby lost my money and I.D.. But I wasn't a quitter, I said, and it was my intention to get a job, and ultimately earn enough money for my own place.

No one argued with my story or accused me of making any of it up. But

I could read their doubts from their expressions. Before leaving home, I was still able to fake twelve, and scam my way into movies at the children's price. After passing for a twelve year old, faking eighteen was quite a stretch. But they respected me enough to pretend to believe me, knowing they'd be told if I wanted them to know my true story.

The time for sleep finally arrived. Pete and Big Bob went their separate ways, and Frank and I got ready for bed. In Frank's case, this involved a quick trip to the bathroom to take another leak, followed by abruptly and unembarrassedly tearing off all his clothes and popping under his covers. He was snoring within minutes.

I was still on guard, skeptical of his altruism, but Frank didn't give off any of the warning signals that Doug had. He hadn't shown any interest in my sexuality and had even joked that night about "screwing" some of the good looking women he'd seen roaming the beaches. I needed to sleep. Thus, wise or not, it wasn't long before I let go, and fell into a shallow slumber myself.

Morning arrived and drifted by. We slept in until some time after ten, before stirring ourselves out of bed. I'd woken several times in the course of the night as Frank got up to waddle over to the bathroom and relieve himself of yet a few more of those beers he'd spent the night consuming. But otherwise the night was uneventful. And I was glad.

We were both famished and Frank invited me out to breakfast (his treat) at the local Ho-Jo's. He was a generous sort while he still had some money; with just five dollars to his name and not a cent in sight, Frank was the sort who would share it all with whomever he happened to be around at the time.

Both groggy, he from his hang-over, and me from a chronic shortage of deep sleep, neither of us were all that talkative. We walked the four blocks to the restaurant in silence, and I realized I felt comfortable with my new friend — ex convict or not, he was an alright guy.

The lobby was crowded, crammed full with families and folks of all ages waiting for their turn to be served. Aromas of pancakes, eggs, bacon, and other breakfast foods permeated the restaurant, making my stomach react with a series of growls and a loud squealing that said "FEED ME NOW!"

Our turn finally arrived a few cigarettes later. I ordered and devoured a huge breakfast of scrambled eggs, wheat toast, hash-browns, crisp bacon, and half of a strawberry smothered waffle I shared with Frank, along with a large orange juice and a frothy glass of milk. The food was greasy and not the best quality, but I was too hungry to care. By the time we emptied our plates, I was so stuffed it hurt to move. It was a most desirable kind of pain.

We paged through a newspaper for a long while, until we grew tired of guzzling coffee. Frank payed the bill and we headed to the beach to see what the day would bring. In the process I forgot about my plan to head to Key West.

Most Beautiful

Compared to some who I might have hooked up with, Frank felt like a relatively safe and protective soul with which to hang. We grokked each other. He respected me, trusting me to follow my own path, and never attempting to boss me around just because he was older. Frank partied with me as he would with anyone else, never adopting the condescending manner of most adults when addressing people my age. We were equals, neither better or more important than the other. At least in the beginning, that is.

After a few days I confided the truth about my situation. I described how after being slapped across the face, I had just snapped and hopped out of the car on the way home from school one day. After I'd finished explaining much of what I'd gone through in the past three weeks, Frank told me he'd figured something like that had happened. He added there was no way I looked like I was eighteen. Then, for the first time since meeting, Frank took it upon himself to tell me what to do, as though my opening up gave him permission. He said he thought I should call my parents to let them know I was alive and well, in case they were worried about me.

It was out of the question. I was too afraid. I felt ashamed for having run, and believed my parents would only be angry with me. They were sick and tired of me always getting in trouble, and the latest incident was just one more time that I had fucked things up, this time worse than ever. I was a bad kid as far as they were concerned, and I believed them.

I told Frank he might be right about what I "should" do, but I just wasn't ready to handle facing my family. Maybe later, but not now.

Frank offered to call them for me, just to say I was alive. But I was afraid the call would be traced. If my parents figured out where I was they might get me arrested and sent to a military reform school, or somewhere else, someplace even scarier.

Frank heard me. He stopped his pressuring for the time being, but every few days he would gently bring it up again. "You don't even have to tell them where you are, just call them so they know you are still alive. They can't trace the call if you keep it short. It's a tough world out there, and your family could be worried that the worst has happened to you. Anything you did wrong must seem really small to them now, compared to the wrong that could have been done to you."

Every time Frank brought it up again I'd go through another bout of guilt and shame. What he said made sense, but I simply wasn't brave enough to risk calling my folks yet. My fears and anxieties for myself outweighed anything I imagined my parents to be going through.

Frank's repeated urgings were one of the few things that bothered me about him. I couldn't get angry though. He was never too pushy, always seeming to sense precisely how much room I needed on this issue.

The better part of our time together was spent focusing on happier subjects. Frank was a free-spirit and just wanted to relish life. We enjoyed daily barbecues at the public grills on the beach, often accompanied by Big Bob, Pete, and a host of other beach bum types. Everybody chipped in whatever money they could come up with to buy all the fixings for an all-American picnic: hamburgers, hot dogs, buns, ketchup (usually from the small packets unwittingly donated by fast-food restaurants), chips, and, of course, beer. We'd just hang out for a temporary forever, eating, drinking, and watching the day go by.

One day the subject of women came up. We'd talked about women plenty of times before, but always in a laughing mood. This time, in a more serious than usual tone, Frank confided that he hadn't had sex for over six years. I jokingly responded that it didn't sound so bad to me; after all, I hadn't had sex in fifteen years and I was still okay. And at the rate I was going, it could be another lifetime before I found a woman who actually wanted me.

Frank was in a different boat, though. I thought it couldn't be all that difficult for someone like him to find a willing woman. At least he was a grown man.

Frank was also a strong man, with tattoos up and down both of his muscular arms. He'd lifted a mountain of weights in jail, since "there didn't seem to be anything better to do," he'd explained. Besides, muscles acted as a deterrent to the bullies in prison. Deadly bullies. His work paid off in the form of a rugged, solid, and at the same time, wiry physique, one which I figured women would go ape shit over.

Nonetheless, he complained that he didn't know how to meet women. The two of us wandered down the shore to an indoor/outdoor bar at the Pompano Beach Pier. It was early evening and we sat on the guardrail surrounding the bar's patio, looking around at the various people enjoying each other's company. To my surprise, no one tried to card me and kick me out for being "underaged." The drinking age was still only eighteen or nineteen then, but it was hard to believe no one noticed how young I looked.

I was in a cocky, spontaneous mood that night, and decided to do something to snap Frank out of his depression. He was my friend and I couldn't just sit by doing nothing, while he felt so dejected. In a sparkling moment of insanity, the solution became obvious: I was going to give Frank a demonstration, illustrating how easy it was to get laid.

"Frank, I want you to just sit here and watch me for a minute. I'm going to show you how it's done." Could it really work? I wondered.

Sliding off the railing, I sauntered up to the most beautiful woman in the bar. She was sitting with a group of people around one of the outdoor patio tables. Her long blonde hair, beautiful blue eyes, and smooth dark skin were just a part of her overall appeal; she also had an easygoing, happy kind of smile.

She looked up at me and I locked eyes, ignoring everyone else in the vicinity. With an ear to ear smile I launched in:

"Hi, you don't know me, but I just want you to know that I think you're one of the most beautiful women I have ever seen. I know this will seem odd, and I won't be offended if you decide not to, but if you're willing, I would really like to lose my virginity to you. I'd begin by making love to you slowly and passionately, doing my best to deliberately bring unimaginable pleasure to every inch of your wonderful body. We could make love for hours."

As I made my little speech, I kept looking deeply into the woman's glowing eyes, feeling an insanely passionate electric chill pass between us. My attention was so focused upon her that I could no longer see any of the other people sitting at her table. Listening to me intently, she broke out into a notably broad grin of her own, portraying the mixture of feelings bubbling up inside her. Her widening eyes and stretched smile made her look flattered, amazed, amused, and just a smidgen embarrassed. It must have been somewhat of a shock to have an adolescent boy approach out of the blue and say such a thing. Feeding off her response, I continued with a playful, "nothing to lose" kind of attitude.

"I've never made love to a woman before, but I've read a lot about it in different books and magazine articles. I'm pretty sure that not only do I know *how* to make love to a woman, but that I would do an extremely good job of it, making you come again, and again, and again."

The woman finally broke out into a laugh. She said she was extremely flattered by my offer, but that her boyfriend (the man sitting right next to her) would be somewhat offended if she took me up on it.

Entirely unperterbed, I smiled a cocky smile and said, "Well, thank you for your time. At least know that you are a spectacularly beautiful woman, and that the man who gets to pleasure you is lucky beyond belief." And

"Most Beautiful" By Nicole Gluckstern

then I walked away.

I smiled at Frank, who was still sitting on the railing. He returned the smile with a look of entertained surprise as I approached another table, where I spied the second most beautiful woman in the bar. When I had her attention, I repeated the spiel I'd just given the blond-haired woman, with perhaps a few refinements. This woman, too, rejected me with a friendly, flattered smile and laugh.

Expecting no success, but having plenty of fun, I went on in this fashion through three other women before achieving a measure of success with woman number six. I wasn't actually all that attracted to her, but had exhausted all the more alluring women within my first few attempts. Number six was an older woman, somewhere around forty, with a thin frame and short, curly brown hair bordering a sun wrinkled face. She sat alone on a bar-stool, at the indoor section of the bar.

I put my foot on the first rung of the stool next to her, and leaning on my knee launched into my speech through a beaming grin. As I spoke, she smiled back and put her hand on my knee.

With slurred speech, and a flirtatious manner she said, "You sure are a cutesy. But don't you think you are just a little too young for me? For chrissake, I'm old enough to be your mother!"

The bartender was too amused by our parley to interfere. Otherwise, I was sure to have been bounced out on my ass.

Moving onto the stool next to the woman I argued that age didn't matter when it came to making love. She placed her hand on my shoulder, leaned towards me, and replied that age did make a difference because it took experience to know how to make a woman happy. She asked where I got the nerve to walk up to complete strangers and ask such risque questions.

Pointing out Frank, who was watching us amusedly from the railing, I explained how I was trying to show him how easy it was to find a willing woman. I relayed how he'd been complaining of being jailed for six years without women, other than those in magazines and on the tube, and how he was clueless about how to find a woman, now that he was out. I was only trying to help him see that all he had to do was ask.

The woman smiled at Frank, waving, then beckoning him over to join us. He looked a bit embarrassed as he ambled our way. She joked, telling him his little friend was going to find a woman before he did. I didn't like being called his "little friend," but smiled anyway. We introduced ourselves and learned her name was Renee. She asked if we wanted to head outside to smoke a joint and continue this discussion in more comfort, at one of our places.

Frank and I glanced at each other, broke into simultaneous grins, and looked back towards Renee, nodding "yes!" Renee's bike was chained to the fence in front. She asked how we got there. Frank told her we were on foot and our apartment was about three blocks away. Renee's place was further off, about a mile and a half in the opposite direction. The pot was at Renee's, so off we went.

Permagrin

Following a few failed experiments we decided the most efficient way to travel was for me to pedal her bicycle while she balanced on the handlebars and Frank jogged alongside. A nineteen-fifties woman's three-speed with wide handlebars, her bike wasn't designed for two; the seat was a tiny triangle, barely able to support one butt.

Somehow I piloted the bike without crashing or dumping her off the steering wheel, though there were a few shaky moments when a fall seemed imminent. Renee laughed, drunkenly, the entire way to her apartment, howling at each close call. She kept shifting her balance without warning, flirting with disaster.

We made it though. Her ground level apartment was in a two-story building that bent around three sides of the leisure patio/pool area. The place was much nicer than the pay-by-the-week roach infested room Frank and I shared. Renee had a modern place complete with a bedroom, a spacious L-shaped living and dining room, a separate full kitchen, and a bathroom. I scrutinized every detail, in my hawkish way. The furniture was new, and unlike the gloomy brown patterns adorning our room, the decor was bright, cheery, and relaxing.

Renee said she worked as a secretary at a nearby law office. She ushered us in and told us to make ourselves at home while she got us something to drink. Frank sat on the fat, cushy sofa, and I sank into one of the matching arm-chairs, letting myself luxuriate in the soft, almost enveloping support it provided.

Renee chatted from the kitchen while she fixed us each a glass of ice water. Shortly, she returned with the sweating drinks on a painted tray and set them on the glass coffee table in front of us. I could enjoy a pad like this.

"Shall we?" she asked, while reaching around the side of the sofa and bringing out the hinged, embroidered box wherein she stored her paraphernalia.

"Yes," we chimed in unison.

Sitting beside Frank, she methodically removed a plump bag of grass, a pack of rolling papers, and a little device for rolling joints. She knew how to use it and quickly manufactured us a compact, perfectly round joint that looked more like a cigarette than the rough pin-joints I could roll. I'd seen a comparable kit before leaving home, and had a sudden vision of similar boxes hiding in their various niches within thousands, if not millions of homes throughout America.

After Renee and Frank each hit off the grass, she offered me a turn. I felt a bit left out, and eagerly seized the chance to sit closer to her on the sofa, mumbling that I wouldn't have to lean so far across the table every time I wanted a hit. Actually, I was just conniving, trying to get closer to her in case what I hoped for was about to happen.

I had an unusual feeling of control. All these pleasantries had come as a direct result of my thoroughly unreserved propositioning of Renee back at the bar. I hadn't overlooked this for a minute. Any conversations we'd had between there and here weren't going to make me forget why we had come together in the first place.

Frank remembered too. Our conversation came to a halt a few minutes later as he started kissing Renee. I didn't know what to do. He began rubbing her breasts, and I figured if he could, I could. I reached out and grasped.

My first "feel!" It was an exciting, yet awkward, situation. I'd never touched a woman in this way, with such blatant sexuality, but where it was leading scared me; so far it was going just like those letters in the magazines, and if it kept up we'd all be naked in a few minutes. I wanted to get as naked as possible with Renee, but not around Frank.

Renee must have been thinking along a similar line, because she pulled back and said that it was "a bad idea" to keep proceeding this way. She declared that she would take Frank back into her bedroom first, and then, once they were finished, it would be my turn. She wanted me to wait outside, in the living room until they were done.

"That's not fair!" I thought. "I'm the one who got us all here. I should go first!"

But I was amazed that I was even getting a turn. I agreed to wait.

Renee led a gleeful Frank by the hand, and the two of them disappeared into the bedroom, shutting and locking the door behind them. The grunting and groaning that soon emanated from the bedroom became a major distraction from my reading. Mindlessly, I flipped through page after boring page of Cosmo, Vogue, and Ladies Home Journal, seeing the pictures and headlines, yet completely incapable of delving into any of the articles.

Time passed.

I smoked.

And read.

And smoked.

Every passing moment added to the nervousness and excitement I felt. Here I was, about to lose my virginity, to have sex for the first time, just like in the magazines.

Eventually Frank emerged from the bedroom, after about two noisy, interminable hours. He was happy, and showed it with a huge, perhaps record-breaking grin across his face. He looked like a little boy, not like the hardened, thirty-six year old, tattooed ex-convict he was. I must have looked pretty elated myself, because now, I presumed, it was my turn.

Renee was quick to deflate my excitement, though. As she came from the bedroom she looked at me and said, "Wow, that was quite a riot we just had in there!" She looked it, wearing a loose fitting robe over her skinny frame and a head of tussled hair.

"I'm sorry, but I think I'm tired out," she apologized. "I have to get up and go to work in a few hours; I need to get some sleep. How 'bout if you come back tomorrow night cutie-pie?"

What a rip-off! Especially after waiting for so long. This certainly sucked, but I didn't see that I had any choice. I'd have to remain a virgin for another day.

A little dejected, I accepted her new proposition. One day wouldn't be so bad. I'd sleep through most of it anyway.

We agreed that I'd return about sixteen hours later, when she was finished with work. Frank and I hung around a little longer, the required amount for politeness sake, and then walked the two miles back towards our room.

Frank wanted to celebrate, and decided to stop at Ho-Jos for another of his huge breakfasts. This was our first time back since the morning after I'd met him. He usually subsisted on bologna sandwiches, Spaghetti-O's and Meatballs, and generic beer. Of course, since he thanked me for his "getting lucky," I was the "man of honor." Not that I was into celebrating; after all, I had initiated everything, yet for some reason Frank was the one who had actually benefited.

After a short nap back at the room, I waited impatiently for the evening to approach. I went out to the beach to pass time watching the surf. My mind was preoccupied with only one all-consuming question: What was going to happen when I returned to Renee's place?

The appointed time arrived. Just as agreed, I returned to Renee's apartment and rang the bell. She came to the door and asked who it was. I said hello and she invited me in.

Renee seemed surprised, as if she hadn't expected me to show. We sat down to talk, her on the couch and me on one of the stuffed chairs. How to start?

Renee spoke first, saying she didn't think that it was appropriate for us to have sex. She asked me how old I was.

"Eighteen," I lied. "How old are you?"

"Thirty-nine," she replied. "I'm old enough to be your mom!" Renee got out one of her photo albums and showed me a picture of a young man. It was her son, and she said he was "only" nineteen. I wondered if Renee was really older than the thirty-nine she claimed, but just wasn't admitting it. Later, when I told Frank and Big-Bob her purported age, Frank laughed, saying she was probably closer to fifty.

It didn't matter to me, I wanted to have sex. I told Renee that age simply wasn't important to me, insisting over and over that I was sure that I wanted her. Replaying my routine from the night before, I promised that if she'd just give me the chance, I'd make her feel unbelievably good across every square inch of her body.

Renee was very reluctant, yet I could tell by her smile and her flirty attitude that she was at least interested. She seemed to want me to convince her that it wouldn't be wrong to make love with me. We talked for what seemed like several hours about whether or not we should, could, and would make love.

Never touching her, I continually, yet politely, attempted to persuade her with my words and my eyes. It seemed silly for us to be sitting in separate chairs, talking about having sex, instead of just letting it happen somehow, but I couldn't think of any better way to go about it; I wasn't going to start kissing her, or anything else, without her permission.

Finally, almost suddenly, she laughed and said, "Well, OK. Lets just go for it and see what happens."

"Holy Shit!" I thought. "This is it! Wow!"

I moved over to her and we started French kissing. My first real love-kiss. It was a lot wetter and sexier than I'd imagined. My hands became increasingly braver in their explorations while we continued exchanging tongue. After a while she pulled back and said we should move to a more comfortable place. I couldn't believe it.

She took me into her bedroom. Less than twenty minutes into my first time at full-fledged necking and I was about to make love.

I was surprised with how matter-of-factly she took off her clothing, simply removing it all at once and placing it on a chair near the bed. No formalities. It was my turn to follow suit.

There was no point in being shy; if I didn't measure up somehow, she was free to let me know. I stripped, quickly, and closed the bedroom door behind us.

And oh, the time that I had!

About five hours later, I left Renee's place with a huge smile on my face.

Close race that it was, I would have laid good odds that my after-the-event grin far exceeded Frank's of the previous morning.

Following Frank's example, this time I headed towards Ho Jos to take my turn at celebrating. I felt a great, bubbling joy, and broke into a galloping run, with my face breaking into an uncontrollable grin. The sun was rising over the ocean and the birds screeched out their morning songs like they shared my delight. I too had a strong urge to sing out a morning song, to tell the world what had just happened to me. Stuck with unremovable permagrin, I found myself smiling and waving at complete strangers as I danced by them.

In spite of how shallow our interaction had been, this was the happiest moment I'd had since leaving home about five weeks ago. After fifteen and a quarter years, I'd done it! Raw, passionate, naked sex.

Hustling

In the course of my weeks in Pompano Beach with Frank, I got in the habit of taking day-trips down to Fort Lauderdale Beach. Fort Lauderdale had a lot more going for it: more people, more stores, and more opportunities — in short, it had a scene. What grabbed me most, was the huge video arcade on the waterfront. From the time I'd first played "Space Invaders," a few years earlier, I'd become an outright addict. Ever since, I'd eagerly played every new game I could find and afford.

Before leaving home I had mastered two games, "Donkey Kong" (the predecessor of Mario Brothers) and "Gallaga," a couple of the most popular games at the time. I'd sought out every publicly accessible video game on the island. Pinball was still hot then, but most of the resorts on Sanibel, and the neighboring Captiva Island, had arcades with at least a few video games, thereby offering plenty of opportunities to feed my addiction.

Sometimes I'd grow so obsessed with a game that I'd dream about it. My unconscious mind would work and rework the patterns needed to solve the puzzles the games presented, ever striving and struggling to advance but one more screen when I returned to an arcade the next day. And I wasn't the only one. Video games draw kids like shit draws flies.

In turn, the kids in video arcades are a magnet to the molesters. It was at the Fort Lauderdale Beach arcade that I met Ray.

Ray was perhaps the most lecherous adult that I'd met up to that point. Unfortunately for me, and most people who ran into Ray, he didn't make this apparent when he first met you.

Ray was a fat, fleshy, unhealthy looking man, with the age wrinkled eyes of a man far past his prime. He had thin, wispy, orange hair and a crooked face that made him look somewhat like one of the Wicked Witches in the *The Wizard of Oz*. He even had wart-like moles sticking out of his chin and nose. Still, his disarming smile and friendly attitude made it easy to ignore his physical repulsiveness.

Ray had two jobs at the arcade. Sometimes I'd see him working inside, making change and fixing problems with the numerous video games and pinball machines. When he wasn't inside, he could usually be found out back working as the parking lot attendant.

I first met Ray when I lied about losing two quarters in a machine in order to get some money to play. When I'd used up my "refund" I asked if he had any work I could do to make some more game money. The disaster had found a way of getting started, and I was the one who made it possible.

Of course, I didn't know it was a disaster at the time. Quite to the contrary, it seemed that meeting Ray was a veritable stroke of luck. Why? Because he offered me a job.

Ray explained that the parking lot out back collected a lot of trash from the litter bugs that parked there when frequenting the beach. A quick glance of the parking area proved his point; there was an assortment of soda can pull-tabs (the sharp-edged kind that are now obsolete), fast food containers, smashed, discarded beer bottles and cans, cigarette butts, scraps of newspaper, and other remnants of the disposable culture centered near the beach. Ray offered me two bucks for every day I gathered the trash and put it in the nearby dumpster.

This was one of my few "legitimate" opportunities to raise cash, so I readily accepted his offer. The work wasn't hard, though I got a bit sticky and slimy from the take-out soda and milkshake cups, and other fast-food garbage. The first time I picked the hot, weed-infested asphalt clean within an hour; after that it took less than thirty minutes a pop to keep up with the new litter. Slimy as the work was, it was a good deal; with two dollars I could buy myself another pack of cigarettes, and have some left over for the arcade.

Another way I managed to "earn" money at the arcade was through betting. Being an expert at both Donkey Kong and Gallaga, hardly anyone could match me, let alone beat me. I'd also memorized some patterns for Pac-Man from a book at a store, and though they only got me through about twenty screens, it was enough to beat most people.

Before betting someone, I'd try to watch them play a game. This way I could be pretty sure whether or not I could beat them. Now and again, I'd first play a two-player game with my potential mark without betting. I'd bait them, playing poorly on purpose to make them think they were better; then they'd be more likely to wager higher stakes.

Then, once they agreed to play for money, I'd let loose, often scoring higher on my first turn than they would in the whole game. I didn't feel too bad about suckering them, as they wouldn't have hesitated to take my money. Besides, the stakes were low enough that I doubted I caused my opponents much suffering. It was hard to get anyone to bet more than a dollar. Still, this small change was enough to keep me playing, which in turn, kept me happily distracted from dwelling on how I was an aimless runaway.

The arcade became one of my hangouts, on the days I made it down to Fort Lauderdale. The parking lot didn't always need cleaning, but each time I visited, I'd find Ray to check if he had any new work for me. I didn't have any problems with him the first few times I came by. He was always friendly, just a guy who liked to chat about different things, and tell lewd jokes about women.

Eventually, his cheery attitude, put together with the familiarity I developed by seeing him on a regular basis, led me to begin to trust Ray. I thought of him as a friend; after all he was helping me out. If I'd only known he was setting me up, in a manner ironically similar to how I set up my video game marks...

But I didn't know.

Back up in Pompano Beach things were about to get a bit harder for Frank and me. We'd been living together for about a week and a half now. Frank was almost out of his "get away from the jail" money, and the rent for another week was due the next day. I never had much money, just what I could scarf up by working for Ray, betting on games, and my other odd ventures. It was rarely more than a few bucks.

We needed seventy dollars and soon, for another week's rent. Frank had done nothing to find a job and seemed to have no intention of changing his unemployed status. Fortunately I had one last resource, the gold chain jewelry I'd stolen from the hotel room in Daytona Beach. If I could find a way to sell it, the money could solve our problem of impending homelessness.

I showed Frank the jewelry and told him how I'd stolen it. He laughed when I shared my idea about melting it down, and suggested we try to sell it to a pawn shop instead. We looked them up in the motel-room's battered and beer-stained Yellow Pages; the closest was a few miles away on the mainland. Frank tore the pages from the phone book and we grabbed a bus.

It was harder to pawn the jewelry than we expected. I didn't have a photo I.D., and only two weeks out of prison, Frank was afraid to risk using his. We had to go to four different pawn shops before finding someone who would to buy it without proof of identity.

The man gave me a pawn card to complete. I made up all of the required information, and signed with a fake name. Then I had to leave my thumbprint in a little rectangle on the card. I figured it was safe enough, as the jewelry bore no distinguishing marks and no one would ever figure out where it had come from. The necklaces and bracelet were simple in design, not much different from the tens of thousands of similar gold chains sold in American department and jewelry stores each year. Moreover, I was over a hundred miles from where I'd snatched them.

The proprietor of the pawn shop, a thin, graying, old fellow slowly and meticulously weighed the jewelry, and then payed me on a "per gram" basis. He carefully counted out almost one hundred thirty dollars, laying them in a compact pile on the counter. This was roughly twice what we needed for the next week's rent, more than enough to keep us going; this was great!

We spent what was left that week on food, cigarettes and beer. Giving nary a thought to the future, we kept to our routine of daily barbecues on the public grills at the beach. And we had company. Both Big Bob and Pete seemed to drop by just as we started cooking, glad to share in our temporary burst of prosperity.

It was on one of these lazy barbecue evenings that Frank taught me a trick he'd learned to protect himself when he was in prison: How to make a knife out of a cigarette butt.

Frank explained that weapons were, of course, prohibited in prison, but there were times when if you didn't have them, you would be in deep-shit danger from those who did. A mushy cigarette butt seemed an unlikely object to turn into a knife, but to my amazement Frank demonstrated how.

First he tore the paper from the butt of a filter cigarette, getting rid of all but the inch long, yellow-brown stained filter. Next, he struck a match and held it to the filter until it caught on fire. As the filter burned, it was slowly transformed into a black and bubbly gel that emitted wisps of stinky dark smoke. Before it burned his fingers, Frank placed the fiery thing on a cement slab and stepped on it, leaning so all of his weight was born through the point of his foot, and the filter beneath. After a few seconds he lifted his foot and bent to pick up the transformed object, a dark black wedge bearing little resemblance to a cigarette butt.

After a brief look at the wedge to confirm it met his standards, Frank handed it over for me to examine. What I held was a very hard material, half a centimeter thick at the base, tapering to less than a millimeter at the point. Frank challenged me to try to bend it with my fingers, and I found that I couldn't. Then he took it back to demonstrate how it worked.

He explained that by burning the filter, the fiberglass of which it was composed was transformed into a compound as hard as rock. If you compressed the material while it was still hot and bubbly, it could be molded into a sharp and pointy shape. In prison, he and his companions worked them into short but sharp blades.

For maximal effect, they would take three of these mini blades and place them between their fingers. When they made a fist, the blades projected from their hand in a deadly array of spikes. The resultant weapon worked like a spiked set of brass knuckles. If someone was punched by a fist armed with these projections, their skin was sure to be shredded.

This was just one of the many cunning and useful survival and criminal techniques Frank had learned about in prison. Later that week, what he'd learned about burglar alarms from a cat-burglar cell-mate of his, was to become central in our planning a dangerous crime that could change our lives forever.

Rape

It was during the beginning of my third week in Frank's company that I finally learned something of Ray's darker side. This was a lesson I would have avoided if I'd had the slightest foreboding. Unfortunately, my instincts and intuitions didn't pick up on Ray's evil designs until the lesson was well under way.

The lesson began soon after I got off the bus to Fort Lauderdale one morning. I'd stopped to check-in and chat with Ray in our usual way. We were hanging out by his little attendant's booth in the parking lot when he casually invited me over to see his house during his lunch break.

He had some video games of his own there and offered to let me play them for free if I wanted. Ray explained he usually drove home for lunch and returned to work about two hours later. It would be no problem to give me a ride.

The video game addict that I was, the idea of playing two hours of free video games got me pretty excited. It was one of my dreams come true! I'd known Ray for a couple of weeks and felt fairly safe with him by now, so I agreed. He played me like a video game, maneuvering me with cunning skill to the perfect position to make the most points: just dangle the fruit of game-bliss, and like a computer junkie, I'd be there. We headed to Ray's house an hour later.

We puttered along in his big old boat of a car until we arrived at his small, middle-class house about three miles away. It was a typical looking two-story home that blended in smoothly with the neighborhood. When we entered, I was surprised to see other kids my age hanging around inside. Ray had never mentioned living with other people, and didn't seem the dad type.

Ray told me they were all runaways, and that he let them stay there for free. He gave me a sweaty can of beer and told me I was free to get started

137

with the Atari in the other room while he fixed his lunch. Needing no further encouragement, I sipped my beer and went into the living room to play a two-player combat game with one of the other kids, leaving Ray to his food. The other boy and I didn't talk much, as we were too busy concentrating on destroying each other's tanks on the screen in front of us.

A few games later Ray reappeared. He offered us each another beer and a couple of little white pills he said would make us feel real good. He called them "Ludes," and promised they would help us mellow out in an undeniably nice way.

Other than aspirin and other over-the-counter medicines, I'd never had any pill drugs before. I was afraid of the pills, small though they were. Warnings about mixing drugs with alcohol, especially depressants, echoed in my mind. I'd heard mixing them could make one terribly ill, to the point of coma or death.

Ray and the boy seemed unaware of these prohibitions, as they each placed a pill in their mouths and swallowed them down with great swigs of beer. The pair looked at me expectantly, waiting for me to do the same. I was too embarrassed to simply admit my fear, but sure as hell wasn't going to ingest a strange new drug in a strange new place. I put the pill in my mouth, but shoved it to the side, between my cheek and gums, to keep from swallowing it as I took my own swig of beer.

I could feel the pill slowly dissolving in my mouth while we talked for a while, but had to wait until they weren't looking before spitting it out. We continued talking about Qualudes and video games for the next few minutes. There was no indication that I'd get my chance; I was growing apprehensive, afraid I'd absorb the drug through my gums if I couldn't get rid of it soon.

Desperate, I asked to go to the bathroom. Ray pointed the way.

With the door finally closed behind me, I reached my finger between my gums and cheeks to scoop out what was left of the melting tablet. What I got was a pasty mash of liquefied pill gunk. I leaned over the sink to rinse and spit out the rest with a few mouthfuls of tap-water. My mouth was beginning to feel as clean as it was going to get, but I wondered if I might have absorbed enough of the pill to affect me. There was little I could do about it if I had.

Looking up, I saw my worried self staring back from the toothpaste-splattered mirror. What was I doing here? I didn't have a good answer.

Neither did my reflection.

Avoiding a dubious delay, I returned to the living room to play some more video games. Ray was back in the kitchen and the boy and I continued to lose ourselves in the games. He looked tired, burnt-out, and was playing rather badly, making it nothing to smear him.

Ray reappeared after a stretch and said he wanted to show me something. Curious, I followed him through the kitchen and into his bedroom. What was he going to show me?

He closed the door and put his arm around my shoulder. I looked up at Ray as he said he wanted me to take off my clothes and lay down on his bed so he could make me feel some "bona fide ecstasy."

For the first time I realized how utterly and revoltingly ugly Ray was. His multiple chins, warty and contorted face, and beady eyes conveyed what I finally realized was a sneaky, manipulative, warped, child-molesting personality. In a flash, it was clear what all the other kids were doing in his home. They were there for Ray to use for his sexual whims.

All of his friendly "help" and conversation at the arcade had been designed to engender trust so he could lure me to his home one day. This was that day. The beer and Qualudes were to get me loosened up, ready for Ray to manipulate like a puppet. He must have thought I was quite drugged from the combination, that I would simply go along with whatever he suggested. If so, he was mistaken.

I was a little buzzed from the beers, but not enough to forget who I was. Since I didn't want him to know I'd faked taking the pill, I pretended to be kind of stupid and slow-witted like the boy in the other room, and slowly enunciated the words: "I don't want to."

Ray argued, saying it would be fun and would feel great, and that afterwards we could go back to the video arcade. Did this mean that if I didn't cooperate, we wouldn't be returning there? I was too afraid to ask. He exerted slight pressure on my shoulders, escorting me towards the bed while he talked.

Ray wanted to have sex with me. In the several weeks I'd known Ray, I'd never suspected it would come to this. He'd never expressed anything but heterosexual interest to me before. In fact, he was always making sexually graphic comments about the women who walked by the parking lot. Ray had been explicit alright, saying things like, "Wouldn't you like to suck those tits," "Boy, what I wouldn't do to get me some of that pussy," and "I bet she gives good head!"

This kind of vulgarity wasn't threatening to me, so it didn't bother me at the time. If anything, it made me feel safer around Ray, as it led me to believe he was heterosexual and was only interested in me as a friend. After what had happened with Doug, I was on-guard for indications, clear or subtle, that men I met might actually be scoping on me, instead of just being friendly.

Ray's constant focus on women made me discount this possibility with him. Frank had also made plenty of comments like that, and he was definitely straight. Therefore, this change in Ray's behavior was a surprise that caught me off-guard.

On some other level I wasn't surprised. This was at least the fifth time that a man had expressed sexual interest in me. It was time to stop being so naive. I could expect to have to deal with this kind of situation as long as I survived as a runaway, if not as a human being.

As I'd done when pressured by Herb and Doug, I argued that I only wanted to have sex with women. Now that I'd given my virginity to Renee, I couldn't claim to be waiting until I first had sex with a female before trying it with a man. Nevertheless, there was no way that I wanted to do anything of the sort with Ray. I tried to explain that I just wanted to be friends with Ray, and not have sex, telling him I was flattered that he was attracted to me, but I could only like women that way.

He argued back, saying that I was being rude after he had been so nice to me, that the least I could do would be to give it a try. At least he was still talking, and not (yet?) trying to physically force me.

I was starting to get an idea of what it must be like to be a woman, to deal with a constant stream of sexually assertive and persistent men I wasn't attracted to. The men were so damn pushy and invasive about their desires. I wanted to be left alone, but they didn't want to hear and accept that.

With the exception of the gnarled old man in the pick-up truck, every one had argued, trying to convince me to change my mind. They didn't respect my simple, polite "No, thank-you anyway." Ironically, it didn't occur to me that this is exactly what I had done with Renee. Maybe this technique worked for them too sometimes.

Like most women with most men, I was much less physically powerful than the men who were pressuring me. I had the very palpable fear of what could happen to me if I said "no" and they didn't care. I couldn't offer very formidable resistance. I could be raped.

Ray was molesting me. He was using his implied power coercively. Ray had set things up to have as much advantage as possible: He was an adult, much larger and stronger than me; he controlled my transportation back to the arcade; he thought he had drugged me and had allowed ample time for the drugs to do their work; and he had me only two feet from his bed, the lone exit out of the room shut tight.

Even if he stopped now, he'd already crossed the line, assaulting me with his abuse of power.

I was damned glad I'd only pretended to take the pills. Even without them I was having a hard time asserting myself. If I'd been sedated as he'd intended by the synergism of drink and drug, I doubt I'd have had much chance of getting out of there without first experiencing physical molestation on top of the psychological.

Somehow, I managed to escape that room without removing my clothes. At least I think I did. I wouldn't give "yes" as an answer, and I don't recollect being raped.

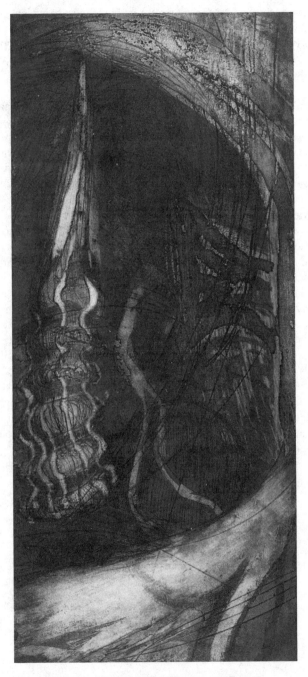

"Windy Night" By Robert Brown

It almost seems as if it doesn't matter, in that I feel certain plenty of other kids didn't get out of Ray's room unscathed, both before and after my visit. My story could just as well have been one of theirs. I merely happened to be one of the lucky ones. If I hadn't been, this page would have been filled with a description of me being raped.

I'd only heard rape talked about in relation to women. But it also happens to men and boys. Frank told me about men being raped in prison. In time, I would have several male friends share their own rape experiences with me. One was gang raped in prison. Another, a gay man, was raped while on a date. And as I was to find out years later, my friend Chris hadn't been as lucky as I'd been that night Herb, the purported film maker, drove us around in his van.

I'd been lucky again, with Ray. Perhaps he didn't want to rape me. Maybe it was the access he had to other boys and girls residing in his home that protected me; he could go to one of them after I left.

I don't really know why or how I got out of there, only that I did. And I was thankful.

I avoided the arcade after that. It was one more place that I couldn't show myself. Not the Don Cesar Hotel the manager had escorted me out of; not the restaurant I wanted to work at in Saint Petersberg Beach; not the entire town of Clearwater Beach after narrowly escaping arrest; not the Daytona Beach motel I was arrested in, or anywhere else those police "authorities" who could recognize me might be; and now, not the Fort Lauderdale Beach video arcade, because I might have to deal with Ray, the child molester.

It seemed I was wearing out my welcome everywhere I went. At this rate, even a state as big as Florida would run out of tourist towns and businesses before long.

Parking Lot

The third week in our Pompano Beach motel was drawing to a close and the next morning it would again be time for Frank and me to cough up the rent. Once again, we didn't have it. Neither of us wanted to end up living on the beach like Big Bob had when he couldn't come up with his rent earlier in the week.

We would have had a good start towards the rent if we hadn't frivolously spent the pawn money left over after paying last week's rent. But woulda, hadda, coulda, shoulda didn't do us any good. It didn't matter where the money had gone, only that we didn't have any now.

There was no more jewelry or anything else of value to sell. If we'd bothered to think about this a week ago, and planned some way to prepare for it, we probably would have been able to come up with enough money within the week. Of course, both our heads were spending the week, along with our bodies, relaxing in the sand, sky, and surf, and pursuing anything but reality. Between the two of us we only had a couple of bucks. We were in a jam.

This was when Frank decided to share his secret. Frank was a pool hustler. He said that if we could come up with a "stake" for him, of about five dollars, he could go into bars and turn it into the week's rent money in a few hours.

This seemed a fairly farfetched plan, and never having seen him play, I had no idea whether he could really pull it off. Frank seemed to believe in himself though, and since I didn't have any better ideas I agreed to help him. We only needed three more dollars.

I went out to the beach and for the first time in my life, I panhandled. Up till now, the closest I'd gotten to begging was to bum an occasional cigarette from someone. This time I approached strangers asking for some change to make a phone call. At ten cents a call I figured it would only take about

"Please Help" By Joel Heflin

thirty people before I had the three bucks we needed.

It was a trifle embarrassing looking all these people in the eye and lying to them, but I got over it quickly enough; the money was for a good cause, our shelter, and begging seemed a lot better than risking arrest for stealing. The biggest challenge was to space my solicitations far enough apart that people wouldn't realize I was making a profession of it.

My figuring was right. It was a whole lot easier than selling sodas in Clearwater Beach had been. I had the extra three dollars within the hour. Now all I had to do was wait.

That evening we went onto the mainland to find pool halls where he could do his work. Frank thought he'd have to go to several places before we finished. Once people saw how good he was, it would be impossible to get anyone else there to bet him. Also, he had to be careful not to bet too much at once. If the stakes were unduly high, and Frank won, his mark might become angry and refuse to pay.

It was easy to relate to this reasoning. Betting at video games involved a similar approach. The key difference was that in pool the stakes were higher and the competition far more likely to become violent if they thought they'd been hustled. Especially if they were drunk.

I was "too young" to go into the bars with Frank. He had me wait in the parking lot, claiming the pool halls weren't like the bar where we'd met Renee. Even if they allowed me in, Frank didn't want me there; it was too risky, he said, because he'd gotten into fights when hustling in the past.

There was nothing to do outside. It wasn't long before I became extremely bored and started thinking how I could be doing just as little, in greater comfort, back in the motel room. I couldn't wander far from the parking lot, because Frank could be coming out at any moment. I waited about two hours, and became increasingly grouchy, staring with hunger at the glowing sign of the pizza place across the street, before he finally reappeared.

Frank bounced up to me with an ever-growing smile beaming from his face. When I asked how it went inside, he reached deep into his front pocket and pulled it inside out, spilling about twenty-five crumpled dollars in ones and fives. He'd actually done it; Frank was a genuine pool shark.

And as I already knew, he was also a genuine drinker. Tonight was no exception, as was made clear by his slurred speech and uncoordinated attempt to show me his winnings. Frank was no lightweight, so I knew he must have had a few more than a few drinks.

It struck me that about half of the money I'd begged for earlier that day was probably used to buy Frank his first beer to sip while he started playing. This pissed me off, as it seemed he could have at least skipped the beer until he'd won a game or two. Even better, he could have gone without any beer, relying on soda pop or water instead.

While he was enjoying himself drinking and playing games, I was stuck outside, doing nothing. On the other hand, he had turned the five bucks into five times that much, hence I didn't have much to complain about. Yet I wondered how much he would have had if he hadn't been drinking. At a few bucks a drink, he must have spent over ten that we could have used.

I asked him about it, and he maintained that he simply *had* to drink while he was in there, or the other guys would get suspicious; growing tipsy was part of his act. There wasn't anything I could do about the money he'd spent, so I let the subject rest.

Undisturbed by my grouchy and suspicious attitude, Frank kept to his happy and silly mood. He bought me a slice of pizza, and we headed to another place about two miles from there. We walked along a busy road, and I began to feel better as I did a few calculations in my head; if Frank could keep up the good work, we'd have the seventy dollars within five more hours. The end was in sight.

I waited for another couple of hours in another parking lot. It was starting to seem my destiny to spend my life hanging out in parking lots; and I didn't even have a car!

It was near midnight when an even more intoxicated Frank came out, this time proudly displaying the nearly sixty-five dollars he'd managed to accumulate. He hooted that the way he was playing tonight, he might be able to come up with enough extra money to keep us in food as well!

As we traipsed another few miles to yet a third bar, Frank got a bit full of himself, loudly explaining how hustling required a real art, and how he was one of the supreme artists. Drunk as he was, he didn't sound like an artist.

Cynically, I told myself that if he was truly such an artist, he wouldn't be struggling to live in a cheap roach motel, two blocks back from the beach. If he were such a supreme artist, he would have it made. But I knew better than to share my thoughts, especially as I was counting on all the craft Frank could muster.

We arrived at the third pool-hall/bar and I was once again left waiting outside. At the rate Frank had been winning, I figured it would take less than twenty minutes before he emerged with his huge grin and a fistful of money.

But twenty minutes came and went. Came and went again. And again. And yet again.

I was becoming both worried and angry at the same time.

What was taking him so long? Had he gotten into some kind of trouble in there? Was he just doing so well that he didn't want to quit? Or was he goofing off, guzzling as much as he could before they closed the bar and kicked him out? I didn't know, and he'd told me not to go inside under any circumstances.

People began leaving the bar and driving away one by one, steadily emptying the small parking lot. Still no Frank.

It was almost two A.M., two hours after our arrival, before Frank finally stumbled out. He was completely smashed, far drunker than I'd ever seen him.

It took a while before he saw me and wobbled on up with his eyebrows stretched to the sky and a pleading look upon his face. He shrugged his shoulders while holding his hands out, palms up, requesting absolution. His whole being was saying, "forgive me Evan for I have royally screwed up and blew our chance to make the rent." Without a word, I knew he still hadn't come up with the five extra dollars we'd needed. The question was: How much was left?

I asked what happened.

He claimed he didn't know what had gone wrong, but he'd somehow lost most of our money. He swore he'd tried his best, but had lost his touch and started losing.

Didn't know what had gone wrong? How couldn't he know?

From the looks of it, he let himself get too drunk. Once he realized he'd blown it, he didn't bother to leave the bar and face dealing with my disappointment. Instead, he just kept forking over what was left on still more drinks and more bad bets.

Tried his best? What a loser! Instead of fending for myself, I'd been counting on an incompetent, dud-headed alcoholic to provide my shelter. That made me a loser, too. I could have panhandled the extra five dollars we'd needed while he was in the bar blowing what he'd managed to build up.

We had less than ten dollars now that the night of drinking and gambling was over. We were lucky the bar closed when it did or we might have been entirely broke. At least we could afford some more smokes and a decent meal. I'd used up all my cigarettes and the pizza hadn't put a dent in my appetite. I was glad we had something left to spend.

The busses didn't run this late, so we had to walk back to the beach. We got back to our motel room by about four-thirty, leaving just enough time for a decent stretch of sleep before check-out time. The manager didn't kick us and our stuff out until noon.

For the first time, I was pissed-off at Frank. I felt like he had not only blown his chance, he'd blown our chance. At least he got to have a good time playing pool and getting drunk; unlike me, he got to enjoy the money both ways, making it and losing it. He'd been so damn close. It was easier to blame him than blame myself.

Once again I was homeless. This time I had some company, but who was that? Frank the ex-con, the pool hustler, the drunk. Yet, for all his faults,

Frank was one of the only people I'd met who had any respect for me. What did it mean if I couldn't return that respect? It wasn't his fault that I'd run away.

Cinderblocks

On the first evening of our mutual homelessness, Frank pulled off a daring supermarket raid, which provided our eats for that night and the beginning of the following day.

He made two trips. On the first he stole mostly cold cuts, and a lot of them. Frank didn't seem to have any particular taste in cold cuts, other than "cheap" that is. He nabbed what he was used to buying, a couple packages of generic bologna and salami. Why he didn't steal some high quality sliced ham or turkey breast, or at least some name brand lunch meats, completely eluded me. He also stole an eight-pack of cheesy looking, no-name hot dogs. Frank's cheap franks. The best score though, was the two-pound tube of low grade hamburger meat, who's pale content only slightly resembled the picture printed on the wrapper. A slightly prolonged stay on the grill boiled off most of the fat.

On his second trip Frank swiped a small bag of coal, a bottle of lighter fluid, and a pack of hamburger buns. To be fair, he deserved credit, because it took guts to take so much stuff all at once. He wore loose, baggy pants and an old button down shirt, and simply shoved everything in at the waist and walked out the door with his stomach bulging. It was a wonder he wasn't caught.

I wondered if it was taking outrageous risks like this that made Frank an ex-convict; he had been caught and convicted for stealing more than once already. Still, it was snooty of me to cop an attitude about him; thanks to Frank I ate a whole lot better then I might have that night.

After his second run, we walked over to the public barbecues to begin cooking up our food. On the way, we bumped into Big Bob and Pete. Big Bob seemed a little dirtier than usual, probably from living outside again. He'd run out of rent money a few days ahead of us. Were we going to look and smell like that in a few days?

Not me. As long as I could get to the public showers I'd make sure I

149

rinsed off every day.

In his typically friendly way, Frank invited them to join us in our little feast. As always, they both accepted and we enjoyed each other's company while dinner was cooking. Pete even decided to chip in and buy us a half case of beggardly beer to make the picnic a little more complete. For my part, I went over to a nearby fast food place and appropriated a fistful of napkins and enough ketchup, mustard, salt, and pepper for all.

It turned out to be a little party, the four of us joking about women with gaping thighs and whatever else we could think of. We didn't talk about where we would be sleeping that night, though I guessed it would be on the beach somewhere with Big Bob. With all the good food, the booze, and the company I didn't really care at the moment. Whatever happened, I wouldn't be alone. I'd be with my friends.

It was dark by the time we ran out of beer. I was pretty tipsy from the three that constituted my share of the half-case. Pete excused himself to go back to sleep at his place so he wouldn't be too tired for work the next day. That left Frank, Big Bob, and me to pack up what was left of our food and things, and figure out where to go next.

Big Bob explained that if we walked a few blocks south, away from the more commercial, touristy part of the beach, we could find a quiet place to sleep. We didn't have much to carry. I'd managed to accumulate another change of clothes, another science fiction book, and little else. Frank's stuff fit in a small shopping bag, and Big Bob had only himself and what fit in his numerous pockets.

After awhile we hit on a quiet-looking area behind some houses and searched for a level place to lay. We couldn't afford to be too picky though, because the most horizontal spots also tended to be the lumpiest. Settling on a location with a slight slope, we spread our things and ourselves on the bare sand, our feet pointed towards the ocean. I used my extra clothes as a pillow.

It was a warm, quiet night. We lay there looking up at the stars and talking until we grew tired. Bob started snoring after a while, so Frank and I hushed up.

As I felt my eyes wanting to close I decided the beach didn't seem such a bad place to sleep after all. I let go and drifted away tracking the sound of the ever pounding, ever rolling surf.

I awoke with an exceptionally bright light in my eyes. Covering them, and turning my head, I saw the shiny black shoes of the person holding the light, and became aware of a deep and commanding voice informing us that sleeping was not allowed on the beach. My eyes focused enough to realize it was a cop, then I noticed another one had his light aimed at Frank.

"Could you please take your light out of my eyes?" I asked, grumpy for being so rudely awakened. It was to no avail. Ignoring me, the two officers continued shining their flashlights back and forth into our three pairs of eyes. Damn it, why couldn't they shine their lights to the side? Jerks.

"Can we see your identification?" the commanding voice bellowed at the three of us. It was clear to us all who had the authority and power in this situation.

Frank sat up. "Just a minute," he said, and started fumbling around in his pocket. Groping for his I.D. he continued, "The boy is my nephew John McGreger, visiting me from Pennsylvania. I don't think he has any I.D. as he is only sixteen." Frank handed over an I.D. card I'd never seen.

"What are you doing here?" came the demanding voice again. "Don't you know there is no sleeping allowed on the beach?"

"I'm sorry," Frank apologized. In a butt-kissing tone of voice like nothing I'd ever heard from Frank's usually foul, yet jovial mouth, he added, "I was trying to show the kid what it's like to rough it camping out. He has it too easy and doesn't even know it, so I thought it would be a good idea for him to try sleeping on the beach one night." I could hear occasional, indecipherable bursts of static-filled voices screeching from one of the cops' walky-talkies.

"Who is this man?" the officer aimed his light at Big Bob.

"I'm Bob Jenkins, a friend of theirs," answered Big Bob. Oh, so Big Bob actually had a last name; the idea had never occurred to me. I wondered if Jenkins' was really it though. When asked for his I.D., Big Bob claimed that he'd recently lost it, and hadn't had time to get it replaced.

I decided to try and say something. Striking off from Frank's story, I appealed, "We're sorry if we did something wrong officer. Uncle Frank just wanted us to camp out for a night. We'll leave if you want." I was trying to sound like an innocent little kid so they might have some pity and not arrest us.

"That's right officers, we'll just pick up and go if you want," Frank chorused.

"Well, if you pack up your things and take off right now, we will let you go with just a warning," the other officer spoke up in a friendlier voice. "It's admirable to want to teach the kid about roughing it, but if we let you stay here, the next thing we know everyone will want to sleep on the beach," he continued.

Ha! Surely not everybody would; the cop obviously didn't know about the sand fleas.

Handing back Frank's I.D. he lectured on, "Camping should be done in the public parks, not on the beach. Just don't let us find you trying to sleep on the beach again, or we'll have to bring you in for vagrancy."

"Thanks officer, thanks a lot!" Frank kissed ass so hard his lips puckered.

"Home Sweet Home" By Mark Klerk

As we gathered our things I asked the friendlier officer, "Do you know if sleeping on the beach is allowed in Fort Lauderdale?"

"I don't know, son," he replied. "You'll have to ask the Fort Lauderdale police that question. Once you're out of our jurisdiction, you're not our problem anymore. I just know you can't sleep here."

"I'm not your son!" I thought, as I gathered up my change of clothes and some of the leftover picnic food. But I knew better than to say it.

Within a minute we were all headed further south along the beach, quite gladly leaving the two officers behind us. We scarcely uttered a word until we were sure the policemen were a few blocks away.

Then, when he was sure it was safe, Frank started uttering a stream of curses at the cops. "God damn, mother-fucking pigs! Don't they have any fucking better things to do than fucking wake up people who are minding their own god-damn fucking business sleeping on the flea infested beach?!? Who the hell do those cock-sucking dickheads think they are?"

Big Bob started chiming in and the two of them laughed as they thought of ever nastier names to call the police, describing them in terms of bodily functions, their sexuality, their favorite hobbies, and their family's in-breeding practices.

Kicked off the beach, and knowing of no other place to slumber in Pompano Beach, we decided to leave. On the move, the three of us wandered on down to Fort Lauderdale Beach. The sun was about to rise by the time we arrived so we didn't bother trying to find anywhere else to sleep. We'd finished off the hot dogs and hamburger the night before, and attacked what was left of our cold cuts, now rather warm, for breakfast.

It was a new day. We sat on the beach and discussed what to do next. The weather had been warm and clear, and Frank suggested that we take it easy for the day, and spend the night on the beach again, in Fort Lauderdale this time. Lacking any better ideas, we agreed to meet at the beach around an hour before sunset. I went off to panhandle enough money for another pack of cigarettes and a slice of pizza. What I wanted most was to play some video games, but I also wanted to avoid Ray, so I had fewer choices.

After pittering away the day, I met back with Frank and Big Bob as planned. The beach was too crowded to sleep on, but none of us were tired enough anyway. We crossed one of the short bridges onto the mainland and aimlessly wandered around downtown Fort Lauderdale.

In time, we came upon a ritzy upper-crust shopping area. It had grown late by now, sometime near midnight, and all the shops were closed. Big Bob and Frank stopped to gaze in the window of a jewelry store and began drooling at the array of sparkling gold and diamond jewelry inside. A sudden vision of the two of them decked out in some of the gaudier stuff made me break into a laugh.

In a dreaming voice, Big Bob declared that if we could get our hands on just a few of those precious baubles, we could parley them into enough money to keep us in style for months. He claimed to know a "fence," who would give us a good price for stolen jewelry, but only if we had enough to make it worth the guy's while. With no one around, the only thing between us and all that wealth was the building.

The road was silent, but well lit, making it hard to be inconspicuous should someone drive by. Frank and Big Bob discussed how to break in without getting caught. Frank tried the door, but it was locked tight. I suggested we check around the rear of the building to see if there was an easier way in. They concurred.

The store's back entrance was along an unlit alley, probably used only for deliveries. It was unlikely that anyone would drive through the alley in the middle of the night, thus it provided ideal cover should we attempt to break through the massive steel door. Frank and Big Bob both tested it, but like the front door, it wouldn't budge. We searched the alley for something to pry it with, but there wasn't much around. It probably wouldn't have mattered anyway, as it seemed even a decent crowbar wouldn't do much more than dent it.

We returned to the front window for a second look, and considered smashing it. Fortunately, Frank noticed the alarm wires attached along the inside. This is where his prison experience helped prevent disaster. One of his cellmates had warned him that if a wired window was broken anywhere near the wires, it would trigger an alarm. It was good we hadn't pulled any harder on the doors, because if the windows were any indication, the doors were most likely wired too.

We needed a diamond-pointed glass cutter and a suction cup to cut the window without triggering an alarm. It was the same problem I'd had when trying to sell sodas; it would take a major investment to do it right. Glass cutters and suction cups were expensive, and if we'd had that kind of cash, we wouldn't be here in the first place.

Growing impatient, I asked my would-be partners-in-crime why we didn't just find something to smash the window with. Even if an alarm went off, we could swiftly reach inside, take sixty seconds to grab whatever we could, then run like hell before the police showed up. Frank thought for a moment, then assented. He figured it would take at least a couple of minutes for someone to recognize the alarm, decide which police car was closest, then have them speed to the store.

Big Bob nodded, and we agreed to try our luck. If we didn't smash the window within a minute of the first attempt, we'd leave anyway, just in case the first blow triggered a silent alarm. It wouldn't be worth being greedy if it landed us in jail.

Now all we had to figure out was how to break the window. It was composed of a heavy security glass, and upon closer examination we realized it was close to an inch thick. It would be difficult to crack.

Big Bob remembered seeing some cinderblocks back in the alley. Sure enough, he led us straight to a small, uneven pile of cinderblocks by a house behind the jewelry store. Frank and Big Bob hefted one each, and practiced swinging them to determine how much power they would yield. Frank was strongest, probably from lifting all those weights in prison, and we decided he would be the one to swing first, and if necessary, Big Bob would follow up with a blow of his own. I would keep watch, tracking time and standing ready to help grab as much jewelry as possible before our minute was up.

We carried the cinderblocks back towards the storefront. Shortly after turning the corner onto the main street, we glimpsed an approaching pair of headlights, a few blocks off and closing. Panicing, Frank and Big Bob quickly dropped the cinderblocks next to one of the sidewalk planters, and the three of us dashed back around the corner.

Another hundred foot sprint, and we slowed to a walk, peeking over our shoulders as the car drove on past the intersection. It looked like any ordinary non-cop car, and the driver probably hadn't seen us. We laughed in relief, but our hearts were all still pounding from the momentary fright. We had yet to do anything illegal, but we'd already let ourselves get scared shitless.

Once we calmed down, we returned to the front of the store for another look. Frank wasn't sure anymore; he said he wouldn't mind risking it alone, he could handle prison, but he didn't want to get me in trouble. He felt responsible for me, like a big brother, and didn't want to lead me astray.

After all this build-up, I was more than ready to take the chance, eager almost. I reminded Frank that it was jewelry *I'd* stolen that had paid for our last week of rent. He couldn't corrupt me; I was already quite debauched. It was worth the risk, I argued, as one big take like this would set us up for months. I was sick of sleeping on the beach with the fleas and cops harassing us.

In a sudden moment of seriousness, Frank brought up the last subject I wanted to hear. He told me I should call my parents and ask to go back home. He said I shouldn't have to be robbing jewelry stores to get by at only fifteen; I should be in school, learning how to make something of myself, not studying how to be a homeless felon with him and Big Bob.

Up till now I'd only committed misdemeanors, not felonies, he explained. Robbing jewelry stores was a hell of a lot more serious in the eyes of the law; it was an entirely different league. If caught, I could be put away for years.

Big Bob agreed with Frank, saying he was ashamed of himself for being so ready to rob a jewelry store with a kid. He'd been in prison too, plenty of times, but he knew how to survive inside; if I were arrested, Big Bob thought

I would be torn to shreds from the start, likely even raped, because I was too small to defend myself. Then, looking at the window, he added that it didn't really matter, because he doubted we could do more than crack the thick security glass without something better than cinderblocks. All this risk would be for nothing.

Try as I might, I couldn't do much to argue with the two of them. I wouldn't be calling my parents any time soon. I still couldn't handle my shame. They wouldn't understand what I'd been through, and were probably still angry with me for everything. I was getting angry, and warned Frank not to push me.

We went back to discussing the break-in. I did my best to convince them I knew what I was getting into and could handle the risk. Besides, if we ran away after a minute as planned, the police would never catch us. We'd be long gone before they even got to the store.

But it was to no avail. Frank and Big Bob were unswayed by my arguments and both steadfastly decided against it. Short of special tools, I couldn't rob the place without their help. I could hardly lift one of those cinderblocks, let alone swing it with much force.

We ended up walking back towards Fort Lauderdale Beach to spend another homeless night sleeping near the waves.

Thanks to the continued good weather, sleeping on the beach wasn't too bad. Other than feeling damp, sticky, and sandy, the only real drawback was dealing with the constant gnawing attack of the sand fleas. It seemed every time I'd manage to forget about them I'd feel another invading my skin, searching for a good place to bite.

Unlike the previous night, my sleep wasn't very deep. Every twenty minutes or so, I woke up, brushed off a sand flea, rolled over, and let myself sink back into sleep once more. The gentle, arhythmic sound of the waves rolling upon the beach below quickly lulled me back to unconsciousness.

A few hours before sunrise, it began to get chilly. Unrolling my makeshift pillow, I pulled a pair of jeans over my shorts, put on my other tee-shirt, and used my other pants as a sort of blanket to keep from shivering. Now I was pillowless, but I didn't mind too much.

It had become easier to handle nippy weather after that night huddling in and outside of the vacant house in Clearwater Beach. This time, it was several weeks later (and warmer) in the summer, and I had enough clothes. Frank lay comfortably to my side, quite oblivious to the fleas and chill, and Big Bob lay motionless beyond him. As I drifted off one last time, a part of me actually felt kind of lucky.

Sand Bum

I'd finally managed an hour or two of uninterrupted sleep, before awakening to Frank tapping upon my shoulder. When my sleep-fog cleared enough to understand him, I realized he was trying to bum a cigarette. It was near five in the morning and I knew I had less than an hour before the sun rose and the beach came alive with die-hard joggers, touristy beach combers, and the city's noisy sand-sifting equipment. I needed that extra hour and I was pissed. Bothering me when I was still half asleep was a sure way to bring out my mean side.

Fueling my anger, there were only three cigarettes left in my pack, and I didn't have enough money to buy more. Frank's waking me from my hard won slumber for no better reason than to bum one of my last cigarettes was the final straw. In that moment, what little respect I had left for Frank simply evaporated, vanishing explosively, like a drop of water dripped upon a hot griddle.

Frank was a fully grown man, yet he couldn't manage to survive any better than me. Now he was waking me, demanding that I support him. I'd begged to get those cigarettes and was in no mood to share. As far as I was concerned he could get off his lazy ass and come up with his own smokes, just like I'd had to do.

Grouchily, I told Frank to buzz off.

He didn't. If I wouldn't give him a cigarette, he was going to take it. Surprising me with his force, he roughly began reaching into my pockets, searching for my pack. What remained of the damp box was tucked inside my sock, alongside my shin, where it wouldn't be crushed when I curled into a ball to sleep. They were in one of the last places he'd think of looking. Still, I didn't want his hands in all my pockets, especially while I was wearing them. I shoved his arms away and shouted at him to leave me alone.

He didn't slow, instead becoming more insistent. His face twisted into a raging snarl. Shaking me by the shoulders he yelled, "Give me a fucking cigarette! Right Fucking Now! And none of your fucking lip, you fucking snot-nosed little shit, or I'll tear the pair of them right off your fucking little smart-ass mouth!"

What a way to wake up.

Frank had never been so enraged in front of me before. I was scared. But also furious. Big Bob began to stir from his sleep a few feet away, but being the sort to avoid confrontation at all costs, he kept to himself.

It was clear the time for slumber was now officially over. Thanks to an electric surge of adrenaline, I was jolted fully awake and alert. My anger at Frank grew, a fiery storm of all consuming rage. If it had been within my abilities, I would have flung him off me, into the ocean where he'd be too busy trying to swim to worry about smoking.

But I was nowhere near that strong, and Frank knew it. My anger was moderated by the reality of my relatively puny and impotent physique, and the waxing realization that I was in danger. In short order, I felt terror. With all my soul I wanted to beat Frank's imposing presence away from me, but it wasn't possible.

"Okay, okay, Frank!" I screamed back. "I'll give you a damn cigarette! Just let me the fuck go so I can get them. You don't have to be such an asshole about it."

He released my arms and backed off about six inches. I reached into my sock, and doing my best to crush the pack (and hopefully mangle the cigarettes inside) as I grabbed it, I whipped it out and hurled it to the side. He couldn't reach them while on top of me.

"There's your fucking cigarettes, you jerk!" I shouted. True to greedy form, he slipped off me and lunged after the pack.

"They're all yours! I hope you're happy stealing from a kid."

As he dove after the cigarettes, I stood up and threw a clutched handful of sand straight towards his face. "You're nothing but an alcoholic, a bum, and a loser," I spat. "And you'll never go anywhere or be anything more than a bum! I'm sick of all your useless shit. I can do a whole lot better without you."

Grabbing my few things, I ran as fast as I could until I'd put about a block of sand between us. When I looked over my shoulder and saw Frank wasn't following me I slowed to a storming walk and continued along the beach. I was overwhelmed, feeling and thinking too much to sort out all at once.

Anger, fear, hurt, determination, righteous indignation, disgust, confusion, and even shame were all churning round and round inside, forming a knot too tangled to untie. A few tears leaked out, and gasping for breath, I choked down the heaving sobs I knew would follow. I was too angry to cry

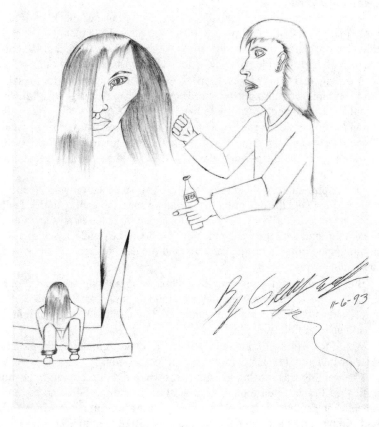

"Joey" By Graywolf

for more than a moment. There was nothing to do with all this anger, nothing but keep on walking.

My constant craving for nicotine resurfaced again, and I longed for a cigarette like nothing else. But, there was no way I'd go back to beg a broken one from Frank. On my own again, I would have to wait until I could bum one from someone else. There was no one in sight, though, so I kept on treading the sand, heading nowhere, just away.

It had been about three weeks since Pete introduced me to Frank and Big Bob. In the beginning I was actually surviving better than I had been on my own. Not anymore.

When I thought about it, I realized I'd actually done as much as (if not more than) Frank in order to support the two of us. I'd stolen the jewelry that paid our rent, I'd panhandled the stake for pool-hustling, and I'd gotten us both laid. The idea of team-work simply wasn't panning out.

Alone again, I could at least keep all my hard-won cigarettes for myself. And I certainly couldn't get any more homeless than I already was. Maybe I could even find another closet to live in.

On the minus side, I once again had no idea where I was going, or what I would do when I got there. Then again, this was no different than while staying with Frank the past few days. Now I could be aimless without any help from him.

On the plus side, I still had my watch. The display said it was Wednesday and I realized the day of the week had no special meaning to me. Half a dozen weeks ago, Wednesday morning meant three more days of school to wait through until the weekend. Now, there was no regularity in my life, nothing anchoring me to the calendar and the days named within. It was just summertime.

But the watch did anchor me in another way. As long as I had it and could see the seconds and minutes continue to pass, I knew I still had a future ahead of me; I hadn't yet sunk to the lowest depths that I might; I wasn't an utter failure.

Would my dad ever know how important it was to me to hold onto his gift? I wondered. It was my most precious possession.

The walking was starting to calm me down. It didn't seem fair to be too critical of Frank. Even though he acted like a sand bum, had no taste in lunch meat, and blew it at pool hustling by letting himself get too drunk, he had still been friendly and respectful to me most of the time. This was the first time Frank had woken me for a cigarette in the middle of the night. Maybe it was only a symptom of his frustration and desperation. And after all, I had just as many problems as he did.

A seed of guilt sprouted inside. Frank would have given me *his* last cigarette. I felt ashamed of myself for saying all those cold, nasty, condemning things. They were probably true, though; he didn't seem headed

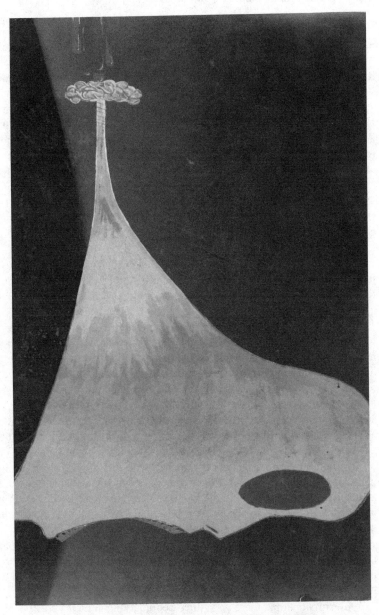

"Don't Wake Me Up" By Cliff Shuffler

anywhere aside from jail.

But where was I headed? I'd already escaped from the police more than once and my lucky streak wasn't likely to hold up forever. For the time being I headed south, continuing along the beach.

It wasn't long before the sun began to rise and light up the surrounding area. There was hardly any traffic along the nearby beachside road, which made sense as all the stores along it were still closed. In a few more hours it would be jammed with traffic, and the stores and beach on either side would be packed with people.

I noticed a lone car slowing down, almost to a stop, just as it passed about fifty yards from where I was trudging along the sand. The car sped up again and continued to drive in the same direction I was headed. When it reached a point about a block ahead, it pulled one-hundred-twenty degrees around into one of the angled beachside parking spaces and sat idling.

As I got closer and saw there were two people sitting inside, I thought about trying to bum a cigarette. A moment later I saw a stream of smoke flowing out from the driver's side window. That clinched it. I changed my course, aiming straight for the car and its occupants.

The driver was a thin man, probably in his thirties, and had an almost full head of short cropped dark hair. The other guy was was a good deal taller and younger, about twenty-five years old. He had curly blonde hair and was also pretty skinny.

They got out of the car and introduced themselves. Greg, the passenger, towered over me at a surprising six and a quarter feet or more. The driver's name was Sam and I was equally astounded to realize he was just about my height, damned short for a full grown man. Sam willingly gave me the cigarette I asked for, my brand even. In turn, he asked my name and what I was doing on the beach at dawn, bumming cigarettes from strangers.

Emotionally exhausted from the explosive confrontation with Frank, and all the garbage it brought up in me, I lacked the right mind-set to make up any new stories. Using my alias was all the fabrication I could manage.

"My name is John and I just had a fight with this guy I'd been living with," I explained. "He woke me up to bum one of my last cigarettes and attacked me when I told him `no.' We were sleeping on the beach a couple miles back that way," I pointed, "but I decided I was sick of him and am going off on my own to find some other place to live."

There was a silent, awkward pause for a moment. Sam glanced over to his friend, Greg, locking eyes for an instant before looking back my way. He finally broke the silence saying they were looking for a live-in maid to keep up on their house cleaning.

Sam explained that there were three people living at their house — he,

Greg, and another man named Mark. They had regular parties there that required plenty of dish washing, ashtray dumping, and so forth. The work paid free rent and food, but no money, and, if I wanted to take it on a trial basis, the job was mine.

After my experiences with Ray, Doug, the man with the gnarled hand, and the other two child molesters before I left home, I was suspicious. It sounded too good to be true. I wanted to proceed with caution. I decided to be straightforward about my fears.

"It sounds like a good deal," I said, "but I want to make sure that nobody expects anything sexual from me. I keep running into people that want me around for other reasons than they say at first and I'm definitely not interested in that."

Sam replied that all three of the men in their house were gay and that many of the people who visited were also gay. But that it definitely wasn't a job requirement.

I told them I didn't have a problem with that as long as they didn't expect *me* to be gay. I would respect them as long as they respected me.

Both Sam and Greg assured me that if I took the job, nobody would try to molest me or make me do anything I didn't want. As long as I didn't hold it against them that they were gay, they wouldn't hold it against me that I was straight. They were perfectly willing to accept me the way I was.

Somewhere inside I knew a spontaneous meeting on the beach at sunrise was a strange circumstance in which to interview for a job and a place to stay. Aside from what they presented of themselves, I didn't know anything about these guys. But I needed help, and for lack of any strong feeling to the contrary, I decided to risk trusting them and took them up on their offer.

They seemed like nice enough folks. After all, they'd given me a cigarette when I tried to bum one, hadn't they? And I didn't have any other prospects now that I'd told Frank to screw off. At least they'd been up front with me about being gay and promised they wouldn't expect anything sexual from me.

It didn't seem any riskier than facing the rest of the day on my own. This could be just the sort of opportunity I was looking for, a chance that wouldn't come twice. I convinced myself it would work out.

Greg and Sam drove me in their beat up car to their place on the mainland. We cruised past the jewelry store Frank, Big Bob and I had contemplated robbing. Following that, I just felt too tired to pay attention to the route we took. After about fifteen minutes we pulled off of a busy road called Sunrise Boulevard, into the driveway of their little home.

The small ranch style house was set back about thirty feet from the north side of the road. In front was a small green lawn with two trees providing a buffer from the passing traffic. Similar looking single-story homes lay on either side, with a six-foot-tall wooden fence providing a boundary between.

As we exited the car I was struck by the early morning singsong of the birds, a melodious tune altogether unlike the seabird screeches I was used to. I imagined the giant leafy green trees must provide abundant shade. Sam led me into the long living room and invited me to feel welcome in my new home.

The living room alone was bigger than the place Frank and I had shared. It had little furniture, merely a sofa, a mismatched stuffed chair, and a low, wooden coffee table to the right, just opposite a television on the left. A slight odor of cigarettes and beer briefly grabbed my attention, but it was no worse than in the motel room I'd shared with Frank. Both the inside and outside of the house were painted white, making it bright in the morning light.

Sam, clearly the more outspoken of the two, offered me a tour of the house. He led me through the arched doorway from the living room into a small kitchen. To our left was the small kitchenette area, with cramped counters, a small sink, a few tiny cabinets, and a mismatched stove and refrigerator. The sink was full of dirty dishes and Sam explained it would be part of my job to keep it empty. The dish drying rack on the small counter next to the sink was bare, waiting for me to get to work at filling it up.

To our right was an equally diminutive dining area. A tiny table was positioned against the wall such that it could comfortably seat one, three in a pinch.

In front of us lay a glass-paned door to the outside. Sam opened it and we walked on through to the backyard. To our right was an attached shed, its door leading directly in from the outside. Sam pointed out the laundry machines, utility sink, and collection of mops, brooms, and other cleaning supplies I would be needing for my work.

But the jewel of the tour was the beautifully landscaped little yard with a curvy light blue swimming pool set smack in the middle. There were narrow decks on either end, on which sat an assortment of lawn furniture: lounges to recline upon, and a matching umbrella-shaded table and chair set. The rest of the pool area was surrounded by a perfectly manicured and extremely green lawn. I pictured myself swimming and relaxing away the long summer afternoons in this yard.

Encircling the yard was the rest of the six-foot privacy fence I'd seen from the front. Several more tall, leafy trees reached over the fence from the neighboring yards. Their branches towered out over the enclosure providing generous shade around the periphery.

According to Sam, I would also be responsible for mowing the lawn and vacuuming the pool once a week, but he would show me how to do that later. I was beginning to think it would be pretty easy to take care of this little place, a good way to earn my keep. It was a nice home, far nicer than anywhere I'd lived since leaving home.

"Where am I going to sleep?" I asked, as we headed back into the house.

"Well there are only three bedrooms," Sam answered, "and there are three of us here already, so until we can figure something else out, you're going to have to sleep on the living room couch."

Finally, a catch. I wasn't too happy about having no privacy. I needed to be alone sometimes. Yet it beat sleeping on the beach, or waiting in parking lots for Frank to blow his attempts at pool-hustling.

I asked who and where Mark, the other guy, was. Sam explained that Mark managed the overnight shift at a nearby twenty-four hour coffee shop. He was due back pretty soon since his shift ended at seven.

Sam led me back through the kitchen to the narrow hallway off the living room. It was lined with four closed doors and a fifth at the end. We peeked in at each of the three bedrooms. Only two had beds and furniture. The third, and smallest, Greg's room, possessed only a lone single-sized mattress sitting on the floor.

Mark's had the most space and the nicest furnishings. Sam explained that almost all the furnishings in the house were Mark's, as he earned the most money; both Sam and Greg were currently unemployed, living off savings left over from their last jobs. They were starting a business together, but were "keeping it a secret" until they worked out all the details.

The farthest door opened into the bathroom. Other than the yardwork, kitchen chores, vacuuming, and general tidying, my last job was to keep it clean. The bathroom didn't look all that bad. It needed a good cleaning, but was a lot less disgusting than the one at Robert's place, where I'd stayed that first night as a runaway.

Sam said I looked tired and could feel free to take a nap if I wanted. I was exhausted after a second restless night of sleeping on the beach. However, it was too bright out and the place was too unfamiliar to allow myself to conk out right away. Being the self-starter that I was, I set right in to wash the dishes and begin earning my keep. Greg quietly prepared some coffee while I tried to figure out where to stack the slimy dishes I removed from the sink to make enough room to wash the others.

How lucky would Frank be? I wondered.

How many more days or weeks would it be before the inevitable happened, and he got himself arrested and sent back to prison again?

Not that he'd mind. In prison he wouldn't have to worry about how to survive from day to day; that would be taken care of for him. "Three hots and a cot," as he put it. He might even prefer it that way. After my brief acquaintance with Frank, I found myself unable to imagine him working at and holding any kind of a job.

Generous or not, my speculation about Frank's character and future would always remain just that: speculation. My angry eyes had captured their final images of Frank during our heated fight on the beach this morning, for I never saw him again.

Sunrise

So here I was, a new resident in an unusual household. One minute I was leaving Frank and Big Bob, my only friends, to strike out on my own again, and two hours later I had a job, a home, and all the food I needed.

The dishes didn't take long, and I was soon faced with the question of how to make myself at home. Drained as I was, I still didn't feel anywhere near ready to fall asleep. Sam and Greg were sitting at the kitchen table, sipping coffee, and asking the expected questions about who I was and how I'd come to be living with Frank. I told them the "I'm eighteen and just finished high-school and set out to make my way in the world" story.

Greg broke his almost perpetual silence, commenting that I sure looked a lot younger than eighteen; he would more likely guess thirteen or fourteen.

I responded with some true stories about how people in my family age slowly. We reach puberty late, but also live a lot longer than most people. My great grandfather lived until he was ninety-three, and only died because he had an accident, falling down and cracking his skull. My dad had last been carded trying to buy a beer when he was twenty-seven, though the drinking age was only eighteen at the time. And my maternal grandfather's hair didn't even begin turning grey until he was in his sixties. Greg listened, but didn't seem convinced.

He also didn't push it. It didn't seem to be all that important, I guess. After all, I was already there. If it truly mattered to them, they would have made a big deal about it before offering me the job. They didn't seem about to kick me out.

Sam helped me get set up to go to sleep. There were no "common" sheets at Sunrise house. Since I didn't have my own, Sam offered to lend me some of his until they could go to the store and buy me some. He said that whenever I was ready, I could set the sheets up on the couch and make myself comfortable.

Just then I heard a car with a racing engine pull up in the driveway. About a minute later Mark, the final resident of the house walked in. He noticed me standing next to Sam and nodded a general hello to both of us as he trudged through the living room on his way to the bathroom.

Sam chose this time to inform me that Mark didn't know of our arrangement yet. In fact, he confided, Mark didn't even know that they were looking for a house cleaning boarder. Sam didn't think it would be any problem though, because Mark was always complaining about how messy the place was. He was sure to be glad that someone was finally going to keep things clean.

Sam asked me to wait in the living room for a few minutes while he went back to talk with Mark. He figured it would go over better if he explained the situation to Mark in privacy, so Mark wouldn't feel too cornered or pressured about making his decision. I lit up a cigarette I'd bummed from Greg and began my wait.

My place on the couch seemed in jeopardy all of a sudden. I wondered if Mark was going to veto the whole idea of my being there. If he asked me to leave I would have no choice. After all, Mark had just as much right as Greg or Sam to make that decision.

When I looked at it from Mark's position I realized how rude it was of the other two to have invited me in before clearing it with him. It was rude to me as well, as it got my hopes up when they just might be dashed a few hours later. I looked at a silent Greg and kept my mouth shut.

After a few minutes he went back to join them. I could hear their muted voices coming from Mark's room down the hall, but was unable to make out what they were saying. I simply had to wait. Greg had left his cigarettes on the kitchen table and I smoked a couple more before they returned an interminable twenty minutes later.

Mark was at the lead and came straight towards me, his hand extended to shake. "Hi, I'm Mark," he introduced himself. "Greg and Sam told me they've hired you to keep our house clean."

He sounded friendly. This was a favorable sign.

I returned his shake and sticking with my alias said, "That's right. I'm John, nice to meet you, Mark."

Now that I could get a decent look, Mark seemed somewhat short for a grown man, probably five and a half feet. He was fairly chubby, with the sort of mid-thirties gut that can come from managing a restaurant and eating too much free food. He wore a speckled gray business jacket, the kind with leather patches on the elbows. Mark also had a very full beard and mustache, kept neatly trimmed in a professional style.

"I'm glad to know you're our new helper and I want to welcome you to your new home." he said, smiling. "We sure could use the help here with these two slobs," he laughed, pointing. "They couldn't manage to keep this house clean if you paid them a fortune to do it, and I've become rather tired of living in a pigsty."

"Seems like every couple of nights there's a party here. I don't mind, really, because I work from ten at night to seven in the morning at the pancake house, and the parties are invariably over by the time I return. But the mess is incredible! Good luck with keeping up with it all; it's not going to be easy."

Something bothered me about the way Mark spoke on and on, but I had to try to mirror his friendliness. "I'll do my best," I answered. What else was there to say?

"I can tell you've been at work already, because normally there would be a pile of dishes in the sink to greet me when I came home." Then Mark launched into the same set of questions strangers always asked: Where was I from, where was I going, and what was I doing to get there? I gave him the same set of answers I'd given Greg and Sam.

Mark seemed impressed. "That's mighty brave of you John, to set out on your own with no resources saved up first. I didn't leave home myself until I was ready to go to college, and I was lucky that my parents were able to help me out with that. You've got a hard road ahead of you John, but I wish you plentiful luck."

I thanked him, and thought to myself that when it came to hard, Mark didn't know the half of it.

Mark excused himself saying he was tired and was going to fix up some warm milk, then go to his room to sleep. "I hope you aren't too loud during the day, because I ordinarily sleep until the late afternoon. You don't have to walk on tiptoes, but I would appreciate a little respect. Not that I'm used to it," he added with a whine.

From the surface, Mark seemed a sharply different breed from the others. They were unemployed, and Mark had a respectable job. While Mark worked all night, the other two were out partying. Mark was neat, while Sam and Greg were slobs. They had little more in common than compatible waking and sleeping hours, and being gay.

Within the hour, the three of them retired to their rooms. Sam was the last to depart, and on his way stopped to tell me I probably had until mid-afternoon before people started moving around again. He added that I should make good use of this quiet time, as it would be my last chance to sleep until early the next morning. He and Greg rarely stayed up to watch the sunrise, he said, so I'd usually be able to get to sleep by three or four in the morning. I'd have to get used to a more nocturnal schedule.

Alone, I pulled the shade and curtain shut to make the room dark enough for slumber. It helped. Light still poured through the small window in the kitchen door, but not too much.

Though I was drained from the past few days on the beach, I wasn't yet ready to fall asleep. I watched TV for the next few hours, finally enjoying the feeling of solitude in a secure space. Until someone else woke up, I had the space all to myself. Luxury!

One of the channels was showing the usual crop of early morning game shows. I watched a string of contestants alternately winning cash and prizes, or blowing their chances with stupid mistakes. If only I could get on one of those shows! I knew I could win.

It was always amusing to watch the contestants get so completely hysterical on these shows. If I had that kind of chance, I wouldn't be jumping and screaming like some sort of blithering idiot. Then again, being on the line in front of a studio audience of hundreds and a television audience of millions might not be as easy as it looked. Or, perhaps the shows' hosts actually made secret deals with the contestants, offering them extra prizes for acting silly.

Speaking of ulterior motives, could I really trust these men whose house I now shared? They'd said they were gay, which made it a possibility that they'd want to molest me; not that I felt gays were more likely to be molesters, just that if they were, I was of the sex they'd want to go after. But unlike Ray or Doug, these guys had been up front about their sexuality and promised not to try anything.

However, I also knew they hadn't been up front about everything. Sam and Greg had acted as though Mark was aware of their search for a live-in housekeeper. Yet, it had turned out the idea was news to him, a surprise awaiting his tired return from a long night at work.

How long had Greg and Sam actually been looking for a housekeeper? What if they'd made the whole thing up when they met me, just to bait me into their house? It was too scary to think about.

My trusting side told myself I was being too paranoid.

My suspicious side argued, asking if there really was such a thing as being too paranoid; after all, wasn't it the "paranoid" Jews that escaped Nazi Germany before the rest of their Jewish neighbors were taken to be killed in the concentration camps? The "paranoid" had been smart to listen to their fears about what might happen.

Yes, it was the paranoid that survived in that case, my trusting side admitted, but these guys weren't Nazis. Unlike Hitler, they had been only friendly, and hadn't threatened or coerced me in the slightest. To exist in this world, you have to let go and trust people, at least some of the time.

Whichever side of myself was closer to the truth, I was too tired to continue this argument right now. Whatever their motives, I could deal with them when they came up, I decided; it wasn't like I was imprisoned. The house was still, the other three were sleeping, so why shouldn't I?

My trusting side won for the time being. I turned off the TV and fell into a much overdue sleep.

I awoke to the sounds of Mark puttering about in the kitchen. He was making his "morning" pot of coffee, though it was four-thirty in the afternoon. I was surprised that I'd slept through his walk down the hall and into the kitchen. I should have awakened when I heard his door open at the end of the hall. And with his chubby frame, Mark didn't seem the stealthy sort.

Waking, I once again sniffed the slight stench of stale cigarettes and spilled beer. I got up, stretching and rubbing the sleep out my eyes, and went over to join Mark in the kitchen. Here, the aroma of fresh brewed coffee overpowered the more noxious odors from the living room.

Mark asked me if I drank coffee.

"Increasingly," I said, and he poured me a cup.

He volunteered that he typically had a pot of coffee before going to work, but didn't bother with breakfast because the cooks at his restaurant made better food, and it was free.

"Do you like your job?" I asked.

"Not really," he frowned. "I would if I owned the place. Then I could relax and count the money like the boss does. The owner is just too demanding. He's always on my back to `Cut costs! Cut costs! Cut costs!' And it's my job to pass it on and be on everyone else's back, telling them not to break dishes, not to put too much food on the plate, not to give water unless the customer asks for it, and so on."

"I don't like having to be such a hard ass all the time, but at least I make some fairly decent money. I'm saving up so I can make a down payment on a house pretty soon. I'm getting tired of living with these two party animals." He looked at his watch and broke off his monologue, telling me he had to go take a shower and dash off on some errands before the stores closed.

The next night Sam and Greg and I were taking it easy, passing a joint around and watching M-TV, when Sam got us back to discussing my age again. He brought it up casually, out of the blue, remarking that I sure looked a lot younger than the eighteen years I claimed, before taking a long toke on the plump reefer.

Oops! Why did he have to bring this up while I was stoned? Caught off guard, my chest constricted, and a long pause developed as my mind mulled over possible responses.

Sam and Greg both seemed cool, I thought. They smoked pot and partied like Frank had. They liked joking around, and didn't act like authority figures or anything.

I decided to trust them, and after swearing them to secrecy, blurted out some of the long story of how I'd run away and was really only fifteen after all. The two of them pushed me for details, and I gave them plenty, but refused to tell my real name, or where I was from exactly; this way, I figured they couldn't betray me by finding my parents.

We sat around in silence. After a while Sam said that it didn't matter to him. As long as I kept doing my job, I was welcome to stay. Since I'd already survived almost two months on my own, he figured I was old enough to take care of myself. As far as he was concerned, my business was my own. He'd want the same respect in my shoes.

When I looked at Greg, he nodded and said that sounded right to him, and he'd go right on calling me "John" if that's what I wanted. He was used to that name anyway. They promised to keep their vow and not tell Mark, who we all agreed would most likely throw a fit if he knew the truth about me. Sam fired up another joint and the conversation moved on to other things.

Every few days there was big party at the house. Some of the parties had over sixty people attending, packing the place like a Manhattan subway car, others had less than a dozen. No matter how many came, the guests never included women, though some of the guys would have gladly accepted sex changes. Most of the guests had met Sam or Greg at Backstreet, a giant gay bar they liked to visit in Fort Lauderdale; Sam had told me it was one of the biggest bars in the world, holding over three thousand people when packed.

When there wasn't a party, there were alwaays at least a few visitors dropping by. They'd typically hang out for a few hours, talking about themselves, exchanging sexually graphic jokes, smoking some grass, and watching music videos. There were two men in particular who came by almost daily; Joseph and Max.

Joseph was a big man, something over six feet tall, but not skinny like Greg. He was well into his forties and had the build of a former football player. Somewhere along the way Joseph had stopped exercising and let his muscles turn to fat. His belly had grown rather round, and his receding hairline just about tripled the size of his forehead.

Almost every afternoon or evening Joseph would arrive spent from a day's work at the shoe store he owned. Of all the regular visitors, Joseph had the best manners, and seemed most like a "normal," mainstream person. Just an average Joe. He did his average job and had average conversations about run of the mill things. Joseph was boring.

The only "unusual" thing about Joseph was being gay, which in Sunrise house, was more the rule than the exception anyway. As average as Joseph was, however, he seemed insatiably attracted to the unpredictable, decadent atmosphere at Sunrise house. He managed to spend the majority of his free time visiting, vicariously soaking up the wild life that was normal there.

Max was another matter entirely. Where Joseph was calm and restrained, Max was excitable and wild. Max was a major Queen. He danced and squawked his skinny six foot frame about like the fairy he was, always needing to be the center of attention. And he was invariably on drugs, especially uppers.

Max's first effeminately voiced words to me were, "Oh look at You! You Cutie-Pie! You need a boyfriend for sure!!! It's a wonder I don't forget visiting these sorry fags, and take you home with me right this instant!"

When it wasn't Joseph, Max was always the first to arrive and the last to leave. I liked Max for the most part, but after a while his voice would begin to wear on me. In a way I was jealous of him, because he was the life of the party, always able to make people laugh, yet never caring if they didn't. Max seemed happy.

Precedent

It was mid-way through the evening of my fourth night at Sunrise house and I was ready for slumber. But I couldn't sleep yet, because there were some guests over, chatting and watching M-TV in the living room, my bedroom. I told Greg how tired I was, and he offered to let me crash in his bedroom until everyone left.

Sometime later I awoke as Greg returned to his room. He was smoking a joint and offered me a hit. I didn't have any particular urge to smoke pot at the moment, but said, "Why not?" and took a drag anyway. Part of what drove me was I didn't want him to think I was afraid of smoking. I also didn't want to wake up.

Greg sat down next to the mattress, crossing his legs Indian-style. I remained where I was, comfortably reclined under the cover as we passed the joint back and forth. It wasn't long before I was completely stoned.

The guests had all left and it was time for me to relocate to the living room. Greg offered to give me a back rub first, to help me relax before dealing with straightening up the living room and making my nest on the couch.

The last time I'd received any kind of massage, it was a professional full-body massage given to me by Laurie, a woman-friend of my father, three months before I ran. Before that, nobody had ever given my body any kind of attention that felt so positive and nurturing. My sister and I had swapped back rubs in front of the television, and though they were alright, they just didn't compare to the relaxation a professional masseuse could give.

Greg's offer brought back memories of the relaxation Laurie had given me; I could use that kind of attention more than ever, now. I knew he wasn't a professional, but as stressed as I felt, any attention would help. Though I'd never had a massage from a guy, I was too stoned to think about where it might lead.

I was clad in my tee-shirt and jockey shorts, the same outfit I'd been wearing to bed (when I had one to go to), since being a toddler. Greg suggested I take off the shirt to make it easier for him to rub my shoulders right. It was warm in the house and I couldn't think of anything wrong with removing my shirt; my lower half was still under the covers anyway. Off it came.

How much would have happened if I hadn't become stoned? It doesn't seem fair to blame the pot alone on my allowing things to go as far as they did. The massage felt good.

Of course, he didn't stop at my shoulders. He did my neck too. Then he moved down my shoulders to do the rest of my back.

With every area that Greg rubbed, another came alive in hedonistic anticipation of having its share of knots removed. As with Laurie's massage, I didn't realize how much tension I carried until I began to relax. Greg was an excellent masseur and I could feel my tension drifting away.

Perhaps naively, I still wasn't suspecting the massage was about to become inappropriate. I focused only on how agreeable it felt, and on how increasingly wasted I was growing. With each breath I seemed to get heavier and heavier; with every heartbeat the pot pulled at my essence, stretching me ever downwards, inwards, and outwards. It felt like I would sink through the mattress, the floor, and the sandy earth under the house, though I knew I wouldn't. What would it sound like if I tried to speak? Would my words come out in intelligible English? This was some profoundly potent grass.

One part of the body leads to the next. To finish rubbing along and around my spine, Greg had to move down to the very top of my butt crack, the part that sticks out when overweight construction workers sit down. It seemed this area should be out of bounds somehow, but what he was doing to it felt phenomenal and I could see how it made a certain kind of sense, so I didn't say anything.

After rubbing around the base of my spine for a while, then returning up and down my back, Greg quietly pulled the cover back over my upper body. He seemed to be finished.

Good. I was relieved he had stopped, short of my butt. Even still, another part of me was actually disappointed, because the places he hadn't touched were waiting their turn and felt cheated.

A minute later, just when I'd drifted back to sleep, Greg started in again, this time on my feet. He'd surprised me back to a semi-conscious wakefulness, but it was a happy surprise as he was continuing to make me feel wonderful. After working on my feet for an eternal ten minutes or so, Greg peeled back the blanket another dozen inches and moved up to my Achilles' tendons and calves. I could feel the delicious sensation of my leg juices being squeezed out from where I'd been unaware they'd pooled. Greg was fully in tune with what he was doing to me, or perhaps it was the pot that made me in tune with what he was doing. In any case, the melody played on, and I felt superb.

Of course, my calves are connected to my thighs, which are in turn connected to my butt again. Over the course of the next forever Greg's fingers followed the flow of my anatomy to this semi-forbidden area. I both did and didn't want my butt massaged. In my indecision I acquiesced, and let him continue. By now, my whole body was tingling, alive with sensual pleasure from the grass and massage.

As his massaging my thighs and butt gently rocked my groin against the mattress, I found myself becoming turned on. I tried to turn myself off, but to no avail. The more he rocked me the more turned on my sinking, floating body became.

I remembered being similarly turned on when Laurie had messaged me, and though I'd been embarrassed, it had turned out alright. She either didn't notice or ignored my erection at the time, and I eventually grew relaxed enough that the blood receded and I fell asleep. Greg couldn't see my body betraying itself, as I was laying on my stomach, and I didn't want to embarrass myself by telling him.

Part of me wanted Greg to stop the massage, but another, more hedonistic part didn't. I tried to think of how to phrase it if I did ask him to stop. Thinking was difficult. What was I supposed to say, "Could you please stop that Greg? It's turning me on too much." It sounded too corny, too embarrassing. Too scary.

Another part of me was disgusted at myself for being turned on by things a man was doing. Nothing I'd ever imagined prepared me for this. I knew I was straight as an arrow, attracted only to women. Then how could I be turned on by a man rubbing my body? Did this mean I was bisexual?

No, it wasn't the masseuse's gender that excited me, but the way I was being massaged. If it were only a woman doing the massaging, I could have enjoyed being turned on without any confusion or guilt. Sure, it would still be embarrassing, but less of an issue.

Even though it was a growing problem, I found myself unable to ask Greg to stop. I was too afraid. Our breathing made the only sounds to break the silence in the room, in the entire house. The confusing combination of physical pleasure, brain-fog from the pot and never completely waking, and the shame and embarrassment about being turned on by a man, all combined to keep me silent for another moment. And another. And still another.

Then it was too late. Before I understood what he was doing, Greg reached under me and touched my penis. The tension had built up so much that even this slight touch caused me to instantly explode into an orgasm. The almost painful waves caused me to curl up in a fetal ball, as the pubescently

"Massage" By Brett M. Damon

small amount of semen ejaculated caused a spreading wet spot in my underpants.

Shit. What had I let happen? I wanted to crawl into the deepest, darkest shadow and hide, permanently.

But it wasn't over. Greg had other ideas. He spoke for the first time in about an hour, telling me it was my turn to help him feel good. He said now that he'd helped me cum, I owed him and had to help him climax too.

Yes, he had brought me to an orgasm, an unwanted one at that, but that didn't mean I wanted to do anything in return. I felt sick. The thought of performing any kind of sex with him disgusted me still further. More than ever, I had no idea what to do or say. Remaining curled up in a ball, I just stared at him, crying inside.

Crouching next to me, Greg unzipped his pants and pulled out his erect penis. It was huge, much bigger than I might have expected, and I was terrified of what he was going to do. A shuddering wave of horror spread through me. God, I wanted to be out of there, but I was too afraid to move.

He laid down next to me and told me to give him my hand. When I didn't move, Greg reached out and grabbed my hand, pulling it over to rest around his penis. He kept his much bigger hand encircled around mine and began squeezing and pulling both of our hands so they jerked up and down his shaft. Then he started thrusting his pelvis so it was like he was fucking my hand. He told me to do it faster and gritted his face in an ugly scowl, his teeth clamped down over his lower lip as he concentrated on thrusting and rocking in and out of my hand.

Looking for someone to rescue me, my eyes wandered over to his other hand. I almost threw up in a sudden fit of revulsion as I noticed for the first time that it was missing two fingers to down below the knuckles. How could I have never noticed before? This was no time to comment about it though.

Finding no impending deliverance, I closed my eyes and waited for it to be over. It dragged on and on, and after a while I almost experienced boredom waiting for it to end. Why was it taking so long?

Greg kept grunting as he rammed back and forth and I was afraid Sam could hear it in his room on the other side of the wall. What would he think if he could? My hand was beginning to hurt from being bent and yanked at such an unnatural angle.

Trying to see it from Greg's perspective, I realized my hand was really just some kind of tool or object for him to use in his masturbation. When I looked at him, his eyes were closed and his face kept contorting into various strained expressions. I was glad he didn't say anything else to me, asking me to do some different thing to his monstrous phallus.

I did my best to detach myself from my hand, just as I would detach when cleaning up some vomit or dog poop. My hand was not me. After

"Price of Freedom" By Kevin Brewer

what seemed like forever, but was probably closer to thirty minutes, Greg screamed out and had his own orgasm. He spewed his gross fluid all over the bed between where we were both laying, getting some on my hand. It smelled. Finally, he let go of me.

Greg rolled his six foot plus body away, and with his implicit permission, so did I. Now what?

I'd just had sex with a man. Now a precedent had been set. After avoiding the lusts of all those other men, this had happened, and it was almost as if the entire lot of avoidances had been for nothing.

Did this make me gay? I didn't think so. I didn't know.

Greg looked over with a smile, and after a drawn out sigh, he said, "That was great!"

"Yeah," I lied. Maybe it was great for him, but certainly not for me. Sure, my climax was intense. Still, I would have forgone it a thousand times if only I'd had a choice. I never meant for it to happen and it only gave Greg an excuse to demand sexual reciprocation, something I didn't want to give. I didn't understand why I'd lied, why I'd agreed when he said it was great; I should have told him it was awful, because later he was to expect more of these kinds of experiences.

I felt deep shame for what had just happened. It seemed the whole thing was my fault because I'd let him keep massaging me. I truly didn't realize what I was in for, though.

Speedy Well-Getting

How do you go on and act like everything is normal in your life right after something very abnormal happens? I had no idea. Even before leaving Greg's room, it felt like everyone in the house, and everyone who came over to visit, would be able to tell what had happened just by looking at me; it was as though I now had a sign over my head saying "'JOHN' HAD SEX WITH GREG!!!"

Somehow I knew that my role in Sunrise house had just changed. There was an invisible new set of expectations placed upon me. I would no longer be "the straight guy," that runaway kid who likes women only. Now I was "Greg's boyfriend." I didn't understand this new role right away, but it became clear over time as I interacted with the others around the house.

The role of "Greg's boyfriend" was not one I wanted to maintain. But how, exactly, was I supposed to explain to everyone that I hadn't wanted to do anything with Greg in the first place? All he'd have to say to defend himself was that it must have been alright with me, after all, I'd had the first orgasm. The whole situation had snuck up on me faster than I could run.

As it turned out, however, this new role offered me a protection of sorts. Small protection yes, but better than none. If I was already Greg's boyfriend, then I wasn't available to any of the other men at the parties who kept making advances on me. All I had to do was say that I was taken, and I would be left alone.

It was probably similar to what happens in prison when an inmate finds a boyfriend bigger than him to offer protection from the other prisoners. Greg didn't have to do anything special to protect me; just be the guy I was associated with. He'd never actually be called upon to fight for me, but men knowing of our relationship would lay off on their advances.

Not that this was clear the moment I left Greg's bedroom. It took several days before the new reality began sifting into place. But I was adaptable;

183

once I resigned myself to accepting this convoluted situation, I went out of my way to take advantage of the protection it offered.

When a man at a party remarked about how cute I was, I'd respond with something like, "You can look, but you'd better not touch. If you do, my boyfriend might come after you. He is very jealous and gets pretty vicious when he is angry."

I'd point, "See, that's Greg over there, that six and a half foot guy. Want to meet him?"

It always worked.

One night, about two weeks after moving into Sunrise house, I realized Joseph was looking to find more than vicarious satisfaction. We were in the midst of another big party. I was busy with my regular housemaid chores, refilling drinks, emptying ashtrays, and picking up dirty glasses in what was now my usual bop-about flirtatious way, when Joseph quietly pulled me aside to make a proposition.

He put on a sly smile and asked if I ever "hustled" to make some extra money. Sure, I'd hustled at video games, but I knew that wasn't what he was talking about. By then I'd learned that hustling was also another word for prostitution.

"No, I've never hustled!" I retorted. "What makes you think I'd ever do that?"

"I don't know," he answered. From the way Joseph was swaying while he spoke I could tell he'd been drinking more than usual.

He went on. "I just figured a good looking boy like you could make plenty of money doing it, that's all. Most of the other young guys who come to the parties here are doing it."

This was news to me. Sure, there were plenty of other boys at the parties, but I'd always figured they were their date's lovers or friends; not prostitutes. I usually avoided talking with the other boys, keeping the discussion to superficial things, like what was on M-TV at the time. Talking or identifying with them would have been an admission of my own youth, and I wanted to be an adult.

On a roll, Joseph continued, unraveling the proposition that from this time onward would change the way I'd looked up to him . "Actually," he locked his eyes with mine, "don't tell anyone this, but if you ever decide to try it, I'll pay you two hundred dollars to let me give you a blow-job. You wouldn't have to do anything except lie there. And with all the cigarettes you're always bumming, I'm sure you could use the money."

His offer confounded me. How could he think I was a prostitute? I wasn't a whore! Did I act some way that made it seem like I was? How was I supposed to respond?

"Thanks for the offer, Joe," I said, angrily, "but I'm not interested. I don't sell my body. Why don't you just jerk yourself off if you're so desperate?"

I was dreadfully uncomfortable and wanted to get away. Quickly. "I have to get back to work now," I excused myself, glaring, and stormed away. Joe didn't have to worry about my repeating what he'd said; it was too embarrassing.

Joe's offer kept circling through my mind while I continued with my cleaning tasks. My deal with Sam, Greg, and Mark was to clean up in exchange for food and a place to stay, but I had no source of spending money. Joe was talking about some big money, and he was right about my always bumming cigarettes, not just from him, but from everyone else as well. I resorted to stealing a carton from the grocery store now and then, but I was smoking more than ever now, and it was too much risk for only a few days cigarettes.

To make two hundred dollars for less than an hour's work seemed a great prospect, but there was just one problem. Even though I was now considered Greg's boyfriend, and I had to let him hump my hand every few nights, I still didn't want to have sex with men. Blow-jobs were in a different league from hand-jobs. I'd gotten used to what Greg wanted, but I wanted to throw up when I imagined looking down at Joseph's balding head while he had me in his mouth.

Later, as I was washing some dishes in the kitchen sink I wondered if there was some way to sell my body to women instead. I was all for having sex with women. Fantasies of getting rich doing what I'd done with Renee began sifting through my head.

Then the questions started to arise: Do women pay for sex? Would they pay me? It seemed unlikely. After all, I was only a boy and they could probably find full-grown men to screw them for free.

Yet, if there were women who paid for sex, where could I find them? Then, if I could find some female customers, wouldn't they just end up being fat, ugly, and old? After all, if they were hot, they'd certainly be able to find any number of horny men to satisfy them.

Who and how could I ask these questions without raising suspicions that I was actually considering the possibility?

All these questions led me back to thinking about Renee again. I wondered if she would appreciate another visit and decided to go and find out as soon as I got the chance.

My chance arrived the next day. I made it arrive, because I couldn't get Renee out of my heads; I was horny and simply had to see if she would go another round with me. Maybe we could even top our first experience. I kept picturing how I'd try.

Now that I'd moved, it required a substantial trek to get there. I had to take three busses and walk a couple of miles as well. If she'd lived closer to Sunrise house, I might have visited sooner.

A few hours of waiting, riding, and hitching found me at her doorstep. I was sweat-drenched from the heat and humidity along the way and suspected I stank of cigarettes. There was nowhere to rinse off so I shrugged and knocked.

Her muffled voice called through the door, asking who I was. It took a moment to explain it was me, and who I was, before the confused tone left her voice and she began unlocking the door. As she opened the door it became my turn to be confused. Something was wrong.

It became clear as soon as spoke. Her lips moved, revealing that her jaw was wired shut with a complex mesh which kept her from opening it in the slightest. Her lips worked fine, and she managed to force her words through her clamped teeth, but it was difficult to tell what she was saying.

Renee invited me in, ushering me toward the familiar couch. She had just returned from work, she explained, and added that I shouldn't stay long because she felt awful and wanted to be alone.

I asked what had happened to her mouth. She explained that the night after our encounter, she'd biked back to the same bar and met a new fellow. He was peddling her home, just as I had the night Frank and I met her, when they'd had an accident.

As before, she was somewhat tipsily balancing on the handlebars while the new man attempted to navigate the roads back to her place. The difference was that unlike me, this man was drunk himself, and when a cat suddenly darted across the street he jammed on the brakes. Hard.

Not surprisingly, Renee hadn't been holding on very tightly, and was thus caught absolutely unprepared. Not slowing as fast as the bike, she lurched head-first from the handlebars. Unfortunately, her jaw was the first thing to hit the hard asphalt and take the brunt of her fall. Her jaw wasn't as solid as the asphalt; it shattered.

As I listened to her story I felt bad for Renee in her tragedy, but also experienced a mounting sense of revulsion. It was like nothing I'd ever experienced before. For the first time I wondered how many other men she had made that bicycle trip back from the bar with. How many absolute strangers had she brought into her bedroom? I knew of three in as many nights. At that rate, given her age, she could have slept with thousands. This seemed inconceivable.

Whatever the number, it was certainly large, and it seemed dirty to think of her with so many different men. My desire to repeat (with variations) the experience we'd shared three weeks before simply disappeared like a wisp of smoke on a windy day. I didn't want her to know how sick I was feeling about her, and was actually relieved that she wasn't up to sex just then.

After sharing her tragedy, Renee excused herself to go to the bathroom.

I wondered how she ate with her mouth wired shut like that. Probably on a liquid diet.

Alone in her living room, my attention focused upon her huge jug of coins. It was one of those thin-necked, five gallon plastic containers used to dispense spring water from office water machines. The jug was emptied of water, turned upside down, and filled about a third of the way up with quarters, dimes, and nickels; no pennies as far as I could tell.

That was a lot of money and I began to wonder if I could get away with stealing it. But I couldn't do that to her; she had only been nice and I knew she worked hard for what she had. I put the thought out of my mind and waited for her to return. There didn't seem to be anything else to talk about and I pondered how quickly I could get out of there.

When she returned, we made small-talk for a while longer, she asking how "my friend Frank" and I were doing and me wishing her "a speedy well-getting." After a polite amount of time we said good-bye and I headed back to Sunrise house, never to see Renee again.

Bit of Truth

The place looked precisely as I'd been told it would. It was a small park on the inland waterway side of Fort Lauderdale Beach, about two blocks from the oceanside beach, and a block from the bridge to the mainland. Palm trees studded an oval lawn that was surrounded by an even greater oval of roadway along which the potential customers were supposed to drive.

On the other side of the road, across a narrow lawn, lay a marina. The same blistering breeze that made me break out in a sweat, also caused the chop making the flotilla of small boats docked there rattle, creak, and bob up and down against their moorings. According to my advisor, if I waited near the side of the street, either casually walking along, or hanging out in one place, potential customers would pull on over and make offers to hire me.

When they stopped, I had to be careful not to say anything until the person in the car made explicit what they were looking for. This way I couldn't be arrested for propositioning an undercover cop. If an officer tendered an offer before I indicated what I was there for, it would be considered entrapment and they wouldn't have any case against me.

Though I'd been told ninety-five percent of the customers were men, I still held to the possibility of landing a job with one of the remaining five percent who weren't. If I was lucky, a wealthy and sexy young lady would pull up soon.

Yes, I was scared, but somehow, I managed to detach myself from my fears. There was just too much for me to be afraid of, to pay it any attention. I had to worry about the police, men trying to pick me up, contracting some kind of sexually transmitted disease, and getting home afterwards.

To top it off, there was a risk of somebody picking me up who wouldn't let me go. The next anybody might see of me could very well be a view of my back as I drifted face down along some canal.

On the brighter side, I knew plenty of prostitutes survived to do it again, and again. If it were otherwise, there wouldn't be quite so many staying in business.

It was late afternoon on a typically hot and humid Florida day. I was wearing my nicest clothing, a blue Izod shirt, white slacks, and the beach-stained sneakers I'd worn everywhere I went for the past six weeks. Though I'd showered just before leaving, my outfit was already sweat-soaked again. I could feel them clinging to my sticky skin. Though I didn't really know what they were looking for, I doubted that I made a very attractive package to would-be clients.

With the exception of two other boys around my age, lingering down towards the far end of the oval, the park was empty. I wondered if the other two were there for the same reason, but I kept to myself. Traffic was sparse around the oval, probably because the road dead-ended at the marina.

It wasn't what I'd imagined, some big "prostitute row" peopled with dozens of prostitutes wearing weirdly cut and revealing clothing, chewing gum, and waiting for customers. To the contrary, it was a well manicured, typical looking Florida park.

How would people who were looking for prostitutes even know to go there? Perhaps I'd come to the wrong spot after all. Maybe I'd misunderstood the directions and was actually supposed to be somewhere else.

Wait a minute! Supposed to be? Ha! More likely, I was supposed to be at summer camp, playing soccer or learning woodcrafts, and looking forward to having dinner in a half an hour; if I was lucky they'd even have pizza tonight.

But I was lucky, right? After everything was tallied up, I had more than I'd left home with; I was still alive, had gotten out of one scrape after another, and was still free to tell about them. It wouldn't do to become sorry for myself. I had a job to do, and it was time to do it.

My instructions had been to just sort of loiter around until someone stopped to solicit my services. But I didn't know exactly how to go about loitering without looking conspicuous. It was kind of a catch-22, trying to seem available to potential clients, yet without looking like a prostitute to the police. I tried walking around the edge of the oval for a while, but my every step felt clunky and awkward. Was I supposed to swing my hips, strut, or just walk like any normal guy?

Finally, I couldn't handle walking anymore, so I settled on leaning back against a palm tree, facing the road, and watching the cars go by. As long as I didn't go right up to any car that pulled over, saying "Hey Miss, I'm a prostitute; want to hire me?" or something else that was equally obvious, I couldn't get arrested for anything. All I had to do was play it cool, the fact that there was nothing cool about it, not withstanding.

It wasn't long before it became clear that I was in the right place, after all. Almost every time a car went by, the driver would slow down and turn their head to look me over. People on their way somewhere don't usually slow down and stare so hard at someone who's merely hanging out by a tree. Problem was, the cars had all been driven by men. I supposed I could deal with a man if I had too; I was already servicing Greg for free. But I was still hanging on to the hope of finding a female customer, if just one women would drive by I'd try to smile real seductively.

But there were no women. A car slowed by the other two boys, they went to the window and talked with the driver for a minute, then got in on the other side. As the car drove past, I saw the driver was an older man. He had his arm around the shoulders of the boy in the middle. That pretty much answered my question about what they were there for.

After perhaps fifteen minutes, one of the slowly cruising cars pulled to a stop just in front of me. The driver rolled down his window and called out, "Hey you! Are you looking for a date?"

A "date?" Shit! That's not what I'd call it.

The guy was clean cut, in his thirties I guessed, and was driving a sporty two seater. He looked like he was in good shape, which scared me as I didn't have good prospect of out fighting him if it came down to it.

"No, I'm not looking for a date, man!" I snapped. "I'm just hanging out here, minding my own business. Why don't you do the same, and leave me alone?"

The man apparently believed me. He cast a disappointed, indignant look my way, then drove off. I wandered off, back to the center of the park, to be as far from the road as possible, settled down in the grass, and lit up a cigarette so I could think about what I was doing.

It didn't look like any women would be hiring me in the near future. If I wouldn't settle for a male customer, I would probably be going home with less money than I'd set off with, considering the bus fare and all.

I took a long drag off my cigarette and decided to risk selling myself to a man. I really needed the money, I told myself. I would just have to make sure not to do anything I hadn't already done for free with Greg.

With one last exhale I determined to face what was coming with all the bravery I could muster. I was feeling pretty shaky when I got back up and walked over to lean against the tree again. For the first time since setting out for this place, I knew I was really going to do it.

About five minutes later a boxy luxury type car started driving around the circle. As with the previous cars, the driver slowed down to look me over as he passed by. I stared back and nodded. He seemed pretty chubby through his window, but I couldn't be sure. After peering at me for a moment he sped up again and continued around the oval.

He repeated the same slow down, look, speed up maneuver once again.

On his third circuit the man finally pulled over in front of me and rolled down his power window to speak. He asked me if I needed a ride.

When I asked him where he was going to, he said he was heading North-wards, along the beach, and would be happy to give me a ride. After all those circuits around the oval I was sure he had more in mind than merely giving me a ride. Herb had been the only one who ever offered me a ride when I didn't have my thumb out. The man might have been just as afraid of getting arrested as I was, so instead of asking me directly if I was for sale, he had asked about the ride.

The open window offered me a good chance to size him up. He was middle-aged, considering his half bald head and the way his fat jowls sagged. He didn't look very tall, though it was hard to be sure with him sitting down, but he was definitely fat, with at least an extra fifty pounds of blub-ber on him.

Like the other fellow who had pulled up, he had the clean cut appear-ance and clothes of a professional man. Unlike the other guy, he looked to be in pretty bad shape. I figured I could outrun him if I had to. He didn't seem like too much of a threat, and since I'd already decided to take the plunge and sell myself, I hopped in.

He started driving around the oval, heading towards the beach. It didn't seem all that different from hitching a ride, at first. And I wasn't usually so particular about who I let pick me up then. I'd accepted hundreds of rides from people far bigger and stronger than me with hardly a second thought when hitchhiking. But this was different; if things went as planned, I was heading for an altogether different destination.

As we turned north on A1A, the beachside road, he asked me if I was "looking for a date." That was just what the man in the other car had done. I wondered if this was the standard way of describing what I was doing; if so, the man knew the lingo, indicating he'd probably done this before.

Hoping to get him to make the first move, I queried, "What do you mean, exactly?"

"Well, um, are you tricking?"

"What's that?" I asked. The meaning seemed clear from the context and the way he said it, but it was a new word to me. Besides, I had to make him make an offer before I admitted to anything.

In a perfectly normal tone of voice he said, "Well, you know, I have forty dollars for you if you want to go on a date." Could this be a normal kind of thing to say? For some people it was. At least he'd made the first move.

It was a pretty safe bet he wasn't a cop, but I decided to ask him, just in case. My advisor had told me that if you ask them directly, the police have to tell you if they are.

"You're not a police officer, are you?" I inquired.

"No," he answered. "Are you?"

Of course I wasn't! How could he even think so for a moment? Who ever heard of a fifteen year old officer? It was probably even against the law to use kids for entrapment; almost everything else we did was.

"No, of course I'm not a cop. I just had to make sure about you before discussing this any farther." Though I had a good idea, I wasn't positive about what he meant by a `date' so I asked. "What would you expect for forty bucks? Because I don't do a lot of things, like I don't do anal sex, and I won't do anything with my mouth either."

"What do you do, then?" he asked, sounding puzzled. "I ought to be able to get something for my money."

How could I be having this conversation?

"What is it that you want to do?" I returned.

"Will you let me give you head for forty dollars?"

Joseph had offered me two hundred dollars for the same thing. But it wasn't the same thing really, because I knew Joseph. It was already impossible to look Joseph in the eye since he'd made his proposition, but if I let him actually suck on my penis, I'd never want to see him or anyone he knew again. There was a chance Joseph would tell other people at Sunrise house, and then everyone there would know. It was bad enough to be known as Greg's boyfriend, but I wouldn't be able to stand being known as a whore.

While two hundred dollars wasn't enough to do anything with Joseph, forty bucks could be enough from this guy. How are you supposed to figure out how much to charge for selling your body? It would take me a couple of days to earn that much at minimum wage, but it was an irrelevant comparison because I couldn't get that kind of job anyway. This would be cash in my pocket, today. And it shouldn't take nearly as long.

In a voice that didn't sound like my own, I answered, "Okay. But that's all. I won't give you head." I was committed. Looking out the window I watched dozens of happy families lounging and playing volley-ball on the beach. They seemed so far away.

"But where do you want to do it?" I added. "This isn't a good place; anybody could see us."

The man laughed. "Not in my car, silly! I've got a hotel room. But what do you say, why don't we go and get some food first?"

I wanted to get the whole thing over with, but I was always hungry, even at Sunrise house, so I agreed. Why the man wanted to eat first, instead of simply getting right to it, eluded me. Maybe he was lonely. Or perhaps this was the way it was normally done.

"Do you like Chinese food?" he asked.

"Sure I do." Chinese was my favorite kind of restaurant food and I hadn't had any since running away. It was too expensive to consider on my non-existent budget. Eating first was beginning to seem like a good idea. It allowed a bit more time to put off thinking over what was about to happen.

The man said he knew the perfect Chinese restaurant and started driving towards the mainland. The radio was set on one of those 'Musac' stations that only play sappy 'elevator' music. I could hear several joyous voices harmonizing some syrupy old love song and wondered if any of the singers had ever tried being a prostitute.

After a few awkwardly silent moments he asked, "So what's your name?"

There was no way I was going to tell him my real name. "Bill," I said. It was time for a new alias anyway. He was `the John,' to use the lingo TV prostitutes used for their clients. I didn't ask his name because I didn't really want to know. I didn't care.

He volunteered it anyway. "Well I'm George. It's nice to meet you Bill."

'George' was probably lying about his name also, I thought. Most likely, he didn't brag about having sex with prostitutes. This activity was presumably a secret. If I knew who he was there would be a chance of my embarrassing him in front of his family and friends. Anonymity was one of the unspoken rules, understood, but not discussed.

He twisted his body and reached out his chubby hand to shake. I didn't want to touch him, but also didn't want to be discourteous so I shook. George said I had a firm handshake and that he respected men with a good grip. "By the way, how old are you Bill?"

"Nineteen," I lied. Not that I had to be afraid of him telling anyone. I didn't want to talk so I didn't elaborate or ask him the same question back.

We rode along in silence for a while longer before he invitingly asked if I'd done this before.

"This is my first time," I answered. A bit of truth had crept into our conversation.

"Oh really?" He had an odd smile on his face and I couldn't tell whether he didn't believe me, or if he was simply happy to hear that, because my answer meant I was undamaged goods or something. Well, I would be damaged before the night was out. I only hoped I could minimize the harm.

We drove without speaking the rest of the way to the restaurant. As we walked towards the entrance, George opened the door and ushered me in ahead of him. As I walked past him, he said "Oh, did you know you have a grass stain on the back of your pants?"

"No, I didn't know that." But now I knew that he'd opened the door for me so he could get a good look at my butt. When I twisted around to check, I realized it wasn't a small grass stain either. It covered the seat of my pants and the upper part of the legs. I should have known not to sit on a lawn with white pants. "I guess I'll have to wash them when I get home."

George told me grass stains don't come out of pants, but that if I did a good job for him he'd buy me a new pair afterwards. What he meant by a good job, I didn't yet know. The whole idea made me somewhat nervous. Maybe he was telling me to be more friendly.

Normal People

After we ordered, George explained that he sold office equipment as a traveling salesman. We ordered wonton soup and eggrolls for appetizers, and I ordered an expensive seafood stir-fry for the main course.

Once the waiters disappeared, George asked what made me decide to stand on the street. I told him I was broke and had been told I could make a lot of money doing this kind of work. "I thought it was supposed to be more than forty dollars per session, though," I added, "but I guess forty will have to do."

George started to scowl, then changed his attitude and said, "Well, I've done this before. There was one other young man that I hired. And my policy is that if you're good to me, I'll be good to you. I always paid the other fellow forty dollars, but I was also generous in other ways, like taking him out to eat and buying him nice clothes."

Fine. So George thought that forty bucks and some new clothes was plenty. I'd already decided and agreed to do the job so there was no point in arguing about it. Forty bucks would get me a couple of weeks worth of cigarettes (I was smoking more than ever now), and still leave me with twenty or so for spending money.

"Well, I sure could use some new pants," I said.

The food was good enough, but it was a poor distraction from the impending encounter. Putting it off only increased my anxiety. It would have been better to get it all over with before, or without, dinner.

We didn't talk about my new job while we ate. Whatever conversation flittered between us was only a thin, almost see-through veil masking whatever George had in mind for later. From the arrival of our egg-rolls, to the ride back to the hotel, all conversation blurred.

Instead of being a participant in the dialogue, I was set back, apart from what we said. I looked on as an isolated and dispassionate observer. It was as though our conversation was between two other people, and it was my job to occasionally prod one of the participants to say his required line.

The hotel was a medium priced place. Nothing fancy. Just a clean and neat room, with the smell of some chemical deodorizer. The room had the same boring setup as a million other hotel rooms in the United States.

This place, this run of the mill hotel room, was the stage where I was to act out one of the most damaging portions of my life. It occurred to me that every time I'd had a similar stage this summer, the play had gotten a little more dramatic. From the first time, when I relaxed a little too much at the hotel in Clearwater Beach and lost my stuff while visiting the pool, to the second, when I stole the jewelry, to the third, when I awoke with the police coming in though the window. And now this time.

The door closed.

The actors took their places.

The curtain rose.

Scene One:

"Here we are," George says.

"Yep," I respond. "So, what do I have to do?"

George stares at me for a long moment before speaking. "Take off your clothes for starters," he drools. A silly, almost guilty smile crosses his face. "I want to see you naked."

This was my job and there was no point in wasting time being shy. "Okay," I return, and proceed to matter of factly remove my clothes, much as Renee had once done in front of me. "Remember," I appeal, keeping my face as serious as possible, "I don't do anything with my mouth, and I won't do any kind of anal sex either."

"That's okay," George answers. "I just want to lick and suck you until you have an orgasm." And then, more commandingly: "Lay down on the bed."

Scene Two:

Following his instructions, I lay down on the bedspread. My penis is as small and limp as it gets and I wonder how in the world will I be able to get a hard-on, let alone have an orgasm, so I can get this over with.

I try to tell him this. "George, I don't know if this will work, because I'm not really excited by any of this."

"Don't worry," comes his reply. "Just give me a chance to put my mouth on you." And smugly, "I'm sure I can remedy the situation."

Scene Three:

George is stripped down to his underwear. He crouches down with his knees on the floor and leans over the bed to start licking me. As his tongue touches me, I feel this sudden wave of nausea and I jolt back a little bit.

I plead, "Be careful of my head; it's very sensitive." This is so sick, I think. And it's not going to be over if I can't get myself to have an orgasm.

Staring at the ceiling, I try to will my blood down there. But it doesn't work. I can feel this disgusting man's beard stubble brushing around on my legs and stomach as he licks me all over down there, making me shiver. It feels like some dirty dish sponge is being wiped on me. I need to get away and turn this into something else; staring at the ceiling is not going to help.

Scene Four:

My eyes close and I try to remember everything I liked about being with Renee. I imagine that it's her licking me. But this isn't quite enough, because I also remember her broken jaw and my feeling that she humps every man she can.

Then I think back further and remember some of the various close calls I'd had with women before Renee. None of them were as close as I would have liked at the time, but I replay my fantasies about what might of happened if the close calls had only gone a little further. I imagine a bunch of different women licking me, and I try to see their breasts and other curves. This works, and I'm able to get a little hard thinking of them.

Meanwhile, there is this thing down between my legs, grunting as it moves around. It sounds kind of like a pig rutting through a mud puddle. I have to turn my fantasies up louder, brightening the colors, bringing the breasts closer, and imagining the feel of smooth skin, so that this grunting thing between my legs won't distract me.

I tense every muscle in my body hoping to accelerate my orgasm. Images of breast after breast, curve after curve, and soft mouth after soft mouth going down on me, flash though my mind.

And finally I do have an orgasm.

Scene Five:

Pulling back to get away from the grunting thing, I return to the room, and remember the grunting thing is a man named George. "I'm too sensitive after an orgasm," I apologize. Looking down at George I see his lips are wet, and become aware of the wetness all around my genitals.

Excusing myself to the bathroom I say, "I'll be right back," and scoot off the bed before he has time to object. I close and lock the door to the bathroom, step into the tub, and begin washing off my penis and everything else down there.

There is only so much soap and water will do, and I don't feel clean. George's voice penetrates the private space, calling me back to the bedroom. After toweling off I grasp the doorknob.

Maybe the hardest part is over.

Scene Six:

When I return to the bedroom I find George laying on his back on the bed, sort of as I had done. George asks me to come lay down next to him, and says that he wants me to put my hand down there, and stroke him while he jerks off. He also wants me to pinch his nipples every once in a while.

This won't be impossible, I think. After all, I'd already done something similar with Greg.

When I lie down, he reaches over and tries to kiss me through my lips. I push him away, but not quickly enough. First, he licks my lips and tries to squirm his slimy tongue between them, into my mouth. I tell him, "I don't do that. Remember?"

My face still burns a little from where his beard stubble scratched against it. How could women find men attractive with stubble like that, I wonder. Dressed in a jacket and tie, George looked like the standard, obese businessman. Most likely, nobody would tend to think of him in terms of being attractive or not when he wore his work clothes; they'd only see a salesman. But this grunting, pudgy creature, with spikes protruding from its face, and its body gyrating as it jerked at its three-quarters hard penis, is a repulsive sight indeed.

George uses his other hand to show me what I am expected to do. He wants me to glide my hand over his thighs, balls, and belly until he can tug himself to an orgasm.

Scene Seven:

It's my puppy dog that I imagine I'm petting. I swirl my hand back and forth across its unusually sparse, rough fur. My puppy dog keeps moving; it's trying to scratch an itch behind it's ear. But I just glide my hand gently over the parts that are moving, thinking to myself that maybe I can help it stop itching.

In time, my puppy barks and spits.

And I wake up again.

Scene Eight:

George is in the bed next to me, moaning about how good that felt. He asks me to go get him a washcloth so he can wipe off the mess. I go to the bathroom and do as he requests.

He invites me back onto the bed and we lay there for a while. In a very dreamy voice he tells me I am a very beautiful young man, and that he is very glad to have met me.

"Thank-you," I say as my eyes roll up into my head. I don't feel very beautiful, and I certainly don't feel like a man. I smoke a cigarette and wait

"Scene Something" By Laura Wells Denton

for permission to dress and leave.

Scene Nine:

We put our clothes back on and go back to pretending to be normal people. The backdrop changes from time to time. From the hotel room, to his car, to the department store where he buys me some clothes, back to his car again, and finally to the parking lot at the donut franchise where he drops me off.

Before he lets me go he asks if I want to do this again exactly one week from now.

No. 'Want to' doesn't capture my feelings about it. "Sure," I agree, figuring it would be best to part on good terms. After all, if a week passed by and I didn't want to show up, he wouldn't be able to do anything about it. George had no idea where I lived.

He opens up his glove box and pulls out a photograph of him with his arm around a boy who looks like he is a year or two older than me.

"This was my last lover, Paul," he says. "This picture was taken aboard my yacht. I used to take him out on it and sometimes he'd ride his water-skis behind while I drove. We had lots of fun together."

The boy, young man, whatever he was, has a smile on his face, but it doesn't seem genuine. I look at the wrinkles around his eyes and see a lying smile, the kind most of us make when we're a bit nervous, but try to smile anyway. He didn't look like he was having "lots of fun."

We arrange to meet at the donut shop one week from now and I get out of the car. I'm forty dollars richer, and have a new pair of pants, a new pair of sneakers, and what's left of the new pack of cigarettes George bought me.

The play is over, I suppose. Sunrise house is about a half mile from the donut shop and I start walking back towards it.

Catalyst

We were having another of our regular parties one night. This party was different however, because this time Max, the party queen, brought a bag of white powder to share with everybody who attended. The powder was a drug called MDA.

Once a good sized crowd had accumulated, Max began walking from guest to guest, scooping tiny mounds of the powder with the tip of a butter knife, and bumping them into people's drinks. He instructed the dose-ees to stir their beverages until the powder dissolved completely, then finish their drinks as they normally would. Max promised the powder would make them feel extraordinarily good, better than they had ever felt before. MDA was called "The Love Drug," he explained; it would give all who consumed it something far more "exciting and new" than they'd find on the finest Love Boat cruise to Fantasy Island.

When Max got around to me, and started to scoop some of the powder into my cola, I told him I was afraid and didn't do heavy drugs. Imploringly, Max promised it was a mellow drug and the effects would only last for three or four hours. He had never heard of anyone having a bad time on it.

Should I believe him? Aside from one trip on mushrooms, I'd never taken any drugs except pot and spirits.

The drug education program back in sixth grade had done a good job of frightening me away from the harder core drugs. I was attending a public middle school in California at the time. The teachers had called an assembly of the sixth grade, where a visiting police officer taught us about the dangers of drugs.

The officer had brought a fishing box with him. He opened it, and instead of lures, flies, hooks, and other tackle, it was filled with trays loaded with drugs and related paraphernalia. Holding up examples from his box, the man told us about various drugs: their names, how they were taken, and their effects on people.

In less than an hour he reviewed marijuana, uppers like speed and cocaine, depressants such as Qualudes, Valium, and alcohol, and the more severe psycho-active drugs such as LSD, PCP, and heroin. His props included everything from rolling papers and scales used for grass, to the spoons, needles, and rubber tubes needed to take heroin. Everything in his box had been confiscated from "real drug users and dealers."

When he finished, our teachers played a film of a teenager going through heroin withdrawal. The boy was dressed in only his undershorts. His thin arms and legs were tied with torn sheets to a small, metal framed bed where he writhed in what appeared to be utter agony. The room was dingy and dark, with cracked paint peeling from the walls providing the only other furnishings. Everything on the screen fit together to spell 'miserable'; it was a lifeless place of death and decay.

A serious, deep-voiced narrator explained that the boy was a heroin addict, one who had been shooting up every day for months, and that this was the only way the poor fellow could kick his habit. The guy simply had to wait in his tied up and agonized state until the heroin passed from his system before he'd be able to have even a chance of handling his life as a voluntarily drug-free being. The narrator explained the teen had actually *asked* to be restrained, because he knew that if he wasn't, his withdrawal pains would grow so intense he would be unable to keep himself from going out to get another dose.

Through time lapse photography, the film showed the kid continuing in his horrible, torturous, writhing for three insane days. He was living hell. As its producers surely intended, the film was terrifying and convinced me to stay far, far away from hard drugs.

When they showed us this movie I'd smoked pot only once. A boy in my class had attempted to sell me some, but I'd found my supply elsewhere. I hadn't known much about grass at the time, and ended up rolling seeds and stems into the joint along with the bud. As I inhaled one of the seeds exploded making a sharp snapping sound and blowing the joint apart in a shower of sparks. I had to jerk back to protect my face from the flying bits of sizzling weed.

The explosion scared me out of trying again until about a year later when I found someone more experienced to teach me to smoke it safely. Even the profound impact of the anti-drug presentation didn't make me fear pot; I already knew plenty of perfectly successful adults who frequently smoked it, and it didn't seem to cause them any problems. My only fear was of blowing myself up through my own ignorance.

But 'hard drugs' were another matter. The film and presentation were enough to keep me wary of any drugs that could be addictive or mind altering. The addictive ones were scary because of the pain I'd have to go through to get off of them; I didn't like pain. Hell if I was going to go through heroin withdrawal! The mind altering drugs, like PCP and LSD, were scary because we were told they could make you lose your mind, never to find it again.

After showing the heroin addict, the film had gone on to show an interview with someone who was severely brain damaged from LSD, then a reenactment of someone else who had gone berserk after taking PCP. The brain damaged woman said she had done LSD over a hundred times. She looked and sounded like a complete idiot. The film showed her explaining how she kept having "flash-backs," where, without any warning, she would see, hear, and feel visions of monsters and other weird things she had seen when tripping years earlier. The woman lost control over her senses during these flashbacks, and they would happen at the most inopportune times, such as during job interviews or while driving in heavy traffic.

The man they interviewed about PCP use had flipped out so violently on the drug that it took half a dozen officers to get him under control. The reenactment was exciting to watch. In addition to making the user strong and aggressively paranoid, the PCP also took away his ability to feel pain. As a result, he smashed a car window with his fist, without even realizing he had broken a bunch of his bones in the process!

So, when Max started sharing his MDA, I was afraid of what might happen. I'd never even heard of MDA before, but when he said it was mind-altering I remembered the film from three and a half years earlier. Why, I wondered, were all these drugs referred to with strings of letters? LSD. PCP. And now MDA.

Not ready to just take Max's word for it, I asked Greg and Sam what they knew about MDA. They both said they'd taken it several times before and enjoyed it completely. They didn't think it was dangerous.

Looking around I saw that dozens of the other people in the room had already mixed it in with their drinks and were casually consuming it as though it was no big deal. As perilous as it might be, at least everyone else seemed to be doing it. I figured that as long as I was in company, I could afford to take the risk, as well. It wasn't as though they were jumping off the Brooklyn Bridge or anything. Besides, if it was to be a "bad trip" we'd all be sharing it together. I went back to Max and said I'd give it a try, making sure to ask for a smaller than average dose, so I could see the effects of taking a little before trying more.

Max happily sprinkled part of a tiny pile of the powder into my soda and stirred it with his finger. Nervous, I took a slight, hesitant sip to see what it tasted like. The cola seemed a bit more bitter and acidic than usual, but not so much so that I couldn't drink it. I decided to go for it, and earnestly gulped the rest of my drink without dwelling upon my anxieties about what might happen.

My drink drained, there were no immediately noticeable effects. I went back to doing my clean-up chores at the party and was beginning to think the drug was bunk. Or maybe I hadn't taken enough. Judging by the background chitter-chatter, every one else in the room seemed to be enjoying themselves just as before.

More time passed and still no perceptible change. I wanted more of the MDA, so I could at least feel some effect. I went back to Max with a new glass of soda. He laughed, saying he'd known I'd be back, and used the knife to scoop a somewhat larger pile into my drink. I gulped the new glass down as before.

I had no idea what I was in for. At first I still didn't think the drug was working. I continued bussing and cleaning. Finally, when I'd practically given up any expectations of the drug working (about twenty minutes after taking the second dose), it hit me.

All of a sudden I felt such a potent, disorienting rush surge through me that I had to sit or fall. In the beginning, the rush was awfully uncomfortable. All the blood was draining from my head and I felt I'd pass out if I moved another inch that wasn't down. This scared me something awful because I had no conception of where it was leading. Was I going to black out? Die?

My heart seemed to be beating a thousand times a minute. I lurched over to a chair by the kitchen table and sank. The discomfort lasted another minute or two before transforming into something else entirely. I started to feel *LOVE*.

Gazing at the people around me, I saw them in a way I'd never seen people before. For the first time in my memory I peered beyond their outward faces, the personas they'd been projecting, straight through all the nonsense, to their core, their basic humanness. It became suddenly clear why this was called 'The Love Drug,' as I had the profound realization that I was looking at my brothers; we were all human beings, together, and I loved us.

Only a few moments before we were just acquaintances and strangers. A few moments before I didn't even know myself. Now everything was simple and clear. All my fears and insecurities had dissolved, and not only did I love others, but for the first time in more than a decade, I loved myself.

I walked outside to be near the pool and the fresh, open air. It hit me that not only was I connected to the people at this party, but I was connected to the neighbors on the other side of the fence as well. I *knew* the fence was just an artificial barrier put up to separate us all. In reality, we were all part of the same family, the same tribe, and the fence wasn't supposed to be.

After gleefully dwelling upon this truth for a while, I began speaking with other people about what I was going through and they all seemed to be sharing it too. We looked in each other's eyes with this "born again" look, like I'd seen Born Again Christians do at a evangelical revival just after the preacher spoke about Jesus's message of universal love. I knew that I was probably seeing the world in much the same way as this guy Jesus was supposed to have seen things.

At that moment I could have seen a good, tender part within the most vicious of people; I would have felt love for the most ruthless murderer. And I most definitely loved my neighbors.

Hell, most of the time I never even thought about my neighbors, but to actually be loving them? This was not something I was used to. But used to it or not, the euphoria of unconditional love poured through me. And for the moment at least, I was connected to every human on the planet: rich and poor; suffering and joyous; white, yellow, red, brown, and black. And not just humans, but every other creature too.

My awareness spread. My attention drifted from feeling connected to people to being connected to the world. The trees surrounding the back-yard tried to start a wordless dialogue with me, but I was too distracted by the movement of the water in the swimming pool to listen just yet. I glided to the edge of the water and gazed through it to the bottom where glistening patterns twinkled back and forth. The patterns were caused by the outdoor lights shining through the wave crests on the pool surface.

Crouching down in awe, I reached my hand into the shimmering fluid. "Wow!" I exclaimed. The water! It was so wet!

Not since I was a toddler had I really and fully appreciated the full tactility of water, the way it slid between my fingers, surrounding my hands, caressingly. I cupped one hand and ladled some onto my other arm, and then my neck, and savored the sensation of the rivulets sliding down, first quickly, then slower and slower, until the flow just petered out and left me wet.

It felt glorious and I wanted more. I removed my shoes, shirt, and socks, and walked down the steps into the pool, calling out to the others milling around the yard to come join me in this discovery. The temperature was perfect and the water welcomed me. There are no words in my English that can fully or even adequately describe what I felt.

Hardly inhibited, I wiggled out of my pants so I could feel even more. I wanted no barrier between the water and myself. I could feel every current and sub current of the water lovingly petting my body. Floating, twirling, frog swimming completely under water, walking and running chest deep, closing my eyes and drifting. I was dancing with the water and we were beautiful.

It was almost sexual, and I was a bit dumbfounded as to why I didn't get an erection. The water was making love with me. I had had sex that summer, but had never made love. This was love making without sex.

Sensing the magic the water and drug worked upon me, other people also began touching and entering the water. Many became equally fascinated. The pool filled with men of various shapes and ages, and after a time I exited to dry off and once again join the clothed world indoors.

Inside seemed gloomier and more synthetic than outside had, but I was still high and didn't get very far before re-engaging in conversation. My housekeeping responsibilities were, for now, thoroughly forgotten. Time drifted by.

At the same time that I felt this euphoria, I had an ongoing, buried sense of physical discomfort. My body was being pushed too far by these chemicals; my breathing wasn't right, and my heart beat far too rapidly. A sense of strung-out tension had spread throughout my body, and I felt like I had to let go of something, but didn't know what or how. It was as though I had some new muscle I'd never used before and it was tensed much too tightly.

Part of me wanted to be off the drug immediately and wished I'd never taken it in the first place. Yet another part was still experiencing the drugged euphoria and wanted to keep opening with people. There was, of course, no quick and easy way to remove the MDA from my system and stop the trip; consequently, the social butterfly in me won out. When I shared this inner battle with others, several expressed they were feeling likewise; it was one of the hidden costs, a kind of tourist tax levied on those who chose to take the trip.

Endlessly mingling, we verbalized about this, that, or the other thing, but the actual content of our conversations didn't matter. While we were talking I was simply loving them for who they were, simultaneously loving everyone else I could perceive as well. This wasn't a sexual sort of love; it had nothing to do with physical lust. It was more spiritual.

Somebody around explained that MDA was basically a chemical analog, an almost perfect copy, of chemicals that occurred naturally in our brains in the first place. What the drug did was massively stimulate receptor sites in the brain, sites that could be stimulated through more natural means, such as feeling the love you normally might for a lover, friend, or relation.

The drug took a shortcut, so no reason or rational was needed in order to experience this love. It cut around all those barriers that we erect to separate our friends and family from strangers and acquaintances, and perhaps going a step further, it circumvented that gap between self and other; there was almost a merging of the two. And the all.

After another hour or two of wandering in and out of the house while feeling incredibly charged on this stuff, I got into a conversation with someone about my family. My love had kept growing and reaching out in concentric circles away from the house, until, along with dolphins swimming out in the Atlantic, I remembered my father, a couple hundred miles in the other direction. I realized I loved my dad, my entire family, more than anything, that I missed them so incredibly much, and that the only thing that had kept me from calling them was my deep sense of shame.

For the first time I fathomed how worried they must be for me. I felt past their anger at me, to the deep pain they must feel not knowing where I was! For all they knew I could be dead! God, I hadn't even called them for over two months now!

I finally understood what Frank had been talking about. The image of their pain grew so much that I broke down and cried to whoever it was I was talking to. He understood and told me I had nothing to lose and everything to gain by calling home; I might as well give it a try. After all, I could always hang up if it got too difficult. At least they'd know I was alive.

He was right. I had to call someone in my family as soon as possible. The question was who?

My dad? No. I wasn't sure whether he loved or hated me. I didn't know, maybe I should call my dad?...

Then I thought of mom. I knew she loved me and wanted to know where I was, but I just felt too ashamed. What could I say to her?...

I wanted to call my sister, but didn't know where she was.

Then I thought of my grandfather, the only other person in my family whose phone number I knew. He must be worried about me, I figured. It would be easier to call him because he didn't have as much to be angry about as my parents. I remembered all the nice things he'd done for me and started to cry again. I couldn't let him worry about me any more.

There being no telephone in the house, I decided I had to go outside and find a pay phone. Now. The closest phone was at the Seven Eleven down the street, but that would be too noisy with all the cars pulling in and out of the parking lot. Besides, I wanted some privacy and was fearful of dealing with people who weren't tripping; I might make a fool of myself in front of them. And if someone realized I was on drugs they might call the police.

I started to wander, with wonder, out along some of the quieter streets off of the busier Sunrise Avenue. It was dark, sometime late in the night, but I didn't bother looking at my watch. Time seemed irrelevant.

A song filled me while I walked. I held my hands out to the sky, tilted back my head, and began to sing to the moon as I walked. It was almost full and beamed down a living warmth I could feel. Giving no power to the previous criticisms of my musical ability, I made up the song, words and tune alike, as I glided forth. The song left my soul and flew free in the balmy night air.

The many trees in front of the people's homes were different somehow.

I had been unready to focus upon them while entranced by the pool. There were no major distractions now.

The trees were alive and three dimensional in a way I'd never noticed before. Of course trees are always alive and three dimensional; they always take up space. But now they were talking to me in a wise and silent tree language. In their wordless way, the trees told me they always look on at what we humans do, and are amazed by our strangeness, by our inability to stay in one place for more than a few moments. Why did we keep killing them to make things we were only going to throw away after one use?

I had so much to tell my grandfather! I jogged down the streets looking for a pay phone. A few blocks later I found one, on a calm corner outside of a closed mechanic's shop. My heart was hammering away, and my breath gone. I had to rest a few minutes before I could speak well enough to use the phone. Lacking money, I dialed the operator and called my grandfather, "collect from Evan." I knew he'd accept.

The phone rang three or four times before the tired voice of my grandfather answered, "Hello."

"This is the operator calling. We have a collect call from `Evan.' Will you accept the charges?"

"Evan? Jesus Christ! Yes! Yes, I'll accept the charges!"

This was it. I hadn't talked to anyone in my family for months. My grandfather said, "Evan? Is that you?"

"Yes Grandpop, it's me," I answered. All my words seemed to have disappeared.

"Where are you? Are you okay?"

"I'm in Fort Lauderdale, Florida, Grandpop. I'm okay. I'm just calling because, because I love you Grandpop and I realized that you and Grandmom must be worried about me."

"Yeah, I'm worried about you. But do you have any idea what time it is?"

I looked at my watch and said "Oh-my-gosh! It's two in the morning." Fuck! I should have looked before. Could he tell I was high? "I didn't realize it was so late," I apologized.

"That's right, it is late," he answered. "But it's alright. It's good to hear you after all this time."

It was good to hear him too. He was just as grouchy as me when woken; I understood. I did my best to hold in my tears. They leaked, then flowed.

"I just wanted you and Grandmom to know I'm okay."

"Thanks Evan. Have you talked to your mom and dad yet?" he asked. "They've been going crazy with fear, not knowing where you are and dreading the worst may have happened."

"No. I haven't called them yet. I'm too afraid," my voice quavered.

"You should call them," he said. "Just don't call them this early in the

"Tree Speak" by Lynette Carpenter

morning. Wait until tomorrow. But make sure you call them and let them know that you're okay; they care about you and they're worried about you. Will you promise?"

I was immediately anxious at the thought of talking with either of my parents, but obediently said, "Okay Grandpop," anyway. I repeated, "I'm sorry for waking you up. I just realized I love you and Grandmom and didn't want you two to be worried about me anymore."

"Thanks Evan. Have a good night and get some sleep."

"Okay. Goodnight Grandpop." He hung up and I listened to the clicking noises until the operator came back on the line to ask if I needed anything else. I hung up and began walking back to Sunrise house. My high had faded away and I felt suddenly exhausted. I wanted to be deep in an unconscious sleep.

Somehow, speaking with my grandfather brought out the kid in me. After all this time as a runaway I'd gotten used to dealing with everyone on my own level; I was an autonomous entity, relating with everyone from a place of adult self-responsibility. Yet the moment I'd spoken to my grandfather I went right back to feeling the child again; I felt like a guilty kid who was doing something wrong (calling so late), and had to apologize to an adult for it.

As I walked, another, more satisfied part of me surfaced through the sea of shame surrounding me. This part felt pride at having done such a hard and dreaded thing, and a new sense of relief and hope from having reestablished contact with my family. I felt better. Even though he'd been irritated by my waking him, I could tell my grandfather had been genuinely glad to hear from me.

The prospect of calling my parents still terrified me, but I'd already gotten over the hump by making that first call. In any case, I could forget about phoning my parents for now, and deal with facing the next hurdle tomorrow.

The feeling of euphoria began to return as I started paying attention to my surroundings again. A flickering, bluish light leaked from one of the many windows along the street and I realized someone inside was still up watching TV. As I passed dozens of other houses along the way, I envisioned most of the people within them sleeping, getting ready to deal with another day, and wished them all sweet dreams.

By the time I returned to the party, three quarters of the guests had left, and the energy of those remaining had declined considerably. People were gathered here and there engaged in quiet conversations, and the largest bunch were clustered around the television set, sporadically commenting on the videos they watched on M-TV.

My body was confused. I was extremely tired and wanted to sleep, but light sleeper that I was, it would be impossible until everyone left and the place quieted down. At the same time, I felt wired, and wondered how I would be able to keep my eyes closed. I was no longer 'high,' more 'fried.'

It was another, too long, two or three hours before Max, the loud initiator and last guest of the whole mind-altered party, finally left. My jaw was tired from too much talking, my ears numb from hours of background chitter-chatter, and my lungs heavy from the two or three packs of cigarettes I'd smoked that day. And my brain was exhausted from thinking and feeling so broadly, deeply, and intensely. The sun was rising by the time Sam and Greg returned to their rooms, leaving me to find the peace of sleep on my own.

Endeavoring to relax, I lay there on my couch-bed waiting. The sounds of the rush-hour traffic picking up outside penetrated the house, and I felt too hot and sticky to tolerate even a sheet over me. My closed eyes were greeted by multi-colored patterns flashing and mutating across my eyelids. I watched these eyelid movies for a long time, wishing they would stop so I could sleep, and regretting having taken that extra scoop of MDA. I felt like a pile of luke-warm shit, steaming and attracting miscellaneous flies on a day so hot I would never cool down. After feeling so much, I just wanted to feel nothing and sleep. Would I ever sleep again?

Eventually. But it was a long, tired and wired wait before I could shut up my mind and senses and simply drift. And my precious sleep was delayed even further; at the moment I was about to fade out, Mark came home from work. He groaned after a look around the party-trashed house, and angrily banged around in the kitchen and bathroom for a long time before finally retreating to his room, and letting me sink into slumber.

Hope

A few nights had passed since calling my grandfather while tripping out on the MDA. Though I hadn't called my parents yet, they probably knew that I was alive by now; my grandfather surely wouldn't have kept my call to himself. But I'd promised, and had put it off long enough already.

It was time to call my parents.

Facing either of them scared me, but speaking with my dad frightened me more. I decided to call my mom first.

Why was I so afraid of dealing with dad? Perhaps because I'd run away from his house and not my mom's; he might be angrier than mom. Or, maybe it was because I'd had more practice talking with my mom. She'd spent about tenfold the time and energy interacting with me as I was growing up. We possessed a mother-son bond that had no equivalent between my dad and me. In spite of this bond though, it wouldn't be easy to call either of them.

I forced myself to a pay-phone and steeled myself to follow through on my promise. But when I finally picked up the receiver and began to dial I found myself gripped by a deep, unnameable, fear. I couldn't do it.

Standing there, the telephone clutched to my ear, I listened to the dial tone, trying with all my might to muster enough courage to make the call. I was stuck. The tone eventually stopped, changing into a recorded, nasally request that I hang up and try my call again.

My mom could wait a few more minutes while I smoked a cigarette. I'd already worked it through in my head, dozens of times in the past two days. My only objective was to let her hear my voice, to let her know I was alive and all right; I'd say nothing beyond that.

Okay. I could do that much. There was no need to drag this out any further. I picked up the phone again. It was now or never. I got another dial tone, began to dial, and found myself astounded by what happened.

213

For a moment, I couldn't remember my mom's telephone number! Were the last four numbers 2702, or 2072, or 7022? I wasn't sure. Only a few months on the run and it had slipped my mind.

After puzzling over the buttons for a minute, it came to me; at least I was pretty sure I had it right. Yet, though the number had only slipped my mind for a moment, it was a big shock nonetheless. How could I forget my own mother's telephone number?

Without dwelling on it I dialed the rest of the number, deposited a bunch of coins, and listened to the phone begin to ring. I wanted to vomit and was just about to hang up when she answered.

"Hello?" It was my mom's voice. A chill tore though me. I hadn't heard her voice for ages.

I paused an eternal instant before speaking.

"Hello Mom. It's me, Evan." I wasn't on MDA now, and a whole host of not-in-love-with-everyone-and-everything emotions were confusing me. What now?

She paused, then said, "Hello Evan, how are you?" Her tone surprised me. She sounded perfectly calm, like it was no big deal to be speaking with her long lost son; it seemed she was having any old conversation with me, as though she'd just seen me yesterday, not like I'd been "whereabouts unknown" for the past two-plus months.

On a conscious level, I hadn't anticipated anything in particular from her, but unconsciously, I had. Without recognizing it, I was expecting some kind of warmth, some emotion. Wasn't it supposed to be a climatic occasion to hear from me after so long? Yet, she sounded almost disinterested.

As we continued to speak she conveyed that she did care about me and wanted to know if I was aiming to come home. But it was through her words, not her voice. While she used words to convey her intended meaning, her tone remained calm, detached, matter of fact. Guarded, I realized.

And I suppose my voice may have lacked emotion also. I cried silently while telling her I just wanted her to know I was okay, but I tried not to let her know about my tears. I told her I had gotten a job that provided free room and board, and lied, saying that I was doing fine. I didn't tell her the unpleasant things. Before ending the call I promised to call my dad soon too, and to call her back afterwards. Whatever gaps had grown between us, I could tell that for better or worse, the pull of family connection was slowly drawing me back in.

The appointed time arrived the next night and I went back to the donut shop to see George again. The forty dollars from the first time was long gone, blown on cigarettes, candy, and video games. I'd decided I could handle going through one more encounter with George. After all, I'd survived the first time alright, and it was better than taking my chances with some new stranger back at the oval.

With a few variations, we reenacted the play again. We went out to a first-run movie and another fancy dinner first. It was a small shock when he called me "Bill," before I remembered that was the alias I'd given him last time. I had to think fast to keep from correcting him, telling my more familiar alias, "John."

After the meal, the sex thing was pretty much the same, the only difference being that this time, while he was down between my legs he paused to ask me if I knew what a "rim job" was. "No," I answered, puzzled, and the next thing I knew his tongue was licking my asshole. I pulled back saying I don't like that. Why in the world someone would want to lick my ass was beyond me.

"It's supposed to feel good," George said. "But if it doesn't, I won't do it." He returned to doing his "normal" thing. I felt like the phone had rung and I'd jumped off the toilet too soon; I wanted to go wipe myself off, but waited until he was done.

This time, when it was all over, I left George's car with a couple of new shirts and a carton of cigarettes as a bonus on top of the forty dollars. Upon his insistence, I agreed to meet him again in another week, but knew I wouldn't show up this time. It simply wasn't worth it; I meant to be finished with prostitution, for good.

My dad was the next one on my list of people to call. It had taken all my will to call mom a few days earlier, and I had to wait for my courage batteries to recharge before attempting the call to my father. Still, when compared to the ten or so weeks before calling anyone, a few more days wasn't that much longer in the scheme of things.

Little did I realize how that first little step, that trip-induced contact with my grandfather, was to set off a whole series of conversations with my family. If I had seen this at the time, I wonder if I still would have made that first call. Continuing this process of reinitiating communication was getting to be a real strain. I made the call anyway.

We talked about many things in the course of that call. Unfortunately, the one thing that stuck in my head after hanging up was one very cold sentence he'd calmly uttered: "I could have hired private investigators and had you found in a day if I wanted to."

God that hurt. I couldn't get it out of my head.

> *"could have...*
> *...found you...*
> *...if I wanted to."*

If he'd wanted to. If he'd wanted to. It kept echoing in my head.

Why did he say that? Didn't he know how it sounded, how it felt to hear those words? Could he have meant to rip my insides so thoroughly by those

"Phone Home" by Travis Mitchell

few words?

What made me ache so deeply was that I believed him. Just as I believed everything else he ever said, I accepted his claims as statements of fact. Implicit within that simple sentence were two basic assumptions. The first was the idea that private investigators *could* find me within a day, and the second was the idea that my dad didn't want to find me, that he didn't care. Two assumptions, and I believed them both.

If I'd thought it through, I would have realized the first assumption didn't hold any water. Within the first twenty-four hours of my journey I found myself over a hundred miles from home, and had been changing my where-abouts regularly ever since. I hadn't developed any sort of routine until moving in with Frank, and even then wouldn't have stood out much from the dozens of other boys on the beaches. The idea that an investigator could find me in a day was ludicrous!

The second assumption wasn't so easy to think away. I'd known my dad for over fifteen years and a part of me understood his logic; if he'd had me found and brought back unwillingly, what would keep me from just leaving again? There would be little point in capturing me if I only wanted to be away.

On another level, maybe he'd taken my disappearance personally, as a rejection of him; maybe he was acting nonchalant to cover his own pain. I didn't want to believe he didn't care about me. I couldn't handle that. But I also couldn't be sure, didn't *know* in my heart whether or not he cared.

Regardless of the assumptions and motivations behind his words, intentions positive or negative aside, how I heard what he said hurt.

As speaking with mom had done, my talk with dad had only intensified the deep sense of alienation and distance I normally felt. There was this seemingly insurmountable barrier between my parents and me, one that now felt higher, thicker, and more unbreakable than ever. Hearing their voices dug at me, reexposing my buried core perceptions of myself as a bad boy, a rotten, worthless person. And, if they only had known what I'd been going through, they'd think I was worse than ever. I longed for them to understand, for some way to communicate who I was and where I was coming from, but it was just too much and I had no idea how to explain it all. So once again I found myself crying, silently.

Sure, there was more to it with my parents, than just the monotone, unemotionality of my mom, and the bland blanket statement that my dad could have found me if he'd wanted to. At the same time that I got these messages, my parents were also asking if I was going to come home, trying to make arrangements to work it out.

I was afraid to go back to the pain I associated with living with my parents; I had been mortally depressed, even suicidal, at home and in school. But I wasn't happy now either. Somehow we came to a compromise that might work.

Maybe I managed to convey my fears of living with them again and having things just return to the miserable way they'd been. Or perhaps they'd come up with the idea first. Whatever the case, in the course of several more phone calls, when all the talking was done, we agreed I would return.

My parents would make arrangements to send me to a mutually agreeable boarding school soon after. This way I wouldn't be on the streets or in party houses anymore, stuck going nowhere at perpetually swifter speeds. And we wouldn't have to risk things going wrong living together again.

My father said I was going to have to repeat the ninth grade, because I'd flunked out in my absence. It was the last week of the school year when I'd jumped from the car. As a result, I'd missed all my finals.

The school's policy didn't allow for missing final exams. They comprised the largest share of the course grades, and by not showing up I was given zeros for all of them. When the weighted zeros were averaged in with my B and C averages, my resulting grades became straight F's. By missing those last few days I'd flunked out! An extra year of school for less than a week's absence!

Still, there was more hope of a sounder, saner future in attending school again. I would at least have a safe place to sleep, and no shortage of food. And harnessing the leverage of the telephone, I convinced my parents to find me a school where I could smoke my cigarettes without getting in trouble. I was an addict and wasn't ready to quit smoking whether or not there was some rule against it. It wouldn't be fair to put me in a school where I'd only be kicked out for the inevitable.

My parents had to care about me, right? They had to love me. Why else would they bother to arrange and pay to take care of me? Why else go to the effort to say that they cared? I needed to believe that they loved me.

Unfortunately, I could also think of other, more selfish reasons for their efforts. Maybe they only really cared about themselves and what people would think of them. What if they were motivated not by love, but because when asked where I was, they didn't want to tell their friends and family that they had ditched me, or that I was a runaway and high school dropout.

By sending me to boarding school they could act proud, or at least shrug their shoulders and say, "Well, we keep trying. Maybe this will help." They could arguably adopt an attitude of "You can't tell us we're not taking care of our kid. It's not our fault that he's such a trouble maker. Look, we're even spending thousands of dollars to send him to a good boarding school!"

There was another, less contemptible motivation, that still allowed for their not loving me. They might just be completely bewildered, only doing what they thought they were supposed to do. As impossible as it was to tell them where I was coming from and what I had been going through, perhaps it was just as impossible for them to convey what *they'd* been going through, what their thoughts and feelings were. Perhaps they were as incapable of speaking their truth as I was mine.

Though there was no shortage of possibilities, I didn't *know* where they were coming from. So, while I had to believe they loved me and were just trying their best to help, part of me also believed that they didn't love me, that to them I was just trouble, and that it was all my fault. In any case, loved or not, boarding school was a chance to make things better. I was set now, counting down towards the day I would return myself to my parents care.

And because of an unexpected turn of events, the time for my return was to coincide with the last day anyone would be staying at Sunrise house.

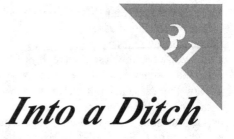

Into a Ditch

Somewhere along the line, sometime during my few weeks at Sunrise house, something snapped in Mark. He was sick of enduring the endless parties and accompanying mess, the constant smell of beer and cigarettes, and his irresponsible, disrespectful housemates. He decided to terminate his lease and move out.

Mark told me he intended to move into a cheap single apartment in a nearby complex, where he would finally have some space that was truly his own. No longer would he return from a long night at work to find crashed-out party-goers had slipped into his room and used his bed as though it was their own. Finding complete strangers in one's bed was for "The Three Bears," he confided.

He'd rather have a house, but it would be too expensive without room-mates. Having an apartment of his own was the only way he could control who entered his private spaces. Mark was moving, and like it or not, when he left, everyone else would have to also.

His name was the one on the lease, and he expected the place to be clean and empty on schedule so the landlord would return his share of the deposit. Just a few weeks away, the move out date was a natural time for me to plan on returning home. Especially, because if I didn't, it looked like I'd be on the streets again; none of my housemates had invited me to join them wherever they moved.

They might have invited me if I'd asked. I'd done a good job, working my ass off to keep Sunrise house as clean and tidy as possible. After growing up in neat and clean houses, I expected relative perfection in that area, and since it was my job I was willing to do what it took to get it. And Greg certainly couldn't complain about me, as he'd used me to satisfy his sexual demands several times by now.

Even if it was an option, I wasn't all that inclined to live with either

Mark, or Greg and Sam. Mark was nice, but boring, and the other two were increasingly dangerous. Sunrise house had transformed from being a safe refuge from homelessness, to a waiting zone, where I purposelessly drifted along with a meaningless tides of days, ever gambling that the sharks, undertow, and other hazards streaming by would leave me unscathed.

Now there was a small but significant difference. I had a plan to go home. As the deadline approached I continued to goof off, work at the parties, get stoned and/or drunk, occasionally be molested by Greg, and run errands to the Seven-Eleven. Time slipped onwards, some times quickly, other times with a dreadful slowness, but for the first time in months, I was grounded to the calendar again.

When the day for my third appointment with George arrived, I intentionally stayed inside Sunrise house watching TV. I was sharply aware as the agreed upon time approached, and then passed, and I felt relieved.

It was sometime during the last week at Sunrise house when we had the party where I saw the boy who I knew was going to die. This was another, typical, MDA gathering where perhaps sixty or seventy gay men and their dates drank, smoked, and did whatever other drugs were available. Most of the guest ranged somewhere between their mid-twenties to their early sixties, with the additional odd assortment of a half dozen or so boys around my age. The boys were the "dates" of some of the older men. They were runaways like me, prostituting themselves just as I had done, but instead of being taken to a Chinese restaurant or a movie first, they were brought to the party.

At the beginning of the party, Max was once again moving around, portioning out MDA from his never empty bag. He looked crazed, and told me he hadn't slept for two days because he'd stayed high on MDA the entire time. To keep oneself tripped out on MDA that long required ingesting ever increasing doses, he explained. The body built up a resistance to the opiate. Max bragged that he'd probably ingested half of one of his baggies of the stuff, and there must have been enough of it pumping through his system in the preceding two days to get a score of MDA initiates rather fried.

It got to be around three in the morning. I was coming down from my own dose, yet still feeling quite awake. I took a break from my duties and found myself sitting with one of the last groups of stragglers, people who hadn't had enough partying or the sense to go home.

I was talking with one of the men about something, when I noticed this boy, the only prostitute who hadn't been taken away, begin to roll a joint. Why he thought he needed any more pot was beyond me. It was beyond him too, it appeared; barely managing to hold onto his folded slip of rolling paper, the boy was altogether unable to distribute his pot evenly enough to make a smokable joint. He'd simply lost his coordination.

It's sad, but in a sick way the boy's efforts became a source of amusement for those of us who watched. His eyes drooped down, just short of being closed, and he spoke with a stuffed, nasal voice, pausing for up to ten seconds between words and never completing a comprehendible sentence. Somewhere between his brain, where the urge to speak originated, and his mouth, which was trying to get out the words, his thoughts and intentions were lost. It was pathetic.

As we sat around intermittently continuing our own conversations and laughing at the boy, I found myself feeling a little ashamed. It wasn't funny. The boy was in pitiful shape and it was depressing to watch; our laughing functioned to suppress this realization, but it was inescapable.

The boy had a reason for pushing himself to devour more drugs, even in his fucked-up state. He had nothing to stay awake and alert for. He was dying; I could see his life-force draining out of him. When I looked deep into the boy's occluded eyes, I saw only a pained abyss, void of spirit; I knew he wasn't going to make it.

Whether reality was so tough for him at that moment that he just had to get a little more stoned, or whether it was simply the result of a long, worn out habit of ingesting any available drugs, I'll never know. It doesn't make a big difference anyway. In either case, the root of his continuing attempts to consume more drug, even though he was too wasted to do so without help, was his need to escape his miserable existence.

If the man who brought him here still had any energy when he decided to leave, he would probably be demanding sex from the boy, ordering him to suck cock, take it up the butt, or something equally gruesome. I don't believe that particular boy was anymore homosexually inclined than me. Yet his eyes told that he'd given up far more than I ever had. He'd do anything he was told. He was worth nothing to himself.

Seeing that boy was the beginning of the end of casual drug use for me. I had already learned that no matter how much I ingested, I never truly managed to forget who I was, to utterly escape. Quite to the contrary, drugs usually managed to add to my troubles, making me feel physically and emotionally ill. Being illegal, they gave me one more reason to fear the police, making it next to impossible to completely relax and enjoy. For every sparkling moment of insight and euphoria experienced on drugs, I had to endure a moment of pain and despair twice as long, as I came down, looked at myself, and saw nothing worthwhile.

The boy epitomized where I might end if I continued my own trend of increasingly frequent and potent drug use. The odds were stacked drastically against his recovery and survival.

How long had he been a runaway?

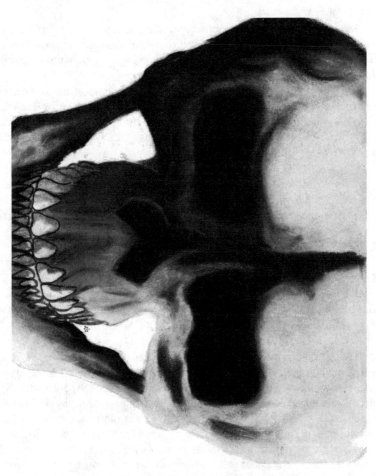

"Empty Pain" By Jason A. Lair

Longer than me.

Did he have any dreams of success left inside him?

Probably not.

Had he ever had any?

Maybe not.

Should he have liked his life as it was?

No.

Could I give him some simple advice that would get him out of his rut of entropic decay?

There were no simple answers.

The only way that boy was likely to survive was with a massive infusion of love, nourishment, and protection. Surely, the men who used him weren't likely to give him such. And that's only what he needed for *survival*. For that boy to actually prosper some day would take twenty times as much energy.

Who has that kind of energy to give to a sick and abused boy? I knew I didn't. What would his customers do when the boy had nothing left in him and couldn't even do the sexual thing he was supposed to? Would they just roll him into a ditch where he might or might not be found before he died?

The time came when everyone, including the boy and his "date," left. It was time to finish straightening up, put the kid out of my mind, and go to sleep. I would be crossing the state to go back home soon.

How was I going to get there?

Rich and Shitty

How exactly was I going to get back to my dad's? There were over three hundred roadway miles between Fort Lauderdale and his house on Sanibel Island, too far to walk in the time I'd allowed. It was important to get there on my own, without any help from my family; I was stubborn and proud, and needed to prove to them I was doing just fine at taking care of myself. I came up with two possibilities.

Option one: I could hitch-hike.

As I figured it, thumbing would involve at least seven different rides, and more likely, twice that many. Each ride would entail the usual host of risks, uncertainties, and frustrations. While waiting, especially on the highways, I'd be vulnerable to hassles by the police. And as always, each new ride carried with it the minute chance that the driver was some sort of psychopath or sex fiend desiring to molest me. On top of all this, there was no way of predicting whether I'd be able to get rides fast enough to make it to Sanibel by nightfall, or the next day even.

Option two: I could ride a bus.

After the ride across the state compliments of the Church of Saint Brendan, taking a bus seemed the easier option by far. The buses were air-conditioned, stuck pretty close to a schedule, and were a hell of a lot safer. All I needed was a ticket.

I called the bus stations and found there weren't any buses to Sanibel. Fort Myers was as close as I could get, and a ticket cost about forty bucks. Once I arrived, I'd still have to thumb a few more rides to cover the remaining thirty miles to my dad's place. Still, I'd hitched this last stretch before, and knew it would be far easier (and much less risky) than begging rides all the way from the other side of the state.

Of course I had the same problem that plagued most of my summer: I had no money.

How was I going to come up with forty bucks?

227

It was three days before my planned departure date and I didn't own anything I could sell for forty dollars. No one at Sunrise house would just give me that kind of cash. Sam and Greg were almost as broke as me, and Mark wasn't feeling very generous after tolerating my rent-free presence for more than a month and being stiffed on the last month's rent by the other two.

Getting a job seemed just as implausible a prospect as ever; at a couple bills a shot, cleaning up Ray's lot had been the best paying non-sexual work I'd managed all summer.

Now that I'd stood George up, it was too late to sell myself to him one last time. There was no way to reach him as I didn't have his phone number or any idea of where he lived or worked. Short of going back to the park and risking another go at prostitution with a complete stranger, I was out of ideas. It seemed I would have to hitchhike after all.

Then I remembered Joseph's proposition of a few weeks earlier. Two hundred dollars to let him give me head. I'd first turned him down because I thought I'd never prostitute myself like that, especially with a guy. After doing so with George, I still refused Joseph's offer because I knew him, and didn't want word of my whoring to get out to anyone else at Sunrise house.

But now I was planning on leaving and never coming back. It wouldn't matter if I couldn't look Joseph or anyone else at Sunrise house in the eye again; I'd never have to. As long as I waited until the last minute, I'd be long gone before anyone else could find out about it.

The two hundred dollars held more appeal than simply paying my bus fare. Once I arrived I'd still have one hundred sixty dollars to buy cigarettes, candy, and whatever else I wanted. That was one hell of a lot of cash to me.

Before I'd run away, my parents hadn't been interested in supplying money to keep me in cigarettes. In fact, I'd been forbidden to smoke, and to satisfy my addiction had to plan my life around sneaking cigarettes. Now, even though they'd finally promised to accept and allow my smoking, it still seemed rather unlikely that they'd actually pay for my supply. And after a summer on my own I was smoking more than ever, nearly two packs a day. The hundred sixty dollars would be more than enough to keep me in cigarettes until I got shipped off to boarding school. Once there, I could secure a part-time job to pay for them.

Two days before I was supposed to leave Sunrise house I gave in to the two hundred dollar temptation and called Joseph to see if his offer was still open. He seemed surprised to hear from me, but was still quite willing to follow through on his proposal. We agreed to meet the next night, just ten hours before I was to split town.

The next day Mark hired a crew to help move his furniture to his new place. No one else at Sunrise house owned much more than clothes and personal effects, so by the time they finished the house was pretty bare. In a moment of moving-day bliss, Mark decided to give me a small black and white television as a going away present. He'd kept it in his bedroom to watch when he didn't feel like dealing with whoever was in the common space. The color set in the living room was also his, but he figured he would only need one now that he'd have his own place.

The four of us spent the afternoon and early evening giving Sunrise house a thorough cleaning. Mark wanted every last cent of his deposit money back. To this end, he had borrowed an assortment of cleaning supplies from the restaurant, and spewed a stream of unwanted suggestions, verging on orders, telling us how to help clean. By the time we broke for pizza, Mark's treat, we'd sponged, mopped, or vacuumed virtually every surface in the house. It was cleaner than ever, and I still had four hours to waste before my rendezvous with Joseph.

At about ten PM, the agreed upon time, I met Joseph by the donut shop a few blocks away. It was the same place George had left me off at after our two transactions. Seemingly uncomfortable with my silence, and the whole insane situation, Joseph made some nervous, joking comments, then drove us in silence to his house. He was no more used to treating me as a prostitute than I was used to dealing with him as a customer. The ride and subsequent small talk as we maneuvered through the rooms and halls of his suburban house, zeroing in on the bedroom, were awkward for both of us, dreadfully more so than things had been with George. This mutually embarrassing encounter was confusing our previous relationship as friendly acquaintances.

Joseph's place surprised me. It was larger than Sunrise house, and yet it was all his. Unlike Sunrise house, however, Joseph's place was immaculate and the expensive furnishings were in tip-top shape. It had thick, clean, pile carpet, quality hardwood furniture, exotic plants, and artsy, framed paintings hanging upon the walls. All in all, it was a typical looking, well maintained, middle-class home.

Joseph didn't propose going out for dinner or a movie beforehand, and didn't intend to go shopping afterwards. All he expected was a simple sexual encounter. And for two hundred dollars that's exactly what I let him have.

Less than a minute after we entered his bedroom, I pulled off my pants and underwear and laid upon the king-sized four-poster bed. Soon after, Joseph started "going down on" me. Once again I detached and bombarded my brain with fantasies about women until my orgasm happened. I pulled back as I had with George before, a view of Joseph's balding head over my belly greeting my return to the room. Both my customers had been bald,

"Receeding" By Robert Brown

and I fleetingly wondered if bald men were more likely to be gay, or more prone to hire prostitutes.

Then, after Joseph got me something to wipe off with, I prepared myself to help to jerk him off, like I'd done to Greg and George. But, to my surprise, Joseph didn't expect anything more. As far as he was concerned, it was over; I'd already completed my job. He told me he would take me home as soon as I got dressed.

On the ride back to the donut shop Joseph shyly wished me luck in my new life back home. He hoped things would work out with my parents and school. When he pulled to a stop in the donut shop parking lot, he handed me two crisp one hundred dollar bills and said good-bye. Trying to be friendly, I said bye to him too, and wished him luck and prosperity selling shoes. He drove away.

I felt rich and shitty. I looked at Ben Franklin's face on the bills and wondered if he'd also prostituted himself when he was a teen runaway.

Not ready to join the crowd at Sunrise house, I wanted to go inside to order coffee and a donut. But I knew they wouldn't be willing or able to break a hundred dollar bill in the middle of the graveyard shift. If they had that kind of cash lying around, they wouldn't admit it to their customers and risk setting themselves up for robbery. On the other hand, I was afraid of letting anyone know I was loaded; some stranger might try to follow when I left and rob me when I was walking along a dark street a few blocks away.

I walked around the neighborhood for a while, keeping my hand protectively clutched around the two hundred dollars in my pocket and thinking about my life.

...In some ways it was much crazier selling myself to Joseph than it had been with George. Joseph knew a little of who I was. He knew I was going home the next day and would have to face my family knowing inside what I'd just done with him. George hadn't known anything about me, not even my real name. What made this time most insane was that even though it was only my third prostitution experience, I was getting used to selling myself. It had become almost routine in some ways...

...Yeah, Joseph, I hoped things would work out with my parents, too. That way I wouldn't have to sell myself to people like you, people who act like friends but really just want to suck on my dick; to use me...

...I didn't have to sell myself though. I could have hitchhiked the greater distance, or panhandled for a bus ticket, or conned another church...

...I just hoped to god (who I didn't believe in) that Joseph wouldn't visit Sunrise house before I left tomorrow!...

After wandering around for a while, my fatigue mounted and caught up with me; it had been a long day with cleaning the house and dirtying myself. I decided to return to Sunrise house for one last night's sleep.

When I walked into the living room, all was dark. Greg and Sam lay sleeping upon the floor. My newly obtained, black and white TV was practically the only furniture left in the house. Someone had hooked it up to the cable line where the color set had been. I guess Greg and Sam figured the living room floor would be as comfortable to sleep on as any other.

There was nothing to do without waking someone up and I was tired of being awake myself. The house was hot tonight. I pictured myself twenty-four hours in the future, back in my own air-conditioned bedroom, floating atop my old waterbed while cozily nestled between fresh washed sheets and blankets, my head resting upon my own pillow, and sinking into a relaxed sleep. Just one more night on a hard floor.

Sweating, I took off my shoes, socks, and pants to prepare for bed. Fearful that someone might go through my pants while I slept, I kept the cash with me. I found a place to lay my sheet, and soon let myself drift to sleep with the two hundred dollar bills clasped firmly in my hand, under my head and the pillow.

Goodbye

How could I have been so stupid?

When I woke up, Greg and Sam had left the room and the money had disappeared from my hand.

"Oh Shit! Shit! SHIT!!!" I thought, as I frantically searched the sheets and floor around where I'd slept. Now that the furniture had all been removed there was nowhere for the money to hide. Other than my clothes, TV, and sheets, there was only the thin layer of beer stained, cigarette burned, wall to wall carpet. I knew right then I wasn't going to find it. I was fucked.

Selling myself to Joseph had been for naught. For a moment that lasted hours, there was only this growing hole in me, a burning, disgusted feeling of loss and anger, as I realized what had happened.

When I asked Greg and Sam if they had found my money, they asked, "what money?" When I told them I was missing two hundred dollars, they wanted me to explain where I had gotten so much money in the first place. I told them it was none of their business, but it was my money and I needed it. They both denied even having seen the money, let alone taking it. Later, I approached Mark, and he also claimed not to know what I was talking about.

No one else had entered the house since my return last night. No one else had left it. There was no where else the money could have hidden itself, without help. Someone had to have taken it, and that someone had to be one of those three men. Perhaps even all three. My housemates. Yet they all denied it.

And they repeatedly asked me where I had gotten two hundred dollars in the first place. A very embarrassing question, one that I didn't want to answer. I just repeated that it was none of their business where I got my money. The only thing that mattered was that it was mine, and no one else's.

I didn't believe Mark would steal from me; he just wasn't that kind of guy. That narrowed it down to either Greg or Sam, or both. But without proof I couldn't directly accuse anyone.

When I kept pressing them, saying I wouldn't be mad if whoever took it would just return my money, Greg got downright hostile. He growled that for all he knew, I was making it up; for all he knew I was so desperate for some cash to return home with that I just dreamed up the money in my sleep.

But I knew I hadn't imagined it. I hadn't imagined calling Joseph two days earlier. I hadn't imagined waiting for him at the donut shop, going to his house, and stripping naked in front of him. I hadn't imagined what he'd done to me. Dreaming up hellish memories just wasn't something I did in my spare time. I'd tried my best to wipe out what had happened, to make the whole event into anything other than what it was.

The two hundred dollars had even *felt* like a whole lot of money. It was more cash than I'd ever had all to myself at one time. All this was way too much to have imagined. I wasn't that crazy!

My bus was scheduled to leave at around eleven, just a few hours from then. I had no way to pay for it now. The frustration overwhelmed me and I cried.

Why now? Did I deserve this? Maybe it was my karmic return for all the stealing I'd done that summer, to have something of mine stolen back.

When I was a little boy, around six or seven years old, my ninety-something year old great-grandfather, "Be-Pop," used to tell me that "when you cast your bread upon the waters, the waves will bring it back to you three times multiplied." In his way, Be-Pop was telling me that if I did good in the world, my life would become rich. And if I did bad... well, I might as well forget it.

I had been doing a lot of bad in the world. In the past few months I'd run away, lied, stolen, and conned. And, I'd prostituted myself. If my great-grandfather was right about the good or bad I put out being multiplied, then my loss of the two hundred dollars was probably only the beginning. Maybe I really deserved far worse than simply losing some money.

Still, it didn't feel simple. How was I to get home?

Maybe this was some kind of message telling me that I shouldn't go home. What if my returning wasn't meant to be?

No. I'd told everyone I was going back. Besides, what else would I do if I didn't go back now? Live on the beach again? Get caught breaking some law and get myself arrested again? Hang out on street corners until I ultimately became as broken as that boy at the party, the one who I knew wouldn't make it?

No. For better or worse I *was* going home, today if I could help it. I had about three hours to come up with the forty dollars.

I had been especially excited by Mark's gift of the television and had imagined bringing it with me to boarding school. But it was time to give up on that idea, because besides my clothing, and my watch, it was the only thing of value I owned. It was the only thing I could sell with any hope of raising enough money to pay for my bus ticket.

Mark was pissed at me for trying to sell it. That wasn't what he'd had in mind when he gave it to me. But it was mine, and what else was I supposed to do?

I tried to sell it for forty-five bucks, but found no takers. The next door neighbors already had a color TV and didn't want to spend money on another one, especially a black and white. Desperate, I went to the pay phone down the street and called Joseph at his shoe store to ask if he'd buy it. He wanted to know what happened to the two hundred dollars he'd just given me. When I told him, he said he felt sorry for me, but he was all tapped out for the time being.

Feeling crushed, I went back to Sunrise house, to sit and figure out what I should do. There was only an hour before the bus was scheduled to leave and I'd exhausted all the potential customers I could think of. It didn't look like there was any hope of coming up with the money and getting to the bus station within the next hour. I would have to forget selling the TV and rely on hitchhiking after all.

Mark was mopping the kitchen floor when I decided to say good-bye. He told me Greg and Sam were out on some errand so I decided to wait until they returned, then offer my final farewells before starting out.

The twosome returned about ten minutes later. I told them how all my attempts to sell the TV had failed and that I was about to leave to start thumbing my way home, but I wanted to say good-bye first. For a reason beyond my understanding, Greg broke down and decided he'd buy the set from me after all, but only for forty dollars. I was more suspicious of Greg than ever now, because he had claimed to be entirely broke just a few hours before. Either he'd been lying then, or he had suddenly come into a bunch of money.

My guess was that Greg had almost certainly stolen my money, after all, and only waited until after he could go out and get some change for one of the bills before offering me the cash. This way I wouldn't recognize one of the hundreds. But there was nothing I could do to prove it, and even if there was, there was no way I could force him to pay me back. Maybe he was buying the TV because he felt a tad guilty for stealing my money. Why else would someone who was so broke buy a crummy little TV set?

Whatever the case, it wasn't worth accusatorially arguing about it. I accepted his last minute offer and asked Sam to give me a ride to the bus. I made it to the bus station with twenty minutes to spare.

Upon hearing the boarding call, I offered an unceremonious good-bye, and finally climbed into the bus that would take me across Alligator Alley and back to Fort Myers. As with almost any Greyhound or Trailways experience, it would turn out to be an overly long ride. The knowledge that I was on my way home after an eternally prolonged summer away, only made it seem longer still. The word "home" didn't even feel right anymore; not after all the different places I'd lived over the past months. It was my dad and his womanfriend's home, not mine. I was merely on my way for a brief visit, before going off to some strange boarding school.

I took a window seat near the middle of the bus and waited to get to the other side of the state. A couple of stops later a man got on the bus and sat down next to me. He introduced himself as "Emillio" and explained that he was originally from somewhere in South America, but he was an American citizen now. Emillio was an older man, probably in his sixties.

With little else to do on the long ride, we got to speaking about different things. I made up some bullshit story about myself, as I did with almost everybody I ran into. It didn't matter that I was going home and didn't really have to hide my identity anymore; I guess lying about who I was had become well-nigh a habit after three months of doing it out of necessity.

At some point Emillio started talking about sexual things. He talked about masturbation, telling me that when he was a kid, my age, he used to masturbate five or six times a day. Though I hadn't intentionally shown any signs of interest, he then proceeded to give elaborate details about the methods he employed during his masturbatory episodes and what his climaxes were like.

After this un-solicited explanation, Emillio turned to questioning me. He asked whether I masturbated, the size of my penis, if I had orgasms, how much I ejaculated, and a variety of other very personal sexual things. Emillio's line of inquiry came as no surprise. Indeed, it was almost predictable after dealing with an endless stream of sexually obsessed men that summer.

As incredible as it may sound, even with all I'd been through that summer, I still didn't know any better than to answer him. Sure, they were invasive questions, but not any stranger than the things people talked about at the Sunrise house parties. I suppose I still naively assumed that if an adult was doing the asking, the questions were legitimate to ask. The only time I didn't follow this principle was when the questions might lead to my identification and/or arrest.

After all the other sexual experiences (both conversational and physical) I'd had with people in the past three months, I was still pretty unsophisticated about how to handle people who pushed past my comfort zones. I could have quite simply said I didn't wish to talk about sexual things and stopped the parley dead in its tracks, but the thought of directly refusing the conversation never occurred to me. As smart as I could be about some things, I was rather dense about others.

What did surprise me, considering the direction Emillio's questions and comments had been heading, was that he never ended up asking me to have sex with him. This was a somewhat puzzling relief after dealing with so many men set on molesting me. Where was he coming from?

Perhaps his line of inquiry was actually a form of molestation in itself, and Emillio got enough excitement from the act of questioning alone, that he didn't feel any need for an actual physical sexual encounter. Or, maybe he wanted a carnal brush with me, yet figured there was no point in asking because he sensed I wasn't interested. He could have simply been too afraid to pursue the idea.

Still, I prefer to think Emillio was, in his rather explicit manner, really only trying to enable me to feel good about passing through puberty; hoping to keep me from feeling guilty or worried about the exploration of my sexuality. After all, the journey through puberty, the growing from a boy to a man, is both an amazing and confusing process! He'd shared how he'd been taught masturbation was a sin and how for the longest time he'd thought he was going to hell for it. Certainly, an unfortunately large number of kids feel ashamed of the strange changes happening to their bodies and of their discovering how to pleasure themselves through masturbation. Maybe Emillio just wanted to relate to the awkwardness of growing up, and had no interest in me for his own sexual gratification.

Whatever Emillio's motives, it was somewhat interesting to have an older adult male, possibly in his sixties, tell me about his own trek through puberty. His simple act of sharing his experience of adolescence was like a mini rite of passage, connecting me to all the others who had traversed the same path on their route to manhood. And, it wasn't like anyone else talked with me about those kinds of things before I left home. Virtually all I'd learned about puberty was that it makes your penis grow, your hair sprout out in weird places, and your voice squeak. For some reason, no one had remembered to tell me anything more.

The ride eventually came to an end. The bus dropped me off as planned at an intersection along US 41, about thirty miles from my dad's home. It occurred to me that I was only a mile or so from the intersection I had stood at three months earlier, waiting for a ride to take me away from school for the day, not yet aware that I wouldn't be going home that day after all. I had come almost full circle.

Now, it was mid-afternoon on an extraordinarily hot, and normally humid August day. Sweat oozing from my pores, I stuck out my thumb and hitchhiked this last part of my journey. The going was slow, but steady, and within two or three hours my last ride dropped me off near the guard booth at the entrance to my dad's neighborhood, about two blocks from his house.

One of the Lucky Ones

By the time I found myself at the foot of his driveway my mind was swirling with thoughts and emotions. Excitement, fear, love, shame, and longing all competed for my attention. My body felt a bursting rush of confused energy, most settling in my chest, and the rest surging from one area to another, trying in vain to find some way to explode out and release the tension. It was too much. I felt insane.

Within three months I had walked, hitched, and bussed myself in a circuit over a thousand miles long; almost always running-away. Now I was walking-towards, or at least trying to. Question was, towards what?

What was going to happen next?

The summer had changed me. Now I had secrets. Bigger secrets than ever before. Shameful secrets. Dad might be proud of me when I showed him the watch, but I wouldn't be divulging what I didn't keep. I knew I couldn't tell anyone in my family, or anywhere else, about my prostitution, or much of anything else from my summer.

I also knew this wasn't "my home" anymore. From this point on, I knew my parent's homes were to be just that: their's. No matter how welcome they wanted me to feel, I would never feel the unconscious sense of belonging I had before.

Though it was beyond thinking about just then, I wasn't to have my own home for years yet to come. And it would take still more years before I would be able to risk telling anyone the most embarrassing parts of my journey.

I wanted this home-coming to be the happy end to the story. But a little less naive than when I started out on this long journey, I knew it wouldn't work out so simply. As long as I lived, there would be no simple, happily-ever-after endings. I still had to sort through the rest of today, tomorrow, and everything else yet to come. And one day, after I had caught up with myself, I could perhaps begin sorting out what had already happened, yesterday and before.

For now, I would do what I could to face the next five minutes. I did my best to keep breathing, and walked up that driveway to go get a very much needed hug from my dad, and try living with my family once again.

It never ceases to amaze me, that as bad as things got for me, I was one of the lucky ones.

Epilogue

So what happened next? Plenty. Enough to fill a succession of books like that which led to the *Little House on the Prairie* television series. Clearly far too much to put in this already long-winded volume. Besides, the point of my story isn't to make myself an ongoing character of interest, but more to illustrate and give a taste of the hell runaways go through in our land, so that you, hopefully, will become more inclined to prevent it.

Nevertheless, it doesn't seem fair to leave you hanging entirely. So I'll tell you a little more about me...

As you read the following, please keep in mind that though this has been my own, individual path, one that will always remain unique to me, it has been a path of healing. The healing hasn't been some quick, instantaneous event as you might wish, but more a journey, an ongoing process, that continues as we do, one day at a time. I believe all of us must consciously seek out our own healing paths for this runaway crisis to end.

In any case, I have been careful to keep this non-inclusive autobiographical outline as condensed as possible while still demonstrating my path.

As you might have gathered, I had a very rough childhood. I was physically and emotionally abused by various people before running. As this book relates, during my time as a runaway I learned about homelessness, hunger, opportunistic child molesters, prostitution, the U.S. economic class structure, and much more while hitchhiking and busing around Florida.

A couple of weeks after returning "home" I was sent off to boarding school, however my family never talked about or dealt with how my running had affected everyone; we never debriefed. The place they sent me to was an exceptional school; but it wasn't equipped to help me or the few hundred other very screwed up kids there to adequately deal with our pain and need for loving nurturance. I hated it.

Not surprisingly, it wasn't long before I got into trouble. My fellow students didn't like me, or believe the parts of my summer journey I risked relating. I had a few sessions with a "therapist" there, but still in virtual shock from my experiences, wasn't able to risk a genuine sharing. Of my own accord, I began to cut down on pot, smoking less and less often. In turn, I noticed my brain was becoming sharper. This helped in some ways, but I still had all my other problems. Five months into the school year, feeling dreadfully depressed and alone, I went off to kill myself by jumping off a tall building in downtown Boston.

Fortunately, I lost my nerve, afraid I'd only paralyze myself in the fall, and getting no second chance, end up confined to a wheelchair for the rest of my life. A homing instinct clicked in and I hitchhiked and stowed away on a train to get to my mom's house near Philadelphia. Mom was away on a business trip, and unbeknownst to anyone else, I hid out in her empty house until she returned. She immediately sent me back to the school, but I was quickly expelled as the school couldn't (or didn't want to) afford the liability of caring for a confused kid who might be disappearing for a week at any time.

Then I lived with my mom in Pennsylvania again, lasting three more seasons in a new public school before another crisis led me to run once more. This time, journeying over three thousand miles to California, it turned out I was leaving both my parents' homes permanently.

I was sixteen, and now a high-school "dropout." In total, alternating between private and public schools in four states, I had averaged about one school per year before this final departure just fourteen months after my return from Sunrise house. And in all those schools, I rarely felt understood or accepted.

A runaway once again. In the months before turning seventeen I shared a house in Berkeley, California with John, a criminally enterprising man, and an odd assortment of other disaffected youth who focused their energy in the "punk scene." John was a twenty-five year old black man, born in the hostile and impoverished environment of the Oakland ghettos. Through John and his family I learned a little more of the language and realities of blacks living in United States urban housing projects, and had still more of the bigoted myths taught me by my community of origin shattered. Notwithstanding, following about six months of living with John I realized we couldn't remain friends, because he, too, abused me.

After seventeen years of feeling like an outsider looking into my own society, I was becoming increasingly aware of its mass-hypocrisy, unnecessary suffering, and my own need to do something about it. But I was still as confused, desperate, and alone as ever. One day, while working a part-time job as a telephone switchboard operator and living out of my car, I read about the Anti-Apartheid movement. The newspaper reported that a few dozen people had started to encamp at the Berkeley campus of the University of California in protest of the school's policy of investment in companies doing business with South Africa's Apartheid government. I empathized with the darker skinned South Africans, who were being legally discriminated against because of a characteristic they couldn't change.

It wasn't all that different from what I was experiencing as a legal "minor" in the United States. Like black South Africans, I had no right to represent myself and vote, no right to be legally employed without special permission, no right to sign a lease with landowners, no right to wander unaccompanied under the nighttime sky, and so on. As a now homeless, disenfranchised, runaway boy determined to join the Anti-Apartheid movement, I decided I could at least add my one body to the mass of those who were protesting at the Berkeley campus. And that I did.

In the next month I blossomed. I found that in giving of myself towards a cause intended for others, I had tapped into a deep well of loving, healing, spiritual energy. Before this, I didn't even know such forces existed.

For the first time in my teenage life, I danced at night under the changing skies. I approached strangers who had also joined the protest with open arms, love in my heart, and a big warm hug for the taking. The last time I could remember dancing with such joyful abandon was back in the first grade. By now I'd given up marijuana entirely, and my highs were completely natural. Spending ever more time at the protest, I watched it grow from around fifty people, to a peak of over five thousand individuals, all gathered in solidarity upon a promenade we protestors had renamed "Biko Plaza." Adding to my aliases, I temporarily renamed myself "Peace-Lover."

One morning I was arrested because I wouldn't remove my body from on top of a plastic tarp the campus janitors were under orders and police guard to confiscate. Along with dozens of other protestors, I resisted, nonviolently sitting Indian-style, and the police had to drag and then carry my limp body away. I was the first one arrested this day, and when the police started to haul me off, a small riot began.

As this was happening I experienced one of the most sacred moments of my life: I felt a profound calm within, as all around me was in almost complete turmoil; the sky was still blue, spotted with puffy white clouds, and I felt as much love for those apprehending me as for those who were trying to free me; from a deep place, a source of knowledge I have rarely touched, I knew I was a part of something bigger than I'd ever experienced, something that connected all life together. To someone who hasn't had an experience like this, it may sound like some flaky, hippie, or "born-again" tale, but it was as real for me as anything I'd ever known. And no, I wasn't under the influence of drugs.

Spiritual experience or not, it had consequences. I spent the next thirty-five days and nights locked in a Detention Center and a Juvenile Hall. The charges against me were "misdemeanor resisting arrest," and "presentation of a false identity to an officer of the law." Had I been a mere eleven months older I could have been out of jail in less than a day.

One of my family members believed "The Communists" had led me astray, brainwashing me into protesting, and he was willing to take me into his custody so he could put me into the Charter Glade mental hospital, a lock-down facility in which his insurance policy would pay $10,000 a month to keep me confined. With that kind of money, they'd have no incentive to let me go. I, of course, wasn't willing to go. Yet if the court found me guilty of my misdemeanor charges I would have no say in the matter; I'd be transferred over to him and this private jail without any sort of due process.

Meanwhile, mostly unbeknownst to me, people I'd met while protesting had formed an alliance in my defense. They had gotten about two hundred folks to sign up as witnesses on my behalf in what would have been my trial. If the trial had proceeded according to law this horde of witnesses would have tied up one of the two juvenile court judges assigned to the Oakland/Berkeley area for several months.

On day thirty-five of my dehumanizing incarceration my charges were officially dropped, "in the interest of justice," as the judge put it. I was released back into my own custody. Free again, I got away from California as fast as possible and settled next among the ten thousand inhabitants of Oberlin, Ohio.

Two months later I met my future wife, Kelli, while waiting on her table in an Oberlin restaurant. In time, we performed our union ceremony over a bowl of chicken soup and declared ourselves married. Kelli was a student at Oberlin College and gave me the much needed gift of unconditional love. She helped me gain strength and supported my healing process. And I helped her in hers as well; she was an incest survivor.

Following another long year that included many odd jobs, a five month attempt to live in Hollywood, California, and half a dozen separate, week-long, bed-ridden bouts with feverish illness, I got myself accepted into Oberlin College as a part-time student. Remarkably, I was eighteen then, right "on schedule" for entering college. I started by taking two courses, and beginning counseling therapy with the wonderful man who ran Oberlin College's psychological services. After two years as a dropout the college level courses were a hell of a challenge, and after nearly two decades of craziness the therapy was even harder.

It was at this time that I first came to the specific, conscious realizations that I'd been an abused child and hadn't been such a "bad boy" all through my childhood after all; rather, I'd only done what most little boys put in my situation would have done. For the first time in my life I let myself mourn for my lost childhood, for the absence of a safe space in which to grow.

Realizing and acknowledging my abuse was, I believe, the most important event in my life. This realization was prerequisite to developing any sense of self esteem, and represented the initiation of my healing. Once armed with the concept of mistreatment, the very word "abuse," as well as a growing recollection and understanding of how seriously I'd been wronged,

I finally had the tools to begin the long healing process.

One of my initial responses to counseling was to become immensely angry at the people who had abused me. How dare they treat me that way! I began confronting my abusers. Though some of them tried to hear me out, and even offered their best attempts at an apology, my abusers weren't (and still aren't) receptive to the notion they had behaved abusively.

I wanted my abusers to unequivocally own their responsibility, to apologize without any "I'm sorry, buts..." Sadly, this idea was simply too threatening for them, and in their confusion, they even tried blaming me for their abusive conduct.

Over time I came to realize that they, too, had been treated in the same abusive fashions when they were kids. My abusers had merely been passing on what they had learned about interacting with people from their abusers. This insight didn't excuse the abuse I received, but it helped me to understand it, and feel a little more compassion for those who hurt me so much. My abusers deserve some credit, because it turns out they have done far more to accept responsibility and apologize for how they hurt me, than those who abused them when they were children have ever done.

My development of compassion was the second most important step in my healing, perhaps in my life. To be able to feel compassion and love for those who hurt me is one of the most freeing abilities. The alternative would be to get stuck in the twin ruts of endless anger and hate, two empty and endless roads that lead nowhere I want to go.

With my new-found understandings, my new sense of community, and my very special wife, my next two and a half years in Oberlin College became a very healing period, one in an exceptionally restorative place. As I regained strength lost from years of constant stress and struggle, I took more and more classes, ultimately enrolling as a full-time student. Once again I ventured into activism, this time through the SANE (nuclear weapons) Freeze campaign and the Oberlin College Men's Center.

Through SANE, I learned about the insanity of the arms race, the scale of potential destruction paranoid military economies made possible, and the interests vested in maintenance of such systems. And in the process, I worked to share what I was learning.

Through the Men's Center, I joined other men in a weekly exploration of our socialization and of how we could redefine what "being a man" meant for us. The examples of masculinity I had been exposed to in the previous years were unacceptable. I didn't want to become a cold, unemotional, and authoritarian war-maker, exploiter, or abuser, only interested in fostering an increase in my personal wealth and power over others.

My time in Juvenile Hall had scared me back into my cold shell, bringing violence back to the surface of my psyche, and I wanted to learn how to dance and joyously hug people again. With a long way remaining to once again reach that open place inside myself, I busied myself with the pursuit of external activities. Eventually, I became the Chair of the Men's Center and co-organized Oberlin College's 1988 Men's Conference, arranging media, speakers, and workshops exploring issues including violence, sex roles, sexism, sexuality, and emotional expression.

After many unsuccessful attempts, I quit my three-pack-a-day cigarette smoking habit on the first day of Fall in my nineteenth year. I made the conscious decision to stop killing myself, to try to live. This life-choice led directly to my forming a reconnection with the rest of "nature."

My wife and I met a ninety year old man named George Jones who led us and others on weekly three-hour nature walks in the relatively wild areas around Oberlin. Through stories, this wizened man of body old and spirit young taught us the names of the various trees and herbs growing around us. Though I'd scarcely acknowledged it before, life was everywhere. George taught me that what some people called "weeds" were actually beautiful, flowering, and even "useful" plants. Later, charging us a mere three dollars for the season, he rented Kelli and I a portion of his back yard, in which we grew our first garden.

At about this time, I also began to explore Earth-centered spirituality. Over the following seasons I participated in a couple of "pagan" covens, following, in an un-dogmatic manner, some of the pre-Christian spiritual traditions found throughout ancient Europe. Both in and out of these groups, I found myself creatively celebrating the cycles of life, growth, and death during the extremes and midpoints of lunar and solar cycles. I grounded myself and began to grow roots.

In my third semester at Oberlin I took an introductory Environmental Studies course which surveyed some of the regional and global ecological crises human actions have manifested. Upon realizing the seriousness of these crises, I determined to devote my life toward helping to bring about a sustainable society that could heal the wounds we have inflicted upon the Earth and ourselves. To this end, I declared Environmental Studies (Bachelor of Arts) as my intended major, volunteered for a summer with the U.S. Forest Service, joined a "green movement" discussion group, and subsequently secured other environmentally oriented jobs and internships as the years went by.

After two and a half years at Oberlin College my financial backer pulled out, and the next one I could find conditioned his assistance on my pursuing a Bachelor of Science degree at a public university. After a complicated search, I accepted his offer. My wife and I yanked our roots and moved to Fort Collins, Colorado, where I could enroll in the Environmental Health program at Colorado State University, and she could enter a graduate program in nearby Denver.

My healing has continued since arriving in Fort Collins. In my five years here I have learned about myself and grown new roots in the local community. I have continued connecting with my environment by exploring my neighborhoods, getting into the mountains, and learning a little about the people who lived here (and throughout America) before me, the original Native Americans. In a local men's group, I continued working to overcome my fear of men. Though I have repeatedly made mistakes, sidetracking and backtracking, I have come to feel good about myself. Now I forgive my mistakes and imperfections, and try to learn from them.

Academically, my final five semesters studying at CSU were mostly spent ingesting the large quantities of status quo science required for my degree. Unfortunately, in my opinion, this has been accomplished in an academic atmosphere sadly devoid of substantive discussion regarding the ethics or creativity involved in the pursuit and application of the sciences studied. Specifically, the professors continually hurled information on technologies and results of research at us students, without ever discussing whether torturing millions of animals or ripping the Earth apart in securing these facts and technologies was our "right," or our wrong. We were taught the marvels of Microbiology, Chemistry, and other sciences without being taught the twin potentials for harmful uses and effects of the very same breakthroughs in knowledge.

Meanwhile, my marriage became more and more turbulent following our move. Though I loved Kelli, I wasn't "in love" with her. I realized I had married out of need for the love she provided, not out of the passion and giving inspired by the more special kind of love. I was weak and on the verge of death before I met her. Her loving support had saved my life, but the relationship of marriage was a lie. It was feeling more and more like an act of prostitution. Though I felt guilty for "using her," remaining married would have been a greater wrong.

Kelli and I divorced seven months after arriving in Colorado. Though we remained best friends for almost two years after our divorce, we were simply unable to get along together, and subsequently stopped communicating about a year ago. Before this, my wife was my most important mentor in a wide variety of feminist theories (personal, political, spiritual, aesthetic, etc.). The stories she shared of her ongoing work as a counselor in battered women's shelters, and as a member of incest support groups, functioned as a constant reminder of the violence and perversion I'd mostly escaped in my five years in Academia. She helped keep me from forgetting where I came from as I finally started to benefit from the power, respect, and wealth that come in our society with growing from a boy to a man, being white, and attending and completing college. What I've learned from Kelli has become integral in my attempts to actualize myself in grassroots pursuits and other avenues.

My divorce and ethically impoverished coursework, along with finally getting rid of my addictive television set, created a vacuum I filled by once again becoming involved in activist work. Once freed, I founded the CSU Campus Greens group in the Spring of 1990 and spent about eighteen months building and developing it. Through my activities with Campus Greens and other groups, I struggled to achieve an integrative "praxis" (synthesis of theory and practice) utilizing the various lenses I'd developed (e.g., scientific, entrepreneurial, feminist, oppressed peoples, former runaway child, psychological, etc.) to effect real, positive change. Participants in Campus Greens focused on a variety of areas including environmental issues, alternatives to abuse and war, personal responsibility and actualization, alliance building, and simply having fun. I kept myself extremely busy with organizing activities, working on presentations, protests, petitions, fund-raisers, recycling, hikes, giving out educational literature, connecting to the national Green Movement, and continually bringing new people into the group.

During my last semester of work on my B.S. degree, I left Campus Greens to continue on its own, and worked with a friend to refound Students for the Ethical Treatment of Animals (SETA). This group grew more quickly than Campus Greens had. It seemed a sign that I had learned through my student organizing experiences and thus rallied people more efficiently. Or perhaps people were simply more interested in working on the single issue of animal ethics than on the more holistic and dispersed approach of the Greens.

In any case, being active in SETA served as great personal reinforcement in my aim to become a vegetarian, and to change many of my patterns that contributed to suffering and destruction of the environment. With the help and encouragement of my peers, I have managed not to eat any birds or mammals for over two years, and intend to eventually eliminate my consumption of all animal derived products, including seafood, dairy, eggs, and leather.

My success as a student activist was hard to gauge. Though I originated and helped organize dozens of events and gatherings in Oberlin and Fort Collins, I lacked a tangible way of measuring how they affected the participants. Was it worth all the effort? Certainly for what I learned, but I don't know about the others.

A high school drop-out, I finally graduated from college in December, 1991, with my Bachelor of Science degree in Environmental Health. Feeling like I now knew less than ever, I pulled back from my external activism and set out to write this book; at least I knew my experiences as a runaway.

Instead of looking for a "job" right away, I risked using up my savings and going into debt to finish this project. After thinking about writing this volume for the previous eight years, I didn't want to postpone it any longer.

When I began this book I told myself it was to help others. As I wrote I came to realize it was helping me. I hadn't told anyone about my prostitution experiences; eight years had passed and I hadn't dealt with them in the slightest. I'd gotten myself so busy with and distracted by schoolwork, activism, and relationships I'd managed to neglect working on myself.

After only a couple levels of introspection and confrontation I'd fooled myself into believing I'd dealt with my abuse and healed. As an activist I gained positive support and recognition unlike anything in my life. For the first time I was "a success;" I was achieving in my academic and organizing work. People kept praising me, telling me I was doing good.

But a part of me couldn't believe I was so good. These messages were in direct conflict with all I'd been told for my first eighteen years. I started to develop secrets.

As scary as it is to admit, there still was, and is, a seed of violence in me, a part of me that is perfectly capable of dishing out the kind of abuse I received. The more I was doing "good" the more I began thinking and fantasizing "evil." I began having fantasies and dreams about hurting people, especially women. This didn't make any sense to me — I really cared about ending abuse, about equal rights, about ending all forms of evil. How could I be thinking and getting excited by such horrible things?

As an activist, and later as a writer, I didn't tell anyone about this. People would hate me, I thought. They'd see me as a hypocrite, working for good while fantasizing something completely different.

After graduating I went to Florida to retrace my steps and take notes for this book. Everything went okay for the first few days, but the closer I came to Fort Lauderdale, the scene of my molestation and prostitution, the more overwhelmed I became. I felt insane and began to imagine having a bazooka and blowing up the people and buildings I passed. It got so bad I couldn't get out of my car to investigate the places I remembered. I had to get out of Florida so I called the airline and pushed up my return by a few days.

Back in Colorado I began to work on writing. I did my best to distance myself from my violent thoughts, to hide them from myself even. As long as I kept them just fantasies, no one would have to know — other than me, no one would be getting hurt.

But it didn't work.

The writing went far more slowly than I'd planned, as though I was procrastinating on getting to the parts of my book that dealt with what I went through in Fort Lauderdale that summer. In college it got so I could put together a twenty page paper in a few days. I'd figured I would finish a first draft of this book within a month or two. But writing my story required a lot more than simply assembling facts and arguments. I had to cope with what I wrote about.

The more I tried to dam up the violence within, the more it built. It grew from a trickle to a surging river and despite my best efforts, the dam began to leak. Though I had a community of friends I grew very lonely because no one knew all of me. Yet I dared not tell them of my dark side.

The months passed, and despite my best efforts at avoiding it, I finally managed to write the Fort Lauderdale portion of my story. I began to risk letting my friends know about my prostitution. They still accepted me. But

I continued to keep the violent side of myself a secret.

Eleven months into this project, my girlfriend of the time had moved to Washington state and I went to visit her. While there, I got in a screaming fight with her and grew so enraged I threw the apple I was eating; I was aiming away from her, but the apple smashed into the wall just two feet from her head. She said, "I knew you were an abuser." I stormed away.

We tried to "make up" and the next day took a trip up to North Vancouver, Canada to visit her aunt. It didn't take long to get into another fight. I left, feeling crazy and incredibly alone.

I needed someone to hold me, but there wasn't anyone. I drove aimlessly through Vancouver and hired a prostitute I saw standing on a street corner. She was fifteen, a runaway. I was disgusted with myself, and wanted to back out, but went through with it anyway. When we finished she told me she had run away to escape being molested by her step-father. I gave her two hundred dollars for the most alienating encounter of my life.

Now I had a bigger secret. I'd moved from fantasy to action. I returned home a few days later, and didn't tell anyone what I'd done. I was the biggest hypocrite in the world, writing a book to end abuse of runaways, while becoming guilty of the same myself. How could I be so fucked up?

Within a month of returning to Colorado I completed the first draft of this book and sent it to forty-eight prospective publishers. I went on a trip to Mexico to walk the beaches and think things through.

When I got there I again became overwhelmed with my loneliness. I saw couples making love in the surf and only felt worse. I left the coast and headed to the interior, to a city called Merida. Merida had over a million residents, virtually none of whom were white or English speaking. I couldn't communicate well with anyone and grew even more insanely alienated. Again, I needed someone to hold me. Again I hired a prostitute.

She was a Mexican girl. Other than the names of American rock groups, she didn't speak a word of English, and I only knew about three hundred words of Spanish. When I got her back to my hotel, she and I undressed. This time I couldn't go through with it. She had a fever and was shivering. I covered her with blankets and we tried to communicate, using a Spanish/English dictionary to look up one word at a time.

In the course of the next two hours I discovered that like the other girl, she was fifteen and a runaway. She'd been raped by her boyfriend and had gone to the police for help. They laughed at her and sent her home. Her boy-"friend" raped her again. She ran a hundred miles to the nearest big city, where I found her. In the two weeks she'd been on her own, she'd prostituted herself five other times.

I managed to tell her how I had been a runaway and prostitute myself when I was fifteen, how my loneliness had driven me to hire her, and how horrible I felt for hurting her this way. I cried and told her one word at a time that she hadn't deserved being raped, that the police should have helped her, that she shouldn't find prostitution her only option, and that the world should be a different kind of place. I told her she didn't have to have sex with me, that I'd still pay her the 300 Nuevo Pesos (about $100) I'd promised, and that I was so sorry.

She reached out and held me. We both shivered, she from fever and me from release, from finally telling someone the truth. I knew that somehow, I'd begun healing from even this part of me, the part that could repeat what had been done to me. We kept holding each other and eventually made love, not as a prostitute/client, but as two lonely people finding a moment of understanding and love in each other. At least this is what I felt. We drifted to sleep experiencing a few illusory hours of safety and comfort in each other's arms.

Then we awoke to reality. I wanted to rescue her, but didn't know how. I didn't understand Mexico enough to help her, and I couldn't stay. I also couldn't bring her to my home in the United States — I had no idea how to get her across the border. I gave her most of my money and left her to survive on her own.

When I returned to Colorado, I felt like I'd at least turned the experience of hiring a prostitute into something more positive than it might have been. Still, I was too afraid to tell anyone about it yet. Who could understand? Who wouldn't hate me? I vowed that no matter how desperate and alone I felt, I'd never use another desperate runaway again. Somehow I would deal with my issues of loneliness, power, violence, and dominance.

I would also deal with my economic reality. After a year of writing, I was seventeen thousand dollars in debt. I found a job that utilized my degree and kept my debt from growing while I waited for publishers to begin a bidding war for my book. In the following months I received forty-eight rejection letters, most saying I wrote well, but the publishers didn't know how they'd market the book. One editor suggested I try rewriting and then publish it myself.

With all the problems I had, I still felt sharing my story and advice was important. I couldn't give up because of a few dozen rejections. Hell, if I quit that easily I wouldn't have survived my teen years. Driven, I began rewriting and built the foundation to make A Blooming Press Co a reality.

I also started being more honest with myself, and began using my diary and poetry to work through the violence within. Something wonderful and amazing began to happen. As I stopped trying to deny my violent fantasies, I found ways to accept this part of myself. Simultaneously, the violence quickly began to subside and lose its power over me.

Soon I began talking with others, and found I wasn't alone in having these kinds of fantasies. Not even close.

Huge entertainment industries have been built on feeding people a torrential river of physically and sexually abusive images. Millions of people voraciously consume them. A look at the covers of thousands of tapes in the video stores confirms this. Violence, especially to women, sells, and sells big.

Feeling slightly safer with these insights, I took a chance and risked sharing my dark side with others. I was sick of feeling alone, a prisoner to my secrets. Even though dealing with them in my diary had lessened their power over me, I knew I wouldn't be truly free until I had no more secrets. Each person who praised my efforts and intentions with this book without knowing the whole story only made me feel more of a hypocrite.

To my amazement, none of the friends I told about my darker side rejected me. In the past few months I've grown strong enough to go one final step and begin sharing about having hired prostitutes. I have still found acceptance. By putting this here in my book, I now have no more secrets. People may accept or reject me, but at least telling the truth has set me free.

Why, when everything was starting to go well for me, did I begin to develop this dark side? Was it simply the natural result of having been abused? Is violence a core part of being human? Was society beginning to rub off on me, the violence merely a product of my environment? Or perhaps I had become so used to feeling guilty and ashamed, that a part of me couldn't handle the acceptance and praise I began to receive in college; maybe developing these secrets was an unconscious way of continuing to be the bad boy I'd always been told I was.

Whatever the cause of my dark side, I know I don't want the accompanying burden of shame and guilt. I want to be centered, honest, and decent. I don't want to perpetuate the cycles of violence and abuse I was exposed to. Acknowledging and facing these negative forces makes it that much more possible.

I will have to continue to work on myself to make sure I don't let that dark seed grow, nurturing instead my healthier tendencies. Knowing at least that I am only one out of the billions of hurt people who have been infected with violence helps give me the strength to face my inner demons without judging myself too harshly. And the more I face them, the less power they hold. The reason I believe people were able to abuse me, is in part due to their never healing their own wounds, never growing strong enough to deal with their own inner demons.

Sadly, I still don't enjoy good relationships with either of my parents. My mom and I stopped speaking when I shared how this book deals with my prostitution; she told me I should be ashamed of myself, and I told her I didn't want a relationship with her until she could accept me for who I am, without judgment and shame. My dad accepted me when I told him what the book deals with, even wished me luck. But when I went to visit him in Florida last week, I ended up in a verbal fight with his wife, culminating with her slapping me across the face and kicking me out of her and my father's home. He blames me.

Ten years after running away, and a mere few days from sending this book off to press, my family relationships still haven't healed. Without compromising who I am and accepting verbal abuse as a way of life, I have no idea how to change this. It feels more important to respect myself, reject abuse, and be alone if I must. This seems crucial to healing.

God, do I want parents who love and accept me, as me. Not having this hurts more than words can say. For now, however, I must (and do) find my family elsewhere.

All of this life history comes together in who I have become. Like most survivors of abuse and the streets, I am exceptionally strong in some areas, unusually weak in others. Without intending it, I have often found myself taking or being given a leadership role in the various activist groups I've joined. I am driven to do my best to help change things for the better and my energy and experience pours out in group settings. Sometimes it is even too much.

In the course of growing up I have repeatedly experienced the power and privilege being an educated white man (even a young one) gives me in this culture; it is my sincere hope to use this privilege to effect positive change. As an abused child and as a runaway in this society, I also experienced lack of power. Remembering this helps me be more sensitive to others who lack power themselves.

Surviving has made me fortunate enough to recognize the special privilege that comes simply with being male in the United States. I don't believe most men, especially white men, are truly consciously aware of their disproportionate power. Having had no experiences to the contrary, or blocking out the painful ones from their childhood, they can't comprehend its absence. They are blind.

Even with my insights and improved sensitivity I've already managed to repeat some of the abuses which I received. Still, I have come a long way.

One of the most profound results of my growth has been a redefinition of the very concept of "power." Our society teaches power is the ability to control people and monetary wealth. I have come to see through this farce. For me, true power is more the ability to be honest, to face all beings including myself with respect, love, and compassion. The wealth I am now concerned about cannot be measured in terms of money. It is to be found in feeling humbly grounded and centered, in establishing friendship and community, in enjoying life and the simple beauties of the world around, and in reaching beyond myself to give and facilitate other's finding similar power.

Currently my goal is to continue to work towards healing myself and add my piece towards healing our society. With all the personal healing I've managed, I still have a long way to go. So does our society.

It is, of course, far easier to look without and see the many areas in which our society is diseased. Such externalizing of energies is very natural for people, especially men it seems. It almost always feels safer to cast one's critical eye without, to see what is wrong with everything else. Still, with all the work needed without, an equally huge labor must be directed within. The rewards are enormous. Yet there are many levels to work through and it is important not to get self-righteous because of a little progress or a few new insights. Healing ourselves and society will require a long, humble, compassionate effort.

As I continue my journey, I'd like to work with others to help find and promote healthy approaches to treat the underlying problems which cause so many of the symptoms most of us are concerned about. The symptoms include running away, abuse and dominance, poverty and homelessness, frequent war, destruction of the global environment, and many other diseases.

The deeper problems seem to stem from the lenses we humans look through when we attempt to figure out what to do. Though they usually remain unseen, our lenses filter our reality in a way designed to help us make sense of our surroundings; unfortunately, these lenses also blind us to important aspects of reality, by filtering out plenty of important information.

Working with others, I desire to develop a more profound understanding of alternative lenses and approaches to problem solving in order to accelerate needed personal and societal change.

It has taken two long years to put this book together. Hopefully my effort will act as a vital seed, spawning healthy growth that far exceeds the expenses incurred in writing it. In any case, however, it has been well worth writing, simply in terms of how doing so has changed me. Focusing my energy inside to sort this period out has helped free me from a burden of debilitating shame and anger I wasn't even aware I carried. I feel much better now.

So what are my next steps? I'll continue to follow up on this book, perhaps going on tour to speak about my experiences and advocate for change. I'll continue to work on myself, seeking inner peace. I'll continue to study and listen. I'll write other books sharing what I learn with whoever wants to read them. I'll have fun, and even fall in love with someone who loves me back, if I'm lucky. But whatever I end up doing, I simply want to continue healing and growing along with the society that birthed me. There is nothing better to do, and directly or not, I'd like to do it with you.

"Kudos to the Warrior"

By Evan Cutler

Uncovering the violence within
tearing, churning, bound by the forbidden
feelings of lust and drive
and guilt and shame.

A beast lies within,
roaring and full of a passionate,
cheerful anger.

Kudos to the warrior eh?
Salute! to the slayer of daemons...
but never our own, eh?

When ...
if you get that far
if *I* get that far
the praise-layer will do it quietly
no-one need ever know.

But the daemons live their vibrant death
tied up in twin ropy vines
of joyful, rapturous, carnage
and pitteriing pattering peating beats of
paranoid stealth.

So good at being stealthy
that the evil hardly gets to leak;
dammed up so damn tight
and just around the corner from the spring source,
so that multiple mechanisms must be devised
to prevent the ultimate explosion.

Racing against nature
to build the dam higher and stronger
knowing it will hold only while I keep busy building.
And when I finally let go...

Whoosh!!!
The devil force will surge forth
entirely intimidating
rushing to merge with the sea of tranquility
like it is supposed to
wreaking a brief carnage along the way
to that which grew in the formerly safe places
along what was once merely the trickling streambed of violence.

All that is now washed away
obliterated
and the daemon forces continue
and do merge
causing the peaceful places to boil
exploding stormy new life clouds of fire and water;

and the concentric gyrations,
echoes of the freed wanton
spread and rumble and rage;

and the dam builder
if not destroyed by the explosions
takes glee
free again to dance in the rain and the wind.

In time
a new creature may thrive and arrive
may see the shattered bone fragments of the stealthy idiot
or the echoes of the dancing fool

and know better ways
easier ways
than dam-building.

Reflections

Scars:

I still bear scars from the traumas I endured as a runaway, especially while at Sunrise house. Much more so than from what I went through in the two months before. Though there were some high points that month, and plenty of moments when I wasn't being hurt, the wounds incurred went deep. The scars are still sensitive, and when brushed or stirred, reflexive feelings of shame, self-doubt, embarrassment, and a real urge arises to avoid mentioning them to anyone.

Still, it's what I went through during this last month that drove me to risk sharing my story in the first place. This is the part that seems most important to tell. Why? Because I'm not the only one with these kinds of scars. In the course of being a runaway, especially the second time, I met too many other kids who were going through similar experiences. I still meet them; they fill the all-night coffee shops in my town today.

If it has been hard for me to retouch these wounds, then it has got to be even more difficult for most other survivors. Most are far less lucky than I. Each and every day of the ten years I've survived since that summer has borne silent witness to over a thousand more children gaining their own set of scars. And far too many of them have died in the process.

I've learned, slowly, that the only way to truly begin healing my set of hurts was to talk about them. Overcoming the shame and guilt which kept me quiet has been the hardest part. Yet once I began taking the plunge and shared my story with people who could listen empathetically, the shame and guilt began to melt away.

Whoever it was that said "the truth will set you free," clearly knew what they were talking about.

Church Con:

When I began this book, I returned to Florida to retrace my journey and jog my memories of that summer. On this trip I found the Church of Saint Brendan, the church I'd conned out of a bus ticket, and stopped to see if anybody remembered me after so many years. To my surprise, the office manager, Margaret, actually did. She recalled they were really worried about me at the time, having believed my story of being mugged on the way to see my grandparents. Confirming my own memories, she recalled how the church bought me a bus ticket to Daytona Beach for about forty dollars, and one of the men there took me out for a hamburger and fries on the way to the station. Margaret called in the "Father," and he, too, remembered me after all those years.

I sheepishly offered to repay them the forty dollars. They wouldn't hear of it. The Father said it would be better to make a donation to my own church; they were happy enough to have me come back years later and let them know I'd survived okay.

Thanking Margaret and the Father for their kindness so far back, I told them a little about my background at the time. I explained how I'd felt guilty about lying to them, but was too afraid they might have turned me in as a runaway to have risked the truth. I simply wasn't ready to return home yet, and though obtained under false pretenses, their help had allowed me to avoid hitchhiking across the state.

Margaret replied that they have suffered much better, more outlandish con jobs than the one I pulled. They just felt thankful I had come back to let them know I was okay, even if it was eight and a half years later. She explained how they'd helped hundreds of people over the years, but rarely heard from them again. By returning to share some of what had happened to me after they put me on that bus, I'd given them a special gift, a reason to keep on giving.

Molestation By Greg:

A decade later, my recollections of the first sexual incident with Greg, when he forced my hand onto his penis, is still one of the hardest things to deal with from that summer. More than any other event this marked a turning point, a transition. I went from being someone who managed to keep all his walls around him, to someone who was caving in under the insanity of it all.

In the course of all my previous molestation experiences I'd been able to keep my integrity, rewarding none of the perpetrators with permission to enter a sexual realm of interaction. Yet, I've thought, what did it matter that I'd fought off all those other molestation attempts, if I was only to succumb at some point anyway? To make matters worse, I felt like this time with Greg it was truly my fault. If I hadn't smoked the pot, if I hadn't let Greg start massaging me, if I'd only told him to "STOP!" before it was too late, then maybe none of it would have happened.

Yes, Greg forced my hand, literally, but he hadn't forced the massage onto me. I felt like it was my fault, and I felt ashamed.

Homophobia (Illogical Fear of Homosexuals and/or Homosexuality):

My sense of shame was compounded because of the fact it was a man who had done this to me: a boy. If I'd been a girl I still might have felt some shame, but perhaps not to the same extent. At least males and females are "supposed" to get it on together. But men and boys, or even men and men, are not. It is forbidden in this society. This gave me more to be ashamed of.

It didn't matter that I personally felt it was okay for two willing, consenting adults of whatever gender to do whatever they wanted with each other. Yes, that was fine for other people, but a part of me still didn't buy that. A part of me bought the social conditioning that says doing anything "gay" is doing the very worse thing possible.

In elementary, middle, and high schools, calling someone a "faggot," a "queer," a "homo(sexual)," or "gay" was one of the most injurious insults you could offer. It was a way of saying, "you are a non-person." Someone hurling those labels at you was asking for a fight, they were challenging your personhood, saying you were less than them and thereby worthy of being stepped upon.

In school, we all had to learn how to be afraid of anyone possibly calling us by those labels. To protect ourselves, not only would we avoid expressing our sexuality that way, but we wouldn't do anything that could be remotely inferred as something a gay person would do. For boys this included things like being nice to each other, showing emotion (especially sadness or tears), or even hugging friends. The only time it seemed okay for boys to hug was after proving themselves athletically on the sports playing field, showing themselves to be "real men." To be fair, these rules aren't universal, but I witnessed them at nine of the ten pre-collegiate schools I attended before dropping out.

Well, there I was. After what had happened with Greg, the very worst insult that could be hurled at a kid in school, especially a boy, could be hurled accurately at me. Hadn't I just had sex with a guy? It didn't matter that I didn't like what had happened, didn't want it to happen in the first place, or would have undone it if I could. I still felt ashamed, revolted at myself.

This one event did for my store of inner strength what pulling a plug from a full bathtub does to its store of water. From then on what was left of my energy and resistance began to drain away. Sure, there had already been a slow leak in my tub. I was already wearing out after the daily litany of traumas such as living in a garbage chute closet, my multiple run-aways from police authorities, eating unhealthy food, living outside, and dealing with one molester after another.

But if anything did, being molested by Greg accelerated the depletion of my strength. I was heading for empty. Knowing no words to explain this to myself, having no way to explain it to anyone else, a part of me knew it was all down hill from then on.

Ten years later, I am armed with an understanding of the concepts of child abuse, child molestation, and adult-child power dynamics. Now, I can look back and intellectually say to myself "Hey! This Greg guy had no business doing anything to you in the first place! Nobody can fairly condemn you for what happened; if they must blame someone, it should be this man, and all the others who were inappropriate with you!"

Yet, even though I know this intellectually, a part of me still feels the shame for what happened. If I looked at the same scenario with anyone else involved, I would feel sadness and pity for them. I would not blame or accuse them of wrongdoing. And yet I have been unable to give myself the same slack; there is still that part of me that hurts. Regardless of how much I intellectually understand what happened with Greg as child abuse and molestation, this part of me continues to feel embarrassed and ashamed, as though I am, even now, a bad boy because of what happened.

Here we can get back again to how I'm one of the lucky ones. Even with all this shame I still feel, at least I survived, and now have the context to say that if it happened to somebody else I wouldn't want them to feel any shame. Thanks to this context, my feelings of shame are surely less profound then other boys-become-men who managed to survive, but not as well as I have.

Insidiousness of the Child Molesting Culture:

It is insidious how this child-molesting culture draws in its children. Once hooked by the shame experienced from a first molestation, they are trapped in a way. The more they struggle to escape, the harder the molesters fight to reel them in.

In some cases, such as in the bedroom of someone who will rape you if you don't comply with their sexual demands, the only way of surviving long enough to become un-hooked is to go with the pull long enough and fast enough to get a moment's slack. You actually have to participate in bringing yourself closer to your perpetrator to develop an opportunity to become free. What makes this so insidious, is that by going along with the perpetrator, you start to feel like you're the person who's responsible for the whole thing in the first place. You helped yourself jump right into the perpetrator's net. It doesn't matter that this cooperating may be the only way to save your strength to get free later. You still end up blaming yourself.

Screwed Up Affirmation:

Making the whole situation even more insidious is that by giving into this kind of molestation, you get a sort of affirmation. Especially in a molestation kind of culture such as existed in Sunrise House. Though there is a part of you that feels shame after the fact, there is another part which says "I'm doing good, people are smiling at me, people are being nice to me." Greg turned out to be the first person that summer to hug me. As disconcerting as the situation was, I needed some hugs.

But the affirmation was confusing. The good feelings gained from this sort of affirmation were actually pretty pathetic, not unlike those a little puppy seems to feel at a college keg party when people are cheering it on to drink some beer. Beer drinking is clearly an unhealthy behavior for puppies. Part of the puppy may even know this, but with all the people cheering it on, it feels like it is doing the right thing. Have you ever seen a dog with that confused look on its face, where it's kind of happy about what it is doing, but also seems to be a little embarrassed? I have.

In Sunrise house it was safe to get that kind of affirmation, to have a man hold onto and hug me. In fact, it was the only form of nurturing available. As most of the people there were gay, there was no danger of anyone declaring "faggot!" and punching or spitting on me. To get the affirmation I needed, I learned to speak in the language of my environment.

Gay Culture Should Not Be Confused With Molestation Culture:

I need to make it clear that I wasn't molested simply because I was living with gay men. Just as there are plenty of "straight" (heterosexual) men and women who manage not to molest children, there are also plenty of gay people who don't molest. Let there be no confusion: *Not all homosexuals molest children!!!*

Child molestation isn't an issue of gender attraction, it is an issue of power. The fact is something on the order of one in four American girls are sexually molested, and the people doing it most often are straight men. Sadly, there are plenty of homes in which straight people create a child molestation culture like that which existed in Sunrise house, with the only difference being that the adults are molesting opposite gender kids. There is nothing wrong or perverted about being gay, straight, bisexual, or asexual. What is wrong is when adults use their unequal power to extract sexual interaction from children.

I feel gifted to have friends of all sexual orientations, and as far as I know none of them are child molesters. It is a dreadful shame to me that ours is a homophobic society. It treats some of my friends with hate and disrespect because of what they share in their private lives and spaces, because of what they feel in their hearts.

My gay and bisexual friends are just as beautiful to me as my straight ones. All are human beings, with positive and negative attributes like anyone else, but the added hate and violence they must endure brings such unnecessary suffering to their lives. It is unfair. I will do my very best to support making our world just as safe and welcoming for them as it is for me. There is no shame in people loving and sharing each other as they feel fit.

Another Example of Screwed Up Situational Affirmation:

When I ran away the second time, just over a year later, I became friends with John, a black man who had grown up in the racially segregated urban ghettos of Oakland, California. John spoke two languages. As a boy he'd been identified as a "smart kid" by a liberal affirmative action program in the neighboring, mostly white town of Berkeley, California. Consequently, he was invited to attend Berkeley's affluent, predominantly white, middle-class schools, five miles away, instead of the underfunded ones in his family's neighborhood. There he learned to speak, read, and write in white middle-class English, "Whitespeak." Simultaneously, he learned not to speak (around white people) his native black ghetto-class English, "Blackspeak."

One day I realized John knew both languages after hearing him make two phone calls in rapid succession: the first to a white business owner in Berkeley, a client of John's promotions business, and the second to his mother in Oakland. In five short seconds, my friend shifted from speaking like a college-educated white person, to sounding like an uneducated black person.

In the first call he said something like, "We have scheduled the Michael Jackson impersonator to perform in front of your store during Friday's lunch hour, when we expect to achieve peak exposure to new clientele." A few moments later, on the phone with his mom, he said something like, "Um-hunh. We gonna go store on de way back and git dat bread you dun ax for."

Why couldn't my friend speak his native "black language" in the middle-class schools? I'm sure he was told that it was "the wrong way" to speak, improper grammar and such. The way his family spoke was something to be ashamed of, to be failed for. But if he spoke the "Whitespeak" he was taught in the Berkeley schools when he returned to his family in the Oakland ghetto, he would be similarly laughed at, scorned, and feared.

When I went with John to visit his family, his aunt asked me "What's yo' baggedy white ass doing hea? Why don't yo go back where yuh belon'?" Now I appreciate her frankness. In essence she was asking: "If I can't go into your neighborhood and be myself, then why should you be allowed into mine?" After a few visits I learned to speak a little Blackspeak myself, because that's the way I had to speak to be affirmed there.

Gay Language:

Adaptable as I can be, staying in the house on Sunrise Avenue gave me an opportunity to learn the "gay language." One, which if I spoke in the general public, I'd probably be beaten up by strangers who justified their attacks by labeling me a "queer." In Sunrise house it was not only okay, but preferable to speak in this "Gayspeak." It was a language of effeminate flirtation. The most pronounced forms of Gayspeak were exhibited by those assuming the role commonly known as being a "Queen."

MDA Max was the most extreme example at Sunrise house. I never figured out what he did for a living exactly. He said he was some sort of engineer. Looking back on it, it seems he was actually dealing drugs. He most likely gave out the free samples of MDA (also known as MDMA, Ecstasy, The Love Drug, etc. (see story)) in order to get people interested in coming back to buy more.

To Max, being a Queen required acting like a snob. He would look down on everything as though he sat on some high in the sky throne. His voice sounded like an aristocratic country club woman, something over sixty years old, except that instead of bragging on about his most recent exotic vacation or his fancy car Max bragged about his sexual conquests. Max exaggerated all the stereotypical high-society female haughtiness, far beyond what any woman would have exhibited. Some in the gay community surely despised Max's effeminate style, but many others seemed to hold it in high esteem, finding themselves either envious of his ability, or attracted by it.

Prostitution:

In this society, and many others as well, prostitutes have been looked down upon, scorned as criminals performing one of the worst acts possible. People don't generally express much pity for the prostitutes. To the contrary, it is quite common to hear folks joke about and ridicule them. I noticed several of my friends and acquaintances casually doing so while I worked on this book; of course, at the time, they didn't know I'd been one once.

On the other hand, there isn't much discussion in our culture about the people who hire prostitutes, most of which are white, middle-class men, members of one of the most privileged sectors of our society. Why doesn't our repertoire of humor include stabs at these men? After all, there wouldn't be any prostitutes if there weren't hordes of people out there to hire them.

Most teen prostitutes (around 95%) are runaways, and most of these were suffering in abusive situations before becoming such. How can we deny what these youth went through, before even leaving home, had a lot to do with their becoming prostitutes in the first place? Why and how can we joke about them? How can you laugh while someone else does?

On a more personal note, my experiences both as a prostitute and a client have all been damaging. While I currently know several prostitutes who claim the work is more than worth their while, I find it very hard to relate. They act unscathed, but I feel my own wounds and don't know how they can be. They contend all work is prostitution, and at least sex work pays well.

As a prostitute myself, I was able to detach and view the work merely as something that had to be done, like washing a toilet. However, no matter how far I separated myself from what I was doing, I couldn't really avoid being and feeling hurt. I was there.

As a client, I felt worse. Yes, I wanted to be close to a soft, warm, loving woman, but paying for that kind of attention made the experience empty. Knowing the power dynamics and desperation that drove the girls to sell themselves only made me feel more rotten.

I hope we can see the day when kids don't see prostitution as their best option for survival and adults don't feel they need to pay someone to care for them.

Drugs:

Though I found most of my drug use to be an unhealthy behavior, with unhealthy consequences, I can't unilaterally condemn drug use altogether. I learned from my drug experiences, and feel using them has expanded my perspective and opened my mind in some beneficial ways.

Many cultures have institutionalized what I might consider healthy drug use for various spiritual and ritual practices. Certain Native American tribes have used peyote and other hallucinogens for vision quests and other purposes. And Jews and Catholics include alcohol in many of their rituals. Coffee, alcohol, and Valium are mainstream drugs, openly and legally promoted, sold, and consumed by millions of Americans. It seems illogical and overly close-minded to blindly assume that all uses of drugs are "bad."

Perhaps that first time I'd done MDA it had actually been helpful, for it acted as a catalyst, leading me to call my family for the first time. But the price was higher than it should have been. The drug wore at my body and left me feeling drained and depressed. Or then again, was I depressed all along, yet simply denying it? Why couldn't I feel love for my family without doing a drug? Why did it take the temporary euphoria to remove my inhibitions about first contact?

As you can see, a lot of good questions arise. If a drug can be used to help one heal and grow, to allow one to make connections they couldn't before, then it may be worth consuming. Certainly the legalized pharmaceutical and psychiatric industries advocate such. The drug problem in our society seems to come not so much from the innate qualities of the drugs themselves, but from the way they are too often used in an overly casual, flippant, and escapist manner.

I am certain that the so called "War on Drugs" is a non-productive use of energy. Apparently, about one percent of American males are currently imprisoned for drug related offenses. Yet if you ask a random sampling of high-school students across America, you'll find that drugs are just as available now, as they were ten years ago. Meanwhile, our government is carrying on little publicized military actions throughout Central and South America, purportedly aimed at destroying the drugs at their source. I suspect the real aim of these actions is to make money for the defense industry and to keep the third world peasants from organizing in their own interests.

Whatever the motivations, if the same energies now being spent on "law enforcement" and punitive actions were redirected towards drug counseling and education, I would expect a far more positive result. Instead of encouraging people to look within to see why there is so much demand for drugs in the first place, our national policy has been to look without and point blaming fingers at scapegoats we can then punish. Legal and illegal drugs alike will continue to be abused as long as we live in a society with so much economic disparity, hate, violence, abuse, and alienation; disease, in short.

Legalization:
Though it is currently an unpopular one, my opinion is that all drugs should be legalized. The fact is, as Prohibition did with alcohol, drug prohibition doesn't stop drug use; it merely makes it a bigger business with higher costs for all involved. As past gangs (Al Capone's for example) fought their turf wars over alcohol distribution zones in the nineteen-thirties, today's gangs fight and kill to enforce their distribution rights. The death and suffering toll is much too high.

Aside from taking this business away from criminals, legalizing drugs has a host of other benefits.

First, it will lower the price. Pot shouldn't cost any more to produce than tobacco. Produced efficiently, cocaine doesn't need to cost more than a few tens of dollars a pound. LSD can also be made for pennies a dose.

Second, it will reduce drug-related crime. With lower prices, drug addicts will find it far less necessary to commit crime to support their habits. In turn, they will less often resort to the shooting, mugging, and thieving currently employed.

Third, society as a whole will save. With less crime, there will be fewer victims. We'll also have a corresponding decrease in criminal arrest, prosecution, and incarceration rates. The savings there alone will be enormous.

Fourth, the drugs can be taxed. Even with a thousand percent tax on marijuana and cocaine, the retail price would still be negligible. We could use the billions of new tax dollars for whatever we wish. I'd vote for funding counseling services, runaway shelters, and educational opportunities. And if we are really so against drugs in this society, we could use the tax monies generated by their sale for drug prevention, counseling, and treatment services, which are currently needed, but far underfunded.

Fifth, with the decrease in crime and the utilization of tax monies to fund good and needy causes, people will grow healthier and happier. This will cut down on the demand for drugs in the first place, as people will feel less need to escape reality.

Six, legalization will allow the ensurement of quality control over the drugs that are sold. Health standards can be set to prevent the sale of drugs laced with harmful toxics like strychnine (rat poison), which is currently used to "cut" street drugs. With good quality control, fewer people will become sick or brain damaged from using drugs, and this too will save societal resources, such as those currently spent on caring for vegetable-people.

Seventh, who needs a seventh point, with six others that are already so good?

Who will suffer from drug legalization? All the criminals, lawyers, prison and mental institution guards, police officers, and military professionals who one way or another make damned good money from the drug trade. Well, let them plant trees or do something else useful. We will be able to afford paying them well with all the money we'll save.

What about all the people who will abuse drugs? Well, allow them to do as they wish, but hold them accountable if their actions hurt others. A free society is supposed to be about self-determination. Let the individuals who can't handle drug legalization screw up their lives if they want to. I'd bet my life there will be fewer problems caused by drug addicts ten years after legalization than there are now.

Volunteering at a Restrictive Runaway Shelter:

When I was twenty-three and had finished college I volunteered at the runaway shelter in Fort Collins, Colorado. This place was so restrictive kids weren't allowed to go to the bathroom without first asking a staff member to pull out a key and unlock the door for them. There was a daily schedule of compulsory activities all the inmates, I mean runaways, had to go through. They weren't allowed outside unaccompanied by a staff member. They couldn't do anything without permission, and the staff was arbitrary about when and how they gave it.

On my second night as a volunteer I witnessed some major problems. One of the boy runaways was in the administrative area being questioned by the police. He was about to be arrested and taken to jail for some crime he'd been accused of. None of the other kids were allowed to enter that area without permission.

A young girl who was staying there told another staff member, call him John, that the boy had her most prized necklace. She'd loaned it to him to wear for the day and was afraid she'd never get it back. She asked John if he would either go up front and get it himself, or let her.

John made no effort to be nice to her or address her concern. He told her he was busy, and she should just go sit down in the other room. He didn't appear busy. In fact, he was standing right where he'd been for the fifteen minutes before that, doing nothing.

The girl started crying, saying John didn't understand, the necklace was her most treasured possession. It had been given to her by her best friend, who she couldn't see any more. The necklace was all she had to remind her of the one good thing in her life.

All John or the girl had to do was walk through that door and ask the boy for the necklace. It would have taken John less than a minute. Instead he got angry and ordered the girl to go away.

The door to the office was unlocked, and I could see through the window that the police were off to one side talking with each other, while the boy just sat meekly in his chair. All that stopped the girl from going through the door herself (or out of the shelter entirely for that matter) was her respect for adult authority. She was a good girl with a reasonable request.

I asked her what the necklace looked like, and walked through that door myself. The police didn't care, and I quickly found out the boy didn't have the necklace after all. It was sitting on a desk in a counselor's office down the hall. I got it and returned it to the girl, thus making her day.

A little later I found out the shelter was in the midst of a crisis. The night before, a girl had been sexually molested by one of the boys staying there. The staff didn't know how to handle it, but decided to separate all the girls from all the boys that night. They pulled a divider wall between the two sides of the big living room and kept the kids from speaking with each other. Because the shelter had a policy of client confidentiality, the staff felt they were unable to tell the kids why they were being separated.

The kids started getting upset and angry. They considered themselves friends, and felt they were being punished by this separation for no reason. When they asked why they were being divided, the staff wouldn't explain, instead throwing their questions back at them: "Well, Tommy, why do you think were doing this?" One of the kids told a staff member that at least half of the kids were planning a mass run from the shelter that night.

A little later the kids and staff had their nightly "group meeting." Instead of the normal procedure of having one big group, the staff decided to have separate boys' and girls' groups. I sat in on the boys' side.

The boys went around in a circle and shared how they were feeling. They were open and honest, saying they felt closed in and punished, and they wanted a no-bullshit explanation of why. I was aware of the staff's reasons, but was in training and remained silent. I watched round after round of the staff member not being honest while the kids were. He was a nice guy in a hard position, and didn't know what to do.

Then one of the kids looked at me and said, "Evan, you were a runaway once. How would you feel in our shoes?"

I told him my truth: I thought they weren't being served fairly or well, the system imposed upon them seemed too repressive, and that having been a cigarette addict at their age I wouldn't have stayed a night under such circumstances. I said I thought they were being treated like they were fifth graders and deserved more respect and honesty than they were getting. The meeting went on for a while longer with the kids never getting an honest explanation for their treatment, then broke up so the kids could get ready for lights-out.

Twenty minutes later a staff member told me a group of boys were having a meeting in their room and wouldn't talk with any staff member other than me. They asked if I would go speak to the kids. It was embarrassing, being picked over staff who had worked there for years while it was only my second day, but I went.

When I entered the room the seven boys told me they were indeed considering a mass run. One of them knew of a party going on that night in an abandoned house and figured they could all get stoned, lay low, and crash there, then go their separate ways the next morning. The shelter had a policy that kids could leave if they wanted, but a half hour later their absence would be reported to the police. The boys reckoned thirty minutes was more than enough of a head start.

It was February, and about twenty degrees out. I asked them if the house was heated. It wasn't. I asked what would happen to them if they got caught. Two of the kids had been court-ordered to the runaway shelter, and would have been sent to Brighton, a youth prison in Colorado, for violating their probation. I asked what Brighton was like. One of the other kids had been there once and said it was much worse than the shelter. I asked what they would do when morning came. Most of them had no ideas.

We talked for about twenty minutes and in the end I told them it was up to them, of course, but that if they didn't have some plan they were likely to freeze all night, and probably get caught in the near future. I pointed out they had nothing to lose by getting a good, warm night's sleep first, then, if they still wanted to run, they could go the next day. I empathized with their position, and wished I had some cure-all suggestion, but I didn't. Lights-out was called, and it was time for me to leave.

I was scheduled to come back on Wednesday, three nights later. On Tuesday I received a phone call from the shelter director, saying that the shelter had reappraised its volunteer program and determined they didn't have the resources to train new volunteers. She told me not to come in on Wednesday after all. She wasn't being honest with me. I argued that no one had taken an effort to train me at all, so discontinuing their program wouldn't change anything.

Then she said the real reason was that I had a Bachelors of Science degree in Environmental Health and their policy was to only use people with Psychology degrees. I pointed out that the other two volunteers I'd met on my first day were only second year psychology students, not graduates, and that though I didn't have a psychology degree, I had studied psychology, counseling, and abuse issues. My ex-wife had been a counselor at a battered women's shelter and for four years had daily shared what she learned and experienced. Further, I'd actually been a runaway, and had a lot to offer simply from having lived through the kinds of problems their kids were dealing with.

The director couldn't argue with that, and said, actually, the real reason they didn't want me there was they felt I hadn't dealt with all of my own issues yet. Hadn't? I'd been dealing with my issues my whole life and was writing a book on them. By now I knew that whatever "the real reason" was, she couldn't be counted on to tell me. The truth was most likely that I was too honest and failed to respect their disrespect for the kids. I was very hurt, as I felt I had a lot to offer.

I asked if the kids ever did the mass run the staff was so afraid of a few nights earlier. They hadn't.

To be fair, some kids may need and want the kind of restrictive environment I witnessed. Yet I must be blind to that need, as I don't relate in the slightest.

Name Changes:

To protect myself from innocent and guilty people alike, I have done my best to change most of the names of people and places described in this book. Though all the events related here-in are true to the best of my recollection, some of the people involved might feel embarrassed or threatened by my recounting of their participation in these events. If I revealed their true identities, they would be perfectly eligible to enjoin me in lawsuits disputing my allegations, lawsuits which I lack the energy or will to fight. I would like to see a day when I don't have to change the names and places to protect child abusers and molesters from answering for their actions, solely due to fear that they might retaliate against me. Not wanting to shame anyone, I wouldn't necessarily include names anyway, yet I should be free to recount my experiences at my discretion.

I am Guilty/Giving Back:

Other names and places have been changed to protect another guilty person: myself. I did indeed steal clothing, cigarettes, and food, and in one instance, jewelry from someone's hotel room. I am guilty of and sorry for committing these crimes. If there was some way I could take them back I would. But the past can't be undone. Without the aid of twenty/twenty hindsight, I honestly didn't know how to survive any better on my own as a runaway. My way of making up for those things I did, to give back more than I took, is to share my story and to give half of the profits from this book to create the Fifteen Fund, a charity intended to give runaways a shot at college. (See the second to last page of this book for a description of how it will work.)

My original intention was to donate that share of my proceeds to a fund designed to help locate, investigate, and prosecute child molesters, to get them locked up in jail. That was before a friend of mine pointed out there are over a million people incarcerated in this country, and before recollecting my own, not brief enough experiences in juvenile jail. After deep consideration I really doubt locking up still more people would be an effective use of that money; imprisoning people in such a dehumanizing environment when they will eventually be released will only make the perpetrators that much more perverted and sociopathic. It is an inefficient use of resources.

All too often, those we imprison for perpetrating physical, sexual, and emotional abuse, are people who have been victims of the very same crimes when they were children. What these "criminals" are doing is often simply, and painfully, just a repetition of what had been done to them. Ironically, a 1992 Denver Post article claims that it costs more to keep the average convict in prison each year than it would to send them to Harvard. Yet, in jail, what they tend to learn is how to be even sicker, so much so, that they are more likely than ever to cause havoc and harm when they are eventually released.

Thus, I've concluded that the money generated by this book would be better spent proactively, to create opportunities for runaways to heal and grow, so they won't become the next generation of child molesters and abusers.

Statistics

Please note: This author does not believe in "facts." All of the following statistics have been extracted out of context from a variety of books and articles. Some will seem to contradict others because the methods and population samples used to obtain them varied. They are only included to help emphasize the magnitude of the problems faced by American youth. Take them all with about a teaspoon of salt. Whether the numbers indicated are fair, or would more accurately be ten times higher or lower, they show that far too many children are suffering unnecessarily.

Please see the *Bibliography* for the sources on the information below.

RUNAWAYS AND THROWAWAYS, GENERAL:

450,000 kids ran away from home in 1988. (U.S. Department of Justice, p.4)

1 to 1.5 million kids run away from home each year. (U.S. Department of Justice, p.11)

Of the 1 million runaway children, upwards of 200,000 may become involved in high-risk behavior, such as drug use and prostitution. (Children's Defense Fund, 1986; Haffner, 1987)

Every 26 seconds a child runs away from home. [approximately 1,200,000/year] (McGeady, p.31)

More than two million young people run away from home each year, and the government estimates that number increases continually. (Rosenbaum, p.261)

13% of high school students have run away at some time. An additional 20% contemplated running away. (Miller, p.2)

12,800 children ran away from juvenile facilities in 1988. (Finkelhor, p.11)

There were 127,100 "throwaways" (children kicked out of their homes) in 1988. (Finkelhor, p.4)

500,000 non-runaway children are homeless each year. (Powers, p.xiii)

100,000 American children wake up homeless each morning. (Hatkoff, p.13)

55% of runaways see no social service agency as helpful or appealing. (Miller, p.5)

15% of runaways are unaware of the free food stamp program. (Miller, p.5)

80% of runaways had looked for work prior to running away. (Palenski, p.84)

Two-thirds of runaways run to the home of a friend or relative. (Finkelhor, p.11)

82% of runaways are accompanied by others when running. (Finkelhor, p.11)

10% of runaways go farther than one hundred miles from home. (Finkelhor, p.11)

48% of runaways run more than ten miles from home. (Treanor, p.118)

More than half of runaways travel less than 10 miles away from home. (Rosenbaum, p.261)

36% of runaways ran away previously in the last 12 months. (Finkelhor, p.11)

47% of runaways are female. (Treanor, p.92)

16% of runaways stay away more than one month. (Treanor, p.118)

About seven in ten teen runaways return home or are reunited with their families. The rest fall victim to violence, crime, prostitution, child pornographers, or starvation on the street. (Rosenbaum, p.261)

ABUSE:

It is widely accepted that there are about 1 million cases of child abuse per year; recent studies show actual numbers may be much higher due to the discrepancy between cases and reported actual cases. (Rosenbaum, p.253)

1.6 million children are abused and neglected each year. (Powers, p.xiii)

Every thirteen seconds an American child is reported abused or neglected. [approximately 2,400,000/year.] (Hatkoff, p.13)

Every forty-seven seconds a child is seriously abused or neglected. [approximately 671,000/year] (McGeady, p.31)

Two thousand children were killed by their own parents in 1976 and 200,000 more were beaten badly enough by their parents to require medical treatment. (National Center on Child Abuse, p.2)

Two thousand children die from child abuse each year. (Rosenbaum, p.253)

Five thousand children are buried in unmarked graves annually. (Nation, p.753)

The average age of a child involved in an abusive or neglectful situation is 7.2 years old. (American Association for Protection Children, p.136)

75% of runaway youth are subject to severe maltreatment in the year prior to running. (Powers, p.4)

36% of runaways run because of physical or sexual abuse. 44% leave because of other severe long-term problems. (FYI Reports, p.1)

Thirty to sixty percent of abusing parents say they were abused as children. (Falroth, p.36)

"Hunter et al. (1978) found histories of maltreatment in 90% of a sample of 10 families reported for maltreatment versus only 17% of the 245 not reported." (Iverson, p.44)

70% of adolescent female prostitutes have been beaten by a family member. (Weisberg, p.93)

HEALTH:

24 % of runaways have tried to commit suicide. (Lerner, p.46)

There are 320,000 births to unmarried teenage women each year. (Lerner, p.29)

11 million American children are without health insurance. (Powers, p.xiii)

7 million American children fail to receive routine medical care. (Powers, p.xiii)

Every 67 seconds a teenager has a baby. [approximately 471,000/year]

(McGeady, p.31)

33% of female runaways have been pregnant. (JAMA, p.1360)

About 250,000 teenagers attempted suicide in 1982. (Rosenbaum, p.176)

2.5 million teenagers get some kind of sexually transmitted disease each year. (Rosenbaum, p.152)

It is estimated that one in seven teens will contract an STD. (Grimes)

4.3% of runaways tested HIV positive in 1990.

0.1% of the total teen population tested HIV positive in 1990. (Treanor, p.12)

49% of homeless adolescents feel at least one of their parents has an alcohol problem. (National, p.2)

At least 20 million children live with at least one parent with a serious drinking problem. (Rosenbaum, p.243)

34% of runaways have a history of intravenous drug use. (Lerner, p.46)

SEXUAL MOLESTATION AND EXPLOITATION:

1.2 million children are believed to be involved in sexually exploitive activities each year. (Campagna, p.3)

90% of the nation's sexual abuse goes unreported. (Stavsky, p.xv)

73% of females and 38% of males adolescent runaways enter shelters with a history of sexual abuse. (Lerner, p.43)

1 out of every 10 families may be involved in various forms of incest. (Rosenbaum, p.243)

48% of adolescent female prostitutes were sexually abused within their family. (Weisberg, p.155)

More than half of adolescent female prostitutes have been raped. (Weisberg, p.93)

PROSTITUTION:

95% of adolescent prostitutes have been runaways. (Weisberg, p.100)

At any time there are 600,000 adolescent prostitutes. (Lerner, p.45)

Some place the figure for teen prostitution as high as 1 million. (O'Reilly & Aral, 1988)

14.1 is the average age of runaways first act of prostitution. (Weisberg, p.71)

26% of runaways have been prostitutes. (Lerner, p.46)

40% of runaways engage in some form of hustling (prostitution). (Palenski, p.90)

28% of male and 31% of female homeless teenagers survive by prostitution. (Berkeley, p.2)

43% of adolescent male prostitutes began prostitution during the same year in which they left home. (Weisberg, p.71)

Two-thirds of adolescent male prostitutes have been arrested at least once. (Weisberg, p.75)

72% of adolescent prostitutes believe they had no other way of supporting themselves at the time. (Weisberg, p.100)

The demand for underage females is approximately equal to the demand for adult prostitutes. (Campagna, p.65)

The median age of first sexual experience among adolescent prostitutes is eleven years old. (Weisberg, p.49)

Two-thirds of adolescent male prostitutes are paid for sex between one and seven times per week. (Weisberg, p.60)

68.1% of adolescent male prostitutes have prostituted for more than six months, 51.1% for more than a year, and 27.7% for more than two years. (Weisberg, p.60)

75% of adolescent prostitutes are introduced to prostitution through their peers. (Weisberg, p.155)

Virtually all types of adults solicit adolescents for prostitution. (Campagna, p.91)

In 1988 the going rate for half an hour of oral sex with a 13 or 14-year-old male was between $5 and $20. (Campagna, p.60)

About one billion dollars is spent on prostitution each year in the United States. (Radovsky, p.68)

It costs about $20,000 for a professionally shot one thousand picture pornographic spread of identical twin girls. (Campagna, p.134)

43% of adolescent prostitutes were physically abused by family members. (Weisberg, p.48)

47% of adolescent prostitutes were emotionally abused in their families. (Weisberg, p.47)

38% of adolescent prostitutes have been sexually abused in their home. (Weisberg, p.48)

72% of youth use drugs while engaging in prostitution. (Weisberg, p.58)

29% are regular users of hard drugs. (Weisberg, p.59)

42% of adolescent prostitutes are heavy drinkers. (Weisberg, p.59)

77% of adolescent male prostitutes use marijuana. (Weisberg, p.59)

27% of adolescent male prostitutes have been photographed by a customer. (Weisberg, p.68)

90% of prostitute-pimp relationships last less than a year. 82% last less than three months. (Weisberg, p.103)

68% of adolescent female prostitutes describe their pimp as someone who abuses them physically. (Weisberg, p.106)

Half of all juvenile prostitutes have been pregnant at least once. (Weisberg, p.114)

OTHER RELEVANT STATISTICS:

93,945 juveniles were held in custody in 1989. (Krisberg, p.2)

88% of juveniles in custody are male. (Krisberg, p.2)

Every 8 seconds of every school day, a child drops out of school. [approximately 570,000/year] (McGeady, p.31)

Every thirty seconds a child's parents divorce. [approximately 1,050,000/year] (Family Tree, Inc., p.2)

Every 36 minutes a child is killed or injured by a gun. [approximately 14,500/year] (McGeady, p.31)

Analysis

Realization of Abuse Prevalence:

Parallel to my realizing I'd been abused, and that my abusers had themselves been abused, I also grew more aware of how much abuse is a problem in our society as a whole. Though they surround us each day, the sheer numbers of affected people are astounding! Nearly one in five children are incested. About the same number are physically abused. One in three women are raped. And according to one recent study, up to seventy-five percent of runaways were subjected to severe abuse in the year before running.

Of course not all kids who run away were abused. However there is an undeniable connection between runaways and abuse, as the rates of all forms of abuse are much higher for runaways than the population of youth as a whole. On the other hand, only a fraction of those who are abused actually end up running away. Exact figures are impossible to obtain as many cases of abuse go unrecognized and unreported, but generally accepted estimates of severe child abuse in America range from one to two-and-a-half million cases a year.

Using the word "abuse" may not have enough impact to get my point across here. I'm talking about severe mistreatment. Around two thousand children are killed by their parents each year. According to the National Center on Child abuse, in 1976 two hundred thousand children were beaten by their parents severely enough to require medical treatment. I've seen no indication that these rates have gone down in the years since.

According to other sources, there are similarly disturbing correlations between prostitution and running away, and prostitution and abuse. Not every runaway becomes a prostitute, but remarkably, almost every teen prostitute was a runaway at some point. And most teen prostitutes were severely abused and molested before engaging in prostitution.

It is especially important to realize that a large portion of those people committing the abuse were themselves abused. According to one study, ninety percent of abusers were abused when they were children, while only seventeen percent of non-abusers experienced childhood abuse. In another study, up to sixty percent of abusive parents claimed they were abused as children. Thus, people who were abused as children seem far more likely to become abusers themselves, when they become parents. To end abuse we will need to find ways to break these intergenerational cycles.

Fighting Back: Power Dynamics and Survival:

A major obstacle to the recipient's standing up and talking about their physical, sexual, and verbal abuse, is that the people who are abused are usually those that don't have the power to fight back. Abusers count on this advantage to allow them to get away with their abuse. This power dynamic often keeps people who have been abused from doing anything to fight back until years after they have left the abusive situation.

Unfortunately, what all too often happens is the survivors of abuse forget or deny what they went through; a part of them doesn't want to think about it because it's too painful to recall. "Besides," they may think, "what's the point in confronting my abuser/s now? It's over, right?" Thus their abuse never gets dealt with, their wounds never heal.

But they're wrong. It's never over. Time passes and what do you know, but one day the former victims find themselves in positions of power over others. Something in them causes them to reenact their abuse on some new, innocent, powerless (less powerful) victim. It's like a pathetic script the actors have no idea how to rewrite.

Ever see one of those Twilight Zone episodes where someone relives the same hour over and over and over again, where all they can do is make minor, insignificant variations in their actions, and yet never break free into a new stretch of living? In a way this is just what happens in the cycles of abuse I have just discussed. Except, instead of an individual person doing the reliving, it is the successive generations; the particular actors change roles as they age. This ends up making it harder to become aware the scene keeps repeating, because by the time it does, the individual's role, and thus their viewpoint, has changed.

Breaking Free:

By writing this book and thereby owning part of my own experience of abuse, I'm choosing to do what I can to break out of that pattern.

As lucky and as strong as I've been, I don't yet have enough power to fully fight back against those who abused me. If I did, this book might include more of an explanation of the critical events that led up to my running away. Unfortunately, one of my abusers has already threatened a lawsuit if I write anything perceived as slandering his or her name. I don't have the emotional or financial resources to waste fighting in courts for my right to explain my formative years as I remember and understand them.

But neither am I blindly accepting the abuse. Instead, I am doing what I can, speaking out and telling *my* story. Hopefully, no one can take that right away from me. I will not take any more abuse. And if I can heal enough, neither will I dish it out, which is what survivors tend to do when they don't deal with the pain of what they survived.

Facing the Pain/Healing the Wounds:

And believe me, dealing with my pain hasn't been easy. Standing up for myself and simply facing what happened, hurt; incredibly. Remembering, reliving, and trying to make sense of my abuse involved a kind of agony. Facing the pain was one of the hardest things I have ever done. But a part of me knew that if I didn't apply the energy needed to deal with my wounds and remove the poison still sitting within, they would fester my entire life, never fully healing. Even worse, they would probably become contagious.

In my mind, virtually every person who has been abused, every person who has abused another, and everyone else who knows these people and is aware of what is going on, has been deeply and severely wounded.

What does this mean?

Wounded Society:

It means that in our society, just in terms of physical, sexual, psychological, and emotional abuse, almost everyone is wounded. It makes sense when you think about the human history in this great land now called the United States of America.

This nation had a very violent birth. Some might say it began with European conquerors coming here five hundred years ago and stealing what another people had. The Native Americans have been left with only a small fraction of their original material and cultural wealth. And yet, as much as we want to distance ourselves from that history, we don't deal with that wound. Deny it as we do, that wound still exists. Even today, Native American tribes throughout this country are having to fight to retain what little our ancestors left them. The only thing that has changed is that the Native Americans now fight within the overwhelmingly unequal legal and economic system forcefully imposed upon them, instead of atop the physically bloody battlefields of days past. Resistant as we are to recognizing it, our United States has been based, from the start, upon abusing another people.

Our cultural history of abuse continued with slavery. The slave masters used physical, emotional, and legal coercion to control the thousands upon thousands of kidnapped Africans and their progeny. Slavery is another form of abuse that has not been fully dealt with in our American society, another wound that hasn't been healed. Over a hundred and twenty years after the legal abolishment of slavery in the United States, it is readily apparent that racial equality is far from reality. The new "we," browns, tans, and all colors alike, still struggle under the debilitating burden of a heap of garbage leftover from the slave days. It's going to take a whole lot more than a few laws mandating equality to recycle this waste into something decent.

Our cultural history of abuse has persisted throughout our five century existence, as people emigrated here from every part of the world. In too many cases these newcomers were runaways themselves, coming to the "New World" to escape mis-treatment. Once here, they never learned how to heal from their torturous experiences. Thus, they unconsciously repeated the exact same behaviors, manifesting generation after generation of continued abuse. The new institutions created by the European immigrants perpetuated the old patterns of abuse. Although they physically conquered the Native Americans and African Americans, and severely oppressed the Asian Americans, it would be unfair to make them out to be complete villains; they were victims and survivors as well.

Many of the European immigrants who came to this land were prisoners arrested in Europe and exiled to the New World for failing to pay debts, or for stealing food when they knew of no other way to feed their families. Others were used to working the land in a futile feudal system where all but the bare minimum they needed to survive was commandeered by the aristocracy and the Church. Later, people came to America fleeing a futile industrial system, where once again all but the bare minimum of their output was taken, this time by the Capitalists, who for the most part were descendants of the former aristocracy. Once in America, these workers fleeing the industrial machines of Europe often found themselves unable to earn more than what they needed to pay out for rent, food, and a minimum of clothing. Many couldn't even manage that much. Still more immigrants were escaping religious or ethnic persecution directed towards them because they were "minorities" in their original land.

The point is, a large part of the history of our current amalgamation of people is one of abuse. Aside from the slaves and exiles, people came here from all over the world hoping to god to find a better place. They came because the places they left were too unsafe or unpleasant in which to live. For most, *running away* to the unknown, even when it meant starting over with little or nothing, seemed their best available option. Once here, they were too busy simply trying to survive, to ever begin to heal from what happened to them before they fled.

Abuse is the Root Cause for Most Social Problems:

It feels like a reasonably fair abstraction to assert that most of our major problems in these United States stem from our history of abuse. People who are hurt and abused themselves, who are physically beaten and told they deserve the beatings, who are told they are lower than shit because of who and what they are, will, if they don't heal, tend to repeat the abuse. They'll justify this repetition of course; almost everyone who abuses has a "reason." Sometimes their reasons seem completely irrational, such as "she looked at me wrong." At other times the reasons may seem (only on the surface) to make perfect sense, such as "You broke the rules; the rules call for this punishment; therefore you must be punished (abused)."

Abuse Continuing on Multiple Levels:

We Americans have grown up with these "lessons" in abuse. And without recognizing it, we are re-teaching them on all levels. On an individual level, with ourselves; on a personal level, with our families; on a gender level, with males and females; on an inter-ethnic level with people of different cultural heritage; on a racial level with people of different skin tone; on a class level with people of different economic and educational realities; on an international level with countries of varying economic and military strengths; and finally on an inter-species or environmental level with humans on top, temporarily taking charge of most other species' destinies.

We abuse ourselves when we engage in internal name-calling, self-destructive behaviors, or the acceptance of abuse from others. On the personal level, families repeat the abuse perpetrated by their elders. On the gender level, women and girls are raped and battered, while men and boys are the cannon fodder for wars and gang violence. Ethnic and racial prejudice continues to rage, as is evident by the support for Neo-Nazis, the Ku Klux Klan, and recent white pride politicians such as the Republican presidential candidate David Duke; the recent Los Angeles race riots after the highly publicized Rodney King verdict are yet another example. Class-based warfare and abuse can be seen in the frequency people with beat up cars are harassed by police simply for driving through wealthier neighborhoods, and the dichotomy of living in a society where homeless beggars share the same streets with highly paid executives.

An example of abuse on the international level is our recent war against Iraq. Before Iraq's invasion of Kuwait, not only had we (the United States) supplied Iraq with weapons, but we'd actually told them that we like it when they invade their neighboring countries. Only a few years before the Persian Gulf War we had encouraged Iraq to invade Iran, one of our "enemies" at the time. Our United States government acted happy when that particular invasion took place, so much so that it even supplied the Iraqis with weapons. More importantly, we supplied the Iraqi leaders with the lesson that large scale, organized killing of people is good, as long as our society doesn't like the people being killed. (We didn't like Iran at the time because its citizens had just had a successful revolution in order to kick out the Western corruption that was bleeding their country dry of resources, while doing nothing for the general populace who lived there.) There was no outcry about rape and murder from the United States then.

Just a few years later, when Iraq invaded Kuwait, our government changed its mind and said, in essence, "attacking and invading countries simply because you think you are right is despicable; and since we think we're right about this, we are going to send in our armies to attack and destroy you." Do you see the hypocrisy? This was just like a parent slapping their child for slapping its sibling. The explicit message is: don't hit; yet the implicit message is: only hit when you are the one with the power that will allow you to get away with it.

And as everybody should remember, we damn well hit Iraq! We directly killed over 200,000 people, and did our best to destroy their infrastructure. Because of this there is now hardly any sanitary water or waste disposal, no electricity, and no irrigation system for their crops. The resultant hunger and disease has killed hundreds of thousands more Iraqis, few of whom had anything to do with starting the war in the first place. One and a half years after the war, the death toll was figured to be well over a half a million of our fellow human beings. Yup, we sure showed them! Oh yes, there is still that rather trivial matter that the fellow we blamed this all on, Saddam Hussein, remains alive and in power.

On the environmental level, we abusively rip the Earth apart in our quest for resources, mainly because we have the power and the self professed right to. We rationalize this. Some with their religions that say God put us here to be in charge of everything, to make the world more "civilized," and "godly." Others simply operate on the greed principle, taking what they want for themselves or their community because they want to and can. After all, if we don't grab these resources someone else will, right? Wrong.

We live in a sick society. I'm only twenty-five years old and could already fill a very long book with personally witnessed examples to support this premise. Others have already written dozens, if not hundreds of such books, focusing in upon some of the many different problem areas.

"Problems" Are Really Symptoms:

What fewer people seem to see, is that these "problems" are actually symptoms of a deeper illness pervading our society. We've had the illness for so long we are almost unable to recognize it. In fact, we have hardly any cultural memory of what it is like to be healthy. However, memory or not, things will continue to get worse until we figure out how to heal ourselves.

Healing Ourselves:

Unfortunately, we don't have enough healers and leaders to do the work for us. If we want to get better, we will have to do the work ourselves. I am convinced that as individuals, families, communities, nations, and as a planetary species, we will either pull ourselves together, face our sickness, and figure out how to heal, or we will destroy ourselves. Scary thing to be convinced of, isn't it?

It is not enough to work on healing only ourselves, or only others, though.

If we deal primarily with our own, personal wounds, by the time we are healed, others who are still sick will be pounding on our doors to take a turn at abusing us. That's what they've been taught to do. And if we don't work on ourselves, but instead opt to create large governmental or community programs to dole out solutions to those who are abused the most dramatically, then we won't be dealing with the real problem. We would only be treating the most pronounced symptoms of our deeper disease. This is like taking Alka-Seltzer to fight pneumonia; the symptoms may recede for a time, but the deeper disease will only get worse.

We are the Problem:

The real problem is that we all go on with our lives, finding as many distractions from our diseased state as we can, while the abuse rages on. Remember the statistics on the pages before this chapter? Like it or not, everyone in our society is a part of the problem. We've been taught that ignoring and accepting the reality of abuse is necessary to our survival. But we've been taught wrong! Actually the opposite is the case. To survive, we must wake up, grow up, and do the work.

So how do we do this?

How do you heal yourself when you are still being abused, and are in the power-less position? When they can, abusers teach that resistance will only bring more abuse. The threat of more force is the coercion used to decrease the resistance. Yet the wounds have a difficult time healing when the abusers keep re-opening them.

How do you heal yourself from the abuse after you've survived it and begun to come into your own positions of power? In many cases, coming into your own position of power requires that you take on the role of an abuser. This role requires that you forget and deny the abuse back when others had power over you.

How do we heal? What are the answers?

What do we do just to deal with runaways?

It is going to be tough, but that's what the final chapters of this book are intended to help us with. They contain suggestions of things we can do on our personal, family, community, state, and federal levels, simply to deal with the symptom of runaway youth, and more generally with the problem of abuse in a sick society. Though my suggestions about dealing with issues around runaway youth do touch the root of the abuse problem, I don't pretend they properly attend to the larger question of societal healing.

To meaningfully address and answer the larger question of healing our sick society will require more wisdom than I command. Fortunately, other people are pioneering, finding the paths our society needs to follow, and some are even writing books on what they discover. All you have to do is find these people and their books, listen to and read what they have to say, and work like hell.

One thing I'm convinced of is that we can't give this job to someone else. We've continually tried to treat the symptoms with programs. For runaways we've developed a system of runaway shelters, which though important and necessary, fall far short of being enough. To achieve real change in our society, such that we will have fewer runaways, fewer cases of abuse, fewer wars, and fewer instances of environmental destruction, we will have to stand up and do the work ourselves.

You, Yes, You:

The sickness will not be healed without your help. Yes, YOU, the individual reader. I know this and can tell it to you because I survived. I was one of the lucky ones. If after reading the small part of my story in this book you think you had it easier than me, then you have been even luckier. As far as I'm concerned, this means that you have a lot of responsibility. Start meeting it today. Please.

Read my next chapters, and when finished, don't put them down. Put them up. Copy or tear out the sections that apply most to you, and place them where you will see them every day, perhaps on your refrigerator, or in front of the toilet, or on your TV remote control. Then, read and think about these suggestions, and figure out what you can do, what you will do to be part of the solution.

Prescription For Change:

The basics are that we have to refrain from using our power solely for our own whims, personal gratification, and self interest, and use it instead to try and make a contribution to the solutions. Until we make peace with our families, friends, and communities; until we make peace with what is left of the original seven hundred indigenous peoples or nations, the original Native Americans who once inhabited North America; until we make peace with the African Americans whose ancestors were brought here in chains to live as slaves, and who currently still suffer from an economic and social disparity; until we make peace with our "third world" (who determined this first/third world ranking system?) neighbors, whom we currently exploit for our own economic gain, as severely as our predecessors ever exploited the slaves; and until we make peace with the web of life and matter we call the environment: we will not be healed.

As enslavers and abusers we are also enslaved. Thus even when we are in our various roles of "abuser," we are still suffering. There is no reason whatsoever to think teens will stop running away from home in America before we free ourselves from these cycles of abuse.

We need a new vision. A new dream of a world in which we would never think of exploiting or hurting our families, friends, and neighbors. It is time.

"It Couldn't be Done"

By Edgar A. Guest

Somebody said that it couldn't be done,
  But he with a chuckle replied
That "maybe it couldn't," but he would be one
  Who wouldn't say so till he'd tried.
So he buckled right in with the trace of a grin
  On his face. If he worried he hid it.
He started to sing as he tackled the thing
  That couldn't be done, and he did it.

Somebody scoffed: "Oh, you'll never do that;
  At least no one ever has done it";
But he took off his coat and he took off his hat,
  And the first thing we knew he'd begun it.
With a lift of his chin and a bit of a grin,
  Without any doubting or quiddit,
He started to sing as he tackled the thing
  That couldn't be done, and he did it.

There are thousands to tell you it cannot be done,
  There are thousands to prophesy failure;
There are thousands to point out to you, one by one,
  The dangers that wait to assail you.
But just buckle in with a bit of a grin,
  Just take off your coat and go to it;
Just start to sing as you tackle the thing,
  That "cannot be done," and you'll do it.

Disclaimer

The following chapters consist of my opinions and perspectives about how to prevent and cope with runaway crises. While I am an expert on my own experiences, have interviewed several dozens of others on theirs, have read many of the books written about runaways, and have given much thought and effort to composing these chapters, I cannot claim my advice will work for you.

I cannot warrant that following my opinionated advice will bring anyone health, safety, or even a slightly improved situation. In fact, following my advice may cause you and/or others more trouble than not.

I have written this material with the best of intentions, doing my utmost to provide balanced and accurate information, but this guarantees nothing. "The road to hell is paved with good intentions," may very accurately sum up the risk involved in following my advice.

> **BE FOREWARNED:**
> **IF YOU CHOOSE TO FOLLOW**
> **ANY OF MY SUGGESTIONS,**
> **YOU ARE DOING SO**
> **AT YOUR OWN RISK.**
> **I WILL ASSUME NO RESPONSIBILITY**
> **FOR DISASTROUS RESULTS.**

Please don't try to buck your responsibility for your own life onto me. Please, please, please! Take what I have to say with a grain of salt, and think for yourself.

Note:

The following four chapters contain my advice for youth thinking of running, youth on the run, parents, and anyone else who cares about runaways. Much of the advice herein overlaps, and I suggest you read all of the chapters whatever your role in runaway crises. As I stated in the *Disclaimer*, the material in these chapters has been culled from my own experiences, my readings of many books and articles, and interviews with scores of runaways, youth crisis workers, and parents. Most of my advice would seem to be basic "common sense," however, this must not be the case, or we wouldn't have such a huge, chronic runaway crisis. I hope it helps.

Please Write:

Please help me make the next edition of <u>Runaway Me</u>, and the soon to be released <u>Runaway Me: Study Guide & Workbook</u> that much better. Send me your comments, suggestions, and criticisms:

c/o: A Blooming Press Co
749 S. Lemay, Suite A3-223
Fort Collins, CO 80524-3900

Thinking of Running?

What You Can do to Deal With the Runaway Crises in Your Life & Society

BILL OF CHILDREN'S RIGHTS & RESPONSIBILITIES:

As growing, not completely mature human beings, all children (defined as those not yet having the rights, privileges, and responsibilities of adults) should have the following:

RIGHTS:

1. To have your basic human needs (food, shelter, & clothing) met.
2. To a safe space in which to grow, learn, and enjoy life.
3. To physically and psychologically nurturing, loving, kind, strong, and healthy parents and/or guardians.
4. To respectful and honoring treatment of your bodies by yourself and others.
5. To never be beaten with hands and weapons.
6. To the sanctity of sexual space; to never be sexually molested by others.
7. To your sexuality, be it straight, bisexual, gay, or asexual.
8. To live free from verbal abuse, such as name calling, being labeled by your actions, being attacked by irrational fits of anger, and being told your feelings are not valid.
9. To be believed.
10. To free, uncensored thought and communication.
11. To an education that will enable you to become a successful adult fully capable of flourishing in your society.
12. To emancipation, when you determine you are ready to fully accept the consequences of self determination and self support.
13. To legal and emotional advocacy, counsel, and representation for the maintenance of these rights.
14. To make mistakes and learn from them.
15. To be heard and respected when you express your needs.

16. To privacy, including the freedom to have private spaces (diaries, bedrooms, etc.) which no one may invade without your permission.
17. Others not enumerated herein.

RESPONSIBILITIES:

1. To respect and honor those who work hard to ensure your rights (parents, guardians, teachers, friends, etc.).
2. To respect the rights of others.
3. To protect yourself to the best of your ability, without infringing upon the rights of others.
4. To work at growing into an ethical, caring, contributing member of society.
5. To go beyond yourself and try to see things from other people's point of view.

For Potential, Current, and Recent Runaways:

I feel so much for what you are going through and wish you strength and luck in your struggle and journey. I was there too at one time, and it was not easy.

So what can I tell you?

Living is a complicated process and the problems you are experiencing may have no simple solutions. In this space I can only touch briefly on some of the issues you are dealing with. I could easily fill a book with a more detailed and comprehensive discussion of these matters. The resources section after these advice chapters is intended to give you further leads (to books, national crises lines, and organizations), so you can actively fill in the gaps in the suggestions I can provide.

Still, I do have a few hundred things to say directly to youth. I have broken my advice for you into two chapters: this one, *Thinking of Running*, and in case you are set on running (or already have), the next one, *Surviving as a Runaway*.

For Youth:

Even when all is going well, being a teenager isn't easy. Your body starts going through the profound changes of puberty. Powerful chemicals called hormones begin rushing through you, making you feel crazy, horny, and restless. New kinds of thoughts creep into your mind, and you begin questioning the values of those around you, the meaning of life, and your place in the world. You want to be liked and loved for who you are, and feel good.

But everything isn't going well in our world, so it's even harder to grow up. Poverty, drug abuse, and all kinds of crime are everpresent. We are bombarded daily with bad news about war, disease, violence, and environmental destruction. Kids in school break into cliques and gangs, groups that are often nasty to those who "don't fit in."

Millions of adults are abusing and sexually molesting many millions of children. Other grown-ups haven't really grown up, and though they don't necessarily commit the more severe abuse, they misuse their power, treating youth without respect, understanding, or love. Governmental and private sector organizations try to help with these problems, but all too often cause more harm than they remedy. Religious organizations also present the promise of a cure, with "God," but the people in them abuse kids just as much as anyone else. To top it off, many adults get so wrapped up in the day to day drama of their own lives, they end up ignoring the needs of youth.

In short, our world is a crazy place in which to be a teenager. It is natural to feel crazy in it.

SOME SERIOUS ISSUES UP FRONT:

Abuse:

There are at least four major forms of abuse: Physical, Sexual, Psychological, and Verbal. Ideally, you and everyone else on the planet should live life free of all four. This is everyone's right, and should you not be having yours respected, feel free to act or find help to defend yourself. If you are abused and can't get it to stop, I suggest removing yourself from the source.

What constitutes abuse should be obvious to all, but just in case:

Physical abuse involves the intentional imposition of damaging physical force by one person upon another. It can be inflicted with weapons (a.k.a. "instruments") or the simple use of body parts such as hands, feet, teeth, elbows, knees, and so on. Many disagree with me, but aside from acts of self defense, I see no justifiable reason for physical abuse. Its sole purpose is to hurt people, an end from which I see no potential benefit and much obvious harm.

Sexual abuse spans a broad spectrum and can take many forms. It involves the disrespectful invasion of one's sexual boundaries by another. It is most often committed by people who have some amount of control or power, upon another person who has less power.

The most obvious form of sexual abuse is rape — brutally forced intercourse. Less obvious forms involve obvious and subtle coercion into sexual interaction at both physical and emotional levels. This coercion can include direct threats of negative consequences for non-participation, promises of rewards, and the use of guilt and shame. Some studies indicate up to one in three girls and one in four boys in America are sexually abused before leaving home.

Sexual abuse does not always involve physical contact. It happens when one person uses words to pressure another into sex. Though many may disagree, by not respecting Renee's repeated refusal to have sex (see story), I was sexually abusing her. The story I shared also had many examples of men sexually abusing me, both verbally and physically.

Psychological abuse involves hurting people by actions that confuse or pain the mind. It takes many forms. Examples include actions that erode the self-esteem of others, the deliberate use of "mind games" to hurt and confuse people, putting people in isolation, imposing control and censorship of communication, lying about other people's motives, guilting and shaming, and deliberately instilling fear as a motivating force. It is often, but not always, inflicted in combination with verbal abuse.

Verbal abuse involves hurting people with words. It includes calling people insulting names, being rude and nasty, and talking badly about people behind their backs. Like the other kinds of abuse, verbal abuse is not justifiable, and should not be accepted. It can be far more damaging than other abuse. Kids who are told they are rotten, worthless, and incapable of accomplishment often believe these labels and do their best to live up to them.

Verbal abuse has far wider acceptance in this society than physical, sexual, or psychological abuse. Almost everyone has experienced it. Almost everyone commits it.

These four kinds of abuse often occur in combination. Sometimes they all occur together, in one brutal act. It is called rape. Currently, up to one in three American women, and an unknown number of men, are raped in their lifetimes.

What to do about Abuse:

Stop it! Don't accept it and don't dish it out. Stand up for yourself, assert your right to be free from abuse. Stand up for others as well.

How?

First, recognize abuse when it is happening. Call it abuse.

When I ran away, I had no idea I'd been abused. I simply thought I deserved all the mistreatment I'd received, like the people who dished it out told me. Before I was eighteen, no one had ever supported me in seeing whippings, paddlings, name calling, solitary confinement, sexual pressuring, and molestation as abuse. I felt worthless and wanted to die.

After getting loving support from my wife and counseling from a good therapist, I began to reevaluate all that had happened. I stopped seeing myself as worthless and deserving of painful treatment. I started to grow healthier and happier. I began standing up for myself. Only then did I stop experiencing abuse.

The second step involves confronting abuse. Let people know you see their behavior as abusive. Try to do so without labeling the person as an abuser. Instead label the behavior as abusive, and do your best to think of the perpetrator as a human being who is merely making a big mistake. Odds are, they are repeating what was done to them when they were in a power-less position. This doesn't excuse the behavior, but it does explain it a bit.

The third step is to communicate that you will no longer tolerate abuse. You have recourse, actions you can take to stop the abuse if they won't. You can escape it, report the perpetrator to authorities and acquaintances, and even sue for damages. None of these steps are easy for any of the involved parties; the win-win solution for all is to get the perpetrator to stop. If they don't think they can on their own, suggest they seek help.

Here in Colorado, a thirteen year old girl just made history by instigating and winning a civil suit against her step-father. He'd been found guilty of sexually molesting her by a criminal court, but she wasn't satisfied. She fought hard to find a lawyer to represent her in civil court, where she sued for damages. She won, and was awarded over a million dollars. Most importantly, she got the abuse to stop.

Abusive behavior becomes an ingrained habit. It may be overly optimistic to expect abuse to stop just because you confront it. In fact, in some cases asking will only provoke an immediate abusive response. Trust your instincts. If you feel this may be the case, be a bit more strategic and arrange for support before you confront the perpetrator. Use the resources section at the end of the book and don't give up until you find the support you need.

Drugs:

As I wrote in the preceding *Reflections* chapter, I believe drugs can have beneficial effects on people. I also wrote that I believe most drugs in our society, legal and illegal alike, are used in an overly casual, flippant, and unhealthy manner. While drugs can open windows of perception that allow one to see things more clearly, they can also become a major obstacle to seeing and thinking straight.

I don't advocate following through upon any major decisions arrived at while under the influence of drugs, without first allowing a significant period of drug-free time to further weigh such decisions. Running away or trying to survive as a runaway can be far more difficult and damaging an experience when one's judgement is continually clouded by a haze of drug induced confusion.

I prefer to live my life without regular drug use. It took three months after I quit smoking pot before I felt my mind grow sharp again. The difference was noticeable and appreciated. I have since found that all of the benefits I'd ever obtained from using drugs can be better achieved without using them.

The chemicals in drugs affect us because we have naturally receptive sites in our bodies and brains for similar chemicals. Exercise of the body and brain produces those chemicals and stimulates those sites in a healthier manner, with fewer side effects. I advocate finding and enhancing your highs and lows without the aid of pharmaceuticals. But as a free being, what you do with your self is your choice and no one else's.

FOR THOSE THINKING ABOUT RUNNING:

I cannot question the severity of your situation, the intense depth of your feeling, or your need to run away for your own protection or satisfaction. But I can ask you to do so.

If you've read my story, you now know some of the problems that can befall a kid who ends up on the streets. And I was one of the lucky ones. I saw kids who suffered far worse.

Up to fifteen runaways die each day in America. Far more are raped, forced into prostitution and drugs, or arrested and locked away in juvenile jails and mental "health" clinics. Hunger, homelessness, malnutrition, and disease are chronic problems for kids on the run.

So what do I advise?

First, don't run unless it is absolutely the last resort; unless you are so endangered by staying where you are, that dealing with the possibility of death and severe abuse on the streets is more acceptable than staying.

Yes, all too many home and life situations are so horrible that they leave no doubt about the necessity of running. However, in most cases it is not necessary or wise to blindly run away. Try facing your situation head on. While it might make sense to move out, it is probably possible to do so in a more planned, better supported fashion, one which doesn't put you in the immediate jeopardy of the unknown.

How do you know if your case is severe enough to run?

Ask yourself some questions:

1. Are you in immediate physical danger? If you stay another minute, hour, or day, do you expect to be attacked, beaten, and injured?

2. Are you in immediate sexual danger? If you stay another minute, hour, or day, do you expect to be sexually molested or raped?

3. Are you in immediate danger of losing your freedom? If you stay another minute, hour, or day, do you expect to lose the ability to run if you are in danger later? Are you about to be locked up in an escape-proof situation?

If you are in grave and immediate danger, then you need help. Look for it, but if there is no one else to help or protect you, then you must help or protect yourself. Take this book with you and get out.

If you are not immediately threatened, you have time to think things through before acting. You are lucky.

Keeping a Diary or Journal:

Instead of just feeling bad and confused, try to start a journal or diary wherein you can sort things out.

After returning from my first runaway episode I started keeping a diary. Unfortunately, I kept falling into the trap of writing only about how bad I felt. I ended up running again, blindly, instead of taking the opportunity to come up with a plan that made more sense.

I didn't feel good about my life at home or at school, but I was never able to get a grip on myself and problem-solve. Maybe you won't be able to either, but it can't hurt to try. If I'd asked myself some basic questions like, "Who will I talk with if things get real bad again?" or "Where can I go to cool off and think things over if I just can't take it anymore?" then when my next crisis came up I would have been prepared to cope. I could have had a plan, instead of being so depressed and confused I thought killing myself the only option, and then being so afraid that I got on a train to I knew not where.

Ask yourself a few questions and write down your answers:
Why do I want to run?
What will happen if I stay?
What is so wrong with my current situation that I think running will help?
What would my life as a runaway be like?
What else could I do?
Who can I talk with about my problems? (See the "Getting Help" section below.)

Read all of the advice chapters and write down any other questions which would be helpful for you to answer. This will give you plenty to keep you busy journaling for some time, then should you choose to run, you will have worked out strategies for success ahead of time.

GETTING HELP:

You are not alone. Though you may not see it, there is help available. Seek it out.

Talking with Parents:

Try talking with your parents. Parents almost always love their children and only want what's best for them. Even most parents who don't treat their kids ideally still love them. Give your parents a chance. They may be able to help you.

First, figure out what you want to communicate.
Write down what your issues are, what you want or need help with, and

what you want from your parents. Depending upon your problems, it may be as simple as just getting them to listen to you without interrupting, or as serious as getting them to stop abusing you.

Problems in your life are shared problems. In too many cases, families label a kid as the "problem child." But when things aren't working out, it is everybody's problem. These issues need to be dealt with as a family, and even as community. If the problems involve poverty, abuse, or drug dependency it may be necessary to get outside help as well.

Second, plan an approach that respects your parents.

Are you upset with how they treat you? Think about how you'd want someone to approach you, if they were upset with the way you were acting. Try to see things from your parents' point of view. Your parents may not deal with you the way you need, want, or deserve, but that doesn't make it right to call them names, shout, or be nasty. Such behavior is abusive. Besides, if you get them on the defensive, they won't be able to hear you. If you don't feel you can handle talking directly, try writing a letter.

Third, ask your parents to set a specific time to hear you out with all their attention.

Trying to talk about serious issues while your parents are busy cooking or rushing off to work won't tend to be productive. If they usually fly off the handle at the slightest provocation, request that they just listen without responding at first, and set another specific time to hear their response, after they've had time to think it through.

Fourth, work out a strategy for success with your parents.

Determine what you need from each other and what you are willing to give in exchange. Write it all down and leave it posted on the refrigerator or somewhere else where everyone will be regularly reminded of what has been agreed. Include a description of how new problems will be resolved in the future.

Fifth, try to be flexible.

Living and getting along with people usually involves compromise. Not everyone can get all of what they want, but if intentions are good, a mutually acceptable middle-ground can often be reached. Then again, if you are being abused, you shouldn't settle for merely less abuse.

Finally, keep talking.

Don't expect serious problems to be solved with just one conversation. Healing and changing takes time and effort. You may have to try several approaches before you find a solution.

Talking with Parents Doesn't Always Work:

In my interviews of twenty current and former runaways, their biggest complaint was that no matter how hard they tried, they just didn't feel understood or respected by their families. Is that your biggest complaint? Are your parents blind to your issues, even after your best efforts to communicate? Are they too controlling? Too abusive? Too busy? Do they just not care enough?

Talking with Others:

Even if your parents can't or won't help, you still aren't alone.

Who else can you talk with? How about other family members, friends, teachers, neighbors, or older kids you respect?

Keep looking for support and you will find it. If your first attempts don't help, look somewhere else.

Counselors:

(also known as Psychologists, Psychiatrists, & Therapists)

There is no shame in getting help. A counselor is simply someone to talk to, someone who can listen and share their experience and perspectives. He or she can be self-trained or prepared by studying at college.

I've seen several counselors in my life. The first two were no help, because I didn't want to see them and they couldn't relate to my problems. But when I was eighteen and started college I found a very good counselor. With his help I began healing from all the crap I'd gone through, started to feel good about myself, and began to be glad I was alive. In the seven years since then, I've found and worked with two other counselors who were also very helpful.

Psychology is one of the most popular majors at United States colleges right now. Hundreds of thousands of Americans have chosen to devote their lives to helping people work through their problems. Many of them have been through similar problems and volunteer at schools, crises centers, shelters, and clinics around the country.

However, be warned, counseling can work both ways. Though it can help, a degree in psychology doesn't guarantee counselors will be any good. In fact, some psychology programs end up giving these counselors methods of "helping" that aren't helpful. And some counselors are still too screwed up from their own childhoods to help anyone else.

For example, Sigmund Freud, the renowned "founder of psychology" seemed to think most problems revolved around "penis envy" for women, and Oedipal complexes (the desire to have sex with one's mother) for men. He even discounted most his female patients report's of being molested by their fathers and step-fathers as "fantasies."

Other college programs teach abusive methods of dealing with kids. Some, backed by the multi-billion dollar pharmaceutical industry, advocate giving kids drugs that only mask problems, not solve them. Another big business involves locking kids up in institutions where they are forced to "behave" or suffer unpleasant alternatives like being tied up, kept in isolation, or the loss of "privileges" like communication with friends. There are plenty of "therapists" who graduate from college and find well paid work in these places.

On the brighter side, many counseling programs teach a variety of helpful things, and produce graduates who can really help you. Some study models of abuse and healing in dysfunctional families, others deal with drug abuse, suicide, and depression, and still others utilize more spiritual perspectives. Good programs enrich counselors with a host of tools they can use to your benefit. These schools teach their students to be supportive listeners, to advocate for your rights, and to help you plan solutions that will work.

Finding a Counselor:

Counselors are human like anyone else. Trust your feelings and look for the good ones. Ask your friends for recommendations. If you wind up with someone who doesn't help, stop seeing them and find someone else.

Many schools have counselors who are paid to take the time to listen to youth and help them find solutions. Ask about what services are available at the administration office. Their time is often available at no charge to you. But before seeing them, keep a few things in mind.

Normally counselors are bound by a thing called client-patient confidentiality; they are not permitted to tell anyone else what you tell them. But many schools require their counselors to break confidentiality and report any knowledge or suspicions they have about your being abused or about your considering suicide. This can get wheels rolling with social workers and mental health professionals that you may not have chosen had you known.

Social workers can be sent to your home to investigate your parents and make a determination of whether you are being abused. With the wrong counselor in the wrong system, the slightest mention of having considered suicide could get you landed in a mental health hospital against your will. If you are being abused or are considering suicide, you deserve help. But it should be *when you decide* you are ready to deal with these issues, not "help" imposed upon you against your will.

Feel free to see a school counselor and open up as much as you want. If you want, ask your counselor about their and the school's policies on confidentiality, and under what circumstances they might break it. Once they've told you, look them in the eyes and ask them if there are any other cases where they might break it. Trust your feelings about their answers.

With a good counselor, you'll have a chance to work out your problems and get the support you need. You have the power to choose what help you ask for.

Some of the most helpful counselors may not have been to college at all.

There are other, equally valid ways to learn counseling skills. Books, volunteer experiences, and reflection can all help prepare people to be good listeners and problem solvers.

Toll-free crisis hotlines have been set up around the country to help people deal with running away, abuse, drugs, suicide, sexuality, and health. The hotlines can provide direct, anonymous counseling, and refer you to other sources of support. See the list in the Resources section at the end of this book.

Books:

Around two hundred thousand books are written each year in the United States. About fifty thousand are published. Not all books are simply for entertainment. There are literally thousands that deal with the struggles you are going through.

Like people, some books are full of crap, while others are rich with wisdom. At their best, writers spend months and years distilling the best of what they have learned into something you can read in a few days. I've found many books to be quite helpful. The bibliography in the back of this book lists some that may aid you.

OPTIONS OTHER THAN RUNNING:

If you decide to leave, it still isn't necessary to become a "runaway" per se. You may have other, more desirable options available to you. Check them out.

Moving in with Another Family Member:

Is there anyone else in your family you can stand to live with? A brother or sister, an uncle or aunt, or grandparents? Would it hurt to ask?

Such a move doesn't have to permanent, though it can turn out that way. If your parents cooperate, moving needn't be a problem. In fact, it could be the best solution for everybody, as it can allow you and your parents a little space from each other, without cutting off the relationship entirely.

One stumbling block to this approach can be the issue of money. Who pays your expenses when you move in with someone else? You may be able to get your parents to chip in some, by explaining that they'd save money by your moving out. Or, you could offer to do work in exchange for being allowed in. Either get a paid job, or offer to do all the dishes, vacuuming, yardwork, and other maintenance.

Moving in with a Friend's Family:

If your entire family seems to present no options, consider friends. Do you have any friends, teachers, neighbors, or other acquaintances you might want to live with? Tell them why you want to move out and ask how they would feel about it. Again, you could offer to get a job or help around the house to help cover your share of expenses.

Emancipation:

Emancipation is the legal term for granting youths the rights, privileges, and responsibilities of adults. It is sort of like an early graduation from school, except it is a legal graduation from childhood. When you get emancipated it is no longer a crime to get a job, rent an apartment, or conduct other business without parental consent. The down side is that you then have to sink or swim like any other adult.

Unfortunately, even if you are as mature as the wisest elephant, emancipation isn't easy to get. The rules vary from state to state, but generally, emancipation requires a judge's consent. To get that you have to demonstrate to the judge that you are "fit" to handle the responsibilities of emancipation. This can be very hard as the requirements often involve "Catch-22" logic, in that you must first have and keep a job, and demonstrate adult responsibility.

Convincing a judge may not be hard if your parents cooperate. However, you probably wouldn't be considering this option in the first place if they were cooperative. If your parents don't cooperate and let you get a job so you can build up a track record, you might be screwed. Also, if you've been in trouble with the law, which is the case for many potential runaways, then you have yet another strike against you. Finally, the younger you are, the less likely you are to be granted emancipation, as judges don't want to get flak from the community for putting "babes" in the wilderness.

If you are interested in emancipation and think you can both handle the responsibilities and pass the stringent requirements, then go for it. Contact your local court, runaway shelter, or whatever other organizations you think might help. Ask what the requirements are in your state and who you need to talk with to get the process rolling. You may need to request a public defender to represent your case. If you get the runaround, go around it, and find someone else who can help you.

Foster Care and Group Homes:

Another option that can beat the streets is getting into a government-sponsored home situation. I've never stayed in such a situation, but I've heard mixed reviews from other current and former runaways about such places. Some placements are quite good, with loving families or organizations that will treat you right and work hard on your behalf. Others can be the pits, worse than the home life left behind. Distressingly, some people become foster parents only so they can receive the extra money paid them by the state, or even worse, so they can molest and abuse kids themselves. Remember your rights, and if you end up in such a situation, do what you can to get out.

How do you get into a foster care or group home arrangement? I'm fuzzy on the details, but generally this is a function of your state's social services department. They usually only get involved in cases of severe abuse and neglect, which they have to verify, and their response times aren't renowned for speed.

Despite your best efforts, you may need to leave. If so, read on.

"IF—"

By Rudyard Kipling

If you can keep your head when all about you
    Are losing theirs and blaming it on you;
If you can trust yourself when all men doubt you,
    But make allowance for their doubting too;
If you can wait and not be tired by waiting,
    Or, being lied about, don't deal in lies,
Or, being hated, don't give way to hating,
    And yet don't look too good, nor talk too wise;

If you can dream–and not make dreams your master;
    If you can think–and not make thoughts your aim;
If you can meet wth triumph and disaster
    And treat those two impostors just the same;
If you can bear to hear the truth you've spoken
    Twisted by knaves to make a trap for fools,
Or watch the things you gave your life to broken,
    And stoop and build 'em with wornout tools;

If you can make one heap of all your winnings
    And risk it on one turn of pitch and toss,
And lose, and start again at your beginnings
    And never breathe a word about your loss;
If you can force your heart and nerve and sinew
    To serve your turn long after they are gone,
And so hold on when there is nothing in you
    Except the Will which says to them: "Hold on";

If you can talk with crowds and keep your virtue
    Or walk with kings–nor lose the common touch;
If neither foes nor loving friends can hurt you;
    If all men count with you, but none too much;

If you can fill the unforgiving minute
    With sixty seconds' worth of distance run–
Yours is the Earth and everything that's in it,
    And–which is more–you'll be a Man, my son!

Surviving as a Runaway

FOR THOSE DEFINITELY INTENDING TO RUN:

Wow! I guess things at home must seem pretty crazy, shitty, and even hopeless. If this is the case then I am sorry for you indeed. But please don't despair.

Running doesn't have to mean the end of your life, your failure as a person, or even an endless road of interminable suffering. In fact some former runaways, such as the renowned Benjamin Franklin, and my unrenowned self, have managed to become quite successful. Though it won't be easy, running away may actually be your best option under the circumstances.

If you truly think this the best you can do, your next step will be to figure out how to make your journey as easy and safe for yourself as possible.

Some questions to consider:

Where or to whom do you intend to run?

Why there and not somewhere else?

Will it be a healthy place for you to be?

A safe one?

How will you eat, drink, sleep, and get clean?

What resources are you going to take with you? Money? Clothes? Food? Toilet articles? Sleeping bag or other bedtime supplies? A multipurpose pocket knife?

How will you carry all your stuff?

How will you get around?

How long do you expect your money to last?

How long do you intend to remain a runaway? A few days? Months? Years? Forever?

Throwaways and Abandoned Youth:

Has your family told you to screw off or leave? Have they locked the doors on you, or moved out without taking you with them?

If so, your leaving does not make you a runaway. Technically, you'd be categorized as a "throwaway," and will have a slightly different set of options available to you. You aren't alone; the U.S. Department of Justice estimates over 100,000 kids are thrown away each year.

Rejection sucks, and parental rejection can be devastating. I'm sorry you have to deal with this. If you're lucky, you will find people who won't reject and abandon you.

Read the following sections for runaways, but when you seek help or deal with authorities, make it clear you were cast out against your will. Whether they like it or not, parents are legally responsible for their children. Governments may be able to force your parents to provide economic support, or charge them with "neglect." And in states where being a runaway is an arrestable crime, you may not be arrestable.

ADVICE FOR RUNAWAYS:

There is so much more to surviving as a runaway than I can cover in this chapter. Below are sections addressing food, shelter, transportation, self-defense, personal hygeine, health (including sexual), money, school, and returning home. I think what I have to say covers most of the the basics, but I'm sure to have left something out.

FOOD:

Do you know how much it costs to eat each day?

Restaurants are expensive. For example, three fast food meals a day may cost around ten bucks. That's $300 in a month, just to eat greasy, unhealthy food. Eating at inexpensive sit-down restaurants will cost more, perhaps twenty dollars a day for three meals plus reasonable tips for the waitstaff. That's $600 a month. In big cities all these prices are even higher.

Store bought food costs much less. You might get by on a few bucks a day for very basic foods. Look in camping books and magazines for suggestions on inexpensive, ready-to-eat foods. The produce and bulk food sections at food co-ops and the giant supermarkets offer basic foods at low prices.

You can save even more if you cook, but for that you'll need a kitchen, or at least some cooking supplies. Pots, dishes, silverware, heat and water sources, and soap to wash the dishes would all help. And unless you shop before each meal you'll need a refrigerator to prevent spoilage of leftovers and other perishables. If you can manage to cook, you can live on fruit, rice, beans, and potatoes all of which are very inexpensive when bought in bulk.

You can get food even if you're penniless. Many towns, churches, and community organizations have programs that provide free food for the poor.

One of the homeless shelters in my town serves a no questions asked breakfast and dinner. All you have to do is show up, get in line, grab some food, and eat. They also give out grocery bags full of donated food to anyone who asks. Use the Resources section to get some leads on finding these places.

One of my tactics was to go to restaurants and offer to work for food. This can backfire if the staff calls the police, as happened to me once. But in most cases people would let me do some dishes, mop a floor, or just give me a meal for free.

Getting on the federal welfare and food stamps rolls is one final option. See the Shelter section below for details.

SHELTER:

Shelter has at least three major functions: It is a place to sleep, a place to stay warm, and a place to keep your things. The first function is the most important. The climate may be warm enough wherever you are, and you may not have anything that requires storage, but no matter what, you will eventually need to sleep.

Where will you stay?

You have several options available to you. They are discussed in order of desirability.

1. Runaway Shelters.
2. Renting a place.
3. Staying with strangers.
4. Stowing away.
5. Hanging out.
6. Welfare.
7. Getting yourself arrested.

Runaway Shelters:

There are around five hundred runaway and youth crisis shelters around the United States. They vary widely in the types and quality of services they offer. I've been to four in my lifetime — three as a runaway, and one as a volunteer counselor. I haven't been happy with what I've seen, but have talked with many runaways who have had good experiences, and were very glad they went to shelters.

On the plus side, shelters can be your best option. Many provide housing, food, counseling, and advocacy of some sort, including help with your parents, the police, courts, job hunting, and educational access. A good shelter staffed with good people can help you work through your problems and figure out what to do next.

Most shelters only let you stay under certain conditions. One biggie is parental notification. Their rules require them to notify your parents that you are staying there. They won't force you back with your parents, but do need to contact them. In abusive situations, they will try to ensure you are protected and won't send you back unless they think the abuse will stop.

Unfortunately, many shelters have problems. Some shelter workers won't like what I have to say. They may blame me for scaring you away, which isn't my intention. I simply want you to be forewarned. If you encounter the kinds of problems I'm about to discuss, don't reject all shelters; you can always go to a different town and try to find a better one.

One problem is some (not all) shelters are overly restrictive. The motivations behind their restrictions are well meaning; they want to protect you. But it may be more protection than you can or want to handle.

For example, some shelters don't allow youth to smoke cigarettes. At all. This isn't a problem for light and non-smokers, but it would have kept me from staying. I had too many other problems stressing me out to add nicotine withdrawal to the list. Regardless of what anyone else wanted to impose "for my own good," I wasn't ready to quit until I reached nineteen years old and had dealt with a host of more important issues. The withdrawal from my three-pack-a-day habit was so intense I had minor hallucinations.

Shelter Staff who Molest:

Not all shelters have the kinds of problems I witnessed at the one I volunteered at (see *Reflections* chapter). But too many have an even more serious one: staff members who molest kids.

When I was sixteen I spent a night at a shelter in San Francisco. The director was a friendly, eloquent, and understanding man. He conducted my intake interview and after speaking for about a half hour we got on the subject of drugs. I told him about my experiences with MDA (a.k.a. X, Ecstasy, The Love Drug, and Adam).

He said, "Normally I wouldn't even think of doing this, but you are an unusually mature and intelligent young man. I happen to have some MDA, and would be willing to share some with you if you come over to my place tomorrow afternoon." I missed doing MDA so I agreed.

The next day, an hour after taking it, he started to try to get touchy-feely with me. I excused myself to go to the bathroom, and while I was in there, noticed several books on child psychology sitting next to his toilet. I came to the sudden realization that he knew exactly what he was doing, and had played my ego like an accordion, pushing all the right buttons to get me to his place. I walked from the bathroom, straight out the front door, and was glad to get away. How many other clients had he pulled this one on? How far did they go?

Another, more publicized example of this problem happened with Father Bruce Ritter, the founder and former head of the Covenant House system of shelters. His 1987 book, Covenant House, tells the story of how he went from letting half a dozen New York City runaways crash at his apartment one night in the 1960's, to building a shelter network which now shelters upwards of 35,000 runaways a year in major cities across the United States and around the world. After his book was published several former clients of his shelter, came out with accounts of how Father Ritter had molested them, or how other staff members had used Covenant House funds to hire them as prostitutes. Father Bruce Ritter was "replaced" by Sister Mary Rose McGeady, the current director of Covenant House. Despite multiple attempts, I have been unable to speak with Sister McGeady or locate Father Ritter.

I wonder if Father Ritter had done more good or harm. He surely didn't molest every kid who stayed at his shelters; maybe his other staff did, but he couldn't have had the time to do it alone. He set his shelters up in areas where many of the kids were being molested anyway, some several times daily as prostitutes. On the other hand, molesting kids at a place where there was a "covenant" (pact or promise) that they would be safe, may have alienated the kids even more than street living. In any case, Father Ritter is now gone, having left an infrastructure which can house tens of thousands of kids a year behind him.

It isn't fair to take a couple of examples of child molesting by shelter staff and presume all staff do this. It simply isn't so. I've interviewed many runaways who had nothing but good, safe, nurturing shelter stays. I've also interviewed some who haven't.

It is natural that child molesters are attracted to work at runaway shelters, just like they're attracted to video arcades and other youth hangouts. They may even go to shelters fully intending to help, not molest, but find they simply can't help themselves. I'd guess the director I ran into and Father Ritter were molested themselves when they were young. Teens do have a lot of sexual energy, and may seem quite attractive in our youth oriented culture.

But kids need to be safe at shelters. Too often, shelters are their only possibility for a safe place. Horny, power craving adults need to restrain themselves, or quit and get help if they can't. The first key to curing a problem lays in honestly recognizing it.

If you run into molestation, don't keep quiet about it like I and the kids Father Ritter molested did. These problems can be rectified where they occur, by removing the staff member and getting him or her into counseling. Report molestation. Make noise. Tell the media. If you don't get results, organize your fellow youth and protest at city hall or some other public place. No one can fight for your rights like you.

So that's a lot said on the downside of shelters, and not much on the up side. If I was a teen runaway now, if I was broke, homeless, and unwilling to return home, I'd go to a shelter. After all I said? Yes. With what I know now, definitely yes.

If I'd known shelters existed before being sent to one by a legal system which was about to send me to criminal trial and possibly jail, I would have given one a chance. With what I now know, when the director tried to molest me at the second shelter, I would have called the police, told the other staff, and the media. I would have tried another shelter.

Let's face it, the streets suck. Trying to learn everything at once with no resources and no support is just too much. I was severely scarred by my street experiences, and was damned lucky to survive.

Like I said, I have interviewed plenty of kids who are grateful they went to shelters. They landed in good ones. Numerous teens have received loving kindness, shelter, food, clothing, help in dealing with their parents, respect in not dealing with them, job training, and foster home placements or help in finding work, cheap housing, and making the transition into adulthood.

You might also consider staying at a homeless shelter. Homeless shelters specialize in helping houseless adults. Some won't take kids, but if you look like you could be over eighteen, you might be able to fake your way in. They are used to housing folks who don't have IDs.

Be careful, though. Adult shelters are filled with a much rougher class of clients. Some of them have severe mental and emotional problems for which they would have been locked in a psychiatric institution a few years back. Some are violent. And most are likely to be bigger and stronger than you. You are far more likely to be attacked or harassed at such a shelter.

How to Find a Shelter:

The resources section lists several toll-free runaway and youth crisis hotlines, all of which can refer you the shelter nearest you. I tried calling all of them in the middle of the night, and found they couldn't offer much more help than that. All but one of the five counselors I spoke with knew next to nothing about federal and state laws regarding youth issues, like employment or the responsibility of shelters to contact your parents. I was surprised by how little they seemed to know. They were simply friendly volunteers who could lend an ear, or use a computer or book to look up places to refer me to in my area. They may call the places for you to give you a lead in, but you take it from there.

If you want to find out what the shelters near you are really like, you need to go to them yourself. I don't know of any which will keep you from leaving if you want to. In some states they may call the police afterwards, but they won't get in your way. If you know other kids who have stayed in shelters you can ask them about their experiences.

Renting:

If you've chosen to forego runaway shelters and have found no opportunities to stay with friends you can try to rent a place of your own.

Renting almost always costs money. Up front. Getting a place for yourself costs most of course, with shared spaces being far cheaper. Sharing a cheap, rundown house or apartment in a small town will cost at least $150.00 or so a month. In a medium sized city it can take over $200.00 each just to share a slum. In a big city it's even more. A nice, yet humble place for yourself might cost two and a half times this much.

Then there is the issue of a deposit. Landlords often require you to sign a one year lease and pay first and last month's rent, plus a security deposit before moving in. The security deposit is to cover any damages you might cause to the rental and can be as much as a month's rent. It is usually returned thirty to ninety days after you move out. All told, you may need the equivalent of three months' rent money just to move in.

Even if you have plenty of money, it can be quite hard to rent a place as a runaway. Many landlords will want to see some form of identification, some evidence which shows you have a history of paying your bills on time, and at least one reference. On top of that, in most states it is illegal for people to rent to "minors" without a parental signature.

Sometimes you can get around the identification, credit references, and signature requirements by sharing a place with someone else who has already signed a lease. And if they're desperate for a roommate they might only require first month's rent up front. One disadvantage to this sort of arrangement is you won't have your name on the lease, and thus no legal recourse if your roommate decides to kick you out at a moment's notice. Still, this may be the only rental option available to you, and no lease is certainly better than having no place to stay.

How to Find Rentals:

Landlords and people looking to share places often advertise in newspapers, on bulletin boards, at college student rental offices, and through private agencies. Most rental opportunities are advertised in the classified sections of newspapers, and the listings are usually broken down into two categories, landlord rentals, and people looking for roommates.

Another popular way of advertising is through flyers and notices pinned to bulletin boards. The best spot to look for bulletin board notices is at places you like to hang out in; odds are that the people advertising there have similar interests and would make more compatible roommates. Other good places include coffee shops, colleges, community markets, and food co-ops.

Many colleges have student and community housing offices. These can be very good places to look because the rentals listed are often geared to college students who may be even more broke than you. College students are more likely to accept young roommates, as most of them are still young themselves, and are thus more likely to empathize with your situation.

Unfortunately, housing offices normally only allow students with college IDs to look at the listings. You can get around this. The listings are often kept in binders which the students check out from the housing desk. Just find a student who looks friendly, and ask them if they will use their ID to check out the books, then let you look through them. It may take a few tries to find a cooperative student, but it should work.

One last source of potential housing is through private agencies such as "Housing Helpers" that charge an up-front fee (usually between $50.00 and $100.00) before trying to match you with compatible roommates. I utilized one of these agencies when I was nineteen and wasn't very happy with the results. It is cheaper to do your own legwork.

All this advice may not help if you don't have any money for rent. You can still use these sources and ask the prospective roommates if they'd be interested in letting you work for rent. You'd probably have your best luck with the ads at community bulletin boards, especially at environmentally and socially oriented food co-ops. I've seen ads at the one in my town asking for people who will exchange gardening and housecleaning for rent, or for a large discount. Still, it is unlikely you'll be able to secure such an arrangement easily.

Staying With Strangers:

Staying with strangers is just that: you don't know the people at who's mercy you place yourself. While it may seem your best bet, it can get you into serious trouble.

Of the five sets of strangers I stayed with in my story, one caused no harm, one attempted to molest me, one led to my watch being stolen, one ended in homelessness, and one led to my molestation. And I feel I was lucky. Going to bed with your host is all too often a price for shelter at stranger's homes. You may decide the risk is better than the alternatives.

Stowing Away:

In my story, I shared several of my methods for stowing away. Stowing away is illegal, and if caught, you will probably end up in jail. But the risk may seem worth it if you're desperate. I don't advise stowing away, but as you might end up doing it anyway, here are a few things to consider.

The easiest places to stowaway in are empty or abandoned buildings, and the quiet parts of large, heavily frequented public access buildings. Abandoned buildings abound in cities, including houses and unused industrial sites. Large public access buildings also abound, including hotels, offices, and the scores of structures on college campuses. In the unlikely event you are out in the countryside, you can probably find an abandoned barn or shed.

Finding these places involves taking risks, being nosy, and poking around where you aren't supposed to be. To make sure a place is empty, you have to enter it. The risk is highest in investigating potentially abandoned buildings. It is hard to explain what you are doing there if the place turns out not be abandoned after all.

I found an empty garbage chute closet in a hotel by opening an unmarked door. What if it had led into the hotel's security center? I would have either turned around and left, or made up some excuse and hoped it worked. It might not have.

Other promising places are basements, boiler rooms, and attics. They're not the most comfortable or healthy places to hang in, but they will keep you warm and dry. In college and office buildings you can often gain access to these kinds of spaces by simply walking up or down some stairs and opening a door. Ideally I'd find a place with two exits or good hiding places so if someone entered (most likely a maintenance technician) I could disappear.

The ideal time to enter such a place is about a half an hour before the building closes for the night. You can get yourself locked in the building and there is a good chance no one will be around all night. You can even leave your hiding place after a while and enter the more pleasant parts of the building, where you might find a couch to lay upon. It is important to be very careful, as night janitorial staff and security guards may roam the halls at any time.

One final option involves camping out. Camping is free, unless you go to a private campground. If it's warm and dry out, you won't need a tent, just a couple blankets or a sleeping bag. If weather is an issue, you can use a tent (check out a Goodwill or Salvation Army store for cheap ones), or make a shelter. Cities and towns are rich with artifacts that can be used to create simple lean-to structures.

It isn't necessary to be afraid of the wilderness. People are your biggest threat, and there a far fewer people in the middle of nowhere than elsewhere. The woods in big city parks are another matter, however. All matter of creeps hang out in some of these places, just waiting to pounce on some vulnerable sucker where no one will see them. Be careful and trust your instincts.

Hanging out:

Hanging out involves similar tactics to stowing away, but the risk is usually lower. So is the reward. You can't sleep while hanging out.

Hanging out during the day is easy. You probably already know how to do it. You can go to malls, parks, or anywhere else you want. However, if you are broke and homeless, your days can be better spent working towards remedying this situation.

Night comes around and you have no money and no place to stay. It's starting to get cold out. Where do you go?

This is when hanging out comes in handy.

If you can come up with about a buck (see the work and money section, below), you can go to an all night coffee shop, order coffee, and stay, stay, stay. It is a good idea to bring something to read. Problem is, you can't go to sleep, and some places will end up kicking you out after a few hours.

Some bus stations are open all night, but they may be the worst place to go. The police and pimps alike regularly search out bus stations to look for runaways. You probably don't want to be found by either.

If you can't find any money, you can wander around and find warm places to stay. The libraries and student centers at many colleges are open until ten P.M. or later. They have plenty of places for students to sit down and study.

After midnight you might have to resort to sitting in stairwells. High rise buildings often have an extra flight of stairs at the top, heading to the roofs. You can take an elevator to or near the top floor, enter a stairwell, and climb to the top. No one is likely to come by.

Welfare:

The welfare system in the United States is the pits. I tried to get on the dole when I was seventeen, but lacked the required identification papers. I still managed to get some emergency food stamps, less than forty dollars worth, but ended up getting mugged for a cigarette while waiting several hours in the stinky lobby.

Welfare's policy isn't too keen on helping youth. They are likely to try to get you to go home or to a runaway shelter. Adults can get emergency housing in designated welfare hotels (danger zones, especially for youth), food stamps, and eventually a small monthly allowance. If you happen to be pregnant, you can also get free, full medical coverage through the Medicaid program.

After my brief experience with Welfare's lines, waits, grouchy employees, and complicated paperwork I came to the conclusion that I could do far better fending for myself. It didn't seem worth the trouble.

Millions of Americans apparently disagree. Once you get on the welfare roles, at least you have a steady income. If you are a minor, and critically homeless and hungry, they can probably set you up with an emergency arrangement within in a day.

They advise getting to their offices early, to avoid the rush. I'd advise the opposite, as they'll waste as much of your time as you let them. I got there at 7:30 A.M., as suggested, and wasn't out until 4:30 P.M., when they closed.

Try to arrive at around two in the afternoon. This will give them enough time to "rush" the paperwork through (nobody rushes at Welfare). If you play the part of a "cute, desperate kid," which you probably are, they are likely to make sure you don't walk out without at least some resolution.

Getting yourself arrested:

If you can't find shelter and would rather forfeit your freedom than put up with another moment of homelessness and hunger, you can get the police to take care of you. I'd rather suffer free than live in jail, but imprisonment might be worth it to you. You could just go to a police station and turn yourself in.

TRANSPORTATION:

Getting around isn't easy for runaways. If you don't have a car, you will be limited to self propulsion, public transit, and hitchhiking. A few words about each:

Walking is free and will almost always get you where you are going. I walked thousands of miles as a runaway. But biking is an even better method of self-propulsion. Even a cheap, used bike will get you twice as far, twice as fast as hoofing it. If you don't already own one, you can probably buy one for less than forty bucks. Check the newspaper classified section for leads. A lock is a good investment.

Sometimes you will need to avoid bad weather or get further, faster than feet or a bike will allow. This is where buses, trains, and planes come in handy. Most bigger cities have low cost mass transit systems, many with reduced rates for youth. To get between towns, private buses are usually cheapest, followed by trains, then aircraft. I managed to stow away on a train once, paying for a fare to a nearby city, then hiding in the bathroom whenever the conductor came by to collect tickets.

Train hopping is an adventurous but dangerous way to travel. A girl in this town recently lost her grip from a slow moving train and sacrificed both her legs in the process. If you succeed in hopping a train, you then have to figure out how to get off. The trains pick up speed, exposing you to viciously cold sixty mile per hour winds, and may not stop anywhere you'd want to be for days. Hoboes who travel the rails are known for being quite violent to train hoppers they don't accept. If they catch you, railway police will arrest you. I don't advise this method of travel.

Hitchhiking can be a last resort method of travel. While I don't recommend it, it is free and may be your only real option. I've hitched hundreds of rides and only experienced a few problems.

Unfortunately, this isn't the case according to the female hitchhikers I've known. For them, any hitching involves routine sexual harassment, and a very high potential for rape. The one time I hitched a large distance with a woman, we were harried by a horny male truck driver to the point that we asked to be let out. Fortunately he didn't argue.

Still, being male is no guarantee of safety. When he was seventeen, my friend Graywolf was raped by one of the truck drivers who gave him a ride. Male or female, there is always a risk of being attacked, or even kidnapped.

If you are set on hitchhiking, consult my story for insight into helpful techniques. Also, if you double up and only hitchhike with a friend you will have a harder time finding rides, but are likely to be somewhat safer. At least you can back each other up in case of trouble.

On last thing to keep in mind, regardless of how you travel, is how will you carry your things? Having nothing but the clothes on your back has its advantages, but the odds are you will want to carry more. On the other hand, the more you carry the slower you can move and the more attention you will draw to your vulnerable situation. Smaller backpacks will allow you to blend in more, making it appear you are just an ordinary student.

Suitcases are the absolute worst form of luggage — they must be lugged. Backpacks are the ideal. They come in many sizes, leave your hands free, and are designed for to distribute the weight of your possessions evenly. Until you have a place to stay and keep your things, I don't advise carrying any more than you can fit in a backpack. If you do have a lot of stuff, it's a good idea to have a modular backpack system, so you can detach a smaller day-pack or fanny pack, stash your heavier things, and move around more easily.

SELF-DEFENSE:

We live in a violent world. Young people are plagued by more violence than most. They are less able to defend themselves than full grown, experienced adults, and are thus that much more likely to be targeted for violent attack.

I've found the best defense is to avoid people and situations with the potential for violence. Rough neighborhoods, drunken people, and getting trapped in closed quarters around people you don't know are obvious examples. Dressing and carrying yourself in ways that don't make you stand out are also important.

Yet, despite your best efforts, it may be impossible to avoid confrontation. This is where a little knowledge of martial arts can come in handy.

Most martial arts are centered in the mind, not in the combinations of physical moves that are so romanticized by the media. Central to most martial arts I've studied is the principle of flowing with the "enemy." This means not resisting their attacks, but channeling them away from yourself such that you utilize the attacker's energy in your behalf. By making this principle central to your being you can de-escalate most violent conflicts without ever entering into an actual physical fight.

There seem to be two main kinds of attacks, those by people who are seeking some kind of ego gratification, and those by people who seek to take something by force. The first is easiest to cope with, while the second can be deadly.

Some aggressors initiate fights because they have a need to feel better about themselves. They feel beating someone up somehow proves they are better. The key to averting physical violence with these people is to help them see it isn't necessary to physically best you in order to feel good. Let them feel better without fighting, or set things up so that they realize they will feel bad about any physical victory over you.

Most often, these attackers start their aggression by making a challenge of some sort, perhaps by name calling, making accusations, or even pushing you. What they are hoping for is any kind of response that will help them justify going off on you. Don't give it to them.

You have little or nothing to lose by humbly acquiescing to their need for ego gratification. They are only attacking because they are weak, and by offering no resistance to their initial attack, all their energy goes right past without harming you. Meanwhile, you have retained all of your energy. You have been strong, the most noble sort of warrior, for you have not let yourself be easily manipulated into a pointless fight. It doesn't matter in the slightest if you could have won such a battle, because unless you are needing childish ego gratification of your own, there is no need to find out.

For example, if the attacker calls you an asshole you can respond by saying something like, "I'm sorry you feel that way. It is not my intention to upset you. Did I do something to disturb you? Because if I did, I didn't mean to."

This kind of response can confuse an attacker. You have honored them by hearing their words and taking them seriously. What they expected, hoped for even, was a disrespectful response, so they could justify escalating the conflict. They may not hear you, and may make yet another attack, but if you keep responding in an honoring way, never talking down to them, they will usually come to see little satisfaction in harming you.

The other kind of attack, one designed to take something by force, can be far more grave a threat. You can try acquiescing, but it may not work. One of the best responses is to get out of range of the assault. Running away often works. Screaming for help can also. If you can't escape, get help, or appeal to the attackers ego, you must either give them what they want or engage and hope for the best. Fighting should be a last resort, but it may be necessary for your survival.

When forced into combat wherein I've decided to fight back, I have found it helpful to go intelligently berserk. Given enough time, I would let the opponent know that I would be doing my best to wreak havoc upon them, and no matter how much they hurt me, I would come back again and again, focusing all my might on destroying them until they either killed me, or promised to leave me alone.

Then I'd let the monster within seem to take over, while maintaining as much conscious control as possible. Like a cat, I'd scream and act crazy, while staying as calm as possible within, so I could coldly calculate how to most efficiently inflict pain. I'd focus on avoiding their blows, then harnessing them in my favor, catching their momentum and adding whatever force I could to it. At my first opportunity, I would escape, for my purpose is not to hurt them, but to defend myself.

There are many good books available on the philosophy and practice of non-violence and martial arts. See the resources section for a few suggestions.

Weapons:

Weapons present several problems.

Most importantly, they can be used against you. An experienced fighter may find it easy to take your weapon. Then you have armed him or her. I don't advise carrying a weapon of any sort unless you know how to use it, are prepared to use it, and are willing to suffer the consequences if it is taken and turned against you.

Second, most weapons are illegal. Besides being one more thing to lug around with you, should you run into trouble with the police, possession of a weapon is only likely to compound your problems.

Finally, having a weapon increases your chances of using it. Since the main purpose of weapons is to inflict bodily harm, possessing one increases your odds of hurting someone. Not only can this get you into legal trouble, regardless of whether you were "justified" in hurting someone, but causing harm to another will stay with you in the form of your conscience. Also, injuring people creates enemies. Should someone survive your counterattack, they may become obsessed with seeking revenge, attacking you when you least expect it.

With all this said, I carried and successfully used weapons for my self-defense while I was a runaway. I'd bought a canister of CS-Teargas, and one time when I was attacked by two men much stronger than me, I pulled it out and sprayed. I didn't hit them, but it served its purpose. They were afraid and backed off twenty feet, the range of the spray, thus giving me time to escape.

I no longer carry weapons of any sort, and have successfully warded off all attacks over the past seven years using the principles of non-violence and martial arts I've mentioned. For a variety of reasons, I encounter far less conflict than I used to. Studying non-violence brings about peace.

PERSONAL HYGIENE:

Staying clean and neat can be crucial to your survival as a runaway. Not only does it affect your opportunity, but more importantly, it affects your health. Being able to maintain personal hygiene (cleanliness) is something most people take for granted.

After a couple of showerless days in the same clothes, people begin to stink. Going much beyond that is a sure way to become diseased. Skin rashes, parasitic infestations of body lice, and fungal infections will take any chance you give them to create a home on your body.

If you smell or look dirty, you will stand out and people will want to avoid you. When seeking a job, a bad odor and unkempt appearance will work against you, turning off most potential employers. Restaurants will not tolerate your hanging out as long. Good samaritans will be less compelled to reach out and help you, not wanting to have you stink up their car or home.

While repelling positive attention, a grimy appearance will act as a magnet to more negative forces. The police will be more likely to notice and question you. You won't be able to rely on the anonymity of blending in with the crowd, and will find yourself challenged as you wonder through semi-public spaces like colleges and hotels. Thus the grosser you get, the harder it will be to turn things around, as you will find yourself getting fewer and fewer opportunities.

When I was a runaway in Florida I had no problem staying clean. There were plenty of showers along the beaches and I scammed soap from the maid's carts in the hallways of hotels. My clothes were often washed right along with my body, and my feet got plenty of time to breathe as I walked the beaches.

But the second time I ran I ended up in a colder, less hospitable environment. There were a couple of months when I lived out of a car, had no access to laundry facilities, and started to get sick. I had few opportunities to take off my shoes or wash my socks, and ended up with a severe case of foot rot. My feet needed a chance to breathe, but they smelled awful. I couldn't take my shoes off at work or the restaurants in which I hung out without seriously offending people (I tried and was asked to put them back on or leave). I resorted to washing my feet in the sink at a Denny's restroom, much to the disgust of customers who happened to walk in while my rotted skin was peeling off under the force of the faucet.

If you get parasitic infections, recognize them quickly and use ointments and powders designed to cure them. Foot rot and athlete's foot produce a slightly irritating itching in the early stages, but left untreated, they can soon become a serious health hazard, causing your feet to burn, bleed, and lose chunks of flesh.

You can do better than this. If you keep your clothes and self clean you can avoid these problems. There are plenty of places to shower — look and you shall find them.

Most YMCAs will let you use their locker room showers for one or two bucks a shot. If you are broke, tell them, and offer to do a little work in exchange for the privilege. Many of the fee based health clubs that have sprouted up across the nation offer similar arrangements. Look them up in the yellow pages to find out where they are.

A word of caution: locker rooms are one of the easiest places to pick up athlete's foot. Soap up your feet and rinse well. If you can, wear sandals when using these showers. Otherwise, minimize your contact with the floor, lifting your toes and walking on the padded heels of your feet until you get them back in your shoes. So what if it looks funny?

You can also resort to sponge bathing. It is far better than no bathing at all. Just wad up a bunch of paper towels, wet them in a restroom sink, and rinse off your arms, legs, and torso. It can be a bit embarrassing when someone walks in on you, so see if you can lock the door until you are finished.

There are two simple tools you won't want to be without: a toothbrush and a comb. Bad breath, decaying teeth, and messy hair won't help you. They are easy enough to prevent.

Washing clothes can be trickier. If you only have one outfit, you will have nothing to wear while cleaning it. The heavier your clothes, the longer they take to dry, and you won't want to be walking around in squishy duds. Obtain at least one extra outfit, and wash one set of clothes while you wear the other.

It costs about two bucks to wash and dry a load at a laundrymat. To save money, you could offer twenty-five or fifty cents to someone doing a small load, in exchange for letting you add a few extra pieces.

Washing clothes by hand is free. Many laundrymats have sinks you can use. For that matter, so do most bathrooms. Then all you need is a place to hang your clothes to dry.

HEALTH:

There are a host of health issues to consider. Other than the hygiene issues discussed above, there are issues of nutrition, sleep, colds and related illnesses, pregnancy, sexually transmitted diseases, and drugs.

Nutrition:

Getting proper nutrition has a direct relationship to what you eat. In turn, your general state of nutrition will determine your energy level and susceptibility to illness. It seems fairly obvious, but you need to eat right to feel right. This requires getting a balanced intake of needed calories, vitamins and minerals, proteins, carbohydrates, fat, and fiber. Living as a runaway tends to make it hard to achieve this balance.

The ready-to-eat foods available at fast food restaurants and convenience stores do not a healthy diet make. It is all too easy to forget about fruits and vegetables when they aren't an option on your menus. The FDA has recently reevaluated the old "four food groups" model of healthy diet, and created a "food pyramid."

The foods at the wide base of the pyramid are supposed to be the base of you diet: grains. Above them are fruits and vegetables, then dairy, then fish, poultry, and meat. Foods with high fat and sugar contents are at the top. The higher you go on the pyramid, the smaller the proportion of your total intake those groups are supposed to represent. I stopped eating all mammals and birds over two years ago and have only felt better for it.

McDonald's and other fast food restaurants have what could be called an inverse food pyramid. They specialize in meats and fats, and offer no vegetables other than fat-soaked potatoes, and meat based "salads." Their idea of fruit is a sugar-filled pie, cherry Coke, or artificially flavored milkshake. You'll have no problem getting enough calories from their menu, but in time you will grow fat and malnourished.

If you find it absolutely impossible to avoid these kinds of restaurants, at least try to buy some fruit or vegetables at a supermarket. They are very inexpensive for their nutritional value. Meats tend to sit in the intestines and rot, and may be the leading cause of colon cancer. Fiber based foods act like a scouring pad, scraping and flushing the decaying matter out of your system. You can also take multivitamins and mineral pills to supplement the nutrients you don't get elsewhere.

Ensuring proper nourishment will be one of your biggest insurances against getting ill.

Sleep:

Getting enough rest and sleep is essential, perhaps more important than nutrition. Your body can eat itself, using up old reserves for a while before symptoms of malnutrition set in. But a day or two with out sleep will be felt immediately. See the section on shelter, above, for suggestions on how to find safe places to crash.

Colds and Related Illnesses:

Even with the best of precautions, almost everyone gets sick periodically. When you are suffering a feverish illness, it is almost impossible to be out and about fending for yourself.

I was lucky, and never got a bad fever while on the run. But by the time I was seventeen my second year on the streets had caught up with me. I was fortunate enough to be living with my wife (now ex-wife) by then, for in the course of the next year I experienced no less than six week-long illnesses.

My fevers sometimes became so intense I was able to sweat-soak my entire wardrobe in a day, changing clothes every time the wetness made me shiver again. Had I not had Kelli's nurturing care, and access to antibiotics, I might have died. There were times I was too weak to make it to the bathroom without crawling.

If you start to feel ill, take care of yourself immediately. Forget all until you are sure you have food and shelter. See if you can get your hands on some Vitamin C and take 500 milligrams up to once an hour to help fuel your immune system. Think about what you will do if your symptoms grow worse. Figure out where you can get medical care if you need it (you can ask shelters which you can reach through one of the hot-lines in the back), and how you will get there if you are weak. Then sleep and drink plenty of fluids.

Should you start to feel seriously ill, it is time to get help. If you wait too long, you might not be able to find your way.

Pregnancy:

Sexual intercourse is the leading cause of pregnancy. People are certainly having a lot of sex, or there wouldn't be over five and half billion people on this planet at this time. If you are a menstruating female, and having sex without using birth control, the odds are pretty good there will soon be more. You will become pregnant.

Pregnancy only makes it that much harder to survive as a runaway. A growing fetus requires a huge infusion of energy merely to survive, and even more to thrive. It is hard enough to get the energy you need as a non-pregnant runaway. But if you become pregnant, you will need more food, rest, clothing, and shelter. Should you manage to bring a pregnancy to term, you will then have the even more difficult responsibility of caring and providing for your infant.

Creating and loving a baby is one of the miracles of life, and can bring parents much joy, meaning, and fulfillment. But it isn't fair to yourself or your potential child to have it happen while you are on the run. To become a good parent you will first need some experience of successfully caring for yourself.

Birth Control:

The only one hundred percent, foolproof way for a female to keep from getting pregnant is to abstain from sexual intercourse (penis in vagina sex) with fertile males. Abstinence doesn't require you to forgo the joys of sexual stimulation. There are other options.

You can still enjoy the pleasures of your body through masturbation. Masturbation is an embarrassing topic for many, and some are even taught it is a sin, punishable by an eternal afterlife in hell. I don't know whether or not there is a god who would send one to hell for doing something that seems to harm no one, but I do know that masturbation won't get you pregnant. Roughly ninety-five percent of American males, and around forty percent of females report engaging in regular masturbation. While I don't advise boring or offending people with your details, I don't feel masturbation is anything to be ashamed about.

Even if masturbation isn't for you, there are many ways to be sexually intimate with another without having intercourse. Don't be fooled into thinking you won't get pregnant if you have penis/vagina sex and the guy doesn't have an orgasm; a small amount of semen is emitted from the penis even without the aid of an orgasm, and that small amount can contain hundreds of thousands of sperm. The key is to keep a penis and any of it's ejaculate (semen) away from your vagina. You can use your own imagination, or refer to a variety of books for ideas. The possibilities are infinite.

If you simply must engage in heterosexual intercourse, you can still do a lot to keep from getting pregnant. Other than sexual abstinence, no birth control method is one hundred percent effective, yet some are better than others. I don't have space for all the pertinent details, but here is a bit of information to guide you on the proper use of birth control pills, Norplant, condoms, and other methods of artificial birth control.

The Pill:

When properly prescribed for your body, and taken daily according to instructions, birth control pills are one of the most effective means to pregnancy prevention. These pills contain hormones (a class of chemicals) that your body produces naturally. The hormones in the pill affect the chemical environment in your body in a way that keeps your eggs from becoming fertilized and nesting in your womb.

But be warned: the pill doesn't always work. If you miss just one day of taking the pill, you may become pregnant. Also, not all birth control pills are the same. It is possible that your doctor may make a mistake and prescribe the wrong dose for your needs, so it may not work as intended. For the same reason, don't try to use a friend's pills, as they are designed for her body-weight and metabolism, not yours. They probably won't work for you, and may even make you ill. Consult a gynecologist for more information.

Norplant:

Norplant contains the same hormones that are in the pill. These hormones are incorporated into a device that is implanted just under the skin in your arm. Norplant implants dissolve slowly, releasing the proper dose of hormones at an almost constant rate for up to five years. It takes away the worry of having to remember to take a pill every day. If properly prescribed and implanted, Norplant may be even more effective than the pill. However, it is also far more expensive than the pill initially, costing perhaps $500.00 per implant. However Norplant costs less in the long run, as it eliminates the need for a monthly prescricption..

Condoms:

In case you aren't aware, condoms are rubberized devices that prevent sperm from entering the vagina during intercourse. They come rolled up in a coinlike shape, and to be effective, must be completely unrolled over the head and down the shaft of an erect penis before the penis is placed in a vagina. The condom must be used during the entire sexual episode, and after the fellow has an orgasm and begins to lose his erection, it can become loose and slide off, spilling sperm inside the vagina. To avoid this, hold the base of the condom firmly when the penis is removed from the vagina. Don't let go, or take the condom off until it is well away from the vagina.

Condoms are not one hundred percent effective for birth control (or the prevention of sexually transmitted diseases (see below)) because they can develop tiny holes that allow fluids to leak out. Try to use new condoms, as aging can lead to their deterioration, and never use the same condom twice.

One last word of caution: don't use oil based lubricants when using condoms, because they can dissolve rubber, thus making them ineffective. For that matter, oil based lubricants can also lead to infections. Water based lubricants, K-Y Jelly for example, don't have these drawbacks.

Other Birth Control Methods:

There are many other birth control methods available. Other devices include diaphragms (fitted by a doctor), spermicide and spermicidal sponges, and surgical implants like the IUD. These all offer varying levels of pregnancy prevention, but none work as well as those methods described above. They can, however, be used along with condoms, the pill, or the Norplant implant.

More permanent birth control can be achieved by surgical procedures such as getting your tubes tied, vasectomy (the male equivalent), hysterectomy (the removal of the womb), and ovariectomy (removal of the ovaries).

Accessing Birth Control Information and Technology:

The pill and Norplant pregnancy prevention methods require a doctor's prescription. You will have to find a doctor and receive a thorough examination to ensure you are prescribed the proper hormonal dose. This may be difficult if you are a runaway. But it isn't impossible, even if you are penniless.

Condoms, spermicides, sponges, and other over the counter supplies may be bought in many supermarkets and drug stores. There is no need to be embarrassed about purchasing them as millions of people use them every day.

Planned Parenthood is an organization that offers low cost and free birth control education and supplies. It has offices around the country. The Resources section in back lists the toll-free number you can contact for referral to the Planned Parenthood center nearest you. Some organizations will supply free information, exams, condoms, and birth control counseling if you don't have any money.

What if You Are Pregnant?

Despite your best efforts to the contrary, you might become pregnant. This might even be why you run away in the first place. Pregnancy can be coped with, but probably not without help.

Contact Planned Parenthood or a shelter to learn about your options. They can counsel you on all your alternatives, from giving birth, to getting an abortion, and help you decide for yourself which of many paths you might pursue.

Sexually Transmitted Diseases:

It is estimated that one in seven teens has a sexually transmitted disease. The sexually active life-style of many runaways puts them at a far higher risk, especially if they are being molested by adults who target many children.

The most common sexually transmitted diseases are genital warts, herpes, syphilis, gonorrhea, and chlamydia. There are others as well. If treated quickly, none of these diseases are likely to kill you, but they will cause great discomfort. Each disease has a different host of symptoms and treatment options.

As of 1991 less than a thousand American teens had been diagnosed with AIDS, but many more are probably infected with the virus (HIV) that causes it.HIV can live in one for many years before any symptoms develop, so it is possible to catch the disease from someone who shows no signs of having it.

The best way to avoid getting a STD is to avoid sex. The second best is to engage in "safer sex" (misnamed "safe sex" by some). Safer sex involves limiting the exchange of blood and other bodily fluids that transmit STDs. This is best achieved by avoiding genital contact, anal sex, and oral sex entirely. Not as effective, but better than nothing, is to use barriers like condoms (read the section on condoms in the birth control section above) and dental shields (sheets of thin rubbery material) when engaging in genital contact, anal sex, and oral sex.

Planned Parenthood and most state and county health departments have a variety of free pamphlets which describe each of these diseases, their prevention, and treatments in detail. These organizations also offer STD testing, treatment, and counseling at low or no cost. If you are going to have sex, educate yourself on these diseases; your life and health are in your hands.

Drugs as a Health Issue:

Using drugs can be bad for your health. Assuming you procure the drugs you intend to, and that they aren't laced with poisons, you will still experience serious physiological reactions. Over time, marijuana numbs the brain, slowing its response time and reducing short term memory. Downers lead to depression. Uppers overtax the heart and other organs. And hallucinogens can lead to long term confusion of the senses, such as is experienced when people have flashbacks.

Also, many drugs are physiologically addictive, and most of those that aren't can lead to psychological dependency. While drugs can have beneficial effects, using them while on the run is more likely to add to your overall stress and make it much more difficult to cope. If you choose to use drugs, I advise saving these adventures for a time when you have achieved greater stability and better support systems.

MONEY:

As should be clear by now, whether and how much money you possesses can greatly determine how you survive. If you are lucky enough to have a couple thousand dollars to start with, you may be able to secure a place, food, clothes, and everything else you need for a few months. You will then have the luxury of time, a breathing space in which to find a job and get more income flowing in.

Most runaways don't have anything close to this kind of money. It's up to you to use whatever resources you do have as wisely as possible. Realistic planning and budgeting is crucial, or you will end up broke. Even a couple thousand dollars will run out eventually, probably in less than three months, even if you are relatively prudent.

How will you get new money?

Work:

Work is the most common, socially acceptable means to getting money. It is probably your best bet.

Do you already have a job lined up?

If not, where and how will you get one?

The most effective way to find work is to look. And keep looking, persisting until you secure it. Searching for work is work. If you want to succeed, make your job hunting a full-time occupation, applying for one job after another, all day long, then starting over again the next day.

Most of the jobs available to unskilled youth aren't very pleasant. The choice work is taken by people with special skills and experience. It may not be any consolation, but almost everyone has to start out at the bottom with drudge work.

As a runaway you will have obstacles to employment that others do not. But with a lot of determination and perseverance, they can be overcome.

Age and Identification Barriers:

Are you old enough to work without parental consent in your state? Are you old enough to work full-time?

Teens are barred from many kinds of work, "for their own protection." Any job that utilizes equipment or methods considered potentially hazardous is off-limits.

According to federal law, fourteen and fifteen year olds may not work in manufacturing or mining industries, and are limited to working a maximum of three hours per school day, eight hours per non school day, and fifteen hours per week. These hours must fall between seven A.M. and seven P.M. during the school year, and no later than nine P.M. during the summer break.

Do you have identification?

As with housing rental, identification is required before getting most jobs. A copy of your birth certificate and a social security card can be enough, but many employers will also want to see a picture ID to make sure you're not using someone else's papers. A birth certificate can be ordered through the mail from the state bureau of records in your state of birth. Social Security cards can be obtained through federal Social Security offices. From the time they are requested it can take six weeks or more to receive these documents.

Also, kids under sixteen usually need a work permit. To get one, you and your parents have to go to the labor department and do a bit of paperwork. Will your parents cooperate?

What if you are too young, haven't a prayer of getting parental consent, and don't have any identification documents? You're screwed, right?

Not completely.

Getting Around These Barriers:

One thing I discovered as a runaway was that there is almost always a back door, a trapdoor, a window, or some sort of hole you can wiggle through if you look hard enough. When something too sheer to climb looms over you, walk around it.

You don't have to resort to drug dealing or prostitution to come up with a few bucks. The risks of getting hurt or caught are too high, and the damage to your core self can be irreparable.

How do you find work? There are plenty of employers willing to ignore government and hire "under the table." The trick is to find them.

Certain employment areas are more promising than others. Construction, landscaping, and agricultural businesses are good bets, but there are possibilities in most areas. When I was seventeen I found both work as a carpenter's helper and office work for an art dealer for five dollars an hour, and later, yardwork for a rich family at eight bucks an hour. None of these employers asked to see identification. I was paid in cash.

I found the carpentry and yard work through ads in small community newspapers. There is less competition for the jobs advertised in limited circulation newspapers than for work listed in the big city papers. Even if you're in a large city, there are sure to be plenty of papers with smaller circulations.

To find the office work I entered an eight story office building, took the elevator to the top floor, and asked for work at every office on every floor. Most of the offices said they weren't looking for anyone right now, or tried to give me an application to fill out, but I refused, saying I was broke, needed work, and was ready to start anything immediately; I didn't have time to waste on paperwork. It took two hours to go through the entire building.

Sure I was tired of rejection, but I didn't quit. I went to the twelve story office building next door and started at the top again. I got a five dollar an hour job at the third office on the fourth floor. They had just fired their receptionist and needed someone to answer the phone, say the boss wasn't in, and take a message. The next day my responsibilities expanded to include filing and typing.

Many colleges have student employment offices that advertise dozens, or even hundreds of part and full time jobs in the community. These employers are looking for young people. As with the college renter's information offices, the student employment offices often require a valid student ID before they'll let you look at their listings. I explained how to get around this barrier in the "*How to Find Rentals*" section, above.

Another way to get work is through "day labor" pools. Many large cities have places where all you have to do is show up in the early morning, and people who need workers simply pull up to the curb, pick a few people from the crowd, and take them off to a job. Day labor is the luck of the draw. Look eager and you're more likely to be lucky.

I found a spot like this in Los Angeles, and ended up hanging drywall for eight hours. I was dropped off eight hours later with forty bucks in my formerly empty pocket. Ask around, and you might find there's a day labor pickup point near you.

Appearance played a big part in my finding work. Keeping myself clean and neat made my job hunting a lot easier. If you like dressing like a hippy or a punk, wearing sloppy, dirty, torn, or marked up clothes, than so be it. I fully respect that a mohawk or wildly dyed hair may be important to you. I like wearing my dangling lizard earring. But the fact is that these things turn off most employers. The choice is yours.

Once You Get Work:

Do you have enough money to last until your first pay check arrives? It usually takes at least two full weeks to get paid after the first day's work. In some cases it can take a month or more.

Do you know how much your first paycheck will bring? Minimum wage, currently $4.25 per hour, pays $170.00 per forty hour week, before taxes. Depending upon your state's income tax rate, expect perhaps $140.00 or so after all federal, state, and city taxes are taken out. (Minimum wage may be raised in 1994.)

How will you cash your first paycheck? Do you have a bank account? A picture ID? Check cashing places that cater to people without bank accounts usually take a few dollars out of every hundred they cash. Some of the larger supermarkets now offer free check cashing services, but they will require an ID.

Budgeting:

How will you spend your money? Even with full time work, if you don't develop a realistic budget, you may soon find yourself broke. Make a list of all your expenses. Then, break your list into three categories: Essentials, Necessities, and Luxuries.

Essentials are the things you can't live without (food, shelter, etc.). Necessities are things you really need, but can last longer without (savings for unforeseen emergencies, toiletries, clothing, bedding supplies, cookware, etc.). Movies, video games, dining out, and gifts should be considered luxuries; they can certainly be nice to have, but you can do without them forever if you need to.

Estimate your weekly and monthly expenses for each item in your essentials and necessities lists. For areas in which you are uncertain, add an error factor of twenty percent on the more expensive side. (If a month passes and you find you overestimated your expenses, you then have a bonus you can apply to the next round of expenses.)

Now compare your total projected expenses to your total after-tax income. If you have money left over you can afford a little luxury, or even better, split it between emergency savings and luxuries. If you don't have enough to cover all your necessities, you will have to cut back. Take care of the essentials first.

What if you don't even have enough for essentials? Scramble! It means you are or will be homeless and hungry.

Panhandling:

"Ask and ye shall receive."

Begging is against the law in many places. Yet it can get you in far less trouble than stealing, drug dealing, or prostitution. If you are broke, and can't find work or help, begging may be your best alternative. Begging can be a dehumanizing experience. I advise avoiding it if possible, but I sometimes found it necessary.

If you do beg, it helps to keep a few things in mind. First, be inconspicuous, so you don't attract police attention. Second, be respectful of the people you beg from — they have no obligation to give you money, so don't cop an attitude just because they give you a hard time. Third, be efficient and get it over with.

The second time I ran, a day came when I was penniless and couldn't find work. My rent was about to be up and I had to pay another seventy dollars that night, or I would find myself homeless once again. I begged.

Begging takes work. I went from store to store and told the workers my situation, saying I was asking every business in the area for a dollar so I wouldn't end up on the street. About one out of three places chipped in. It took about five hours to come up with the required cash.

Before this day, I'd only begged on the street, asking people for change to get food. Sometimes they'd hand me some money, and once in a while they'd give me an apple or some other food. Some people would get angry, others would ignore me, and now and then someone would accuse me of lying. I had to deal with much rejection and scorn.

Do your best to avoid begging. It is hardly worth it.

Prostitution:

Prostitution is hell on earth. I hated it. It hurt me. Don't do it. Stop now if you already do. You can get diseases that will kill you or make your genitals rot. Prostitution puts you in dire risk of being killed, raped, beaten, mutilated, held against your will, and ripped off. And in this society, you can experience a heap of shame and guilt.

I have nothing against free beings choosing to engage in prostitution, or even hiring prostitutes, as long as both parties do it of their own free will, not out of desperation or the need to exploit. If it is truly your desire to prostitute yourself because you think you'd like or love the work, that is your choice, and you shouldn't be burdened with shame. But that is not why most runaways resort to prostitution.

You deserve far better than this. It simply isn't worth the ten, twenty, forty, or even couple of hundred bucks you might get per shot. Not for what you risk.

If you ignore my advice and do as I did, not as I say, at least try to protect yourself. I know of no safe way to be a prostitute. But I can think of safer approaches.

If you are going to do it, you could minimize your risk by only prostituting yourself at places where you might gain protection if you need it. Find your clients elsewhere, and agree to meet them on neutral ground, like at a big, expensive hotel. Whatever you do, don't go into you client's space, don't get into their car, don't go to their home, and don't go to some cheap motel where no one will respond to your screams. If they get you on their own turf, anything may happen. They may even have a dungeon and lock you away where no one will find you, ever.

At least meeting at a big hotel has a few built in protections. First, the client has to register to get a room, which requires an ID. This way there is a record of their presence. If something awful happens, they can be tracked down and held accountable. Also, at big hotels, everyone has to enter and exit through the lobby. If you try to escape, the customer will be reluctant to follow; you can make a scene by screaming "RAPE!" and "HELP! PLEASE HELP!!!" Still, there is little to stop them from raping and abusing you when you are locked in some hotel room.

Avoid or escape pimps, as whatever they say, they are merely trying to exploit you. If you let them, most will take you for all you're worth, get you hooked on drugs, and discard or abandon you when you need the protection they'll promise. They may even try to sell you into slavery. Don't let their threats paralyze you with fear.

There is almost always a way out, an escape. If you become cornered, plot and plan so the moment an opportunity presents itself you can make an escape. Don't go anywhere they've ever known you to be, or anywhere they might think to look. Though there are plenty of good police departments and officers, the police might not help you if you go to them alone. Many police look at prostitutes as total losers, worthy of nothing but mistreatment. Go to a school or shelter and demand help. You have a much better chance of finding some teacher, principle, or counselor who will make sure you receive the help you need.

But don't let yourself get into a position where you have to put this advice to the test. Just don't prostitute yourself. It isn't worth it.

Drug Dealing:

As I explained in the Analysis chapter, I believe drugs should be legalized. I know several people who used to deal illegal drugs, and say they feel quite good about doing so. They made money, but for two at least, dealing was more a statement of honor and freedom; they firmly believe that regardless of what any government declares, every person has an inalienable right to ingest whatever drugs they choose.

However, with the way things now stand, I can't and don't advocate becoming a drug dealer. Dealing drugs may seem tempting because of all the money you could make. Like prostitution though, it is laden with so much risk that it just isn't worth it. When you deal drugs you go from having the protection of the system, to being a wanted criminal. If you get caught, you will go to jail. If convicted you will stay in jail, for a long time.

Assuming you don't get caught (though you probably will if you deal for any period of time), you will still have problems. Drug users and others will try to steal from you. Some will be desperate or crazy enough to attempt killing or hurting you. If you start carrying weapons to "protect" yourself with, you can face additional criminal charges, have your weapons taken and used against you by someone who knows what they're doing, or end up a murderer, with someone's dead body on your conscience.

When trying to buy drugs to sell, you need to have a bunch of money up front. If the dealer just takes your money, then refuses to give you the supply, what are you going to do about it? You certainly can't go to the police.

If you have the money to invest in drugs, use it for something else. Invest in yourself. Drug dealing can be a ruthless, <u>dead</u>-end business, and simply isn't worth it. Especially for small fry runaways who already have the decks stacked against them.

Starting a Business:
Someone once told me, "You can't get rich working for someone else." This premise is one of the reasons millions of Americans have started businesses of their own. The rewards of a successful enterprise can be enormous. On the other side, so are the risks. On the order of three out of four first-time businesses fail.

To succeed in business you need to offer some product or service people value at a price they are willing to pay. This seems simple at face value, but the trick is to determine what you can offer, and where you will find people willing to give their hard earned money for it. The profit is the difference between the cost of what you sell, including all the energy you put into preparing and marketing it, and the price you get for it.

It can take a substantial effort to get started in business. Aside from investing in the skills and materials you wish to sell, you may also need to conform to the legal environment in which you operate. When I tried to sell sodas on the beach (see story) I quickly discovered that I needed a government permit to do so. Without an ID I had no hope of getting that permit.

When I was seventeen I tried selling light bulbs. It seemed like a good idea because I could buy a case of one hundred light bulbs for less than twenty-five cents apiece. I figured I could easily sell them door to door for fifty cents, a one hundred percent profit. What I forgot to compute was how much time it would take to complete a sale. After an hour of knocking on people's doors I'd managed to sell four light bulbs for a giant $1.00 in profit. Even after giving many away, I didn't have to buy another light bulb for years.

If you want to go into business, I recommend selling something with a very large profit margin. Some people sell ten thousand dollar cars in the same time others take to sell one hundred dollar sets of steak knives. If they are both making ten percent on their sales, the car dealer has made one thousand dollars to the knife dealer's ten.

SCHOOL:

What about school?

When I ran the first time I missed the last three days of the school year and thereby failed all of my final exams. This turned most of my C and B averages into F's, causing me to flunk the ninth grade.

Do you intend to attend school while on the run? If so, where?

Starting at a new school in a new town involves a bunch of paperwork, paperwork the schools expect your parents to sign. Also schools cost money. Some public schools may not accept you unless you (and/or your parents) are legal, taxpaying residents of the town you are in. Private schools want cash in advance.

Or, do you intend to forget about school, to drop out?

When I ran the second time I became a "drop-out." As I'm sure you know, this is not a generally advised practice in our society. Drop-outs are said to have fewer and poorer opportunities for advancement, and fewer skills to help them find work in the first place. Studies show their average lifetime earnings to be less than half that of average college graduates.

However, not everyone is average. In my case, I managed to get into college, in spite of dropping out. I found a back door and started by taking a few courses as a part-time student. After I'd proved myself for a couple years, and built up my abilities to handle a full-time course-load, I applied. They couldn't argue with me as I'd already succeeded. It took me five and half years to get a four-year degree, but I did it. Now I have more employment opportunities, and at my last job earned more than twice as much per hour as I ever did before.

I don't regret dropping out. I hated high school. It was a prison where I wasn't safe from bullies, kept getting in trouble for smoking cigarettes, and was forced to study things that seemed to have no connection to the hell I was living through. Indeed, since then I have needed very little of what I studied there. The lessons I learned by living on my own, though painfully acquired, have proved far more valuable.

In contrast, I loved college. The course work was ten times harder than anything in high school, but I choose what to study so it meant something to me.

Still, please remember, I was one of the lucky ones, one of the exceptions. You are not me, and there are no guarantees this approach will work for you. Most people won't get into college without finishing high school. And dropping out brings up more questions than it answers.

For example:

Can you do so legally? Some states require you to reach a certain age (usually sixteen) before they will allow you to withdraw. Some also require parental consent, even if you are legally old enough.

If you drop out without following whatever process is required in your state, you will then be considered "truant." In some states this is regarded as a serious enough crime for your arrest and incarceration in a detention home, where they can force you to go to school. Because many of the inmates in detention homes have such undeveloped skills, the coursework offered at them is often at the grade-school level.

And let me stress, although I was eventually able to overcome the disadvantages of dropping out, it took years. In the meantime I experienced a lot of pain and suffering, sometimes so intensely I wanted to die. And I didn't manage college on my own. By the time I turned eighteen I'd been struggling for years, working one crummy job after another, and never bringing enough money to pay for more than survival. I got help paying for college, first with a loan, then with support from my parents.

RETURNING HOME:

Sooner or later, around seventy percent of runaways return home. Going home is rarely a simple matter. Depending upon why you ran and what you experienced while away, you and your parents will have a variety of important issues to deal with.

What did you go through while on the run?

You may have been overcome with feelings of fear, shame, anger, loss, doubt, and/or despair. If lucky, you found a safe place to stay and received some caring support from those around you. Or you may have gone through hell, desperately struggling to survive and being preyed upon by harmful people or systems.

What was it like for your parents?

Most parents care dearly for their children. Yours may have been terrified, plagued with nightmare images of the dangers you were experiencing. They may have felt deep hurt, taking your disappearance as a personal rejection. Or they may have been panicing, concerned you would get into some kind of trouble for which they would be held legally accountable. Anger, guilt, loss, shame, confusion, and a host of other feelings are all natural reactions for parents of runaways.

Why did you run?

Your parents may have no idea. You might not know yourself. Making sure everyone understands your motivations is a prerequisite to determining how to prevent a future runaway episode.

Are things going to be any different upon your return?

If you ran because of problems with how your parents were treating you, what will keep these problems from recurring all over again? The same question applies if you ran because of difficulties at school, at work, or inside of yourself. You and your parents may or may not have given much thought to how things need to change for the best.

When I returned, my family and I never dealt with the root problems which precipitated my running. We never discussed what they or I went through while I was gone. I was sent off to boarding school filled with more problems than ever. Just a few months later I found myself feeling suicidally depressed, and ran once again.

Dealing with all these issues isn't easy. It requires hard work. Yet if you don't all make the effort, another runaway episode is far more likely.

HOW TO COPE WITH RETURNING:

This is a big question. Addressing it properly could take far more than a book-length discussion. Unfortunately, I must limit my discussion to a few paragraphs here.

Debriefing:

The first issue is debriefing. It may be quite difficult, but you and your parents need to share what you have been going through, both before and during the runaway episode.

A key to a good debriefing is to take turns listening to and honoring each other's experiences. One way is to just sit down as a family and go around the room taking turns sharing what you thought, felt, and experienced. It is crucial that each person be allowed to speak without interruption.

You must resist the urge to reach in with an impulsive response to what someone says, even if you have some important reply or feel what they are saying is unfair or even flat out wrong. For one thing, feelings are never wrong; everyone has a right to feel however they do. It is when people start making assumptions about someone else's feelings and motivations that problems arise. But more importantly, it is not possible to truly hear someone when you are busy waiting for a chance to say something of your own.

One way to manage letting people speak without interruption is to use a "talking stick." Some Native American tribes used talking sticks during the meetings of their highest councils. The meeting would start with a moment of silence, where the stick lay in the center of the circle of people gathered. Whoever felt they had something to say would lean forward, get the stick, and begin speaking. It was then their turn to speak, for as long as they wanted, without interruption. Everyone else present had the responsibility of listening without responding. When finished, the speaker would return the stick and someone else could have a turn.

This technique can produce much better results than simple dialog. For running away even to be an issue, it is likely that you and your family haven't had the best of communication skills; if you did, problems wouldn't have grown so serious in the first place. Talking about deeply emotional issues in your family's normal conversational pattern is apt to lead to raised voices and a fight.

Another helpful approach is to make sure you really heard and understood what each person said. A good way to do this is after each person has their turn with the stick, go around the room and have everyone else repeat what they understood the speaker to have said. This is still not a time to answer the points their speech brought up in you.

For example, if your dad said he felt like you were trying to hurt him by staying out late one night, you would say "If I understood you correctly dad, you are saying you feel my staying out was done to hurt you." You wouldn't say, "That's not why I stayed out; it was because I missed the bus and had to walk home!" This simple act of echoing back gives everyone a chance to feel like they were really heard. It can cut down on misunderstandings, because if you don't echo what they felt they said, they can have another chance with the talking stick to make themselves more clear.

You may need several sessions to feel fully debriefed. After each debriefing session, take some time to rest with what you have said to and heard from your family. Think about it, digest it, and even better, write about it.

If you and your parents can't manage talking and listening without help, you can seek a family counselor to work with you. Even if you never went to a shelter, the counselors there may be willing and able to help.

Planning for Success:

Though some issues may need to be negotiated before your return, there is sure to be much left unresolved. After debriefing, you and your parents need to plan and make agreements for living with each other so the same set of problems doesn't recur. Refer to the *Talking with Parents* section in the *Thinking of Running?* chapter for ideas.

That's all the advice I could fit in this chapter. I hope it helps you.

So do you still want to run away?

If you already did, do you intend to stay that way?

Well, either way, it is your life. I wish you all the luck and strength you can manage. The decks are stacked against teen runaways, but I promise you, that if you make it to adulthood, life can and probably will get much better. It has for me.

Then you can help us turn this crazy country around.

Advice to Parents

BILL OF PARENTS' & GUARDIANS' RIGHTS & RESPONSIBILITIES:

As human beings charged with the care of children and the responsibilities of adulthood, all parents and guardians should have the following:

RIGHTS:

1. To receive respect from children for the love, support, sustenance, and shelter you provide.
2. To set healthy and appropriate bounds for your children and yourself.
3. To sufficient time and space for yourself to maintain the balance required to meet your responsibilities.
4. To call a time-out, if necessary, in order to keep from abusing children in your care.
5. To seek legal, psychological, and financial help if you are unable to meet your parenting responsibilities on your own.
6. To make mistakes and learn from them.
7. Others not enumerated herein.

RESPONSIBILITIES:

1. To respect the rights and needs of children.
2. To provide positive love, support, sustenance, shelter, and educational access to the children in your care.
3. To refrain from verbally, physically, psychologically, and/or sexually abusing children.
4. To prevent others from abusing the children in your care.
5. To respectfully listen to the needs and wants of children in your care.
6. To explain the reasons behind the limits and bounds you set for your children.

7. To continually work on further developing your parenting and coping skills; to try your best.

8. To seek help from others when you find yourself unable to meet your responsibilities.

9. To allow your children to make mistakes, to be forgiving and non-judgemental.

For Parents and Guardians:

I've used most of my available space and time writing my story and the advice sections for teens. I only have a few brief pages to advise you directly. However, most of the material in the preceding chapters applies to you as well as youth. Please read them. Doing so will greatly improve your insight into what your teens may be experiencing, and how you can help them cope.

Parenting isn't easy, even when all is going well. Simply meeting a child's food, clothing and shelter needs is quite an accomplishment in this world. Going a step further to help them develop good habits, healthy self-esteem, respect for others, and a host of other desirable traits may have been next to impossible to manage amid all the other challenges you've been coping with.

Here you are, keeping busy with work and building a home, meeting one obligation after another, and suddenly your kids are approaching or are well into their teen years. Raising a teen is no piece of cake, especially if you've exercised the best in parenting skills, been nothing but loving and supportive, and given all you can to enable your child to grow happy, healthy, and wise. You've had a dozen years of practice treating your kids as children, but they are changing, no longer simply children, yet still far from adults. Just when you thought you had your parenting down to a science, the old rules no longer apply. It's time to adjust your role to the new needs of the youth in your care.

When people experience stress, they tend to fall back on the coping tactics they are most familiar with. If you didn't receive healthy and nurturing parenting during your childhood, how will you manage to give it to your children? Unless you have focused on developing alternatives, you are likely to treat your children exactly the way your parents treated you. This may not be a problem if your parents had healthy coping strategies. But if they didn't, if they treated you abusively, resorted to drinking, violence, name calling, or arbitrary forms of punishment, then you are likely to do the same with your children.

In the course of interviewing over twenty current and former runaways I found one common thread. Almost every one claimed something to the effect of:

"If I had just felt like my parents heard, understood, and respected

me, I wouldn't have run. I didn't want them to always give me my way. I just wanted to feel like what I had to say meant something, like they understood how I felt, like they cared."

How do you make sure your kids feel understood and cared for? Here are eleven keys to focus on. If you work hard on each of these you are almost certain to reduce the odds of a runaway crisis occurring in your family. The choice, of course, is yours.

ELEVEN KEYS TO HEALTHY PARENTING:

1. Don't abuse your kids.

a. Never hit them, no matter what. There is no excuse whatsoever.

b. Never have sex with your children and never put them in situations where some other adult is likely to molest them.

c. Don't play mind games. Don't make and break promises. Don't lie. Don't use guilt and shame.

d. Don't be verbally abusive. Never call your children names. Never put your children down. Label their actions, not them. Your kids are always good, though their actions might not be so good.

e. Be consistent. Don't promise one thing, then break that promise just because you feel like it.

f. Be fair. Avoid making and changing the rules just because you feel like it. Treat all of your kids with equal respect and attention.

2. Remember your childhood years.

Remind yourself of how you felt fifteen to fifty years back, when you were a teen. Get out a pen and paper and try answering the following questions: What was important to you then? How did you feel about your changing sexuality? How did you want to spend your time? Did your parents treat you with love and respect? Did you feel like they understood you? Did your parents treat you fairly? How did it feel when they didn't? What were the things your parents did to you that you vowed never to repeat when you became a parent? What did they do right? Have you kept these things in mind after all this time? How did your parents discipline you? How did it make you feel? Did their disciplinary techniques lead you to fear your parents? Or did they make you feel better about yourself? What could they have done better?

3. Listen to your kids.

a. Give your kids space to say what is on their mind. Let them share whatever they are feeling. Regularly. Set aside some time each day, or at least a couple of times per week, when you simply listen, without condemning or punishing your kids, no matter what you hear. Create a safe space where your children feel they can say anything, as long as they do so without being abusive towards you. Don't punish them for being honest.

b. Ask them about how they are feeling, what's important to them, what they want out of life today, tomorrow, and in the longer term.

c. Take time to think and reflect upon what they say. Don't get trapped into reflexively responding with the first feeling or response that comes to mind.

d. Let your kids know you have heard them by summing up what you think you've heard and asking them if you got it right. You will often find that your first interpretation of what you hear isn't what your kids are trying to communicate.

e. You don't have to agree with your kids. But save your arguments until sometime after they have finished speaking. Allow some quiet time after hearing their words, so you and they can reflect upon what has been shared. This will lend far greater protection from off the cuff responses that lead to bad feelings for everyone. By taking this time you set an example for your kids. You teach them how to listen, and how to reflect upon what they hear. In time they will begin to incorporate these principles into their own interactions.

4. Talk with your kids.

a. Explain the reasoning behind your decisions. Don't take the seemingly easy way out of saying "because I said so..." It isn't easier in the long run. Your kids deserve to know the reasons behind your conclusions. If you don't know your reasons, be honest and say so.

b. Share the way you feel. Let your kids know you love them, let them understand your concerns and hopes and dreams. Own your feelings as feelings — not absolute rights and wrongs.

c. Respect your children's intelligence and naivete. Respect your own as well. Teenagers can think things through and often see angles that won't occur to you. At the same time, you are blessed with at least twice as many years of life-experience as they, so you are sure to see aspects to problems that won't occur to your children. Your children can learn much from you, but remember, talking and listening is a two way street; you can learn much from your children. Respect and honor the seeds of wisdom in your children and they are that much more likely to blossom.

d. Make sure to let your kids know the major problems in your life weren't caused by them. Too often, kids blame themselves, thinking they are the reason their parents get divorced, have money problems, or develop depression or other mental health problems. A few words to the contrary, where you explicitly tell your children these kinds of problems aren't their fault, can go a long way towards preventing misplaced self-blame.

5. Set healthy limits and boundaries, yet respect your child's needs to

broaden their experience and grow.

a. Protect your children from abuse and other harm.

b. Allow your children the freedom to explore and learn on their own.

6. Respect your children's rights to be who they are.

a. Agree to disagree. Don't expect your children to have the same beliefs as you. They are individuals with minds of their own. They will develop their own opinions, values, interests, goals, and ways of expressing themselves. This is their right. Respecting their freedom of thought and expression doesn't mean allowing them to disrespect or abuse you; they have a responsibility to honor and respect you. But that doesn't mean they have to be a carbon-copy clone of your dreams for them.

b. Let your children explore their need for personal expression. Your home is yours, but let their rooms and bodies be theirs. Individuals need some space and privacy of their own. You may not like how your teens want to decorate their walls or bodies, but as long as such expression doesn't intrude upon your rights to a safe place to live, don't try to control it. Let your children decorate their walls with flowers or psychedelic posters as they so chose — it is unlikely to cause any harm and should be their right anyway. Let your kids wear their hair and clothes as they wish, no matter how immature or insane you feel their choices to be. Have some faith in your children; experimentation is natural and over time they will grow through many phases of aesthetic appreciation. Besides, who's to say the way you like to decorate your house and body is what your kids should ultimately decide upon? Getting uptight and controlling about your children's artistic expression is silly and immature.

7. Make room for mistakes.

a. Don't arbitrarily punish or condemn your children just because they make mistakes. Everyone makes mistakes; they are a normal part of life. If you trust your children will learn from their errors, they are much more likely to. Not only that, but they will more often come to you for advice. If instead, you harshly punish children for their mistakes, they will try to hide them from you, afraid they will only be punished if they share the truth. This fear based withholding cheats them of the opportunity to learn from your wealth of experience.

b. Don't act so perfect yourself. Share some of the biggest mistakes you've made and what you've learned from them. Let your kids know what you've learned the hard way and they may be able to learn without suffering like you once did. When your children see you are just as human as they, that you have dealt with many of the same problems they are struggling with, they will feel less alone with their own looming problems.

c. Let your children know they always have a home with you, even if they make a huge mistake. Some kids run because they make a mistake like wrecking the car, getting in trouble with the law, or taking some drug that is "blowing their mind," and are afraid you will no longer accept them, or even worse, punish them harshly. If you let them come home no matter what, they will be far better off than trying to hide out in the elements or some stranger's home. Sooner or later all mistakes can be overcome. Trust that your kids will learn from their mistakes and they will.

8. Be there for your children.

a. Do your best to meet your children's basic food, clothing, and shelter needs. If you can't manage this on your own, seek help.

b. Set aside time to be with your children every day. Take the time to play with them. Take other time to communicate.

c. Tell your children you will help them work through even the hardest problems. Then follow through when they come to you for help.

9. Be flexible.

a. Strive for an atmosphere of mutual respect.

b. Compromise (see the Talking with Parents section of the *Thinking of Running?* chapter).

10. Study Parenting.

Contrary to popular belief, good, healthy parenting doesn't come naturally. It is a learned behavior. Parenting, the nurturing of a being from the dependency of infanthood to the independence of adulthood, is one of the most complex and important tasks befalling a family. In fact, it is arguably the single most important function of family.

And the more complex society has grown, the more important this function has become. It is absurd to think all that is needed from you will come without effort and study. Even if you had ideal parenting as a child yourself, our world has changed so incredibly much in the years since your childhood that there is much more to learn. All you can do is your best, but to empower your children with the skills, values, self-esteem, and overall health they will need to thrive as adults in the world, your best will be better if you take the time to study.

There are many ways to study parenting:

a. **Books.** There are literally hundreds of books offering insight and advice into the parenting process. The wider the variety of the books you read and review, the richer will grow your parenting tool-kit. No one or even half dozen books will tell you everything you need to know, and some will even offer bad advice, but the more you read, the more you will learn.

b. **Classes.** Many schools and colleges offer free or low-cost parenting classes. Take advantage of these. Not only can you learn from the course material and instructors, but also from the other parents taking the trouble to study. By networking with other parents you can share strategies for success, and learn from each other's mistakes.

c. **Counseling.** A good counselor can help you work through the areas you are having difficulty with. They can also help you resolve some deeply buried, unresolved issues you have from your own childhood. If you are having a hard time dealing with issues of discipline and respect, anger and violence, or love and nurturance, there is a good chance this is because of the way you experienced your early years. Counseling can help you deal with these difficult issues in a supportive environment. Read my comments on counseling in the preceding chapters for advice on finding a counselor who's right for you.

d. **Journaling.** Keep a diary and use it to work through the difficult issues that face you as a parent. A diary is a wonderful place to safely test ideas, ask questions, and explore answers. Use a journal to keep notes on the strategies you try and the results that follow. Review your journal periodically to see what you are learning. Again, read the appropriate sections in the preceding chapters.

11. Get Help.

Don't be afraid or embarrassed to seek help when you need it. If you can't meet your children's basic needs, if you are abusing them or can't stop others from doing so, or if you are simply in a quandary about how to best deal with a problem, find the help you need. If you are just too overwhelmed to give your children what they need and deserve, perhaps the best you can do is find someone else you can trust to care for them while lending what time, energy, and financial support you can. Whatever the case, it's your responsibility to do your best for your children, and that may require seeking help. Consult the resources section and read the other chapters for ideas on where to find the support you need.

WHAT IF MY CHILD RUNS AWAY?

If one of your children runs you clearly have serious problems in your family. Avoid the cop-out of saying it's the runaway who has problems. You all have problems or the kid wouldn't have run. Now you have even larger problems. If you haven't sought help it is time to do so now. Read the other advice chapters and consult the Resources section.

You need to deal with the powerful emotions you are sure to feel. You need to understand why your child ran. You need to determine what to do if he or she returns. And you need to cope with the possibility your child will never come back.

I empathize with some of what you must be feeling. It is normal for parents of runaways to feel a confusing mixture of fear, anger, rejection, loss, doubt, anxiety, guilt, shame, and even relief. It can be a hell of a lot to sort out, too much even. When I ran, my dad became so knotted up with feelings that his arm developed a mysterious aching pain.

It is okay to feel all that you do. Don't try to fight your feelings. Do try to sort them out. Find people to talk with. Consult with runaway shelters, get counseling, read books, keep a diary, cry, and do whatever else it takes to come to terms with what you feel.

Also, begin trying to figure out why your child ran. Were you or someone else abusing them? Were they too afraid or ashamed to deal with you? Were you being too strict for their needs? Do they have a problem with drugs? Was your child feeling suicidal? Did your child just want to start living on their own? The possibilities are almost endless.

If you are in contact, ask them why they left and what they need from you to want to return. Don't argue with their reasons — they are their reasons. Take notes and study them. Think about them. You will need to understand why your child left to have any hope of getting him or her back and avoid having the same problems occur all over again.

Will your child come back?

Do you want them back? Are they welcome? Let them know if they are. In any case, you do have a legal and ethical responsibility to take care of your children. If you can't or don't wish to meet it, you must take care to ensure someone else does.

If your child does come back, how will you handle it?

Read the section on debriefing in the previous chapter. How will things change so your child doesn't feel a need to resort to running again? About a third of runaways run again within one year of returning. It will take a lot of hard work on everyone's part to maximize the chance this isn't the case with your child. Even still, your child may elect to run again.

What if your child won't or doesn't come back?

"If you love someone, let them go." It's good advice. Be as supportive as possible and give them the freedom to return. It will do neither of you any good to try and force a runaway back home. They will only leave again, and will resent you for disrespecting their wishes. Everyone has a right to self-determination, even teens, as long as they don't intrude on the rights of others.

And whatever you do, barring their being a danger to others, do not get your child locked up in some mental health or drug crisis institution against their will! I know some will strongly disagree with me, but help can not be successfully forced upon people. If your child is locked up, help them get out.

Some Runaways Never Return:

Depressingly, some kids will never return because they die. If this happens to your child, you aren't alone; about five thousand runaways die each year. This breaks down to around one in two hundred. I can't really advise you on how to handle the death of your child, but perhaps you could take the energy you would have had for them and give it to a child who has no loving family caring for them.

If your child is in touch with you, but doesn't want to come back, you can at least be supportive. Most children grow up and move out eventually. Do what you can to enable yours to survive better, so they don't end up dead or suffering unnecessarily. Offer to help them work things out. If they want to get emancipated, cooperate. Let them know you will co-sign a lease, help them stay in school, chip in a bit on basic necessities (you save money when they move out anyway), and try to be there however else you can.

Supporting your child doesn't mean giving them a free ride while they just goof-off and party their life away. It means helping them get to the point where they can take care of themselves. It's hard getting started on your own as a teen; you can help make it much easier for your child, and continue healing and building your relationship at the same time.

I have much, much more to say about your role in preventing and coping with runaway crises in your family, but I'm out of time and room. I hope what I have written helps at least a little. Just keep trying to be loving and decent parents. I know it can be tough. Good luck!

Advice to Others

This chapter is for everyone else who wants to help prevent and cope with teen runaway crises. It has sections for friends and family of teens, do-gooders in general, former runaways, shelters, schools, social workers, and governments. All of you people and organizations have a lot to offer. Many are already doing good work. Please keep it up. To the rest of you: You are needed too!

Unfortunately, space limitations necessitate a far more limited discussion of these issues than is warranted. Please forgive me for what I have had to leave out and my lack of elaboration on what I have included. If you've read the rest of this book you will have found many other ideas both explicit and implied.

FRIENDS & FAMILY:

Your love and support may be the most important factor in helping potential and actual runaways. Just being available to listen to and hug troubled teens can make a world of difference for them. When I ran I felt entirely alone. There was no one with whom I felt I could share even a little of what was going on inside of me. If there was, I might of worked through my problems and found it unnecessary to run in the first place. I would have had someone to go to when I felt really confused.

You may be a troubled teen yourself. In any case, whoever you are, reaching out to someone can help more than just them; it can help you. Ironically, being there for someone else can help alleviate your own feelings of loneliness and desperation, make your problems seem a lot smaller than they otherwise would.

Let the youth you care about know it. Tell them you care and are there. Ask questions to help them open up, and let yourself be genuinely interested in what they have to say. Then go a step further: reach out and offer moral and material support if they need it.

If a teen you care about is being abused, help them get the abuse to stop. Let them know you'll stand by them if they want to report the abuse, and help advocate for them with the agencies that get involved in such matters. Help them in challenging their abusers. Open the door to your own home as a place for them to get their bearings, should they need to get away. If they can't find institutional support in ending the abuse, help them make the noise required to demand that support.

If the teen decides to run (or already has) your caring help is especially needed. Consider inviting them to live with you while they try to work things out. If you can't or are unwilling to manage that, at least lend some time and material assistance. Runaways can really use help, from someone they can trust, with most aspects of survival, including getting around, job hunting, finding food and shelter, and everything else. Simply offering them a place to shower, a meal, some clothing, a ride to a shelter, or some advocacy can be a gift some of them won't find anywhere else.

Helping runaways sometimes involves taking risks. Their parents may be afraid and see anyone doing so as an enemy. If they discover you are helping their child there is a chance they will threaten you directly, with legal or even more unpleasant consequences. On the other side, the runaway may potentially pose a threat to you, as some have developed plenty of problems. By the time you start helping them, stealing, vandalism, or drug use may be a normal part of their life. These are chances you may have to take, as you may be the only one on the runaway's side. Don't let a little fear or a few bad experiences keep you from reaching out.

DO-GOODERS:

There is definitely a place for "doing good" for runaways. Your help is needed. Some runaways don't have family or friends who will support them, and crisis organizations can't currently offer runaways all the help they need. Sure you can donate money to help these organizations, but what you can offer in personal time and attention is far more valuable. Money can help, but we can't just buy this problem away.

What's needed from you includes all the things mentioned in the "For Friends & Family" section just above. If you can offer a runaway some compassionate assistance, without making sexual demands like so many "helpers" do, you may make that crucial difference that saves their life. If you don't know of any runaways, they are easy enough to find. Look in all night coffee shops, especially in the wee hours of the morning, and most especially in the smoking sections. Other good places include bus and train stations and video arcades.

Consider volunteering at or for a youth crisis shelter or other organization geared to prevention and/or coping. With a little training and a lot of self study you can offer one-on-one crises counseling in person and over the phone. These organizations also need help with getting the word out about their services, fund-raising, administration, youth advocacy, expanding and maintaining their facilities, and just about everything else they do. Perhaps you could even help start an organization in your community if one doesn't already exist.

If you have a business, consider hiring runaways and other youth. Yes, they are more likely than adults to be a bit flaky, and not always work the hours they commit to. Yes, their skills are usually less developed then the adults you could hire. Yes, they may not have the legally mandated working papers. And yes, it may cost you more than they net you to hire them. But hiring runaways isn't about making money; it's about giving them a chance to learn and grow while meeting their basic needs. It took me working a lot of jobs before I grew mature enough to keep one with out flaking out. But when I couldn't find work, I had to resort to very undesirable survival tactics.

Whether you own a business or not, you may consider mentoring a teen, taking them on as an apprentice in your work or hobby. Ours is an overly age segregated society. Youth are too often left on their own, with too few options other than hanging out and goofing off. We need more adults to reach out and share their valuable experience, knowledge, and friendship with youth. Being a mentor, be it job or hobby related can make a world of difference for a teen.

In summary, youth need adults who won't use and abuse them to reach out and offer what caring support they can. Unfortunately, many of the adults who do reach out, only do so because of ulterior motives that cause much harm. By the simple act of being there, you can be a do-gooder and displace these child molesters and abusers. Don't take advantage of runaways. Help them.

FORMER RUNAWAYS:

You have a very unique and special gift to offer the current generation of troubled youth: you've been there. One way or another you've managed to survive through the traumas of being a runaway, probably learning a host of painfully acquired lessons along the way. Not only can you offer the kinds of help described above, but you can relate to the newest batch of runaways better than just about anyone. By being a friend and sharing your experiences, you can help runaways avoid the pitfalls you've had to deal with.

Runaways will respect you more than anyone, because they'll know you've been there too. You can be more than a friend. You can be a role model. And reaching out to help others in similar boats can help you to heal some of the scars you probably still retain. Read what I say in the *Shelters* section, below.

SHELTERS:

Read what I wrote about my experiences with runaway shelters in the story, and in the *Reflections* chapter. Many good suggestions are implied within. Then, whether you work with shelters or not, do more to help improve the shelter services now provided.

Being the obvious place for runaway youth and their families to seek help, most shelters and their workers find themselves overwhelmed with the demands placed upon them. While dealing with a chronic shortage of needed resources, shelters are expected to provide, at minimum, food, clothing, and a place to stay while runaways work out their crises. This may be hard enough, but shelters also have to cope with the demands of providing counseling for youth and families, advocacy, and help in making connections to educational, legal, physical and reproductive health, and long term services.

Basically, with just a few paid staff and an inadequate supply of volunteers, shelters are expected to take one of the most abused and neglected contingents of society, and deliver all the services families are "supposed" to be providing. Frankly, this is expecting too much. Yet there is little choice, as there are up to two million runaways per year, too many of which know of absolutely nowhere else to go. There is no hope of this changing until parents and others stop abusing and molesting children, and until people in general get off their butts and reach out themselves.

The most important thing shelters can do to help current runaways is to hire and promote former runaways. There is a tendency for some organizations to focus on hiring college graduates with degrees in counseling, social work, and other areas that may be helpful for runaways. However, schools can't teach what it is like to be a runaway. Former runaways, even without specialized university training, have been through an even more important school, the "school of hard knocks." What they've survived will make them invaluable in charting out how to best serve current generations of runaways. Take advantage of their wisdom and make them an important part of your team.

Kids need shelters to be safe. Shelter workers need to refrain from abusing and molesting the children they care for. If you are guilty of these crimes, stop it now! Get help. Be honest with yourself and others. And don't let other staff abuse your kids. Confront suspected abuse by your co-workers. Make it clear to your "clients" during each intake interview that they have the right to be treated healthily and your organization will support them in exposing such abuses. Post a bill of runaway rights and responsibilities, in large print, where every client will see it regularly.

Runaway youth also need to be treated with nurturing respect. Forgive me for telling you your business, but I've seen too many know-it-all psychologist counselors addressing runaways with condescending attitudes. Periodically check-in with yourself and challenge yourself not to be condescending.

Some policies that discourage kids from seeking help include those of non-anonymity, no smoking, restrictive and hierarchical rule and punishment systems, and mandatory contact with the runaway's families. I am aware these policies are often dictated by the legal environment in which shelters operate, but they are counterproductive. If the real goal is to serve the interests of runaways, to keep them off America's tragically dangerous streets, such policies need to be changed to make room for runaways who are unwilling or unable to conform to them.

Many runaways are naturally and justifiably paranoid. They've been hurt and betrayed too many times to trust some new organization that promises help. Requiring kids to identify themselves and contacting their parents scares runaways off. Even though no negative consequences are likely to come of these actions, runaways don't know and believe this. It would be better to waive these requirements than leave the kids who won't accept them to the streets.

Make room for kids who smoke. Many shelters do, but many others don't. Once people are addicted to cigarettes they will smoke whether or not you allow it. Yes, smoking is bad for human health, but so is being on the streets. Runaways are dealing with enough difficulties without adding the simultaneous burden of nicotine withdrawal. Set aside a room for smoking, or at least let smokers go outside when they need their fix.

Restrictive rules can make shelter management easier on the staff, but they also scare off runaways in need of help. The shelter I volunteered at required a staff member to unlock the bathrooms every time a youth needed to use one. This was an absolutely ridiculous, disrespectful rule. A host of other rules may be intended to help or protect runaways, but the greater the number of constraints clients are forced to operate in, the more likely they are to reject shelters. Perhaps other youth want and need tightly regulated systems wherein they aren't required to think for themselves, but kids who are like I was don't. A solution might be to have some shelters with complicated rules and others with a bare minimum.

Shelters should have enough staff to handle the counseling needs of all their clients. Kids need to be able to talk in confidence with adults about anything, including abuse and molestation, committing crimes, and drug use. This means that no matter how serious the content of their disclosure, the confession of a murder for example, the staff may not tell anyone else without first obtaining the consent of the youth. Runaways can't be expected to work through their issues without talking about them, and they won't feel free to talk if they aren't safe in doing so.

Finally, runaways need to be free to come and go from shelters as they wish. They need to know that no matter what, as long as they don't behave in ways destructive to the shelter or it's other clients, they have a place to go when they need it.

Some of my suggestions may seem rather extreme, especially to shelter workers who are used to maintaining restrictive shelter environments. They are extreme. But, again, if the goal is truly to keep runaways off the street and to help them resolve their crises, shelters need to conform to runaway's needs, not impose someone else's expectations upon runaways. If there is a basic respect for the integrity and growth potential of each runaway, the runaways will eventually come around to developing trust with the shelter.

I know many of you are working hard at shelters, doing your best to help out with an endless tide of seemingly hopeless situations without burning yourselves out. I applaud your efforts. Trust me when I say you are making a difference. You are heroes and sheroes, and America needs more of you. Please keep up the good work, and no matter how hopeless things seem to be, please, please, please don't give up!!!

SOME COMMENTS ON PROBLEMS WITH OUR SCHOOLS:

If American schools truly met the needs of youth, including runaways, there would be fewer dropouts and fewer runaways. It is clear that our public and private school systems aren't meeting this challenge, and this is a dreadful shame. It is well past time for radical, evolutionary and revolutionary change in how and what we teach our children.

I have no regrets whatsoever about becoming a high school dropout. I experienced most of my pre-collegiate schools as hostile, insensitive, disrespectful, and completely unhelpful environments. They were unmotivating prisons in which I was coerced into suppressing my creativity, individuality, interests, and intelligence in the interests of making me and the other students more convenient to manage as we were herded from one lecture to another. About the only good they did me was pass on some basic reading, writing, and mathematical skills.

Too many of the teachers were mean-spirited, uninspiring, and prone to arbitrary, unfair usage of their authority over us. Of the exceedingly few teachers I met who were the opposite in nature (caring, inspiring, interesting, and generally enabling), I witnessed one get fired for his evolutionary energy.

It is unreasonable to expect more of our schools when our society so undervalues their services. Readying successive generations for adulthood and full, healthy participation in society may be the single most important function of any institution we have. Yet our society offers better rewards and performance incentives to those who work in almost any professional occupation other than pre-collegiate education. Being a capitalistic culture, the one message that does get across is the self-interest motivated accumulation of capital. Thus it is no surprise that many of our most talented citizens scarcely consider making education their chosen occupation; they can earn much more elsewhere.

On top of this, there is often ittle support for those gifted citizens who forgo better paying career opportunities in the noble hope of making a positive impact in our schools. Of my idealistic friends who jumped through all the university hoops required to allow them to teach, all have found themselves extremely frustrated when they smashed into the monolithic walls built into our schools to maintain the status quo. They are not allowed to express innovation, are overloaded with more students than they can properly attend to, and find the bureaucracies running the schools completely noncooperational with their attempts to change things for the better.

If my talented friends compromise long enough to climb the ranks of the bureaucracy to the point where they will be the ones with the power to control institutional change, yet another generation or two of youth will pass through these systems unhelped. Even worse, the act of compromising for so long will deaden my friends to change, such that by the time they are "in power," they will probably have become used to the status quo themselves and forgotten their idealism.

The fact is, our school systems are outdated, based on archaic, now obsolete functions. As I understand it, the practice of an instructor writing information on a blackboard while a roomful of students copies it, originates from Catholic monks in the days before the printing press was invented. This is how copies of the bible and other books were made; one person copied the contents of a book to a board, while a roomful of monks copied the same material to create a new set of books.

The practice of sitting kids in rows, ever restricting their freedom as they moved through the years, and their class changes signaled by the changing of bells had a similarly obsolete origination. The Industrial Revolution was gathering steam and needed a large influx of workers who could regiment themselves to the requirements of assemblyline work; workers had to have basic reading and arithmetic skills, take orders, be on time, and sit in one place for about an hour at a time.

Our world has changed drastically since the Industrial Revolution. For example, it is estimated that the total body of accessible human knowledge doubles on the order of every eighteen months. The purposes behind the design of our schools are no longer applicable. We now need a far different kind of individual to graduate from our schools, one who can intelligently and creatively adapt to ever changing environment around them. Yet by their very nature, the design of our schools creates the very opposite, in fact breeding out the attributes our youth need to thrive after school. The few students who challenge or don't conform to these unhealthy systems are punished and/or cast out.

I suspect the high school dropout rate would be even higher if our system wasn't so sadly successful at this. By the time they make it to high school, their massive ingestion of television combined with the rigid structure of their education, has created hordes of passive, un-free-thinking cattle, who wouldn't know how to challenge or reject these systems if they wanted to. The problem is when they graduate, they are nowhere near ready to cope with the complicated world around them. Those who get their college educations paid for get a four or five year grace-period to make up for lost time, but most of the rest are cast out to sink or swim.

SCHOOLS:

So what can schools do to help runaways and other youth? Change radically. I'm about out of space so I will list just a few of the many important ideas. I would prefer writing a few paragraphs on each, but oh well.

1. Teach kids the things they need and want to know. These sentiments are echoed by the scores upon scores of other survivors I've spoken with. Make their education more pertinent to their lives, less abstract. Sure, the history of warfare in Medieval Europe is somewhat interesting, but kids need to know about how to be self-sufficient (how to live in this world.). This necessitates a study of:

a. Nutrition, food acquisition and preparation.

b. How to set up a household: renting and buying housing, setting up and paying for utilities and telephones.

c. Household maintenance: what is required to maintain a home, auto, and other valuable assets.

d. Financial management: how to open bank accounts, create and balance budgets, pay bills, secure and manage credit.

e. Searching for and securing paid work, or starting a business.

f. Rights and responsibilities as a youth and later as a citizen: freedom from abuse, due process, taxation, respect for others, etc.

g. Shopping: how to purchase quality products (e.g. cars, computers, clothing) at reasonable prices.

h. Health care: exercise habits, how to find and utilize dentists, doctors, optometrists, and holistic health care professionals, how to recognize and treat illness.

i. Sexual health: Birth control, STD transmission and prevention, sexuality, etc.

j. Parenting: how to plan for and cope with becoming a parent, non-abusive child-raising techniques, fiscal requirements of parenting, etc.

k. Computing: how to use computer hardware, software, and information services.

l. Drugs: an honest discussion of what are the licit and illicit drugs, their effects, and the health consequences of using them.

m. Survey of services: What public and private sector services are available today (including insurance, counseling, accounting, legal counsel, welfare, social security, etc.), what are their functions, and how does one use them.

n. Physical, Sexual, Psychological, and Verbal abuse: definitions, prevalence, coping strategies, and how to end it.

2. Allow runaways to attend for free. Only require that they maintain their GPA at acceptable levels to stay enrolled. Don't charge runaways for lunch.

3. Create and maintain support groups for runaways, abused children, and troubled youth.

4. Make room for kids who smoke. Once they are addicts they will smoke whether or not you allow it. Don't set them up for failure by making it against the rules.

5. Create and enhance opportunities for youth to develop their creative, problem-solving, and cooperative abilities, so they can better cope with the complicated problems they will need to face as citizens in our changing world. Brainstorming sessions, circular (put chairs in a circle) dialog-based peer-to-peer discussions, and group projects can all help in this area.

6. Teach crisis management skills by having youth work through various scenarios such as what would they do if they felt like running away, if they knew their friend was being abused or molested, if they were feeling suicidal, or if their parents suddenly died in a car crash.

7. Bring a variety of mentors into the classroom from the professional world. Take advantage of the wealth of experience out there. Regularly expose youth to the people living and coping with the real world. Have these mentors share what they do and how they do it, their challenges, and dreams. Then encourage these mentors to take an even more active role, inviting students to come join them at their work site and learn by first hand participation.

SOCIAL WORKERS:

Keep working. Work harder. Make noise when you don't have the resources needed to investigate and cope with abuse, provide health care for needy youth, or help them with job training, welfare programs, and counseling. Remember to honor and respect youth and others for the hurdles they are dealing with. Do your best and please, please, please DON'T QUIT!!!

GOVERNMENT AND THE PRIVATE SECTOR:

Again I must resort to a brief list. I apologize.

1. Fund shelters. Reduce the legal requirements for securing funding, as even "substandard" shelters can be far more helpful than no shelters. Make helping runaway and throwaway youth state and national priorities. Build more shelters. Advertise their existence.

2. Fund intentional communities and other alternatives to the dysfunctional families breeding so many teen runaways.

3. Provide free and low cost counseling that is respectful of the needs of runaways and their families.

4. Subsidize apprenticeships and work experiences for youth so there is more incentive to give runaways a leg up.

5. Decriminalize hiring of and renting housing to teens.

6. Provide free and sliding scale sexual education, birth control, family planning, and abortion services.

7. Create free and low-cost access to needed preventative and disease treatment health care for all youth.

8. Make it easier for runaways and other youth to secure free or price controlled food.

9. Create and maintain more opportunities for healthy social activities for runaways and teens in general. Adults have bars, nightclubs, all manner of restaurants, social clubs, and many many other opportunities to meet and socialize with other adults. Kids have few options outside of school, especially when they are broke. The network of Boys and Girls clubs is good, but doesn't meet the needs of many teenagers, and they have no place for kids who smoke.

10. Change the laws to decriminalize crashing in abandoned buildings. Runaways and other homeless people are better off with a roof over their head, even if it is "substandard," than being exposed to the elements.

11. Mandate the listing of toll-free crises numbers in every phone book in the United States under plain English listings like "Help available at this number," "Runaways get help here," and "Suicide, you don't have to kill yourself."

12. Get the police off the backs of runaways. Make protecting kids from abusers more of a priority than arresting and incarcerating truant and homeless youth.

13. Ensure access to free or low cost legal aid and advocacy for all runaways.

14. Make it easier for youth with uncooperative parents to become emancipated. Eliminate the Catch-22s discussed in the *Surviving as a Runaway* chapter.

15. Provide guaranteed options for college level education for all runaways and throwaways. Eliminate the Catch-22 requirements for consideration of parental assets in determining their aid packages, as parents of runaways often refuse to cooperate with anything that would help their children grow and excel.

Concentrate on developing additions to this list.

Everyone:
Some people may argue that good services will only encourage kids to run away. Perhaps this is true to some extent, but remember that the fact is: most kids only run when dealing with what faces them at home is more terrifying than what awaits in the outside world. Youth with loving, nurturing home lives are very unlikely to run.

In any case, the current reality is that when kids do run, they are burdened with a debilitating array of challenges, and often suffer severely. This suffering is not necessary and we owe it to future generations to call a halt to it as soon as possible. We can do it. We should do it. But we aren't doing it. Please WAKE UP!

Taking immediate and comprehensive action to heal our serious societal diseases of abuse, molestation, inadequate education, youth homelessness and hunger, etc., will cost quite a lot. To do it right will take an enormous investment in time, personal healing, money, and societal resources. In some ways it will make the great wars we've fought look like nothing.

But it will be economical over the long term. Our descendants will live less pained, healthier lives. For every youth we protect and nurture we will reap enormous societal savings. Overall there will be fewer sexual diseases, including AIDS, fewer depressed people, fewer suicides, fewer drug addicts, fewer crimes, fewer prisoners, fewer prisons, and less violence.

Simultaneously, the next generation will be composed of more educated, better adjusted, contributing members of society. As we begin to see the fruits of this kind of labor, we will become less likely to repeat the cycles of abuse and neglect that created initial high runaway incidence in the first place. We will feel better as individuals and a society, for our hearts will feel more peace. We'll experience less guilt and pessimism for failing the next generation as we currently are. Our sense of community will grow. We will feel more love for our neighbors. I'm talking about real, meaningful, "family values."

As Stated in the Beginning of This Book:
"We don't inherit the earth from our ancestors, we are simply borrowing it from the children."
And don't you dare forget it.

Acknowledgements

There are so many to thank for their help, direct and indirect, on this book. Being human, I am sure to have forgotten some. I offer my apologies.

First, I want to thank my immediate family. Thank you Mom, Dad, and Jodie, for all the love and strength and support you have been able to give me, even under difficult circumstances.

To Mommy: If it hadn't been for all the hugs and love and support you've shared, if it hadn't been for all the ethical philosophy you've exposed me to, if it hadn't been for all the thought and planning you've devoted to directing my education, and if it hadn't been for all the times you've forgiven me in spite of your anger, I wouldn't have been strong enough to survive so well as I have. I love you so much and am so glad and fortunate for the examples you have set. I have learned so incredibly much from your being strong even when it meant your being alone. And on top of all that, you were my first living example of feminist praxis. I will always love you.

To Daddy: Thank you for your support, even when I was too angry at you to even begin to understand from where you were coming. Your planning and work generated the income that clothed and sheltered me and paid for my education over the majority of my life. While my mom's actions have provided an ongoing example of the strong, vocal type of support, you have provided an ongoing example of strong silence. What you have shared with me has been so crucial. Though I don't yet know how to express it, I identify with you in unspoken ways that can only be between a father and a son. I respect, understand, and love you more than any words will ever express.

To both my parents: Please know this book is not about finger-pointing; it is about healing. The fact that I have been able to write this, in a world where not one of the millions of other runaway survivors in my generation have written similar books, is in large part due to your influence on me, your nurturing and your examples. Please be proud to know I love you. Aside from me, you have been the most important people in my world. You have both performed in the 99.99+ percentile in the areas you have focused, and I'd love you even if you hadn't. Thank you both. I miss you.

To my sister, **Jodie Elizabeth:** I love you and owe you much for the love, support and understanding you have given me. More than anyone, you have witnessed and shared the world we both grew up in. I love you and am honored to be your friend. We are so different and yet so similar. You were the first person I shared some of the events of my summer as a runaway with, and you loved and honored me. I don't know if I would ever have had the courage to share those things with anyone again if you hadn't still loved me. Thank you.

To my grandparents, **Grandmom Jean and Grandpop Victor:** You trusted and supported me when I asked, when I didn't know where else to seek help. I don't think I would have had the strength to begin and finish college without your help. I was lucky to have you both; I love you both. Thank you.

To **Mommom Blanche:** You knew and honored my pain. I love you. Thank you.

To **Granny:** Thank you for being there as a friend when I moved back with my mom. Your support helped much. I love you and Poppop both.

To **Kelli Jo Gilbert:** You rescued me. I am almost certain I would not be alive without the love you managed to give and share. I hurt so much when we bumped into each other, and you held me and loved me for so long that I could finally start to breath again. You supported me through my pain, then my anger, then my denial, then my anger again. You shared your amazing strength and intellect and beauty and anger and pain with me. Kelli I love and respect you so much. Thank you.

To **Kresta Meriki Stouffer:** You were my bestest friend while I wrote most of this book. You gave me more feedback on its content than anyone else, and helped my writing and my self be so much stronger in the process. I love you Kresta. Thank you.

To **the families of Kelli Jo Gilbert and Kresta Meriki Stouffer:** Thank you for inviting me into your lives. I love you. Thank you.

To all the teachers and professors who put that extra loving energy into my education: I remember you all. Thank you.

To all the people who treated me with loving decency and support while I was a runaway, particularly during the second and permanent time, especially **Steven Kevin Wilson and Carolyn Betinsky** and a multitude of people whose names escape me: Thank you.

To **Scott Alyn,** who subsidized the cost difference so I could afford to print this book on recycled paper, who let me use his FAX machine and laser printer for this project, who read early drafts and shared editorial feedback: You helped tremendously and served as a role model, proving business can be conducted with a conscience: Thank you.

To **Evan Manvel,** who helped create the statistics pages in this book, who gave me ongoing editorial feedback and moral and emotional support: Thank you.

To **John Schiller,** of Channel Z Graphics, who spent twice the time I paid him for to do the computer graphics for the cover: Thank you.

To **Ann Carr**, of Carr & Associates, who spent at least twice the time I paid her for, writing and refining cover and brochure copy: Thank you.

To **Ethan Knipp**, who spent around a hundred fifty hours working on the page layout and formating of this book: Thank you.

To **Sara MacDaniel, Barbara Cuzzort, Christy Fisher, Stephen Maye, Liz Stork, Shelly, Alyn Mctavish, Jackie Eis, Judy Adams, George Cameron Bishop, Tom Cummings, Lisa Holmes, Robyn Haus, Sean Lacy, Mark Major, Jo Quinn, Ann Carr, Alyn McTavish, Shamus Moon, Ethan Knipp, Pandora K. Smolinski, Keli Lippert, Liz Ellis,** and a host others who have shared editorial feedback on various drafts of this book: Thank you.

To **Heather Joa Campbell, John Kefalas, Latona, Laura Dawn Wells, Kari Mayberry, Roxanna Butler, Shari McLane,** and other friends who have offered emotional and friendship support while I worked on this book: Thank you.

To the **members of Penpointers** who offered an intensive critique of several chapters: Thank you.

To **John Thompson, Don Cook, and George Cameron Bishop,** all of whom have devoted professional time and energy to counseling me and supporting my healing: Thank you.

To the **more than twenty current and former runaways** who let me interview them: Thank you.

To the members who have co-participated in Anti-Apartheid, Men's, Greens, SETA, SANE, Peace, Christian, Jewish, Wiccan, and co-counseling groups with me: Thank you.

To **Rick Benzel** who first suggested I take a spin at self-publishing this work: Thank you.

To other important friends, including **Abram Nalabotski, Sean Hannish, C. Bret Murray, John (Trey) Rice the third, Rolfe Hegwar, Curtis MacCartney,** and others: Thank you.

To the over fifty professional editors and four agents who agreed to look at my book to consider its publication: Thank you.

To the people who helped me transcribe and photocopy some of the various permutations of this book: Thank you.

To **Gretchen Wilson, a.k.a. ERIS,** who worked so hard to create original cover art from deep within herself: Thank you.

To **Eric Hill,** who let me use his illustration of *"ENOCK"* for the back cover: Thank you.

To the artists whose works fill have enriched these pages: **Jason Lair, Ragz T. Rejected, Andrew Ehrnstein, Ann Miller, Bret Damon, Greywolf, Nicole Gluckstern, Joel Heflin, Robert Brown, Laura Dawn Wells, Chris DeHerrera, Cliff Shuffler, Kevin Brewer, Lynette Carpenter, Travis Mitchell, Stephanie Horser, and Mark Klerk:** Thank you.

To the directors and workers at a host of runaway organizations who have provided ongoing support and feedback on this book: Thank you.

To **Laura Thomas,** director of the National Runaway Switchboard: Thank you for being willing to support my work with your name.

To **the staff at Avogadro's Number, Deja Vu, Paris on the Poudre, Seattle Blues Cafe, and Perkins:** Thank you for your ongoing smiles and encouragement while I spent seemingly endless hours writing and editing at your restaurants.

To **the regulars at the above mentioned cafes,** who offered ongoing community and support for this project: Thank you.

To **the professionals at copyshops, printshops, photo and computer graphics studios, answering services, fulfillment centers, Library of Congress, Bowker Books, and Quality Books:** Thank you for your patience and energy in answering myriad questions.

To **the makers of Framework III (Ashton Tate), Pagemaker 5 (Aldus), AST computers, and DOS 6.2 and Windows (Microsoft):** Your tools are first rate and have cut years off the time required to make this book. Thank you.

To **the members of C.I.P.A.:** Your advice and energy has been very helpful in my publishing effort. Thank you.

To **Dan Poytner,** author/publisher of the Self Publishing Manual: Your book has been invaluable. Thank you.

To all of the **teachers and employers and co-workers and fellow students** who sensed my immense need and reached out a bit to help and love me when I needed it: Thank you.

To all those who have lived and died fighting, writing, speaking, and enabling for truth and love and rights and fun: Thank you.

To **everyone else who has lent support in some way:** Thank you.

And **perhaps most importantly, to all the great spirits and the animals and plants and winds and rains and other forces of nature and the universe,** to all you who have shared your life and beauty and strength: Thank you.

Yes, I wrote and lived this book. But I couldn't have done so without the help of all the above-mentioned people and forces, and plenty of others as well. You have helped make my life rich.

Artist's Credits

Much creative talent and work went into both the cover design and the illustrations contained within this book. Most of this talent is available for hire. For more information, please contact Athena at A Blooming Press Co, 749 S. Lemay Ave., Fort Collins, CO 80524-3900, or call us at (303) 482-0705.

Cover Art:

Front: "*Runaway*" by Gretchen Wilson, a.k.a. "ERIS."

Back: "*ENOCK*" by Eric Hill.

Both Gretchen and Eric have created a variety of excellent artwork. It is time their talents are discovered. They are interested in exhibiting and selling their existing works, and in creating commissioned pieces.

Computerized Cover Design:

By John Schiller of Channel Z Graphics, (303) 493-1834. John is an extremely dedicated Computer Graphics expert. Though A Blooming Press Co could only afford to pay him for ten hours of design work, he generously donated at least another twenty hours towards the completion of this project and the computerized design of the promotional brochure used to sell the book.

Cover Copy:

By Ann Carr of Carr & Associates. Ann is a writing, design, and marketing consultant, dedicated to producing her best. Though A Blooming Press Co could only afford to pay her for four hours of copy writing, she has donated many times that, reading this book, and working on multiple drafts of the cover and sales brochure copy.

Illustrations:

"*Prison*" (p.59) by Ann Miller, 1025 Sherman St. #101, Denver, CO 80203, (303) 832-7571. "I'm a cartoon drawer."

"*Night Forest*" (p.97) & "*Massage*" (p.178) by Brett M. Damon, 1024 So. Pratt Parkway, Longmont, CO 80501. "Brett just went crazy and may be a little hard to reach... Insecurities do not accomodate the soul; the soul accomodates insecurities."

"*Squeezy*" (p.23) by Chris DeHerrera, 3618 Platte Dr., Ft. Collins, CO 80526, (303) 225-0290. "Music is everything... Ran away in seventh grade because of stepdad."

"*Don't Wake Me Up*" (p.161) by Cliff Shuffler, 700 East Drake, Apt. F1, Fort Collins, CO 80525. "A flute with no holes is still a flute, but a donut with no hole is a danish." (his favorite line from Caddyshack.)

"Joey" (p.159) by Graywolf (now homeless). "Hi. I'm a nineteen year-old gutter punk and I've been living on the streets since I was 8. I've been on drugs, in jail, and raped."

"3 items only" (p.40), *"Please Help"* (p.144), & *"Arrested"* (p.90) by Joel Heflin, 326 Scott Ave, Fort Collins, CO 80521. "Joel Heflin is a young artist from the Fort Collins area. Please write if you wish to correspond or obtain an issue of his home spun 'zine, Figtree."

"Empty Pain" (p.224) by Jason A. Lair (a.k.a. Genie Smurf), 912 Wood St. #5, Ft. Collins, CO 80521, (303) 484-2965.

"Precarious Perch" (p.47), *"Price of Freedom"* (p.180), & *"Getting out of Here"* (p.111) by Kevin Brewer. "Kevin is a survivor of childhood ritual abuse."

"Scene Something" (p.199) by Laura Wells Denton.

"Tree Speak" (p.209) by Lynette Carpenter.

"Home Sweet Home" (p.152) by Mark Klerk, 1605 Westinghouse Ct., Fort Collins, CO 80521, (303) 493-3015. "Freelance Plus."

"Most Beautiful" (p.124), *"Gift"* (p.117), & *"Kinder, Gentler Nation"* (p.107) by Nicole Gluckstern, 1619 Peterson Pl., Ft. Collins, CO 80525, (303) 495-0450. "Nicole Gluckstern is a part-time college student who currently resides in Fort Collins with delusions of artistic ability..."

"Pain" (p.54) by Ragz T. Rejected (a throwaway). "Your basic every-day fucked up street punk, with an odd realistic Christian twist."

"Windy Night" (p.141) & *"Receeding"* (p.230) by Robert Brown.

"Fetal Thoughts" (p.67) by Stephanie Horser, 6067 S. Lima Way, Englewood, CO 80111.

"Streets" (p.81) & *"Phone Home"* (p.216) by Travis Mitchell.

Layout and Design:

By Ethan Knipp, 1799 S. College, Lot 28, Ft. Collins, CO, 80525 (303)484-0473. Ethan is an expert in a variety of computer technoligies. Though he had never used the most recent version of Aldus PageMaker used for this book's layout, he managed to quickly adapt to its features. In a matter of a few insanely brief weeks, Ethan layed out the entire contents in a manner even Benjamin Franklin would have been envious of. Like both Ben and I have been, Ethan too is a runaway.

Bibliography

Ackerman, Robert J.; Graham, Dee. Too Old to Cry: Abused Teens in Today's America. 1990. (ISBN 0-8306-3407-X)

Arenberg, Gerald S., et al. Preventing Missing Children. 1984. (ISBN 0-936320-21-4).

Artenstein, Jeffery. Runaways: In Their Own Words, Vol. 1. 1990. (ISBN 0-312-93132-8).

Brenton, Michael. The Runaways. 1978. (ISBN 0-316-10773-5).

Campagna, Daniel S.; Poffenberger, Donald. The Sexual Trafficking in Children. 1988. (ISBN 0-86569-154-1).

Children's Defense Fund. Building Health Programs for Teenagers. Washington, DC. 1986.

Connors, Patricia; Perucci, Dorianne. Runaways: Coping at Home & on the Street. Rosen, Ruth, ed. 1989. (ISBN 0-8239-1019-9).

Dryfoos, Joy G.. Adolescents at Risk: Prevalance and Prevention. 1990. (ISBN 0-19-505771-6).

Editors of Go Ask Alice, 1971. (ISBN 0-380-00523-9).

Falroth, Jeanette Willan. Child Abuse and the School. Palo Alto: R & E Research Associates. 1982.

Finkelhor, David; Hotaling, Gerald; Sedlak, Andrea. Missing, Abducted, Runaway, and Thrownaway Children in America. Executive Summary, May, 1990. U.S. Department of Justice.

Grimes, D.A. "Sexually Transmitted Diseases." In Wallace, H.M.; Ryan Jr., G; Oglesby, A.A. (Eds.). Maternal and Child Health Practices (3rd ed., pp. 347-356). Oakland, CA: Third Party. 1988.

Haffner, D.W.. AIDS and Adolescents: The Time for Prevention is Now. Washington, DC: Center for Population Options. 1987.

Hatkoff, Amy. How to Save the Children. New York: Fireside. 1992.

Hupp, Susan C.; Thompson, Travis, editors. Saving Children at Risk: Poverty and Disabilities. 1992. (ISBN 0-8039-3968-X)

Iverson, Timothy J; Segal, Marilyn. Child Abuse and Neglect: An Information and Resource Guide. New York: Garland. 1990. (ISBN 0-8240-7776-8).

Janus, Mark D., et al. Adolescent Runaways Causes & Consequences. LC 86-45037. 1987. (ISBN 0-669-15280-3).

Kapadia, K.M. Young Runaways. 1971. (ISBN 0-318-36941-9).

Krisberg, Barry; DeComo, Robert; Herrera, Norma. National Juvenile Custoddy Trends 1978-1989. San Francisco: U.S. Department of Justice. 1992.

Lerner, Richard. Early Adolescence: Perspectives on Research, Policy, and Intervention. 1993. (ISBN 0-8058-1164-8).

Lovell, Ann. Lost & Found. 1986. (ISBN 0-575-03405-X).

McGeady, Sister Mary Rose. God's Lost Children. Covenant House. 1991.

Miller, Dorothy. Runaways, Illegal Aliens in Their Own Land:Implications for Service. LC 79-11682. 1980. (ISBN 0-275-90525-X).

National Association of Social Workers. Executive Summary: 1992

Update to a Natiional Survey of Programs for Runaway and Homeless Youths and a Model Service Delivery Approach. 1993.

O'Reilly, K.A. & Aral, S.O.. "Adolescence and Sexual Behavior: Trends and Implications for STD." In Sexually Active Teenagers, 2, 43-51.

Palenski, Joseph. Kids Who Run Away. LC 83-62298. 1984. (ISBN 0-88247-727-7).

Powers, Jane L; Jaklitsch, Barbara. Understanding Survivors of Abuse: Stories of Homeless & Runaway Adolescents. (ISBN 0-669-20902-3).

Redmond, Rosanne & Mark. "The Paradoxes of Covenant House." In Commomweal, 18 May, 1990.

Redpath, Ann. What Happens if You Run Away from Home? 1992 (listed date, however, not actually published yet). (YA) (ISBN 1-56065-133-4).

Redpath, Peter A. Help Me! My Child is Missing! LC 84-71207. 1985. (ISBN 0-936049-00-6).

Rosenbaum, Alvin. The Young People's Yellow Pages. 1983. (ISBN 0-399-50846-5)

Rossiaud, Jacques. Medieval Prostitution. 1988. (ISBN 0-631-15141-9).

Rudman, Jack. Runaway Coordinator. 1991. (ISBN 0-8373-3467-5).

Runaways in Texas: A Statistical Estimate, 1985. 1985. (ISBN 0-89940-852-4).

Rutter, M.D., Peter. Sex in the Forbidden Zone. 1989. (ISBN 0-87477-486-1).

Sorel, Julia. Dawn: Portrait of a Teenage Runaway. 1986. (ISBN 0-345-33923-1).

Stavsky, Lois; Mozeson, I.E.. The Place I Call Home. 1990. (ISBN 0-944007-81-3).

Switzer, Ellen. Anyplace but Here:

Young, Alone & Homeless: What to Do. 1992. (ISBN 0-689-31694-1).

Treanor, Timothy J.; Treanor, William W.. 1992 North American Directory of Programs for Runaways, Homeless Youth and Missing Children. 1991. (ISBN 0-944678-01-7).

U.S. Department of Health & Human Services Editorial Staff. Runaway Homeless Youth: FY 1985 Annual Report to the Congress. 1986.

U.S. Department of Justice. America's Missing & Exploited Children: Their Safety and Their Future. U.S. Department of Justice. 1986.

U.S. Department of Justice. Missing, Abducted, Runaway, and Throwaway Children in America: First Report: Numbers and Characteristics National Incidence Studies. U.S. Department of Justice. 1990.

U.S. Department of Justice. Missing & Exploited Children: The Challenge Continues. U.S. Department of Justice. 1988.

U.S. Department of Justice. National Juvenile Custody Trends 1978-1989. U.S. Department of Justice. 1990.

Vance, Mary. Runaway Children & Youth: A Bibliography. (Public Administration Ser.: P 2420) 1988. (ISBN 1-55590-810-1).

Walsh, Joy; Fuda, Siri, eds. Life Junkies: On Our Own. 1990. (ISBN0-938838-51-2).

Weisberg, D. Kelly. Children of the Night: A Study of Adolescent Prostitution. 1985. (ISBN 0-669-06389-4).

Resources

NATIONAL HOTLINES:
National Runaway Switchboard
800-621-4000 (hotline), 312-880-9860 (business)

The National Runaway Switchboard is a toll-free crises line operated by Chicago's Metro-Help. It operates twenty-four hours a day, year-long, and is designed to serve the needs of at-risk youth and their families. The phone lines are staffed by trained volunteers who use crisis intervention and active listening techniques to help callers identify their problems, explore options, and develop a plan of action. Their services are secular (non-religious), non-judgemental, and non-directive. Volunteers try to give callers factual information and confront irrational perceptions and solutions. They also offer message-relays (communication between runaways and parents without disclosing location of runaway) and referrals to over 8,000 social service agencies nationwide.

Runaway Hotline
800-231-6946 (hotline), 512-463-2000 (business)

P.O. Box 12428
Austin, TX 78711

The Runaway Hotline is a twenty-four hour a day toll-free nationwide hotline for children who have run away, are thinking about it, or have been thrown out of their homes. Like the National Runaway Switchboard, the Runaway Hotline serves as a nationwide information and referral center for runaways and throwaways needing food, shelter, medical assistance, counseling, and related services. The goal of the hotline is to keep troubled youth safe and off the streets, so they can avoid becoming victims of crime and molestation, and to serve as a communication link between runaways and their families.

Covenant House
800-999-9999 "Nineline"

Covenant House, one of the largest privately funded child care agencies in the country, provides food, clothing, shelter, medical care and counseling to 35,000 adolescents under the age of 21 each year. Founded in 1969 by a Catholic Priest, today Covenant House has shelters in New York, Toronto, Fort Lauderdale, Atlantic City, New Orleans, Houston, Los Angeles, Anchorage, and in three countries in Central America. The Nineline provides referrals and counseling for youth in need.

OTHER HOTLINES:
Boys Town:
800-448-3000

This hotline offers twenty-four hour short term youth and family crisis counseling geared towards problem-solving, dealing with issues including abuse, suicide, runaways, parenting, school problems, and drug and alcohol problems. Boys Town offers nationwide referrals to a variety of social service agencies. Boys town also operates a broad range of programs, including several short and long-term residential facilities, and a national training center.

CDC National AIDS Hotline:
800-342-2437

The purpose of the Centers for Disease Control (CDC) twenty-four hour AIDS Hotline is to inform and educate people on AIDS, it's prevention, diagnosis, and treatment, and to refer callers to other sources who can help them further.

CDC National STD Hotline:
800-227-8922

Hours: Monday through Friday, 8 A.M. to 11 P.M. Eastern Standard.

The CDC National STD Hotline offers referrals to low and no cost clinics, disseminates information, and discusses treatment, diagnosis, and symptoms of sexually transmitted disease.

Childhelp USA Child Abuse Hotline:
800-4-A-CHILD (422-4453)

The Childhelp USA hotline is apparently the only national twenty-four hour toll-free hotline for child abuse. It's purpose is to take calls from anyone dealing with abuse and connect them with the agencies set up to report and deal with abuse in their state and locality.

Children's Rights of America Youth Crisis Hotline:
800-442-HOPE (4673), for crises.
800-874-111, for child abuses

The Children's Rights of America hotline offers support and crisis counseling for runaways and other youth. The make refferals to attornies in many areas, offer advocay for youth in abusive situations, and aid law enforcement and parents in locating youth.

GED Hotline:
800-626-9433

The GED hotline sends callers information on where and how they can take the GED high school eqivalancy examination in their area.

National Center for Missing and Exploited Children:
800-843-5678

National Counsel on Child Abuse & Family Violence:
800-222-2000

Hours: Monday through Friday, A.M. to 5 P.M.

National Literacy Hotline:
800-228-8813

This hotline focuses upon increasing literacy in America. They will send callers information on where and how they can get help learning to read, or volunteer in helping others to attain improved literacy.

National Resource Center on Child Abuse and Neglect:
800-2-ASK-AHA (227-5242)

Hours: Monday through Friday, 8:30 A.M. to 5 P.M. Mountain Standard.

National Youth Crisis Hotline (Christian Based):
800-448-4663

The National Youth Crises Hotline offers twenty-four hour crisis counseling, based upon the belief that

Jesus Christ is the ultimate solution to teen runaways and problems facing teens in the world today. When a teen is on the street their objective is to get them immediately off of it, back to their parents or to the runaway shelter nearest them. They refer teens to a nationwide a list of shelters. (Personally, I have my doubts about Jesus Christ being the "ultimate solution" to the problems facing teens, however I'll leave this decision up to you.)

OTHER NATIONAL ORGANIZATIONS WORKING ON YOUTH ISSUES:
American Youth Work Center
1-202-785-0764
1751 N Street, NW, #302
Washington, DC 20036
The Center's mission is to assist the staff and management of community based youth service organizations throughout the U.S. and abroad, and to improve services to children and youth. Founded in 1984, AMYC activities include publishing <u>Youth Today</u>; advocating for youth; organizing domestic and international conferences and training; distributing reports, studies, and videos on youth issues; and providing consulting and technical assistance.

National Clearinghouse on Runaway and Homeless Youth
301-608-8098
PO Box 13505
Silver Spring, MD 20911-3505
The Family and Youth Services Bureau (FYSB) created the National Clearinghouse on Runaway and Homeless Youth (NCRHY) to serve as a central resource on runaway and homeless youth issues. NCRHY acquires, analyzes, and distributes the latest information about successful program approaches, available resources and current activities relevant to the runaway and homeless youth field. FYSB's goal in creating NCRHY is to facilitate communication on strategies for addressing the causes and consequences of youth runaway episodes and homelessness.

National Network of Runaway and Homeless Youth Services
202-783-7949
1319 F Street NW, Suite 201
Washington, DC 20004
The National Network's mission is to "challenge the nation and ourselves to provide positive alternatives to youth in high-risk situations and their families." Their programs include advocacy, public education, information dissemination, technical and training assistance, and an annual symposium. The Network represents over 900 agencies that serve youth and their families.

National Resource Center for Youth Services
918-592-1841
202, West Eighth
Tulsa, OK 74119-1419
The National Resource Center is a national clearinghouse which addresses the specific issues of adolescents and their families. NRC is dedicated to bridging the gap between needs and services and to providing direct support to youth-serving professionals. NRC offers a rich catalog of books, tapes

and videos, as well as direct training and consultation on a wide variety of youth issues, including curriculum development, runaways, foster care, substance abuse, independent living, decision making, conflict resolution, suicide prevention, and fund raising.

SUGGESTED READINGS:

To help get you started, below are a few dozen leads to books that could help you in dealing with the crises in your life. I have read or reviewed most of these (marked with dots), and feel they represent some of the best of what's out there. The rest are included based on having interesting titles and reference information, and on recommendations by others which I have lacked time to follow up upon. Use your libraries and bookstores to find further leads, and read on!

Also, see the *Bibliography* immediately before this section for many of the over forty books and articles I read or referred to while writing Runaway Me: A Survivor's Story. Some are quite technical while others are for a more general audience. Almost all offered me some valuable insights.

Coping With Abuse:

Abused Boys: The Neglected Victims of Sexual Abuse. Hunter, Mic. 1991. (ISBN 0-449-906299).

•Allies in Healing: When the Person You Love Was Sexually Abused as a Child, a Support Book for Partners. Davis, Laura. LC 90-56423. 1991. (ISBN 0-06-055299-9); (0-06-0968834)

•Beginning to Heal: The First Book for Survivors of Child Sexual Abuse. Bass, Ellen; Davis, Laura.

1993. (ISBN 0-06-0553308); (ISBN 0-06-096927X)

Beyond Survival: A Writing Journey for Healing Childhood Sexual Abuse. Brady, Maureen. LC 91-59056. 1992. (ISBN 0-06-2552945).

•Breaking the Deadly Embrace of Child Abuse. Jorgensen, E. Clay. 1993. (ISBN 0-8245-12146).

•Breaking Free from Domestic Violence. Brinegar, Jerry L. LC 92-11973. 1992. (ISBN 0-89638-263X)

•Broken Boys - Mending Men: Recovery from Childhood Sexual Abuse. Grubman-Black, Stephen D. 1992. (ISBN 0-8041-09400).

Child Victim of the State: The Shocking Documented Account of a Child Cruelly Abused by the Very System Created to Protect Him. Davidson, Carla. Reiner, John, editor. LC 90-86376. 1991. (ISBN 0-962892009).

•The Courage to Heal: A Guide for Women Survivors of Child Sexual Abuse. Bass, Ellen; Davis, Laura. LC 91-58463. 1993. (ISBN 0-06-0969318); audiocassettes (ISBN 0-89845-8331).

Do Tell Someone!: Inner Turmoils Surrounding Sexual Abuse Victims. Houston, Yvonnia M. Robinson, Kathy, editor. LC 90-84068. 1991. (ISBN 0-962823503); (ISBN 0-962823511).

•The Education of Little Tree. Carter, Forrest. 1976. (ISBN 0-8263-0891).

•For Your Own Good: Hidden Cruelty in Child-Rearing and the Roots of Violence. Miller, Alice. 1990. (ISBN 0-374-522693).

Growing Beyond Abuse: A Workbook for Survivors of Sexual Exploitation or Childhood Sexual Abuse. Nestingen, Signe L.; Lewis, Laurel. 1991. (ISBN 0-962870307).

•The Healing Way: Adult Recovery From Childhood Sexual Abuse. Kunzman, Kristin. 1990. (ISBN 0-06-2553631); (ISBN 0-06-2553836).

•In Love & In Danger: A Teen's Guide to Breaking Free of Abusive Relationships. Levy, Barrie. LC 92-41914. 1992. (ISBN 1-878067265).

Love, Lust, & Handcuffs: Understanding the Sex Abuser. McCrary, Sharie. LC 92-45167. Soon to be published. (ISBN 1-880489031).

The Me Nobody Knows: A Guide for Teen Survivors. Bean, Barbara & Bennett, Shari. LC 93-12624. 1993. (ISBN 0-02-9020158).

Pressing Toward the Mark: A Guide to Healing for Victims of Sexual Abuse: Incest, Child Molestation, Rape & Sexual Harassment. Nero, Jacqueline E. 1992. (ISBN 0-963221302).

Preventing Adolescent Abuse: Effective Intervention Strategies & Techniques. Barth, Richard P.; Derezotes, David S. 1990. (ISBN 0-669-209031).

Scapegoating in Families: Intergenerational Patterns of Physical & Emotional Abuse. Pillari, Vimala. LC 91-3452. 1992. (ISBN 0-87630-6393).

The Singing Bird Will Come: Living with Love, Strength, & Joy, a Book for Incest Survivors. Blaha, Dionne C. LC 92-64113. 1992. (ISBN 0-942421477).

•Verbal Abuse Survivors Speak Out on Relationship & Recovery. Evans, Patricia. 1993. (ISBN 1-558503048)

•The Verbally Abusive Relationship: How to Recognize It and How to Respond. Evans, Patricia. 1992. (ISBN 1-558501339).

•Victims No Longer: Men Recovering from Incest & Other Childhood Sexual Abuse. Lew, Mike. LC 89-45839. 1990. (ISBN 0-06-0973005).

Working with Adult Survivors of Child Sexual Abuse. Jones. 1992. (ISBN 1-85575-0171).

Creating Our Future:

•One Hundred Fifty Ways Teens Can Make a Difference. Salzman, Marian; Reisgies, Teresa. LC 91-2965. 1991. (ISBN 1-56079-0938).

•One Hundred Things You Can Do for Our Children's Future. Louv, Richard. 1994. (ISBN 0-385-468784).

•Rebellion with Purpose: A Young Adult's Guide to the Improvement of Self & Society. Sidy, Richard V. 1993. (ISBN 0-963374419).

Financial Management & Job Hunting:

•Electronic Job Search Revolution: Win with the New Technologies. Kennedy, Joyce L. 1994. (ISBN 0-471-598216).

•Healthy Parenting: An Empowering Guide for Adult Children. Woititz, Janet G. LC 92-18058. 1992. (ISBN 0-671-739484); (ISBN 0-671-739492).

•Money Doesn't Grow on Trees: A Parent's Guide to Raising Financially Responsible Children. Godfrey, Neale. 1994. (ISBN 0-671-778057).

•Piggy Bank to Credit Card: Teach Your Child the Financial Facts of

Life. Barbanel, Linda. 1994. (ISBN 0-517-880490).

•What Color is Your Parachute, 1994. Bolles, Richard N. 1993. (ISBN 0-89815-584-3); (ISBN 0-89815-5681).

•Surviving Unemployment: A Family Handbook for Weathering Hard Times. Beyer, Cathy; Pike, Doris; McGovern, Loretta. LC 92-32402. 1993. (ISBN 0-8050-20500).

•Surviving Without Your Parents' Money, Princeton Review. Martz Geoffrey. LC 92-38342. 1993. (ISBN 0-679746269).

•Zen & the Art of Making a Living: A Practical Guide to Creative Career Design. Boldt, Laurence G. LC 93-17225. 1993. (ISBN 0-14-019469X).

Non-Violence & Self Defense:

Best Handbook to Secure Living. Crandall, Clifford C., Jr. 1993. Paper. $9.95. (ISBN 0-963660500).

•Children and the Martial Arts: An Akido Point of View. Homma, Gaku. (ISBN 1-556431392).

•The Gentle Art of Verbal Self-Defense. Elgin, Suzette H. 1985. (ISBN 0-880290307).

•Learning to Live Without Violence. Sonkin, Daniel; Durphy, Michael. 1989. (ISBN 0-912078847).

•Living Non Violence. Bhardwaj, Arya. 1986. (ISBN 1-55280757).

•Still as a Mountain, Powerful as Thunder: Simple Taoist Exercises for Healing, Vitality, and Peace of Mind. Dong, Y.P. LC 92-50442. 1993. (ISBN 0-87773-688X).

Take a Firm Stand: The Young Woman's Guide to Self Defence.

Grosser, Vicky; Mason, Gaby & Parmar, Rani. 1993. (ISBN 1-85381-3907).

•Teen Violence. Lang, Susan. 1991. (ISBN 0-531-110575).

•Victories Without Violence. Fry, Ruth, compiler. 1986. (ISBN 0-943734-061).

•Zen in the Martial Arts. Hyams, Joe. 1982. (ISBN 0-553-260782).

Parenting:

•Attention Deficit Disorder: A Different Perception. Hartmann, Thomas. 1993. (ISBN 0-88733-1564).

•Discipline Without Shouting or Spanking: Practical Options for Parents of Preschoolers. ?nell, Barbara; Wyckoff, Gerry. LC 84-527. 1984. (ISBN 0-88166-0191).

•I'm On Your Side: Resolving Conflict With Your Teenage Son or Daughter. Nelsen, Jane; Lott, Lynn. 1991. (ISBN 1-55958-0593).

•Parenting Teens With Love & Logic: Preparing Adolescents for Responsible Adulthood. Foster, Cline; Fay, Jim. LC 92-64090. 1992. (ISBN 0-89109-6957).

•Positive Discipline. Nelsen, Jane. 1987. (ISBN 0-345-348567).

•Raising Your Spirited Child: A Guide for Parents Whose Child is More Intense, Sensitive, Perceptive, Persistent, Energetic. Kurcinka, Mary. LC 90-56376. 1992. (ISBN 0-06-0923288).

•Strong Mothers, Strong Sons: Raising Adolescent Boys in the 90's. Caron, Ann. 1993. (ISBN 0-8050-24999).

•Tough Questions: Talking Straight With Your Kids About the

Real World. Kitzinger, Sheila; Kitzinger, Celia. 1991. (ISBN 1-55832-0334); (ISBN 1-55832-0326).

•We Did the Best We Could: How to Create Healing Between Generations. Dwinell, Lorie ; Baetz, Ruth. 1993. (ISBN 1-55874-2697).

Rights of Youth:
•Protect Your Legal Rights: A Handbook for Teenagers. Dolan, Edward. LC 83-81862. 1983. (ISBN 0-671-461214); (ISBN 0-671-495666).

Shifting the Burden of Truth: Suing Child Sexual Abusers - a Legal Guide for Survivors & Their Supporters. Crnich, Joseph E.; Crnich, Kimberly A. 1992. (ISBN 0-963160834).

So, You Have to Go to Court!: A Child's Guide to Testifying As a Witness in Child Abuse Cases. 3rd ed. Harvey & Watson-Russell. 1991. (ISBN 0-409-906115).

•Teen Dads: Rights, Responsibilities & Joys. Lindsay, Jeanne. 1993. (ISBN 0-930934-776); (ISBN 0-930934784); (ISBN 0-930934792).

•Teen Legal Rights: A Guide for the 90s. Hempelman, Kathleen. LC 93-37509. 1994. (ISBN 0-313287600).

Runaways (a few Books not included in the Bibliography):
Life Junkies: On Our Own. Walsh, Joy; Fuda, Siri., editors. 1990. (ISBN 0-938838512).

Runaway Children: How & Where to Find Facts & Get Help. Reed, Robert D.; Kaus, Danek S. Parker, Diane, editor. LC 92-53768. 1993.

(ISBN 0-88247-9377).

Runaway & Homeless Youth. Rothman, Jack. 1991. (ISBN 0-8013-0539X).

Street Kids: The Tragedy of Canada's Runaways. Webber, Marlene. 1991. (ISBN 0-8020-57896); (ISBN 0-8020-67050).

Self Esteem & Personal Growth:
Authenticity: The Being of the Self, the World, & the Other. Kuhry, Robert. Parker, Diane, editor. LC 92-50860. 1993. (ISBN 0-88247-9784).

•Born To Win: Transactional Analysis With Gestalt Experiments. James, Muriel; Jongeward, Dorothy. 1971. (ISBN 0-451-141954).

•How to Win Friends & Influence People. Carnegie, Dale. 1990. (ISBN 0-671-723650)

Learning to Love Yourself Workbook. Hendricks, Gay. 1990. (ISBN 0-13-5284562).

•Love Is Letting Go of Fear. Jampolski, Gerald. LC 79-52027. 1988. (ISBN 0-89087-3445); (ISBN 0-89087-2465).

Secrets of Self Acceptance. Walters, J. Donald. 1993. (ISBN 1-56589-0434).

•The Way to Love. De Mello, Anthony. 1991. (ISBN 0-385-249381).

•Way of the Peaceful Warrior: A Book That Changes Lives. Millman, Dan. 1984. (ISBN 0-915811-006).

What to Do until Enlightenment: Healing Ourselves ... Healing the Earth. Alpert, Stuart W. Tick, Edward, editor. 1991. (ISBN 0-89391-8040); (ISBN 0-89391-8059).

•When Anger Hurts: Quieting the Storm Within. McKay, Matthew;

Rogers, Peter D.; McKay, Judith. (ISBN 0-8239-14127).
1992. (ISBN 0-934-986770); (ISBN 0-934986762).

•Your Mythic Journey: Finding Meaning in Your Life Through Writing and Storytelling. Keen, Sam; Valley-Fox, Ann. 1989. (ISBN 0-87477-5434).

Sexuality & Health:

•Changing Bodies, Changing Lives: A Book for Teens on Sex & Relationships. Bell, Ruth. 1988. (ISBN 0-394-755413).

•Coming Out: An Act of Love: An Inspiring Call to Action for Gay Men, Lesbians, and Those Who Care. Eichberg, Rob. 1991. (ISBN 0-452-266858).

•Coming Out Right: A Handbook for the Gay Male. Muchmore, Wes; Hanson, William. 1991. (ISBN 1-55583-0218).

•Is It a Choice?: Answers to Three Hundred of the Most Frequently asked Questions about Gays and Lesbians. Marcus, Eric. LC 92-56425. 1993. (ISBN 0-06-2506641)

•Sex & Sense: A Contemporary Guide for Teenagers. Kelly, Gary F. 1993. (ISBN 0-8120-14464).

•Take Care of Yourself: Your Personal Guide to Self-Care & Preventing Illness. 5th. ed. Vickery, Donald M.; Fries, James F. LC 92-48678. 1993. (ISBN 0-201-632926).

Teens:

•Bringing up Parents: The Teenager's Handbook. Packer, Alex J. LC 92-36625. 1993. (ISBN 0-915793-482).

•Coping with Cliques. Peck, Lee; Rosen, Ruth, ed. LC 92-12380. 1992.

Index

<u>Notes:</u>

Notes:

Author's Services

Consulting:

Evan Cutler is available to consult with teens, parents, and organizations on a host of issues related to runaway crises. Evan will do his utmost to apply his wealth of personal experience to problem-solving around your issues. He specializes in helping clients develop healthy, respectful, and realistic strategies for success.

Public Speaking:

Evan is an experienced public speaker. As a student and community activist, he has led numerous presentations and workshops, addressing groups ranging from three people up to sixteen hundred. His experience includes speaking at national conferences, churches, high schools, colleges, and meetings of grassroots community groups.

Previous presentation topics have included this book, the national runaway crisis, abuse, teen sexuality, the connections between war and abuse, and personal and organizational healing. Evan will cater a presentation to the time, subject, and group participation needs of your organization.

Advocacy:

Evan is motivated to advocate for positive change. He can eloquently present assertive, yet respectful arguments advocating children's rights and organizational change. He is also available to testify in court as an expert witness on runaway issues.

Writing:

Evan is available to write articles and provide excerpts from this book for inclusion in your organization's publications.

Compensation:

Evan provides services on a sliding fee basis, giving discounts to economically disadvantaged individuals and nonprofit organizations. Twenty-five percent of all writing, advocacy, speaking, and consultation fees collected in 1994 will be donated to the Fifteen Fund.

Evan Cutler may be contacted through A Blooming Press Co, (303) 482-0705, 749 S. Lemay, Suite A3-223, Fort Collins, CO 80524-3900.

FIFTEEN

15

FUND

Half of the profits from this book will be used to create the Fifteen Fund, the first-ever college and job-training scholarship fund for runaways (structured as a 501(c)3). One hundred percent of donations made in addition to, or instead of book purchases, will also be added to this fund.

Though a high-school dropout, I was lucky enough to receive support for college. Someone reached out and helped me when I couldn't manage college on my own. Unlike the majority of my college peers, I had been on the streets and deeply appreciated the opportunity I was being granted. I didn't waste it. The process of working towards and earning my Bachelor of Science degree in Environmental Health transformed me and opened a world of opportunity.

Now I want to give back. If successful, this fund will provide one, or a number of youth, a chance like the one I received. There are literally tens of thousands of worthy young men and women who have earned their scars in dysfunctional families and on our American streets. A small investment in these youth will pay giant dividends for our society.

All recipients of Fifteen Fund scholarships will be required to sign what I call a "karma contract." This contract is a promise that when they finally reach a point of above poverty-line self sufficiency, they will begin giving back. They will be committed to giving away a small percentage of their time and earnings, either to further the Fifteen Fund, or to promote another cause they find dear to their heart.

Thus, if this works, your support of the Fifteen Fund will be a seed that spawns several generations of growth. Administrative costs will be kept to a minimum, as the Fifteen Fund will rely as much as possible upon volunteer management, accounting, and legal work.

Your support will go to those it is intended for — a generation of survivors that needs your aid more than anything.

The first candidate for a Fifteen Fund scholarship is a seventeen year old runaway named Dave. Dave is a survivor. He has kept himself together through a lifetime of poverty and abuse, the Los Angeles riots, two months of imprisonment for putting colorful graffiti on abandoned industrial buildings, and day after day of living on the inhospitable streets of America. With all he has going against him, including homelessness, Dave has managed to secure and hold a dishwashing job. He is exceptionally intelligent, artistic, and ready.

Please help give Dave a chance.

ORDER FORM

☎ **Telephone Orders:** Call 1-800-210-TEEN. Have your VISA or MasterCard ready. *All other inquiries:* please call 1-303-482-0705.

▤ **Fax Orders:** 1-303-482-9848

✉ **Postal Orders:** A Blooming Press Co, 749 S. Lemay, Suite A3-223, Fort Collins, CO 80524-3900

❏ **Please send me** _____ **copies** of *Runaway Me: A Survivor's Story* at $14.95 each. (Discounts available on bulk orders; write, fax, or call for schedule.)

Books: _____

Sales Tax:
  Colorado residents add 3% ($.45/book)
  Larimer County, CO residents add 6% ($.90/book)

Tax: _____

Shipping and handling:
  $3.00 for the first book and 75 cents for each additional book. (Allow up to four weeks for delivery.)
  Air Mail: $4.50 per book (Second day air.)

S&H: _____

I also wish to contribute:
  ❏$5 ❏$10 ❏$25 ❏$50 ❏$100 ❏$_____
  to the **Fifteen Fund**, a college scholarship fund for runaways. (See back of this page for details.)

Fifteen Fund: _____

❏ **Please add my name** to the *Runaway Grapevine* mailing list so that I may receive more information on runaway issues.

Payment:
(Please Print)

❏ Check or Money Order (payable to: *A Blooming Press*)
  Company name: _____
  Name: _____
  Address: _____
  City: _____
  State: _____ Zip _____-_____

There is a 75 cent surcharge on telephone orders.

❏ Credit card: ❏ VISA ❏ MasterCard
  Card Number: _____
  Name on card: _____
  Expiration date: ___/___
  Signature: X _____

Phone Order Charge: _____

Total: _____